International Energy Policies

International Energy Policies

Edited by

Giray Saynur Derman

Cambridge
Scholars
Publishing

International Energy Policies

Edited by Giray Saynur Derman

This book first published 2022

Cambridge Scholars Publishing

Lady Stephenson Library, Newcastle upon Tyne, NE6 2PA, UK

British Library Cataloguing in Publication Data
A catalogue record for this book is available from the British Library

ISBN (10): 1-5275-8560-3
ISBN (13): 978-1-5275-8560-7

TABLE OF CONTENTS

Part II: Region-Based Analysis

Part III: The Effect of Global Energy Policies on Developing Countries

INTRODUCTION

Primarily energy obtained from fossil fuels (coal, oil and natural gas), which has been stored for hundreds of millions of years, started to be used intensively with the industrial revolution. Then, nuclear and renewable energy produced add diversity to the energy resources.

Energy has become the basic principle of life today. Political transformations, wars and conflicts experienced at an unbelievable speed for the sake of owning energy resources, led mainly by oil and gas, reveal what an important role the energy factor has in the world. The fact that energy reserves are clustered in certain geographies of the world and that the need for energy increases in parallel with the ever-increasing world population emerge as the main determinant of energy policies. As it is well known that the resources are limited and the human factor is helpless at this point, all countries are putting into effect the rules of law to play the right card and are already putting into effect some measures that will ensure their future. Countries with very high consumption rates put forward many legal texts in order to establish their energy supply security. The European Union is one of them.

All kinds of political decisions taken to ensure energy security and the strategies, plans and practices developed for the realization of these decisions are called "energy policies". Energy policies can also be defined as strategies, plans and implementation objectives developed to manage the economic, diplomatic and political interaction between the actors that produce, process, distribute, consume and control/affect the global energy flow (energy regime) in line with the interests of the country. Besides, energy policies have to consider issues such as climate change and environmental security at least as much as energy security.

The concept of "energy security" refers to the situation in which the supply of energy is permanently secured at the requested place, time, in sufficient quantity, in quality (not causing environmental problems) and at reasonable prices. In other words, energy security is the continuous supply of energy from reliable, clean and diverse sources/countries at reasonable prices and in high efficiency; access to sufficient amounts of energy resources from a stable price and stable source, by means of transport that is not actually threatened (pipeline, suitable sea routes, etc.) and within the framework of fair distribution; rational and efficient use of energy in the

World. It can be defined as the continuous availability of energy services that the economy needs. By energy policies, it is meant all kinds of political decisions taken to direct the flow of energy in this sense and the strategies, plans and practices developed for the realization of these decisions. Energy policy can also be defined as the strategies, plans and implementation targets developed to manage the economic, diplomatic and political interaction between the actors that produce, process, distribute and consume energy in line with the interests of the country. “Energy” and “modern politics” have become two intertwined concepts that cannot be considered separately. Although energy creates a cooperation ground for producers through organizations such as OPEC, OAPEC and OPEC+, there are often market share struggles between producers, struggles between producers and consumers, and most importantly, the efforts of big states to control energy valves in order to establish hegemony over both producer and consumer countries. It is a major source of conflict for many reasons.

On the other hand, the main responsible for problems such as environmental pollution and climate change/global warming is the dimension of energy use in modern life. Climate change is not only a problem related to the quality of life and the environment, but has become a problem that threatens the human race and global security. In this respect, energy is one of the most important components of governance in global politics. Therefore, the energy sector, which consists of alternative sub-sectors such as nuclear and renewable as well as fossil fuels such as oil, natural gas and coal, is one of the most important factors in terms of foreign policies and the functioning of the international system, as well as the domestic policies of the countries. It is and especially one of the main determinants of the interaction between domestic and foreign policy. Fossil fuels are responsible for the emission of gases such as carbon dioxide and methane into the atmosphere that cause climate change, in short, the environmental problems experienced today. For this reason, energy security policies cannot be carried out by relying on companies that seek short-term profit and aim to survive in the sector at all costs. Market instruments are insufficient in solving problems such as resource diversification; such as production, transportation, refinery and storage, the construction of adequate infrastructure at the national level in matters and preventing the use of energy as a political weapon by the producer, hegemon and transit countries. Because more than 70% of fossil fuel resources at the global level are in the hands of the states. The share of investments made by the states in matters such as production, refinery and distribution is quite large. Therefore, energy security must be based on long-term strategies with strong political footing.

Today, global energy policies are mainly determined by oil and natural gas. The regions that shape the basis of these policies are the Middle East, Central Asia and the Caspian regions, which have the largest share in terms of reserves. The most important region of the world in terms of Oil and Natural Gas is the Persian Gulf. Kazakhstan has also the largest oil resources in Central Asia mainly concentrated in the Caspian Sea region. Revenues from oil exports is the primary source of income for the state budget of Kazakhstan and essentially important for the entire economy of Kazakhstan. Europe is the major market for Kazakhstan's crude oil. There is an important global competition in the exploration, production and delivery of oil and natural gas to international markets. There exists many problems in marketing the resources of Russia and Iran, which are important actors in the global energy markets and despite the ongoing issues USA, EU, China, India and Turkey are trying to implement multi-dimensional policies in order to obtain the energy they need from alternative sources uninterruptedly, cheaply and safely. Turkey is a hub between the energy producers and consumers and has a strategic importance for oil and natural gas which makes it a candidate country to become an energy market in the future. For this reason, it is of great importance for Turkey to ensure resource diversity, supply security and continuity in oil and natural gas imports, and to develop energy transportation projects.

Nowadays the world energy system is at a crossroad. The current global trends in energy supply and consumption are clearly not sustainable, from an ecological, economic or social point of view. However, that can - and must - be changed. There is still time to change the course. It is no exaggeration to claim that the future well-being of humanity depends on how well we manage to overcome the two key energy challenges we face today: securing a reliable and affordable energy supply and swiftly switching to a more efficient and environmentally friendly energy system, the low-carbon one. It doesn't take anything less than an energy revolution.

In this book, international energy policies are analyzed from a general perspective with the inclusion of future consumption provisions. The energy policies of regional and global actors such as the European Union, United States of America, Russia, China, Turkey and Kazakhstan are particularly evaluated.

The International Energy Policies book is organized in three divisions. In the first part, under the title of Country Based Analysis; Mesut Hakkı

Caşın analyzed the energy resources of the USA. After that Kutay Karaca and Müge Yüce evaluated China's Middle-East policy based on energy perspective. Then, Meral Balcı studied the energy problems in Turkey. Arzu Al and Hayri Kaya evaluated the energy politics of Russia. Sina Kısacık analyzed Russia's reformed energy policy during the Crimean crisis. Emrah Ceylan and Mert Gül studied energy from the perspective of Japan. The second part of the book analyzes the energy from the perspective of regional concerns. Asia Pasific's energy policy has been prepared by Deniz İstikbal. Hasan Korkut, Endris Mekonnen Faris and Hamza Preljevic figure out the relationship between energy and politics in the Western Balkans. Energy policies involving Latin America is scrutinized by Gökhan Katıtaş. After that Ferit Belder examined the Middle East's energy policy. Alaeddin Yalçınkaya has prepared the Caspian Basin's energy policy. Meanwhile the Blacksea Basin's energy policy has been prepared by Meltem İrteş Gülşen. In the third part authors contributed under the title of The Impact of Global Energy Policies on Developing Countries. Gülden Ülgen, İpek Yurttagüler and Sinem Kutlu Horvath scrutinized the effects of unstable oil prices in developing countries. After this section Giray Saynur Derman analyzed how energy affects on the Kazakhstan's foreign policy. Meral Balcı and Serkan Yavuz examined the evaluation of TurkStream Pipeline in terms of Turkey and Russia while Furkan Kaya researched the main parameters of the importance of Cyprus in the context of eastern Mediterranean energy security. Finally Bilgin Birlikseven reviewed the renewable energy. A book can hardly cover all the matters and issues about energy and policies of the whole world, however we tried to gather all the current important hot topics in this book.

All economic activities somehow interact with national and global politics, but in the modern era, the energy sector has always been one step ahead in this regard. In this book, the interaction of energy-politics and energy international relations is examined with the aim to emphasize the importance of energy policies in terms of political and economic aspects under the title of Energy / World Energy Politics. I would like to thank all the authors and their valuable contributions for their publications.

Prof. Dr. Giray Saynur Derman

PART I:

COUNTRY-BASED ANALYSIS

CHAPTER ONE

U.S. GLOBAL ENERGY'S DOMİNANT LEADERSHİP ROLE AND EURASİAN ENERGY SECURİTY PARAMETERS İN THE 21ST CENTURY

MESUT HAKKI CAŞIN*

Introduction

For decades, U.S. presidents have pursued energy policies aimed at reducing America's dependence on foreign oil. The first Commander-in-Chief to achieve the goal of energy independence could be President Donald Trump, with the United States expected to become a net energy exporter by 2021 next year. But in typical Trump fashion, this is not enough. The new goal: energy dominance. Spurred by America's continuing oil and natural gas boom, the Trump administration is promoting the export of U.S. energy products all over the world, and along with these, the country's values and worldview. When the White House rolled out its new energy policy in June 2017, officials reiterated America's need to become self-reliant. An energy-dominant America "means a secure nation, free from the geopolitical turmoil of other nations who seek to use energy as an economic weapon," U.S. Energy Secretary Rick Perry said in 2017. The main difference, however, is the focus on exporting energy and influence. "An energy dominant America will export to markets around the world, increasing our global leadership and our influence," Perry said (Mai, 2019). On the one hand, for hydrocarbon-holding and producing states, the security of demand is of great significance for them. On the other side of the coin, for energy-hungry states, the security of supply is a vital issue in contemporary times. The states that are situated in these two groupings need the hydrocarbon trade in order to sustain their current political, economic, security and social

* Prof. Dr. Mesut Hakkı Caşın, Faculty of Law, Yeditepe University. E-mail: mesutcasin@hotmail.com.

systems. Therefore, in this sense, these two groups necessitate each other, and this necessity has resulted in the complex relations between them. Especially since the fall of the Soviet Union at the beginning of the 1990s, there has been great competition between the U.S.-led and Russian-led hydrocarbon transportation projects. This competition occurs within the context of pipelines and liquefied natural gas (LNG) transportation by tankers. In this regard, an important game-changing development happened in the U.S. at the beginning of the 2010s with the advancement of shale gas and oil technologies in the world energy market. Following this development, the U.S. has become an important net energy-producing state and has been prioritizing the export of its natural gas resources to the world's markets via LNG. But there exist some problems before it.

In this context, Washington has also been attaching ever-increasing significance to the alternative natural gas transportation projects that aim to bypass the Russian Federation in the Southern Gas Corridor, namely the Trans-Anatolian and Trans-Adriatic Pipelines. Also, as part of this grand strategy, it has tried to develop multidimensional policies, including sanctions against the implementation of Russian-backed natural gas transportation projects, that is to say, the Nord Stream, in which projects are exclusively developed for European energy markets. By taking into consideration these abovementioned parameters, this paper will try to discuss the noteworthy energy security parameters put forward by the U.S. towards the Eurasia region in the 21st century. Washington's liquefied natural gas exportation in the 21st century will be elaborated in the first part of the paper. Washington's policies towards the implementation of the Southern Gas Corridor will be discussed in the second part of the paper. Washington's disapproval of Russian-backed Nord Stream II natural gas pipeline projects will be analyzed in detail in the third part of the paper.

The Liquefied Natural Gas Export Policy of the U.S. in the 21st Century: Can It Be a New Game Changer in Eurasian Energy Geopolitics?

The United States' energy policy from 1973 to the present has been a sequence of initiatives based on a strategy of "oil avoidance." The purpose of the 1973–74 Arab "oil weapon" was to force changes in the policies of states towards the Arab-Israeli conflict. This is a stance that can be traced across all administrations, starting with President Richard Nixon during the Arab oil embargo in 1973. This began with the 1973 oil crisis, when the oil to avoid was from Middle Eastern suppliers, and has lasted until today, when the prevailing electrification policies of coal and nuclear power development – the energy options the United States has favoured – still predominate. The U.S. "National Energy Policy" report calls for greater energy efficiency, modernized energy infrastructure and increased energy supplies. The policy is a comprehensive package of proposals whose main objective seems to be to satisfy the ambitions of the energy industries either by easing environmental rules or by opening public lands for exploration. The policy makes, however, no reference to the Kyoto Protocol. The U.S. electricity sector is in the midst of a major change as power producers shift from coal to natural gas as their primary fuel. From 2007 to 2013, coal's share of the U.S. electricity mix declined from about half to just 39%, while natural gas generation's share grew from 22% to 27%. Higher coal prices, standards aimed at limiting harmful pollution from coal-fired power plants, and sharp declines in natural gas prices driven primarily by U.S. shale gas production are leading utilities to choose natural gas over coal to meet electricity demands. The choices being made in the power sector today to replace retiring coal power and meet our growing electricity needs merit further examination because they will have major consequences for the country's economy, health and climate for decades to come (Deyette et al., 2015, pp. 1-5).

In 2007 and 2008, there was a fast upturn in the internal production of the United States' natural gas. It might be asked if the energy industry had predicted the solemn decline in terms of its domestic production within the United States and if LNG had been seen as the only response to this problematic. Nonetheless, subsequently, there were some effective technological advancements. The energy industry began to comprehend that an original improvement was happening in which numerous energy companies were focusing on prodigious international LNG projects that were thought to be essential to counterweight the strong reduction in the natural gas reserves of the U.S. After this development, shale gas production would withstand the upsurge, which was entitled the "Shale Gale". Because of the escalation in supply and the further progression of capacity, expenses would drop. In that manner, shale gas has established itself to stand cheaper than conventional natural gas resources. For instance, in 2000, shale gas formed merely 2% of the gas supply. Since 2012, it has constituted 37%, and within twenty years, it may perhaps attain 65%. Shale gas has helped out the conversion of the U.S. natural gas market. It has similarly started to become effective in climate change and energy security considerations. On account of the swift and widespread growth of shale gas and its effects on the markets, in the 2010s, it was assessed as the most central innovation in the energy field since the start of the 21st century. So, with the shale gas revolution, North America's natural gas basin, now estimated at 3,400 trillion cubic metres (tcm), will possibly be supplying the remaining consumption phases for over a hundred years. Besides, President Barack Obama underlined that *"Recent innovations have given us the opportunity to tap larger reserves – perhaps a century's worth – in the shale under our feet. The potential here is enormous".* When observed within the context of natural gas, the United States ensures an encouraging state of affairs. For the statistics issued by BP in 2016, the natural gas reserves of the United States were 10.4 tcm as of the end of 2014, which is equivalent to 5.2% of the world's recoverable natural gas reserves. Likewise, natural gas production in that year equated to 728.3 bcm and consumption was measured at 759.4 bcm. Between 2013 and 2040, a 45% upsurge is estimated in natural gas production, owing to the anticipated production to be attained from the fields currently possessing low penetrability (Kısacık, 2017, pp. 233-236).

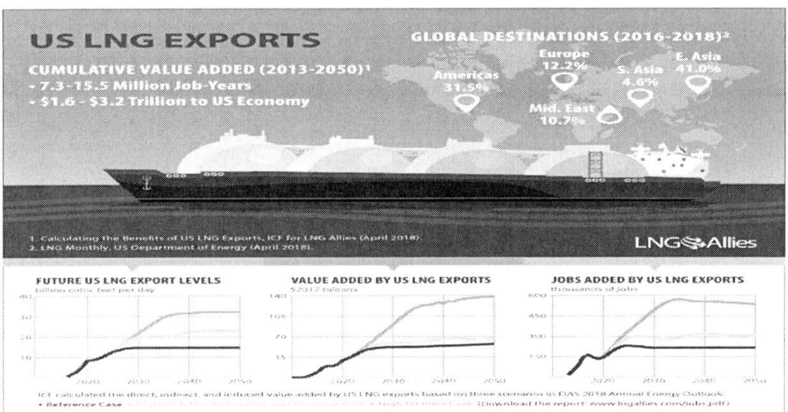

Figure 1: US LNG Exports. Source: USEA, n.d.

It should also be considered that the values and the volumes of natural gas are related in the spot market. In today's world, most LNG trades connect the natural gas price to the oil price. Nonetheless, in the U.S., as a result of the shale gas revolution, this association has been wrecked, and the common 7:1 ratio between natural gas and oil prices has augmented to more than 20:1. This condition aids the affordability of the United States' LNG exports when compared with LNG exports from Qatar and Russia, breaking the linkage between oil and natural gas pricing. Along with this, LNG contracts are typically secured to particular routes which disallow trading. In that sense, LNG exports from the U.S. will not encounter antitrust commercial procedures and, for that reason, one can straightforwardly indicate the appearance of a spot market. As a final point, the potential LNG exports from the U.S. are supposed to disconcert Gazprom's pricing policy in Europe, which is also causing the lowering of natural gas prices all over the world. Kristīne Bērziņa from the Latvian Institute of International Affairs put forward the following considerations on this issue in 2013:

> The shale gas revolution may possibly have some impacts on Europe. Firstly, the Qatar LNG that was reserved for the American market has shifted its route to Europe, which means an extra gas source for the continent. Secondly, the spot market in the United States has clearly put forward that the natural gas price is not obliged to be determined by oil prices, which has permitted European gas importers to renegotiate their long-term deals' terms with current suppliers. In that sense, for instance, ENI, PGNiG and EON would get more suitable terms with Gazprom. Thirdly, Washington possibly will export its less expensive gas to Europe as of 2018. Within that context, it should be mentioned that the shipping of gas bonanza to foreign countries can be realized after the approval of two LNG exportation projects by the US Department of Energy. Even though much gas is anticipated to go to more lucrative Asian markets, the European buyers have already contracted for American supplies. (Caşın & Kısacık, 2018, pp. 339-340)

As said in the European Parliament's detailed analysis of possible oil and gas exports from the U.S. to Europe that circulated in February 2016, LNG terminals positioned in Europe undermine the efforts to branch out natural gas sources not only from the U.S. but also from Australia, Iran, Qatar, Tanzania, Angola and Mozambique. On the other side of the coin, the construction of new LNG plants in the E.U. is favourable for long-term forecasts of Washington's natural gas exports to the Union. On the other hand, two commercial terms have got to be fulfilled for the bourgeoning of the United States' LNG trade with the E.U., which are that the prices paid by European buyers for the United States' natural gas are required to remain modest with regard to the lower prices of Russian natural gas and the prices that U.S. firms obtain in order to trade in natural gas in the E.U. should be similarly parallel with the higher prices in Asia. However, when the present energy prices are taken into consideration, it is most likely to be commercially impracticable for Europe to import U.S. LNG in the short run, for it must contend with other gas resources conveyed through European pipelines and LNG. The potential race between the current LNG market and new Russian gas pipeline projects might further reduce natural gas prices. In that sense, the European LNG demand may either surge or drop. Nevertheless, strategic circumstances are specifically reducing the dependence of the E.U. on Russian natural gas supplies and, likewise, the need to differentiate suppliers could assist in comprehending the energy investments outside market conditions (Kısacık, 2017, pp. 238-240). Furthermore, the forecasts on LNG demand remain undefined. Within that framework, two scenarios can be set forth as follows:

- A scenario grounded on high demand anticipates that the demand for LNG will sharply increase by 42% within the next 10 years and reach 113 bcm as a result of decreasing coal use within the European Union. Of this increase, 90% of the demand will be met by Australia and the United States, however Russian gas consumption will not decrease in a significant manner.
- A scenario grounded on low demand envisions a minor rise in terms of gas importations due to uncertainties and truncated economic growth (Caşın & Kısacık, 2018, pp. 341-342).

Consequently, the U.S. cannot be a substitute natural gas supplier for Europe in adjacent terms owing to the non-appearance of its LNG export plants and reduced prices of its LNG. When the long-term situation is deliberated, it is much more favourable despite the fact that the LNG capacities are anticipated to upsurge in a significant manner within the coming decades. Nevertheless, the percentage of U.S. LNG that might be held in reserve for meeting European demand is not adequate for playing a game changer role within the framework of the E.U.'s energy security. For instance, in June 2016, Paris announced that it was in search of a ban on LNG imports from the U.S. due to environmental and electoral factors. In this context, the contracts taken out by EDF and ENGIE with LNG companies from the U.S. could be annulled. When we come to Berlin, considered the prime natural gas market of Europe, it has at no time thought of acquiring U.S. natural gas. It has not built an LNG import facility. Berlin remains more focused on its efforts to grow natural gas imports from Moscow through the prolongation of the Nord Stream pipeline's connection with the Eastern hydrocarbons supplier in an original project termed Nord Stream 2. The situation in Poland, which contains the major market of Central and Eastern Europe, is interesting in that sense. On the one hand, due to the energy security considerations, an expensive LNG facility at Świnoujście on the Baltic coast was built by Warsaw in order to bring in profitable Qatari natural gas. On the other hand, as a result of pressures within domestic politics, Poland has been encouraging the use of CO_2-belching coal for electricity production and also benefiting from it as input in the chemical industry in order to protect its mining industry situated in southern Poland. Thus far, the natural gas pipeline interconnectors positioned in Central and Eastern Europe that exist to supply non-Russian natural gas to Slovakia, Bulgaria and Ukraine have been gradually moving ahead. In the near term, the only spot markets in the E.U. seem to be in Finland and Sweden due to the fact that their steel industry and maritime fleets are considered to benefit more from natural gas and LNG as fuel sources to decrease carbon emissions and thus stick to COP21 climate obligations (Kısacık, 2017, pp. 241-243).

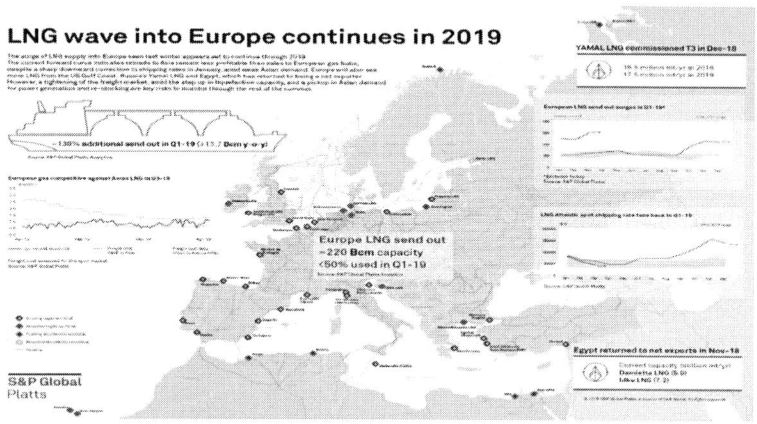

Figure 2: LNG wave into Europe. Source: S&P Global Platts, 2019.

Additionally, in terms of Europe, among the 25 large-size operational LNG import facilities, only two of them are positioned in former Soviet Union countries, namely Poland and Lithuania, which are the more hydrocarbon-dependent countries, while the remaining ones are situated in Western and Southern Europe. There are another six new LNG import facilities that are being constructed with two wide-range terminals in the Canary Islands and four small-range facilities, meaning break bulk facilities. There are also 21 new regasification facilities which are projected across Europe in the wide timeline of the forthcoming eight years. But the LNG outlook for the ex-Soviet Union states (except the Baltic States and Russia) is in serious contradiction with the continuously advancing LNG capabilities of the E.U. For now, within this region, there exist no effective LNG importation or exportation plants, principally because most of these states, encompassing the five Central Asian states and also Armenia and Azerbaijan, do not have any exits to the open seas.

Moreover, Ukraine and Georgia have declared their intentions within the context of the construction of regasification terminals. On the other hand, the Russian Federation, now the prominent natural gas exporter through pipelines, does have targets for the expansion of its LNG export capacity with four more plants. At the moment, Moscow's sole LNG liquefaction facility is positioned on Sakhalin Island in the Far East (Grigas, 2017, p. 80).

According to the well-known rating agency Moody's report entitled "Global Liquefied Natural Gas Industry: Market Imbalance Will Continue Beyond 2020, Keeping a Lid on Prices", it is projected that global LNG prices will remain low in the post-2020 period on account of the arrival of a fresh supply while the demand coming from the world's top exporters will continue declining. In that sense, the global oversupply will stand to reach virtually 55 million tonnes annually in 2019. It is likewise specified that imports to Japan will shrink to 80 million tonnes per year, and for South Korea, the demand will intensify. Additionally, the fresh gas supply will upsurge by 44% from 2020, which translates to 455 million tonnes/year, in common with the implementation of LNG projects in Australia, the United States and Russia that will cost a total of $750 billion. These projects have been the consequence of a growing demand from Tokyo after the tsunami and nuclear shutdowns in 2011 and similarly enormous shale gas supplies from Washington. Furthermore, it is indicated in this report that the global supply capability is much more than demand, but the LNG offtakers of Washington will continue to determine their offtake volume and trading price decisions by taking into consideration the negligible cost of production. This cost will remain effective on the global LNG costs in the post-2020 period (Caşın & Kısacık, 2018, pp. 346-347).

Within this context, in the early 2010s, the energy expert Daniel Yergin discussed the importance of the U.S. shale gas revolution and pointed out that it may upset the appearance of an oil-centred market, because U.S. shale gas decreased North America's natural gas prices in an important manner compared to oil prices within the rest of the world. For Yergin, thanks to unconventional natural gas, "the appearance of this new resource in North America represents fundamentally to hold a worldwide effect which shows that the natural gas market turns out to be a global one from now on". But as of 2015, numerous early proponents of U.S. LNG exportations, namely the Atlantic Council, highlighted their worldwide energy security considerations, which were anticipated for the provision of increased differentiation, competition and energy security for global and regional markets via the enlargement of the volume of worldwide LNG supply. It is important to mention that in order to gain open access to U.S.

natural gas and oil markets, hard work will have to be done on the depoliticization of the energy trade and on augmenting the energy security policies of Washington's allies throughout the world, as most of them are still largely dependent on foreign energy suppliers in terms of hydrocarbons importation to meet their energy needs. But in this sense, of all the institutions, the Brookings Institution has been operating in a more cautious manner. They emphasize that as Washington's sponsorship for exportation is constrained primarily to not imposing any fundamental limitations via the regulatory process, the success of future exports is largely dependent on the global market. For Brookings, while Washington remains determined to be a central worldwide LNG supplier, it will encounter both LNG and pipeline competition from countries with geographic advantages and also from the internal output and new energy resources that are suppressing the LNG demand within the significant energy markets in Asia. Moreover, Gal Luft underscores that the surplus occurring in the worldwide market and decreasing energy prices since 2014 contribute to the unpopularity of U.S. LNG exportation. Here, it is significant to point out that the response to North America-centred natural gas remains not to construct multibillion-dollar LNG plants down the coasts of the United States with an expectation of selling natural gas to far-away markets where it is no longer desired. Luft and other experts underscore this in order to support the usage of internally produced natural gas and LNG within the context of the U.S. transportation sector; to exemplify this, as of 2015, just 1% of internally produced natural gas was used as automotive fuel. The economic slowdown in China, the recession experienced in Europe, the probable eventual reopening of Japanese nuclear facilities and the increase in LNG exportation from Australia remain the major concerns for the LNG industry in the U.S.A. Despite these short-period difficulties, the creation of export infrastructure will help the U.S.A. to better determine its condition within the market when demand begins to overhaul supply (Grigas, 2017, pp. 90-91).

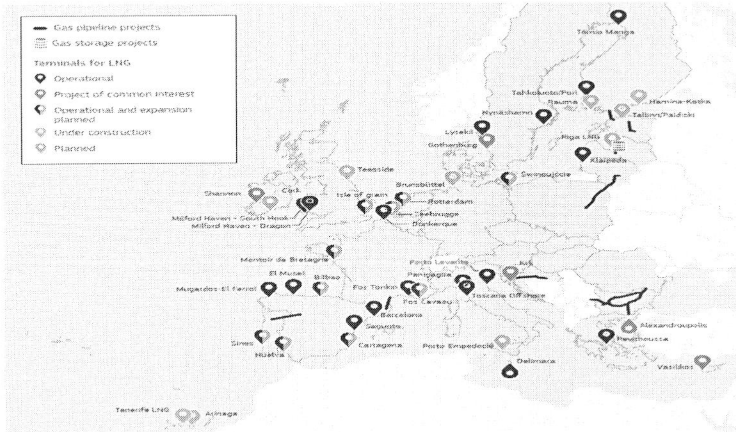

Figure 3: The European LNG Infrastructure. Source: CEEP, 2019.

According to the projections made by the International Energy Agency (IEA), it is expected that the LNG exports of the U.S. will reach 100 bcm in 2024 and that Australia and Qatar, the existing market leaders, will be replaced by the U.S. At the same time, it is projected that the largest LNG importer, Japan, will be replaced by China with an import rate of more than 100 bcm. The global LNG demand reached a record level of 432 bcm in 2018 with a 10% increase primarily due to China's rapid development in recent years. According to the IEA, the 18% increase in terms of China's natural gas demand in 2018 was the result of Beijing's environmental policies that have been transforming most industrial and residence consumers from coal to natural gas in order to decrease pollution. The IEA anticipates that due to the economic slowdown in China, the speed of natural gas consumption in this country will decrease by 8% by 2024. According to the projections of the IEA, the production of the U.S. as the greatest natural gas producer in the world will rise to over 1 tcm, and therefore its share of global production will increase to 23% (Küçükkaya, 2019).

The Prominence of the Southern Gas Corridor in the U.S.A.'s Eurasian Energy Strategy

Ambassador Richard Morningstar, Special Envoy for Eurasian Energy, U.S. Department of State, commented that the first element of Washington's Eurasia Energy Strategy is to embolden the development of new oil and gas resources while similarly stimulating efficiency and preservation in the use of all energy resources and new technologies. When the White House discusses fresh natural gas production in Azerbaijan or Turkmenistan, this is not for the benefit of the White House, but then again it is important because it can make a contribution to the global natural gas supply, which helps to increase global energy security. This policy correspondingly embraces Washington's intention to sponsor European energy security. Washington's ambition to support Caucasian and Central Asian producer countries in search of alternative transportation for marketing their vast hydrocarbon resources is the final pillar of this policy. After the disintegration of the Soviet Union and away from the boundaries of the former Ottoman Empire, the newly independent Central Asia, mainly Turkic in terms of cultural heritage, is now calling. The lively commercial and cultural outreach of Ankara is a promising source of strength for the modernization, secularization and ultimately democratization of this energy-rich albeit geopolitically unsettled region. It remains very important to discuss that, in the meantime, Moscow is searching to establish a monopoly on direct foreign access to Central Asian energy exports; consequently, Ankara's expanding regional role can play a catalyst role – in mutual collaboration with Baku and Tbilisi – in securing Europe's unrestricted access across the Caspian Sea to Central Asia's hydrocarbon resources (Kısacık & Avcı, 2015, p. 467).

In the shifting energy geography, Turkey, as the newest, dynamic and proactive actor possessing structural features, plays a fundamental role in the providing of regional security for the transference of clean and reliable energy resources. Ankara's contiguity to such a geography, where more than 70% of proven hydrocarbon resources in the world are present, has produced the definition of this region as the "Silk Road of the 21st Century", which includes many of the world's most noticeable energy producers, that is to say, Russia, the Caspian Basin and the Middle East, and European consumer markets. Turkey is a significant country situated between fast-growing energy markets and the world's prominent energy producers. Turkey imports roughly 70% of its energy resources from foreign suppliers, which annually cost about $60 billion. As a result, it can simply be termed as an "energy-dependent" country. Within the context of prevailing energy security demands, Ankara has to develop all-inclusive strategies in order to meet its energy needs from trustworthy and environmentally friendly resources at a reasonable cost with a continuous supply (Kısacık & Kaya, 2017, pp. 110-111).

Baku's 7 bcm of recoverable oil and 1.3 tcm of gas reserves remain noteworthy for both itself and for the global energy supply. Other South

Caucasus countries, namely Georgia and Armenia, are critically important in their transit standing for the transference of these resources to world markets. Within this process, Moscow has attempted to direct the demanding interests of Western energy firms to principally Baku's hydrocarbons. The $8 Billion Production-Sharing Agreement of Azerbaijan's oil resources was contracted on September 20, 1994 between the State Oil Company of the Azerbaijan Republic (SOCAR) and international energy companies. Furthermore, the creation of the Azerbaijan International Oil Company (AIOC) to oversee the exploration, production and partaking in Azeri-Çırak-Güneşli (ACG) oil fields in the Caspian Sea has had a central role in the operationalization of the Baku-Tbilisi-Ceyhan (BTC) project. Washington and Ankara, aiming for resource variation, lessening the dependence on Moscow and underlining the independence of Azerbaijan, introduced the implementation of the Baku-Supsa line together with a Moscow-offered pipeline. The intergovernmental framework contract granting official status to BTC was contracted between the Presidents of Azerbaijan, Georgia and Turkey during the OSCE Summit on November 19, 1999 under the sponsorship of the then-US President Bill Clinton. The ground-breaking ceremony of BTC occurred on September 26, 2002. On account of this, Azerbaijan's political and economic independence has been strengthened. In this way, Ankara and Tbilisi have also augmented their strategic impacts (Erhan & Gürbüz, 2013, pp. 308-314; Grigas, 2017, pp. 208-209).

Ukraine signifies an analytically imperative transit country not only for Russia but also for Europe's energy security, in that more or less 70% of the Kremlin's gas resources are conveyed to Europe through Kyiv. Russia followed a discounted price policy for Ukraine, which was $50 for 1,000 cubic metres of gas, until 2004. But then the Orange Revolution in 2004 wholly transformed the Russian attitude towards Ukraine. When Viktor Yushchenko came to power in Ukraine, he began to pursue pro-Western foreign policies, highlighting his country's intended membership of NATO and the E.U. Moscow powerfully condemned Ukraine for that and, in response, professed the authentication of market rules in energy associations with Ukraine. The Kremlin similarly stopped funding Ukraine's energy and pressed for Ukraine to pay its gas debts earlier, which was vetoed by Kyiv. Moscow reacted to this by cutting off natural gas supplies to Ukraine in 2006 and 2009, which had an extreme impact on the European continent as well. After the incidence of these energy crises, both Moscow and Brussels initiated moves for the development of substitute gas pipelines, aiming to bypass Ukraine, in the post-2009 period (Kısacık, 2017, pp. 167-184).

In consequence of increasing gas consumption volume in Europe and the increasing dependence of European countries on Russian gas, Azerbaijani gas has arisen as a fresh alternative in terms of resource variety. The aforementioned Russian-Ukrainian crisis further amplified the prominence of Baku's gas volumes. The Shah Sea Basin remains relevant due to possessing significant reserves of roughly 1.2 tcm of gas. Even though production in the Shah Sea II field was foreseen to commence in 2014, its date of being active was put off to 2018 owing to the conflict between Ankara and Baku on gas prices in the Shah Sea I field following Turkey's inconsistent policies during its "Armenian Opening" process. The additional natural gas to be drilled from the Shah Sea II field would initially be conveyed to Turkey through the Trans-Anatolian Natural Gas Pipeline (TANAP), crossing the whole country, and then with the Trans-Adriatic Pipeline (TAP) to Europe (Sürmelioğlu-Parlar, 2018, pp. 35-51; Grigas, 2017, pp. 209-211). After the discussions between Ankara and Baku in the framework of the High-Level Strategic Cooperation Council on October 25, 2011, the TANAP agreement was contracted. Turkey aims for the transference of Turkmen gas to European markets via TANAP. For this purpose, Turkey and Turkmenistan developed a memorandum on gas exports to Europe in Turkish President Recep Tayyip Erdoğan's official visit to Ashgabat at the beginning of November 2014. In this way, Turkey will likewise propose a different transportation route for Caspian natural gas into the energy-hungry markets of Europe. TANAP will respectively assist in Turkey's goal to turn out to be one of the principal energy hubs for Europe (Caşın & Kısacık, 2018, pp. 202-203).

On June 12, 2018, the TANAP project was officially instated with the involvement of Erdoğan, Ilham Aliyev, the President of the Republic of Azerbaijan, Aleksandr Vučić, the President of Serbia, Petro Poroshenko, the President of Ukraine, Mustafa Akıncı, the President of the Turkish Republic of Northern Cyprus, and the related officials in Eskişehir, the pipeline's domestic exit point in Turkey. This pipeline remains intensely supported by the U.S. in terms of providing its European allies with energy security, which was also underlined by Sandra Oudkirk, Deputy Assistant Secretary in the U.S. Bureau of Energy Resources, as follows:

> Oudkirk told journalists ... that TANAP would bring diversification of supply and energy security to European countries and to Turkey. "TANAP is a strong additional element for energy security for Turkey and Europe," she said and added, "The U.S. government supports the project on a policy basis. We are supporting it even though there is no direct investment in it." [...] "The launching of TANAP on Tuesday is really good news. There are lots of bad, challenging and difficult news around the world, but TANAP is

> universally good. As the U.S., we consider energy security for ourselves and our allies as very important." [...] Oudkirk also said that two criteria are central when the U.S. considers support for a European gas project, the first being the effect of the project on Ukraine and the second related to energy security. "Turkey is a big country and economically diversified," the official said, adding that Turkey with its many energy resources is very different to that of other European countries like Bulgaria that is 100 percent reliant on Russian gas. "When we look at the projects such as the Nord Stream 2, TurkStream's second line and the former South Stream, we consider two things. First, we look at the effect on Ukraine as the Russian government no longer wants to transit gas through Ukraine. That would be very bad news for Ukraine," she said. She added "the second thing we look at is energy security for countries in Europe. We fully support diversification of energy supplies." (Temizer & Erdoğan, 2018)

The prominence of TANAP and Ankara-Baku relations was articulated by President Erdoğan as follows:

> Azerbaijan have adapted to the changing geopolitical landscape and rapidly become the shining light in its region. The projects we jointly have conducted such as the Baku-Tbilisi-Ceyhan Oil Pipeline, the Baku-Tbilisi-Erzurum Natural Gas Pipeline, the Baku-Tbilisi-Kars Railway and TANAP are leaving their mark on the entire region. Turkey is one of the biggest investors in Azerbaijan. Hopefully, Azerbaijan will soon become one of the biggest investors in Turkey as well. (Presidency of the Republic of Turkey, 2018)

The importance of TANAP was also voiced by President Aliyev as follows:

> Baku-Tbilisi-Ceyhan, Baku-Tbilisi-Erzurum oil and gas pipelines, the inauguration of TANAP this year are historic projects. By implementing joint projects, Azerbaijan and Turkey redraw [the] energy and transport map of Eurasia. [...] The importance of our countries is growing. (Trend News Agency, 2018)

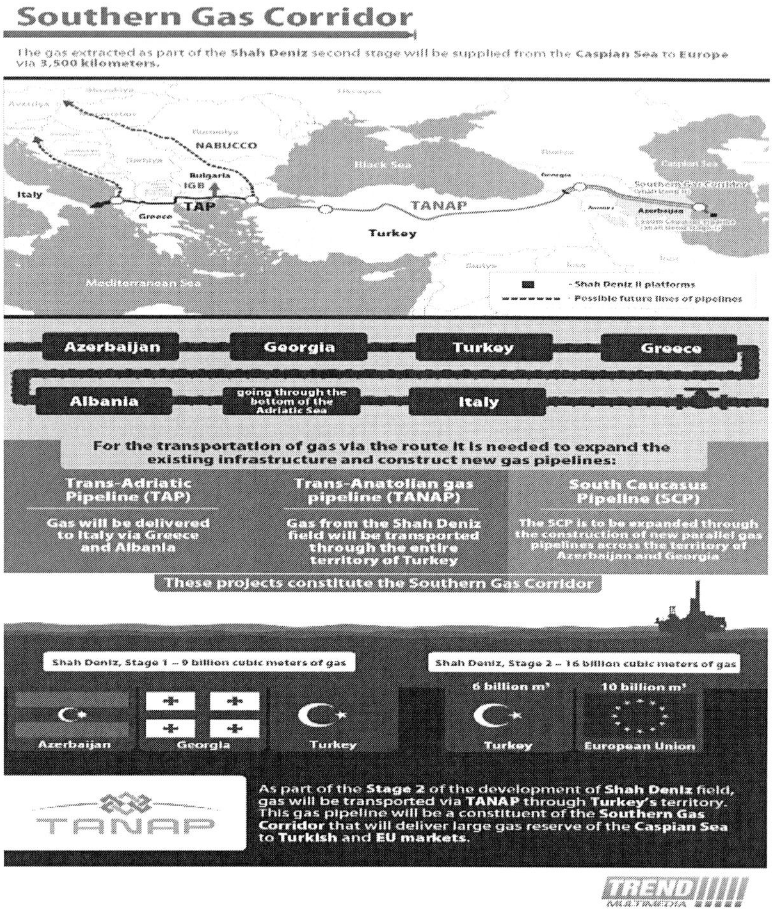

Figure 4: Southern Gas Corridor. Source: Trend News Agency, n.d.

The American Opposition towards the Russian-German Nord Stream 2 Natural Gas Project

Nord Stream is a project that will transport natural gas through a pipeline assembled underneath the Baltic Sea between Russia's Vyborg province and Germany's Lubmin province (Nord Stream AG, 2016). When the twin pipelines, each of them 1,224 kilometres long, are completely operative, a gas flow will be realized between Germany and Russia, depriving them of the necessity for any transit country. This makes the project a sui generis one. This project is foreseen to carry 55 bcm of gas annually. While Gazprom stands as the principal shareholder in this project with 51%, the German BASF Wintershall and E.ON Ruhrgas possess 15.5% shares each. Of the remaining shares, 9% belong to the Dutch N.V. Nederlandse Gasunie, and another partner in the project, specifically the French company GDF Suez, holds 9% shares as well. In this way, the Russian-German control in the project is equivalent to 82%. The Baltic countries and Poland have countered this project with plausible reasons (Kamalov, 2008, pp. 288-291). Gazprom selected the former German Chancellor Gerhard Schroeder as the head of the project with the expectation of breaking Northern European countries' opposition. It was planned that when the project would become functional in the last quarter of 2015, these two pipelines would be capable of providing 55 bcm of Russian gas to the E.U. for at least 50 years.

The first line of Nord Stream became operative in November 2011 and stretched to its project volume of 27.5 bcm. The second line, planned to have the same capacity as the first line, was finished in April 2012 and turned out to be functional as of October 2012. Studies on the realization of third and fourth lines continued. Subsequently, Gazprom, E.ON, Shell and OMV reached an MoU/Good Will Protocol for Nord Stream 3 and 4, adding another 55 bcm to the total capacity on top of the previous 55 bcm, on June 18, 2015. After this signing ceremony, the top executives of Gazprom, BASF, E.ON, ENGIE, OMV and Royal Dutch Shell reached a deal on a Shareholding Agreement for the enactment of the Nord Stream 2 project, which planned to upturn gas supply to the E.U. market, at the Eastern Economic Forum held in Vladivostok on September 4, 2015. The project would be advanced by a new project company entitled New European Pipeline AG. For the contracted document, Gazprom would possess 51% shares in the project company. E.ON, Shell, OMV and BASF/Wintershall would have 10% shares each. The remaining 9% of shares would be controlled by ENGIE. The extension of one of these pipelines to England remains under discussion. With this line, it is aimed to convey gas to England, the Netherlands, France, Denmark and other E.U. members (Örmeci & Kısacık, 2018, p. 324).

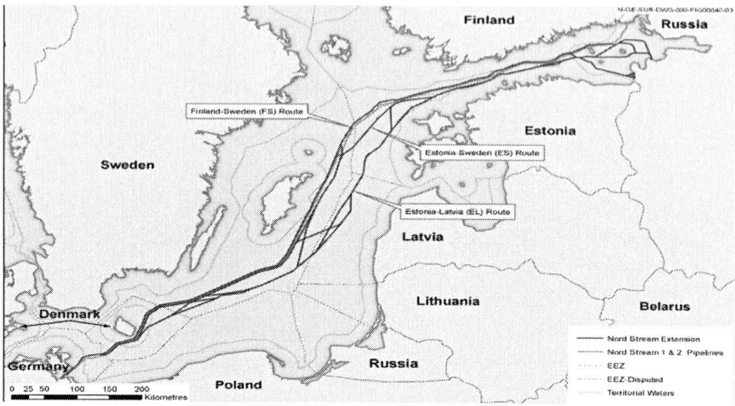

Figure 5: Planned Extensions to Nord Stream 1 and 2. Source: Michalopoulos, 2015.

It is clear that this project is certainly a very significant one within the framework of the Kremlin's economic and strategic interests. One noteworthy fact has to be revealed in that regard. When the E.C. approves countless decisions in the dynamic topics explicitly lessening the reliance on Russia, differentiating resources and ensuring security of supply, the project which will upsurge the dependency of Europe on Moscow in natural gas is being implemented under Berlin's leadership. When the E.C. recommends to the European Parliament that, in terms of energy resources' importation, a non-E.U. member country ought not to possess above 30% shares in view of the security of energy supply and resource diversification goals, it must be underscored that the prioritizing of this project over these recommendations remains a meaningful issue to be deliberated over. Principally Berlin, but other capitals as well, stand firm in considering only their interests after the determination of their particular circumstances. In such conditions, the interests of countries or companies far outweigh the Union's interests and policies (Pamir, 2017, p. 301).

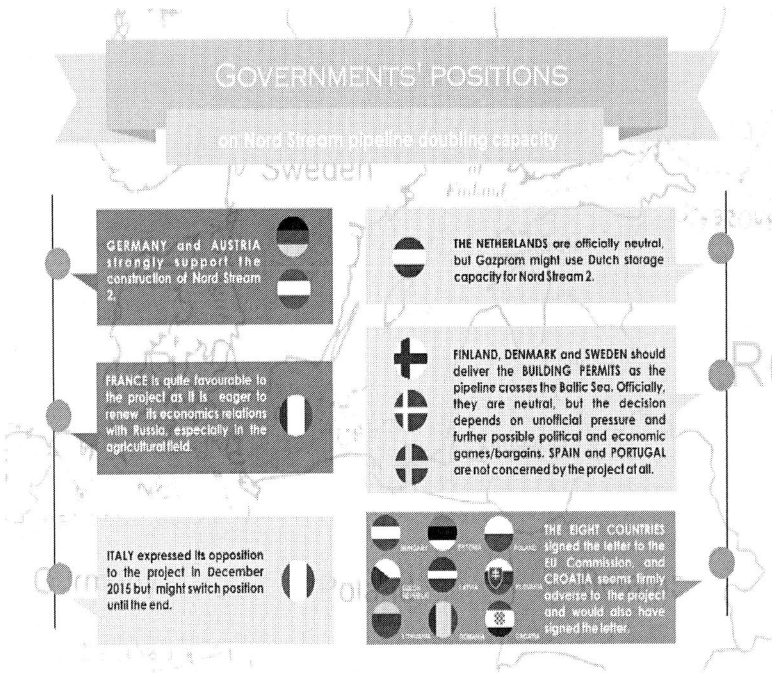

Figure 6: Governments' Positions on Nord Stream Pipeline Doubling Capacity. Source: Votewatch, 2016.

On June 9, 2016, a Good Will Protocol was signed by Nord Stream 2 AG and Allseas Group for the laying of the first line of this pipeline in the Baltic Sea. Following this development, on April 24, 2017, this pipeline's financing agreement was signed between Nord Stream 2 AG and ENGIE, OMV, Royal Dutch Shell, Uniper and Wintershall. These five European companies committed to meet 50% of the pipeline's cost. A group of countries within the E.U., led by Poland and the Czech Republic, opposed the Nord Stream 2 project owing to several reasons, including environmental issues and the further increasing of Gazprom's monopoly. The European Union has mentioned that it demands that its member countries make their own decisions and take initiatives. One of the discussed subjects was the suitability of this project to the European Union's Third Energy Package. The Nord Stream 2 AG underscored the unnecessity of this process and also underlined that this project is irrelevant to the Third Energy Package. On the other hand, E.U. officials claimed that the continental (land) part of this pipeline has to be evaluated within the context of the package. While the discussions were ongoing, due to this complex process, it was assessed that the project would be delayed until towards the end of 2019 (Pamir, 2017, pp. 301-302).

But this natural gas pipeline project developed by the Russian Federation has been criticized by both European countries like Poland and Ukraine as well as the U.S.A. The opponents of this project have been underscoring that the Nord Stream 2 natural gas pipeline project will increase Europe's high dependence on Russia. Another criticism in that regard has been put forward by Poland and Ukraine due to the fact that, in the event of Nord Stream 2 becoming operational, they might lose an important amount in transit fees, estimated to be $3 billion. In order to prevent this natural gas pipeline from becoming operational, Washington has been intensively carrying out several methods such as sanctioning countries and companies that have been working with the Russian Federation in order to realize this project. The latest development on this issue was the introduction of a bill by U.S. Senators Ted Cruz (R-TX) and Jeanne Shaheen (D-NH) on May 14, 2019 that would impose sanctions on vessels involved in fabricating the projected Nord Stream 2 natural gas pipeline and other Russian energy projects. Cruz underscored that *"Nord Stream 2 threatens Europe's energy security and America's national security. The United States simply cannot allow Russia to dominate Europe's energy future"*. In parallel with this, Shaheen highlighted that Russian President Vladimir Putin "*is dangling the prospect of cheap gas in front of some of our closest allies to monopolize the supply of energy in Europe and bring increased instability to the continent. This pipeline has the tremendous potential to compromise energy security throughout the continent for decades"*. This initiative came onto the agenda after TASS, Russia's official news agency, referred to Gazprom Deputy Chairman Vitaly Markelov underscoring that simply 40 km remains to be constructed of the 800-km Russian part of the planned pipeline from Russia to Germany under the Baltic Sea (Snow, 2019).

Conclusion

In this paper, the main energy security parameters of the U.S. in the Eurasia region within the 21st century were discussed. In the first part, the place of LNG exports in Washington's energy security policies was elaborated. Secondly, the reasons why the U.S. has been strongly supporting the Southern Gas Corridor that aims to transport the vast natural gas resources of Azerbaijan to European markets via the Trans-Anatolian and Trans-Adriatic Pipeline projects were set forth. Thirdly, the reasons why Washington has been strongly disapproving and trying to prevent the Moscow-Berlin-sponsored Nord Stream 2 natural gas pipeline project from becoming operational were examined.

To maintain its valuable position in the European gas supply and bypass Ukraine as a transit state, Moscow has been attaching special importance to the new natural gas transportation projects to Europe since the occurrence of the gas crises in 2006 and 2009 between Ukraine and itself. The noteworthy projects that have been developed in this sense are the South Stream and Nord Stream projects. The South Stream was advanced by Russian and Italian energy companies in 2007 with an envisioned capacity of 63 bcm. Nevertheless, numerous significant developments have delayed the operation of South Stream, specifically the high cost of the project, projected to reach €29 billionand the E.U.'s pressure on countries such as Bulgaria not to agree to the authorization of Russia regarding this issue because of Russia's Ukraine policy. In the aftermath of the breaking out of the Ukraine crisis in November 2013, discussions on South Stream were put off and, in answer to this, Moscow presented the TurkStream project together with Ankara in which the associated contracts between them were concluded, and this pipeline was anticipated to be operational by the end of 2019 with twin pipelines operating with a capacity of 15.75 bcm each. Other significant pipelines in that regard are Nord Stream 1 and 2. The first line has remained functional since 2012. Gazprom and its European partners have been intensifying their efforts with regard to implementing Nord Stream 3 and 4, which will also hold a 55-bcm capacity. This project is one of great standing for Russia due to the straight transference of natural gas to Europe (Germany), bypassing Ukraine. Within the context of the Nord Stream 2 natural gas pipeline becoming operational, Russia is about to complete all the permissions from the related countries that the pipeline will pass through. In that sense, Gazprom is determined to complete this pipeline at the end of 2019 or at the beginning of 2020 at the latest. On the other side of the coin, the U.S. and some of its European allies, especially Poland, France and Ukraine, have been making intensive efforts to prevent this pipeline from becoming operational. In that sense, Washington has preferred to adopt sanctioning policies towards the participants of this huge natural gas project. But the participants have not stepped back from their current stances. The competition on whether or not this project will become operational between the proponents of Nord Stream 2, led by Moscow, and thc opponents of the project, led by Washington, is likely to continue in the coming years, and this struggle will form one of the hottest topics that will be followed within the international arena.

Although Europe's dependency on Russian natural gas will withstand this struggle in the next few years, Europe will attempt to increase its initiatives to lessen its continuing addiction to Russian natural gas by attaching special importance to such alternatives as the Southern Gas Corridor. In parallel with this, it will strive to work on the probable addition of the Eastern Mediterranean's, Turkmenistan's and Iran's natural gas resources to this corridor due to the inadequacy of Baku's natural gas reserves (single stanch supplier) in order to meet the European demand in the 2030s, estimated to be above 600 bcm. Nevertheless, all of them will be expected to be involved in the aftermath of the resolution of problems within these regions. When the official statements made by the U.S. administration are examined in detail, Washington's powerful support for the full realization of the Southern Gas Corridor can be clearly seen, with the reasoning of the provision of European energy security and the successful implementation of a natural gas corridor, bypassing the Russian-proposed and Russian-dominated natural gas pipeline projects, namely TurkStream and Nord Stream. Also, the competition between the U.S.-sponsored Southern Gas Corridor and the Russian-backed Turk Stream and Nord Stream 2 natural gas projects becoming fully operational will be closely followed in the international arena within the context of Eurasian energy security in the 21st century by the related parties.

Accompanying this point, since the 2010s, the energy security parameters in Eurasia have been under the effect of shale gas development in the U.S. With the discovery of shale gas and oil, Washington has turned out to be a net energy exporter; in other words, one should talk about the gradual decreasing of U.S. energy imports in recent times. Also, with the intention of helping to decrease its European allies' ever-increasing dependence on Russian natural gas, Washington has been proposing several LNG transportation projects to Europe. But it should be clearly put forward that, due to environmental concerns in Europe, the preference of using domestic energy resources of some European countries like Poland and the preference of some European countries like Germany to develop more energy relations with Russia, the transportation of U.S. LNG to Europe is highly unlikely in the near and longer terms. Consequently, the current and probable energy security parameters of the U.S. will be closely influenced by its struggle with the Russian Federation within the context of establishing domination in terms of Eurasian geopolitics within the 21st century.

References

Caşın, M. H. & Kısacık, S. (2018). *Avrupa Birliği Enerji Hukuku ve Güvenlik Algılamaları.* Çağlayan Kitap & Eğitim & Yayıncılık.

CEEP. (2019, March 15). *LNG imports from the U.S. continue to rise, up by 181%.* https://www.ceep.be/lng-imports-from-the-u-s-continue-to-rise-up-by-181/

Deyette, J., Clemmer, S., Cleetus, R., Sattler, S., Bailie, A., & Rising, M. (2015). *The Natural Gas Gamble: A Risky Bet on America's Clean Energy Future.* Union of Concerned Scientists. Retrieved August 17, 2018, from https://www.ucsusa.org/sites/default/files/attach/2015/03/natural-gas-gamble-full-report.pdf

Erhan, Ç., & Gürbüz, A. (2013). Azerbaycan'ın Enerji Politikası. In. Ç. Erhan (Ed.), *Kafkasya'nın Yükselen Yıldızı İlham Aliyev Döneminde Azerbaycan* (pp. 297-351). Atatürk Araştırma Merkezi.

Grigas, A. (2017). *The New Geopolitics of Natural Gas.* Harvard University Press.

Kamalov, İ. (2008). *Putin Dönemi Rus Dış Politikası: Moskova'nın Rövanşı.* Yeditepe Yayınevi.

Kısacık, S. (2017). *The Ukraine Policy of the Russian Federation and The Paradigms in European Energy Security* [Unpublished doctoral dissertation]. Yeditepe University, İstanbul.

Kısacık, S., & Avcı, T. (2015). An Assessment of the Pipeline Projects for the Transportation of Caspian Basin Hydrocarbons within the Context of Energy Strategies of the United States, the Russian Federation, and Turkey. In H. Işıksal and O. Örmeci (Eds.), *Turkish Foreign Policy in the New Millenium* (pp.463-502). Peter Lang.

Kısacık, S., & Kaya, F. (2017). Turkey's Unique Energy Corridor Role at the Center of Eurasia in the 21st Century. *Marmara Üniversitesi Siyasal Bilimler Dergisi / Marmara University Journal of Political Science*, *5*, 93-105. http://dergipark.gov.tr/download/article-file/301437.

Küçükkaya, E. (2019, July 23). *IEA: ABD ve Çin LNG Ticaretinde Lider Olacak.* Enerji Portalı. https://www.enerjiportali.com/iea-abd-ve-cin-lng-ticaretinde-lider-olacak/

Mai, H. J. (2019, March 15). *America's Oil and Natural Gas Boom Continues To Reshape Foreign Policy.* The Well News. https://www.thewellnews.com/americas-oil-and-natural-gas-boom-continues-to-reshape-foreign-policy/

Michalopoulos, S. (2015). *Σύγκρουση στην Ευρώπη για την επέκταση του ρωσικού αγωγού Nord Stream 2*. Euractiv. https://www.euractiv.gr/section/energia/news/sigkrousi-stin-evropi-gia-tin-epektasi-tou-rosikou-agogou-nord-stream/

Nord Stream AG. (2016). *Nord Stream – Operations*. Retrieved September 15, 2016, from http://www.nord-stream.com/operations/

Örmeci, O., & Kısacık, S. (2018). *Rusya Siyaseti ve Rus Diş Politikasi Teorik Çerçeve – Tarihsel Arka Plan – Örnek Olaylar*. Seçkin Yayıncılık.

Pamir, N. (2017). *Enerjinin İktidarı: Enerji Kaynaklarını Elinde Tutan, Dünyayı Elinde Tutar!*, 3rd edn. Hayykitap.

Presidency of the Republic of Turkey (2018, September 15). *Turkey is Azerbaijan's most important partner in trade, economy and culture*. https://www.tccb.gov.tr/en/news/542/98586/-turkey-is-azerbaijan-s-most-important-partner-in-trade-economy-and-culture-

S&P Global Platts. (2019, June 5). *US promotes 'freedom gas' but prices, not politicians, drive LNG flows*. https://blogs.platts.com/2019/06/05/us-freedom-gas-prices-lng-flows/

Snow, N. (2019, May 15). *Senators' bill would impose Nord Stream 2 sanctions*. Oil & Gas Journal. https://www.ogj.com/general-interest/government/article/17279280/senators-bill-would-impose-nord-stream-2-sanctions

Sürmelioğlu-Parlar, D. (2018). Türkiye-Azerbaycan İlişkileri. In G. Tüysüzoğlu & A. Özkan (Eds.), *Soğuk Savaş Sonrası Türkiye'nin Kafkasya ve Orta Asya Siyaseti* (pp. 25-59). Detay Yayıncılık.

Temizer, M., & Erdogan, H. (2018, June 12). *US strongly backs TANAP for energy sec.: US Official*. AA English. https://www.aa.com.tr/en/americas/us-strongly-backs-tanap-for-energy-sec-us-official/1172823

Trend News Agency. (2018, September 15). *President Ilham Aliyev: By implementing joint projects, Azerbaijan and Turkey redraw energy and transport map of Eurasia*. Trend News Agency. https://en.trend.az/azerbaijan/politics/2952195.html

Trend News Agency. (n.d.). *Southern Gas Corridor*. Retrieved July 29, 2019, from https://en.trend.az/infographics_page.php?id=178

USEA. (n.d.). *Economic Benefits of US LNG Exports*. Retrieved July 29, 2019, from https://usea.org/event/economic-benefits-us-lng-exports

Votewatch. (2016, April 26). *The national and European politics behind Nord Stream II*. https://www.votewatch.eu/blog/the-national-and-european-politics-behind-nord-stream-ii/

CHAPTER TWO

CHINESE ENERGY POLICIES AND THEIR IMPACT ON FOREIGN POLICY IN THE MIDDLE EAST

R. KUTAY KARACA* AND MÜGE YÜCE**

Introduction

The 18th National Congress of the Communist Party of China (CPC) in 2012 points to a historical turning point in Chinese foreign policy in the Middle East as China then adopted a more comprehensive and strategic approach towards the region. In the first year following the 18th National Congress of the CPC, Xi Jinping 习近平 announced the Belt and Road Initiative (BRI) in 2013 and realized a historic visit to the Middle East in 2016. Moreover, the Chinese government also published the first official Arab Policy Paper reflecting the new perspective on the Middle East in 2016.

This critical change in China's Middle East policy sparked a heated debate in the international system and even in international relations (IR). There are various theories and reasons to explain the new Chinese approach to Middle Eastern affairs. However, the prominent reasons given have been the energy factor and China's increasing dependency on imported energy from the region. In 1993, China's oil consumption exceeded oil production, and China began to import oil. After about two decades, the secure limit of the dependency on imported energy exceeded in 2009 (Karaca, 2012, p. 93). As a result of the growing oil imports, China imported 15.2% of global imported oil in 2017. China was the second-largest importer after Europe, surpassing the United States (US). And the Middle East was the largest oil exporter in 2017 with a share of 35% of the total (BP, 2018, p. 24). Even

* Prof. Dr. R. Kutay Karaca, Social Sciences Institute, Aydın University. E-mail: rkkaraca@gmail.com.
** Müge Yüce, Ph.D., Atatürk University. E-mail: mugeyuce@gmail.com.

though China is trying to diversify its energy supply sources, the Middle East still provides 56% of the total crude oil imports of China (Qian, 2014, p. 51).

Within this context, most Chinese specialists assert that Beijing will establish closer relations with oil-exporting countries tout court because of the soaring demand for imported hydrocarbons by the start of the twenty-first century (Legrenzi & Lawson, 2015, p. 62). This is especially the case for the energy relations between China and the Middle Eastern countries. Indeed, Chinese leaders have committed themselves to energy diplomacy and heartened energy collaboration with Middle East oil-producing countries in recent years. Under the current circumstances, following through on energy cooperation with these countries is inescapable for China's security (Qian, 2010, p. 65). Nevertheless, the energy relations between China and the Middle Eastern countries also have critical importance for the Middle East and even for the international energy markets. Because of the fact that the Middle East has approximately 72% of the world's total oil reserves and China alone accounted for 23.6% of the world's total energy consumption in 2018, energy relations between them have a great capacity to change the geopolitics of energy. Therefore, the growing political and economic ties between China and the Middle East necessitate a comprehensive and multi-dimensional analysis in terms of the changing regional and international geopolitical landscapes.

In terms of the regional level, Middle East has suffered from social and political instability since mass movements called the Arab Spring began in 2011. The Arab Spring not only changed the social and political structure of the region but also caused a new reckoning of the Great Powers in the region. Crises in Libya, Yemen and Syria turned into international issues between the Great Powers and divided them into two camps: the US and Western countries on one side and Russia, China and Iran on the other. Moreover, the changing balance of power in the region escalated the tension between Saudi Arabia and Iran, which are the main partners of China in the Middle East.

In addition to regional turbulences, the changing dynamics of the international system are another factor that affects the Middle East policy of China. The global financial crisis of 2008, the internal challenges of the European Union such as populism, Brexit and social integration concerns, the changing foreign policy vision of the US under the Obama administration, the growing threat of terrorism and the emergence of ISIS have been the main determinants in the formation of the Middle East policy of China. The period after 9/11 in particular caused a breakdown in relations between the United States and Middle East countries (Qian, 2010, p. 76). The Middle

East remains unstable, especially since the Arab Spring. This instability causes a risk of interruption in energy flows to China. Beijing, as a net energy consumer, has to operate within an unsteady geopolitical context in terms of the Middle East (Troush, 1999).

Accessing energy resources in a secure and stable way does not only mean guaranteeing economic development for China. Rather, energy security is considered a guarantee for social welfare, the rapid modernization of the army and the continuity of the regime. The inter-dependency between energy security and domestic stability has directly affected China's foreign policy. Therefore, China perceives establishing relations with countries that have energy resources as a priority (Karaca, 2012, p. 93).

In the current situation, China is building stronger ties with Middle Eastern states and is trying to expand its influence in the region. Now, the Middle East is considered as one of the privileged regions in general Chinese diplomacy. As Pan mentioned, "It has reached the point that not knowing China's Middle East policies means not understanding Chinese diplomacy as a whole. Nor can one understand the Middle East without knowledge of that region's relations with China" (Pan, 1997, p. 35). Chinese Foreign Minister Wang Yi 王毅 also stated in 2014: "China's political role in the Middle East will only grow. There is no way back" (Lyall, 2019).

Within these given conditions, this study tries to shed light on the changing nature of China's Middle East policy and to analyze the possible impacts of their increasing inter-dependency on the near future of these bilateral relations. The main hypothesis of the study is that the traditional political stance of China will remain couched in terms of Middle Eastern affairs. In contrast with mainstream IR specialists, it is asserted that China has to maintain its Middle Eastern relationships in a balanced and impartial position. To justify the hypothesis, this study is divided into three main sections. In the first section, the historical background of China's Middle East policy is examined from the 1950s to the end of the Cold War. The second part of the study tries to present the interactions between increasing energy consumption and the changing political behaviour in Chinese foreign policy. In the last section, the efforts of the Chinese leadership to balance regional and global interests are evaluated. According to the main findings of the study, the historical meaning of the Middle East has undergone a big transformation in the eyes of the Chinese leadership. Hereupon the Middle East is considered a region that directly affects the internal and international policies of China. When it is analyzed in detail, China's Middle East policy shows a great harmony of continuities and changes to balance the national and global interests of China.

Historical Background of China's Middle East Policy

The Middle East is located at the confluence of Asia, Africa and Europe and links the three continents with each other in terms of geopolitical considerations. As a result of this strategically important geographic location, the Middle East is considered as a centre of the transportation network between the eastern and western hemispheres. This geographically strategic location of the Middle East has provoked the Great Powers to vie for control over the region. Therefore, it is widely believed that a growing power that has certain global interests cannot neglect to gain influence over the Middle East. In this context, there is a heated debate about China's position in the Middle East. In recent years, Beijing has had an increasing motivation to expand its influence over the Middle East, and China's overseas interests have extended to West Asia and North Africa (Gao, 2014, p. 67). Concordantly, the foreign policy of China in the Middle East has transformed and adapted to the new developments in regional and international politics. To understand this revision, it is vital to reveal the traditional meaning of the Middle East for China.

In the historical sources of China, the Middle East is not considered as an independent geographical region in its own right but in relation to the neighbouring regions that connect the Middle East to China. In the official documents of China, the term used for the Middle East today is West Asia 西亚 (xī yà), which is used in connection with Central Asia 中亚 (zhōng yà) (Shichor, 2018, p. 47). However, due to the growing importance of the Middle East, Chinese leaders not only consider the region to include West Asia and North Africa but also refer to the region of the Broader Middle East 大中东 (dà zhōng dōng) as a part of Central Asia and South Asia (Scobell, 2018, p. 19). So, the Middle East is traditionally perceived as a region that is not directly related to Chinese national interests. However, especially since the 1990s, the traditional approach towards the Middle East has undergone a big transformation as a result of the growing Chinese economy.

Before the 1990s, China's Middle East policy was shaped by the general principles of Chinese foreign policy, such as non-interference in internal politics, respect for sovereignty, and mutual benefit from its relationships. In this context, China's first direct contact with the Middle East was realized in 1955 through the Bandung Conference in Indonesia. At this conference, Prime Minister Zhou Enlai 周恩来 developed direct relations with the participants and became the main architect of the Middle East/African policies of China between 1955 and 1974 (Olimat, 2014, p. 4). China, which was not then a member of the United Nations and was officially recognized by just a few countries in the international system, made direct contacts at the Bandung Conference to expand its diplomatic, cultural and commercial relations. China gained the support of the countries of the region at this conference, especially with its support for the national independence movements in the Third World. After this conference, China's contacts in the Middle East until the early 1980s were motivated by its efforts to export the ideological thoughts of socialism and support the anti-imperialist revolutionary movement in the region (Evron, 2016, pp. 4-5).

The main reason for its efforts to expand political relations with Middle Eastern countries was based on the "Intermediate Zone" theory developed by Mao Zedong 毛泽东. According to Mao, the Middle East is located in the Intermediate Zone, which is vital for controlling international relations. Mao pointed out that the main field of interest lay not between the two worlds but rather in the vast zone that separated the two rivals (the US and the USSR). Therefore, the Intermediate Zone became a new ally for the socialist camp because it served as a protective buffer (Gillespie, 2004, pp. 111-112). The conceptualization of the Intermediate Zone determined China's political stance on the developments in the Middle East and shaped Chinese policies towards regional crises such as the 1952 Egyptian Free Officers Movement and the transition of Gamal Abdel Nasser to the government, the formation of the Baghdad Pact in 1955, the Suez Crisis of 1956, the 1958 Lebanese Crisis and the 1958 Iraq Coup staged by General Abd al-Karim Qasim (Olimat, 2014, p. 64).

Apart from the ideology-based geopolitical approach towards the region, relations with the Great Powers and especially decreasing Soviet influence in the Middle East was another motivation to force China to be more active in the region during the Cold War. Indeed, Masannat (1966, p. 216) says that Sino-Arab relations cannot be understood without reference to several relevant factors on the international scene. Any realistic approach must consider the role and objectives of the Great Powers. John Calabrese, who focuses on Sino-Middle Eastern relations, also argues that China's Middle East policy is a reflection of Beijing's relations with the US and the superpowers (Calabrese, 1991). During the 1971-1989 period, China developed its foreign policy in the Gulf Region and the Arabian Peninsula in accordance with three main principles to limit Soviet influence (Bin Huwaidin, 2002, p. 108):

- De facto rapprochement with the US
- Maintaining political relations with Gulf Region and Arabian Peninsula countries
- Developing economic relations with the countries of the region

In this context, the most explanatory reason for China's intervention in the Middle East and its entry into the region is the necessity of the Cold War conditions (Calabrese, 1991, p. 3). It was especially the changing atmosphere of the international system from 1971 and regional developments that contributed to the growing relations between China and the Middle Eastern countries. The positive impact of the votes of the Middle Eastern countries during the process of China's UN membership application and the loss of influence of the Cultural Revolution from 1974 opened the way for China to show interest in the region. China took the side of the Arab countries during the 1973 Arab-Israeli War and supported the 1973 oil embargo decision. After the decision of the oil embargo, China aided the efforts of the countries in the region to reduce the influence of the Western powers over them and to pursue an independent foreign policy. The deterioration of the relations between the countries of the region with the Western bloc during the 1973 oil crisis, the crisis in Afghanistan in the late 1970s, the Iranian Islamic Revolution in 1979 and the Iran-Iraq War was an accelerating and encouraging development for the Middle Eastern countries to establish diplomatic relations with China (Olimat, 2014, p. 35). During the 1980s, the most important development that revealed China's basic perception of the Middle East was the Iran-Iraq War (1980-1988) (Neill, 2014, p. 208). Beijing sold significant amounts of arms to both sides but, at the same time, maintained its neutral stance in the political conflict between Iran and Iraq (Dillon, 2004, p. 50). Beijing was motivated by the great amount of economic gains and foreign exchange reserve obtained through arms sales during the war (Rashida, 2010, p. 137). Indeed, Iraq and Iran were the largest consumers of Chinese arms sales during the 1980s (Bitzinger, 1992, p. 87). According to the SIPRI Arms Transfers Database, these two countries alone accounted for 40% of all Chinese arms sales between 1980 and 1990 (SIPRI, n.d.). More sophisticated weapons systems, improved marketing techniques and the contacts which Chinese officials had established in the non-military sphere facilitated China's emergence as a major arms supplier to the Gulf countries, primarily Iran, Iraq and Saudi Arabia (Calabrese, 1992, p. 473).

Since the end of the Cold War, the main aims of Chinese foreign policy have been searching for energy security and expanding overseas markets and investment opportunities. China's Middle East policy seeks to promote economic and energy relations (Chaziza, 2016, p. 25). Its dependence on energy imports, which began to be clearly felt after 1993, is the most important element highlighted by studies dealing with China's Middle East relations. According to Neill, who sees energy as the primary factor in China's relations with the region, the Middle East is still China's most important oil resource, although the increasing oil demand has necessitated Beijing to diversify its energy supply sources (Neill, 2014, p. 206). In terms of oil prices, transportation and geographic factors, the Middle East should be China's main source of oil (Qian, 2010, p. 68).

The meaning of the Middle East has transformed from the traditional one of a "remote location" to a "main region to supply energy resources" to China. Indeed, Dongfang Xiao 东方 晓, Secretary-General and Vice President of the Chinese Middle East Studies Association, defines the Middle East by its strategic location, energy resources and defining characteristic of Islamic religion (Xiao, 2013, p. 98). Given the growing importance of the region for China, it is asserted that Beijing's traditional political stance based on respect for sovereignty, non-interference in domestic affairs, a win-win strategy promoting mutually beneficial economic relations and refusal of foreign military presence in other countries will be inadequate to ensure its vital interests. By relying on this assertion, some experts believe that China will have to become an influential regional actor in competitive cooperation with the US, which is the dominant great power in the region (Dorsey, 2017, p. 1). Within the context of recent developments in global and regional policy, the Middle East is associated with four main security factors for China in the twenty-first century (Scobell, 2018, p. 11):

- Main region of competition between the Great Powers over sphere of influence
- Rich energy resources
- Inclusion within China's national interests
- Role as the geostrategic junction of the world

Summarizing the relations between China and the Middle Eastern countries for the period 1950-1990, it is possible to say that Chinese foreign policy was entirely different before and after 1978 in the Middle East. The main factors forming Chinese foreign policy before 1978 were its socialist-communist ideology and its efforts to regime-export, while after 1978 they were economic gains and profits after the reform and opening-up policies. After the implementation of the reform and opening-up policies, Beijing tried to enhance its relationship with the Middle Eastern countries in spite of the security concerns over the ties between Uighurs and the Muslim world. Indeed, China still considers the region as a strategic zone to control fundamentalist and radical Islamist movements. Therefore, there is already a contradiction for China to balance national and international security concerns in the Middle East. In terms of the increasing energy consumption,

Beijing still depends on Middle Eastern crude oil. The next section will explain this dependency.

Impacts of Energy Consumption on the Foreign Policy of China in the Middle East

The Middle East policy of China has mostly been considered as a reflection of the Chinese thirst for energy. This phenomenon is quite understandable as China is the largest energy consumer while the Middle East is one of the regions which has a great amount of rich natural resources. Indeed, China accounted for 24% of global energy consumption and 34% of global energy consumption growth in 2018, and it was also the largest contributor to global growth for the 18th consecutive year (BP, 2019b, 1). Energy supply security is contemplated as a prerequisite for the economic rise of China by many politicians and academics. However, unlike other forces in the world, securing energy supplies for China not only ensures its sustainable economic development but also increases the welfare of the people, the rapid modernization of the army and, most importantly, the maintenance of the regime (Karaca, 2012, p. 93). Therefore, China adopted the "Go Out Policy" in its 10th Five Year Plan published in 2001 (Vendryes, 2012, p. 5). The "Go Out Policy" 走出去战略 (zǒu chū qù zhàn lüè) is considered the beginning of China's decision to expand relations across the ocean in the energy field, and three important oil companies (CNPC, Sinopec Group, CNOOC) were encouraged to engage in activities such as oil exploration, extraction, refinery and pipeline construction, especially in the Middle East (Dorraj & English, 2012, p. 175).

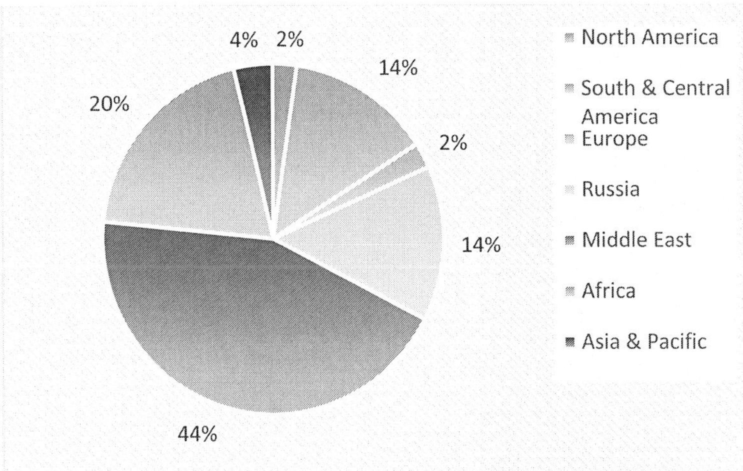

Figure 1: Chinese Oil Sources by Region – 2017. Source: BP, 2018.

The "Go Out Strategy" mainly aims to diversify energy supply sources and strengthen mutually beneficial cooperation in international energy markets (Qian, 2010, p. 66). As can be seen in Figure 1, the Middle East has been the main oil source of China as a result of the implementation of the "Go Out Strategy". China's energy interests in the Middle East lie beyond oil and gas transfer and cover all areas of energy cooperation such as energy exploration and exploitation, mortgaged contracts with risks, two-way investments, renewable energy development and asset acquisitions (Qian, 2014, p. 48-49).

The Gulf region and the Middle East are also the main sources of LNG as well as oil imports for China. Therefore, smooth access to energy necessitates securing pipeline and maritime routes all over the world, but especially in the Gulf region and the Middle East. In this context, maritime security has become increasingly important for China's LNG imports. The natural gas trade, as LNG is imported by China, grew by 46.51% in 2017. Australia is the main LNG source country, while Qatar is in second place with a share of 19.6% (BP, 2018, pp. 34-35). Aside from Qatar, other Middle Eastern countries that supplied LNG to China in 2017 were Oman, Algeria and Egypt (BP, 2018, p. 34). Moreover, it is estimated that China is going to consume two times more natural gas in 2040 (BP, 2019a, p. 2).

As a result of its high dependence on energy imports from the Middle East, Beijing has been forced to take control over energy trade routes. Major oil-exporting countries in the Middle East such as Iraq, Saudi Arabia,

Kuwait and the United Arab Emirates transfer oil through the Strait of Hormuz, with 85% going to the main energy consumer countries of Asia. For China, about 36% of its crude oil imports are transported through the Strait of Hormuz. Therefore, China would face a significant challenge in oil and gas imports in the event of the Strait of Hormuz being blocked (Qian, 2014, p. 56). With such heavy dependence on strategic checkpoints to import oil, the US' strategic domination over sea lane communications from the Strait of Hormuz will be perceived as a major threat to China's energy supply. So the main target of China's oil strategy is to avoid such a threat (Troush, 1999). Approximately 43% of imported oil from the Middle East has to pass through the Strait of Hormuz, while 82% of all Chinese maritime oil imports must pass through the Strait of Malacca (Bender & Rosen, 2015). To control the energy trade routes, Beijing has initiated great naval-based projects focusing on the Indian Ocean. One of the most important naval-based projects is called the "String of Pearls", and it is claimed that Chinese-sponsored port projects are part of a concerted plan by Beijing. Under the String of Pearls project, Chinese companies have been involved in the construction, expansion or operation of numerous commercial port facilities in the northern Indian Ocean, including at Gwadar (Pakistan), Hambantota and Colombo (Sri Lanka), Kyaukpyu (Myanmar), Lamu (Kenya) and Bagamoyo (Tanzania), and several others (such as Sonadia in Bangladesh) have been proposed (Brewster, 2017, pp. 276-278). In this context, China increased its military presence on the Strait of Hormuz, the Strait of Bab al-Mandeb and the Suez Canal, built ports of call in the Gulf countries, Egypt, Israel and Iran, and held a joint naval exercise in Iran and the Strait of Hormuz in 2017 (Kliman & Grace, 2018).

from / to	US	Europe	China	India	Japan
Iraq	15.8	26.7	19.5	21.6	1.4
Kuwait	7.1	9.8	18	11	11.3
Saudi Arabia	13.1	10.3	14.6	9.5	17.7
UAE	0.8	0.3	8.1	13.1	30.1
Other Middle Eastern Countries	0.3	18.4	30.9	14.6	11.2

Table 1: Share of Oil Exports from the Middle East to its Main Customers (%). Source: BP, 2018, p. 24.

It can be clearly seen in Table 1 above that Middle Eastern oil resources have become the main source for Asia-Pacific countries such as China, India and Japan. Table 1 also shows that Iraq, Kuwait and Saudi Arabia are China's major oil sources in the Middle East and that the share of the US and Western countries is on a decreasing trend. In this situation, the increasing energy consumption of Asia-Pacific countries will sharpen the competition to access Middle Eastern energy resources in the foreseeable future. This is to say that the new geopolitics of the energy competition will definitely affect the foreign policy of the major powers including China. Within this context, Beijing has already decided to reshape its foreign policy towards the Middle East.

Reshaping China's Middle East Policy

The regional and international power shifts present both opportunities and challenges to China in terms of securing energy supply. Under this condition, China finds itself in a contradictory situation in terms of basic principles of foreign policy in the Middle East. According to Qian, it is inevitable and safe for China to promote energy cooperation with Middle Eastern oil-producing countries. The geopolitics of Middle East countries has already changed (Qian, 2010, p. 69). As a result of the last developments, the traditional Chinese political stance that follows the principles of respect for sovereignty and never intervening in internal issues and taking a side on Middle Eastern conflicts has to change, and it must be more active in the region. In fact, Beijing has started to make a political, economic, cultural and diplomatic leap towards the Middle East. This actively balanced diplomacy towards the Middle East is looked upon kindly by the countries in the region. China, as a permanent member of the UN Security Council (UNSC) and the largest rapidly developing country, is playing an increasingly important role in the international arena and in Middle East affairs in particular (Qian, 2010, p. 77).

China has three main channels to expand its influence in the region:

- Economic and financial cooperation
- Major investments such as the BRI to promote stability through increasing the welfare of the region
- Participation in UN peacekeeping operations in the region and UNSC vetoes to be an active member of regional issues

China's trade volume with the Middle East rose by 87% from 2005 to 2009 and reached approximately $222 billion in 2012. Now, China is ranked as the top destination for the Middle East's exports, surpassing the United States (Kāzemi and Chen, 2014). According to World Bank trade statistics, the Middle East and North Africa (MENA) region accounted for 5.5% of total Chinese exports and 6.23% of total Chinese imports in 2017. In addition, the MENA region's imports from China are worth $34,627 million, with a partner share of 12.25%, and China is ranked first in this regard (WITS, 2017). Chinese economic ties are blooming, especially with the Gulf countries through the Gulf Cooperation Council (GCC). The GCC unites the Persian Gulf, which connects the Mediterranean and the Gulf of Aden to the Indian Ocean, the South China Sea and the Pacific. Moreover, mutual relationships between China and the Gulf states move beyond energy exports. In 2014, China and the Gulf states enhanced their relationships by accepting an action plan for the years from 2014 to 2017. Both sides decided to develop cooperation in a wide range of areas from politics to health and sports (Sevilla, 2017, p. 94).

Besides the need to protect its investments and secure energy supply from the region, China has a strategic interest in the stability of the Eurasian countries because Beijing is worried about the risk that the uprisings in the Middle East, North Africa and Central Asia will spread to Xinjiang (Dorsey, 2017, p. 1). China's overall relationship with the Middle East underwent its most significant transformation under the BRI in 2013. Indeed, the Middle East was designated as a "neighbour" region by Beijing in November 2013 at the Third Plenary Session of the 18th Central Committee of the Communist Party of China and falls within Beijing's top-priority geostrategic zone (Lyall, 2019). Beijing aims to increase employment and prosperity in the region through investments within the scope of the BRI and thus contribute to the resolution of instabilities (Calabrese, 2018, p. 181).

The BRI project gains its meaning when analyzed in the context of the changing policy of the US in the Middle East and Sino-US relations. In particular, the Middle East gained strategic importance against the "rebalancing" strategy of the Obama administration in Asia-Pacific. The US initiated this "rebalancing" strategy with an increase in US military power projection in the Asia-Pacific region. Therefore, the Middle East is becoming increasingly important in the implementation of China's neighbouring strategy as well as in China's relations with major powers, especially new Sino-US relations (Gao, 2014, p. 67).

With the decreasing influence of the US in the Middle East, China is becoming a more active power in the region's issues. To contribute to the stability of the region, China adheres to the principles of mutual benefit and win-win in production capacity cooperation with Middle Eastern countries (Yao, 2016, p. 8). The changing geopolitical view of the Middle East has also been reflected through the declaration of the BRI, and the Middle East has gained more importance for Chinese diplomacy under the BRI. Indeed, the prioritization of the Middle East within the BRI has seen China become the largest trading partner of the Arab League and Iran, as well as a key partner of Israel. This is to say that Beijing's Middle East policy is to focus on energy security on the one hand while it tries to enhance China's status in the region on the other through growing economic power to balance against, but not directly oppose, US influence (Lyall, 2019).

Another important channel for Chinese diplomacy in the Middle East is UN Peacekeeping Operations (UNPKO), especially since the 2000s. China provides personnel and equipment support throughout the Middle East, such as to UNPKO, such as the United Nations Truce Supervision Organization (UNTSO) in Palestine, the United Nations Interim Force in Lebanon (UNIFIL) and the United Nations Mission for the Referendum in Western Sahara (UNMINURSO). The first Chinese casualty occurred on the night of July 25, 2006 during an Israeli airstrike when one of the Chinese UN peacekeepers – Lieutenant Colonel Du Zhaoyu – was killed in southern Lebanon (Kemp, 2010, pp. 5-6).

Outside the UNPKO, Beijing has effectively increased its influence in Middle Eastern affairs through its UNSC membership. In recent years, the UNSC has discussed two prominent issues related to the Middle East region: one of them is the uranium enrichment programme of Iran, while the other is the Syrian crisis, ongoing since 2011. Beijing maintains its traditional diplomatic principles such as non-interference in internal politics on the Syrian crisis and has vetoed UN Resolutions that aim at foreign military intervention or regime change in Syria. However, China has changed its "fundamental position" on the Iranian nuclear issue and has actually voted against Iran at both the International Atomic Energy Agency (IAEA) and the UNSC (Wu, 2015, p. 55). Since 2006, Beijing has supported and voted for four UN Resolutions – 1696, 1737, 1747 and 1803 – which all enabled the UNSC to impose sanctions on Iran.

The Beijing administration, which has the will to contribute to conflict resolution and regional peace through UN missions in the Middle East, is convinced that the ongoing instability in the region can be prevented by economic development and increased welfare. In explicating Chinese foreign policy perceptions, Wang Jisi, Dean of the School of International Studies at Peking University, notes that "the perceived changing power balance between China and the United States has prompted many Chinese to expect, and aspire to, a more 'can-do' PRC [People's Republic of China] foreign policy". According to Hudson, this expectation requires reconstituting the historic Silk Road, both in its terrestrial and maritime dimensions, to guarantee a secure flow of oil, gas and other bulk resources. This means building and dominating a new Eurasian "super region" through an economic assistance programme for South Asia, Central Asia, the Middle East and the Caspian Sea region (Hudson, 2013, p. 460).

Even though its instability has steadily grown since the Arab Spring, the politically chaotic situation has contradictorily been the driving force for China's deeper entry into the region. According to Calabrese, the instability that arose with the Arab Spring also led to the creation of a justification for legitimacy through the discourse that the BRI would bring peace to the region through prosperity and development (Calabrese, 2018, p. 181). It is also important that the results of the Arab Spring have not only affected its Middle Eastern relations but also its competition in the South and East China Seas. As Sevilla asserts, the events of the Arab Spring awakened Asian policymakers to their over-dependence on Middle East energy suppliers. Because of the rising prices of basic services and commodities after the instability caused by the Arab Spring, growing Asian economies feel under pressure about their energy security. Indeed, Asian economies have increased their efforts to import more secure sources of hydrocarbon energy supplies and have become more assertive in protecting their interests in the Middle East region. The sharpening competition over Middle East oil has also caused a more aggressive political stance on their claims in the energy-rich areas nearer to home – notably in the South and East China Seas (Sevilla, 2013, p. 94).

When we draw a framework for Chinese diplomatic attitudes towards the Middle East, it is possible to say that China has maintained a pragmatic, non-interventionist stance regarding the big issues. Beijing has always stayed in an impartial position in the Palestinian-Israeli conflict, and in regard to the Syrian crisis, China has advocated for a political solution supplemented by its humanitarian efforts to help build hospitals in Jordan for Syrian refugees (Kāzemi & Chen, 2014). Beijing also actively participates in solving problems and puts forward ideas about the major issues in the Middle East, such as the Palestinian-Israeli issue, the Syrian crisis, the Iranian nuclear issue and the fight against ISIS and other terrorist forces since 2013 (Gao, 2014, pp. 69-70).

The changing dynamics of the international balance of power, recent developments in the energy markets and the eliminating of geographical distances with developing transportation technologies are forcing China and the Middle East to build increasingly close relations with each other. However, these closer relations have led to a heated debate that China is trying to become "the new hegemonic power" in the global energy markets by replacing the US and also that Middle Eastern countries are going to be more dependent on China (Shu, 2013, p. 38). In contrast to Western discourses accusing China of being a hegemonic power, Beijing has never given up following a non-interventionist and pragmatic approach towards the Middle East. Especially since the Arab Spring, China has promoted peaceful solutions to conflicts and called for respect for territorial integrity and sovereignty (Yao, 2012, p. 17). In terms of the current developments in the Middle East, Beijing would like to stay as a supportive ally for all the countries in the region. Despite its assertive and aggressive policy towards East and South Asia, China has pursued a more moderate way with regard to Middle Eastern affairs. Energy is still the most important factor that forms this moderation. Beijing is trying to secure its energy supply security by contributing to the economic and social welfare of the region and is taking important steps to further its influence there.

Conclusion

The Middle East cannot be considered as "a remote region" for China any longer. As recent developments such as the Arab Spring, the emergence of ISIS and the increasing rivalry between Iran and Saudi Arabia show, Middle Eastern issues have the capacity to directly affect China. This is also the case in terms of the Great Power relations. Even though Beijing has always supported Arab regimes economically and diplomatically, China feels under increasing pressure to maintain its relationship with the US and the international community. Indeed, Beijing has shown its support for international norms by voting for sanctions on Tehran over the Iranian nuclear issue. Taking a more clear stance on Middle Eastern issues, Beijing has to balance its national, regional and international interests. At this point, energy supply security is located at the conjunction of this triple structure of interests.

Even though there are many variables that have a complex interdependency with each other in the region, energy supply security will remain the main concern for China in terms of its foreign policy in the Middle East. Beijing has already begun to re-construct its relationships with Middle Eastern countries. The most prominent policy of this re-construction can be seen in China's energy relations with Saudi Arabia, which has become the main energy supplier to China, surpassing Iran in the mid-2000s. When we analyze China's increasing ties with Saudi Arabia and its turn from its traditional stance on the Iranian nuclear issue, it can be viewed as Beijing trying to balance its interests by replacing Tehran with Riyadh. This diplomatic flexibility has always been a part of pragmatic Chinese foreign policy since the 1980s. Therefore, it is possible to say that China's Middle East policy has great harmony in its continuities and changes.

References

Bender, J., & Rosen, A. (2015, May 13). *This Pentagon map shows what's really driving China's military and diplomatic strategy*. Business Insider. https://www.businessinsider.com/this-map-shows-chinas-global-energy-ties-2015-5

Bin Huwaidin, M. (2002). *China's Relations with Arabia and the Gulf 1949-1999*. Routledge.

Bitzinger, R. A. (1992). Chinese Arms Sales to the Third World. *International Security*, *17*(2), 84-111.

BP. (2018). *Statistical Review of World Energy 2018*. https://www.bp.com/content/dam/bp/business-sites/en/global/corporate/pdfs/energy-economics/statistical-review/bp-stats-review-2018-full-report.pdf

BP. (2019a). *Energy Outlook 2019. Insights from the Evolving transition scenario – China*. https://www.bp.com/content/dam/bp/business-sites/en/global/corporate/pdfs/energy-economics/energy-outlook/bp-energy-outlook-2019-region-insight-global-et.pdf

BP. (2019b). *Statistical Review 2019. China's Energy Market in 2018*. Retrieved August 2, 2019, from https://www.bp.com/content/dam/bp/business-sites/en/global/corporate/pdfs/energy-economics/statistical-review/bp-stats-review-2019-china-insights.pdf

Brewster, D. (2017). Silk Roads and Strings of Pearls: The Strategic Geography of China's New Pathways in the Indian Ocean. *Geopolitics*, *22*(2), 269-291.

Calabrese, J. (1991). *China's Changing Relations*. Pinter.

Calabrese, J. (1992). Peaceful or Dangerous Collaborators? China's Relations with the Gulf Countries. *Pacific Affairs*, *65*(4), 471-485.

Calabrese, J. (2018). China's 'One Belt, One Road' (OBOR) Initiative, Envisioning Iran's Role. In A. Ehteshami & N. Horesh (Eds.), *China's Presence in the Middle East: The Implications of the One Belt, One Road Initiative* (pp. 174-191). Routledge.

Chaziza, M. (2016). China's Middle East Policy: The ISIS Factor. *Middle East Policy*, *23*(1), 25-33.

Dillon, M. (2004). The Middle East and China. In H. Carter & A. Ehteshami (Eds.), *The Middle East's Relations with Asia and Russia*. Routledge.

Dorraj, M., & English, J. E. (2012). China's Strategy for Energy Acquisition in the Middle East: Potential for Conflict and Cooperation with the United States. *Asian Politics & Policy*, *4*(2), 173-191.
Dorsey, J. M. (2017). China and the Middle East: Venturing into the Maelstrom. *Asian Journal of Middle Eastern and Islamic Studies*, *11*(1), 1-14.
Evron, Y. (2016). China-Japan interaction in the Middle East: a battleground of Japan's remilitarization. *The Pacific Review*, *30*(2), 188-204.
Gao, Z. (2014). The New Development of China-Middle East Relations since the Arab Upheaval. *Journal of Middle Eastern and Islamic Studies (in Asia)*, *8*(4), 63-80.
Gillespie, S. (2004). Diplomacy on a South-South Dimension. In H. Slavik (Ed.), *Intercultural Communication and Diplomacy* (pp. 109-130). DiploFoundation.
Hudson, M. C. (2013). Geopolitical shifts: Asia rising, America declining in the Middle East? *Contemporary Arab Affairs*, *6*(3), 458-466.
Karaca, R. K. (2012). Çin'in Değişen Enerji Stratejisinin Dış Politikasına Etkileri (1990-2010). *Uluslararası İlişkiler*, *9*(33), 93-118.
Kāzemi, A. V., & Chen, X. (2014, February 28). *China and the Middle East: More Than Oil*. The European Financial Review, https://www.europeanfinancialreview.com/china-middle-east-oil/
Kemp, G. (2010). *The East Moves West: India, China and Asia's Growing Presence in the Middle East.* Brookings Institution Press.
Kliman, D., & Grace, A. (2018, June 14). *China Smells Opportunity in the Middle East's Crisis.* Foreign Policy. https://foreignpolicy.com/2018/06/14/china-smells-opportunity-in-the-middle-easts-crisis/
Legrenzi, M., & Lawson, F. H. (2015). China's Gulf Policy: Existing Theories, New Perspectives. *Middle East Policy*, *22*(2), 58-71.
Lyall, N. (2019, February 16). *China in the Middle East: Past, Present, and Future.* The Diplomat. https://thediplomat.com/2019/02/china-in-the-middle-east-past-present-and-future/
Masannat, G. S. (1966). Sino-Arab Relations. *Asian Survey*, *6*(4), 216-226.
Neill, A. (2014). China and the Middle East. In T. Dodge & E. Hokayem (Eds.), *Middle Eastern Security, the US Pivot and the Rise of ISIS (Adelphi Series 54)* (pp. 205-224). Routledge.
Olimat, M. S. (2014). *China and the Middle East Since World War II: A Bilateral Approach.* Lexington Books.
Pan, G. (1997). China's Success in the Middle East. *Middle East Quarterly*, *4*(4), 35-40.

Qian, X. (2010). China's Energy Cooperation with Middle East Oil producing Countries. *Journal of Middle Eastern and Islamic Studies (in Asia)*, *4*(3), 65-80.
Qian, X. (2014). Protecting China's Energy Interests in the Middle East. *Journal of Middle Eastern and Islamic Studies (in Asia)*, *8*(3), 48-69.
Rashida, H. (2010). Sino-Iran Relations Current Developments and Future Scenario. *Policy Perspectives*, *7*(1), 135-153.
Scobell, A. (2018). Why the Middle East matters to China. In A. Ehteshami & N. Horesh (Eds.), *China's Presence in the Middle East: The Implications of the One Belt, One Road Initiative*. Routledge.
Sevilla, H. A. (2013). The 'Arab Spring' and South China Sea Tensions: Analyzing China's Drive to Energy Security. *Alternatives: Turkish Journal of International Relations*, *12*(3), 94-107.
Sevilla, H. A. (2017). China's New Silk Route Initiative: Political and Economic Implications for the Middle East and Southeast Asia. *Asian Journal of Middle Eastern and Islamic Studies*, *11*(1), 83-106.
Shichor, Y. (2018). Vision, revision and supervision: The politics of China's OBOR and AIIB and their implications for the Middle East. In A. Ehteshami & N. Horesh (Eds.), *China's Presence in the Middle East: The Implications of the One Belt, One Road Initiative*. Routledge.
Shu, X. (2013). The United States' Strategy Towards the Middle East Oil and China's Energy Security. In Y. Guang (Ed.), *China-Middle East Relations: Review and Analysis*, vol. 1 (pp. 38-50). Paths International.
SIPRI. (n.d.). *Arms Transfers Database: TIV of arms exports from China, 1980-1990.* Retrieved August 27, 2019, from http://armstrade.sipri.org/armstrade/html/export_values.php
Troush, S. (1999, September 1). *China's Changing Oil Strategy and its Foreign Policy Implications*. Brookings. https://www.brookings.edu/articles/chinas-changing-oil-strategy-and-its-foreign-policy-implications/
Vendryes, T. (2012). The "going out" strategy: economic moves with political consequences. In *Facing the Risks of the "Going Out Strategy"* (pp. 5-6). European Council on Foreign Relations,
World Integrated Trade Solutions (WITS) (2017). *China exports, imports and trade balance by country and region 2017.* Retrieved August 27, 2019, from https://wits.worldbank.org/CountryProfile/en/Country/CHN/Year/2017/TradeFlow/EXPIMP
Wu, F. (2015). China's Puzzling Energy Diplomacy Toward Iran. *Asian Perspective*, *39*, 47-69.

Xiao, D. (2013). Chinese Strategic Option: Approach to the Greater Middle East Initiative Through the Hinterland. In Y. Guang (Ed.), *China-Middle East Relations: Review and Analysis*, vol. 1 (pp. 97-109). Paths International.

Yao, K. (2012). The Upheaval in the Middle East and China's Middle East Policy. *Journal of Middle Eastern and Islamic Studies (in Asia)*, *6*(3), 1-27.

Yao, K. (2016). Opportunities and Challenges of China-Middle East Countries' Production Capacity Cooperation. *Journal of Middle Eastern and Islamic Studies (in Asia)*, *10*(2), 1-19.

CHAPTER THREE

TURKEY'S ENERGY POLİCY

MERAL BALCI* & YEŞİM KARADENİZ**

Introduction

Since current practices in the usage of energy are at an important turning point in the history of humanity and is a crucial resource for [1] health, transportation, economy, technology, environment, urbanization, and daily use tools in human life, energy has a very central importance (Doster, 2017: 87). In the definition provided by the Ministry of Energy and Natural Resources of the Republic of Turkey's website, the concept of energy is explained as the ability to do work. It should also be noted that energy categorized among eight main varieties – potential, kinetic, heat, light, electric, chemical, nuclear, and sound – will not be lost, so much so that energy can continue to exist by transforming into another kind of energy.

In addition to the definition and importance of the concept of energy, the increasing consumption of primary energy has led to the examination of its background. The fact that there is a large population and income growth behind energy consumption shows that it is too important to be ignored. Recent research shows that the world's population will rise to 8.3 billion in 2030. It is explained that around 90% of the estimated population growth will result from non-OECD countries. Therefore, non-OECD countries are expected to contribute 70% to the global GDP growth and 90% to global energy demand increases due to the developing industrial and urban factors. The share of fossil fuels, which constitute 82% of the primary energy resources in the world, is estimated to decrease to 64% in 2035, according to the new policies scenario. Within this framework, the ratio of coal is estimated to be 25%. According to these estimates, the ratio of natural gas

* Assoc. Prof. Dr. Meral Balcı, Faculty of Political Sciences, Marmara University. E-mail: mbalci@marmara.edu.tr.

** Yeşim Karadeniz, Ph.D. student, Social Sciences Institute, Yıldız Teknik University. E-mail: yk.ky.yesim@gmail.com is suggested to be around 22% or 24%. Moreover, while the share of nuclear energy in primary energy sources is 5.6%, it is predicted that it will increase to 7%. The share of renewable energy resources in 2035 is estimated to be 14% according to the current policies scenario and 17% according to the new policies scenario. The amount of energy used in electricity generation is expected to increase by 49%, with an annual average of 2.1%, by 2030. It is anticipated that there will be a 31% increase in the primary energy consumption used in industry, and this estimated rate constitutes 25% of the primary energy growth rate in the world. In addition, nuclear energy is expected to have an average annual growth rate of 2.6%, and hydroelectric power is expected to have an average annual growth rate of 2%. The growth rates of nuclear energy and hydroelectric energy in total are higher than the growth rate of primary energy. The highest growth in fossil resources is natural gas, with an average annual rate of 2%. Natural gas is followed by coal, with an average annual growth rate of 1.2%, and oil, with an average annual growth rate of 0.8% (T.C. Enerji ve Tabii Kaynaklar Bakanlığı, 2015, p. 80).

1. Turkey's Energy Resources

When the energy potential of the Republic of Turkey is analyzed, energy resources can be divided into two: exhaustible (fossil) and renewable energy resources. Exhaustible energy resources are those such as mineral coal, lignite, oil, and natural gas, but they are not productive in terms of resources other than lignite. Hydropower, wind, solar, geothermal, and biomass energies have significant potential for renewable energy resources.

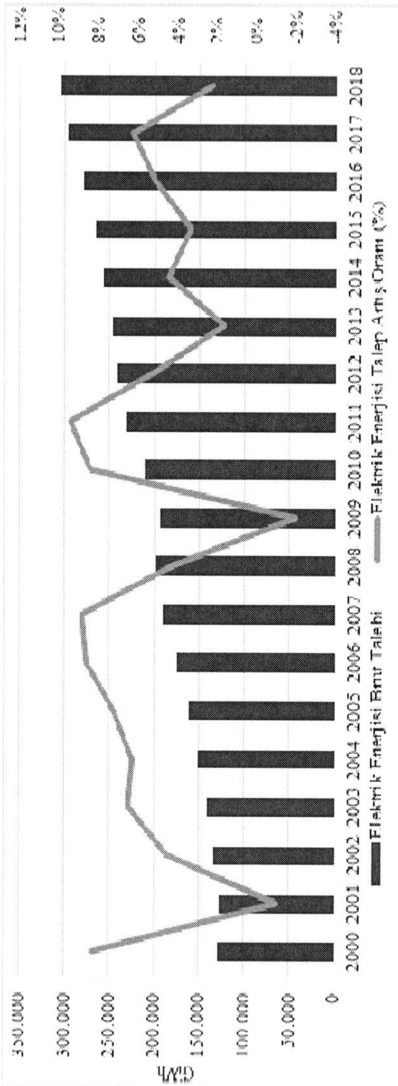

Figure 1: Gross Demand/Demand Growth Rate of Electrical Energy. Source: Ministry of Foreign Affairs of the Republic of Turkey, n.d.

1.1. Turkey's Non-Renewable (Fossil) Energy Resources

Energy resources that can be depleted do not have an important place in Turkey. Although the Middle East and Caucasus regions are rich in oil and gas deposits, Turkey is not able to accommodate these energy resources in terms of geological features. This is also true for coal; only lignite reserves can meet Turkey's needs in terms of exhaustible energy resources. Within the framework of the data obtained, Turkey has taken first place among the members of the Organisation for Economic Co-operation and Development (OECD) as the country that has increased its energy demand the fastest in recent years (Yılmaz, 2012, p. 35).

When the oil resources of Turkey's exhaustible energy fuels are analyzed, it can be seen that this increase first started in 1945 with the discovery of oil in Raman, and today, oil production is observed especially in the Adıyaman and Batman regions (Erdoğan, 2016, p. 53). Following this process, with the "Petroleum Law" enacted in 1954, Turkey was divided into 18 different oil fields and allowed domestic and foreign private companies to conduct oil exploration and production activities. Today, many companies, especially TPAO, still continue these activities (Yılmaz, 2012, p. 39). In the framework of the oil reserves announced in 2017, it has been suggested that Turkey has 324 million barrels of oil (Türkiye Petrolleri Anonim Ortaklığı, n.d.). The medium-sized oil reserves held by Turkey are defined as small, comparatively speaking. Because Turkey does not have productive reserve fields with more than 500 million barrels of oil, this is the data that confirms that there is no efficient source. Within this framework, the ratio of small areas is 93%, and the ratio of medium-sized areas is 7% (Türkiye Petrolleri Anonim Ortaklığı, n.d.). The total proven oil reserves worldwide amount to 1.7 trillion barrels, which can cover 54 years of consumption. Of the remaining oil reserves, 60% are located on land, 37% under the sea, and the rest at the North Pole. With the emergence of new technologies such as recoverable petroleum resources, multi-stage hydraulic fracturing, and other similar technologies, the use of this data in the determination of welding locations is increasing (T.C. Enerji ve Tabii Kaynaklar Bakanlığı, 2015, p. 16).

When we examine exhaustible energy resources within the framework of natural gas, Turkey's natural gas production started in the Trakya-Hamitabat region in 1970 (Erdoğan, 2016, p. 57). Today, natural gas production can be carried out in land areas as well as in marine areas. Production activities are also carried out in Akçakoca, a North Marmara natural gas field (T.C. Enerji ve Tabii Kaynaklar Bakanlığı, n.d.-c). Natural gas production is carried out by TPAO and other companies. While 36% of the existing reserves are in the production areas of TPAO, 64% are in the production areas of other companies (T.C. Enerji ve Tabii Kaynaklar Bakanlığı, n.d.-c). Turkey, which is not rich in natural gas resources, generally uses this energy as electrical energy and for the purpose of heating, and it imports the vast majority (94%) of the natural gas it consumes (Özalp, 2018, p. 35).

In terms of coal resources, Turkey has more reserves than oil and natural gas. 1.6% of the world's coal reserves are in Turkey (Tiftikçigil & Yesevi, 2015, p. 35). Turkey, which often uses its coal reserves as a means of generating electricity, has 1.3 billion tonnes of coal reserves, 506 million tonnes of which are visible. In addition, it has approximately 14.2 billion tons of lignite reserves, of which 13.9 billion tons are visible (Tamzok, 2016, p. 41). The most important mineral coal reserve in Turkey is in Zonguldak. The data of the Zonguldak Basin, which has been mined for many years, is produced from the fields of Armutçuk, Üzülmez, Kozluk, Karadon, and Amasra (Yılmaz, 2012, p. 38). The highest level of coal production was reached in 1975 with 4.8 million tons. However, in the following years, coal production reduced and decreased to 2.5 million tons (TKI, 2013). The inability of domestic production to respond to existing needs has led to increased coal imports in recent years. Coal imports, which started in 1973 with 16,000 tons, increased to 30 million tons in 2012. Russia, Colombia, the United States, Australia, and the Republic of South Africa are among the leading countries where coal is imported from (TKI, 2013). Coal production in Turkey is carried out by Turkish Hard Coal Enterprises and private companies. A total of 1,234,033 tons of coal was produced in 2017. Of this amount, 823,042 were produced by Turkish Hard Coal Enterprises, while 410,991 were produced by private companies. When the May 2018 coal consumption report is examined, it can be seen that 37.475 million tons of coal were consumed in Turkey in 2017, and 3.29% of this consumption was obtained from Turkey's own resources (T.C. Enerji ve Tabii Kaynaklar Bakanlığı, 2018, pp. 26-27).

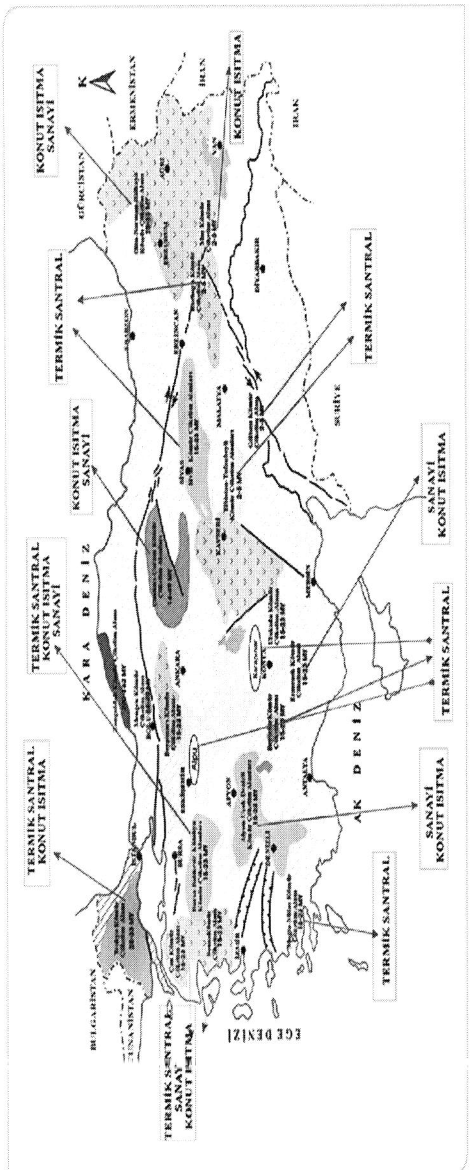

Figure 2: Turkey's Coal Fields and Uses. Source: Maden Tetkik ve Arama Genel Müdürlüğü, n.d.

Nuclear energy activities in Turkey started in 1955. In the first stage, a cooperation study was carried out with the USA as a first step in order to use nuclear energy activities for peace (Ergün & Polat, 2012, p. 48). The Atomic Energy Commission (AEC) was established and is the clearest step in this context. In 1957, Turkey became a member of the International Atomic Energy Agency (IAEA), but concrete steps toward the installation of nuclear power plants took place at the nuclear summit, which was organized in 2006. At this summit, the promotion of private enterprise was announced, and these incentives became concrete with the agreement signed with Russia for the construction of the Mersin Akkuyu nuclear power plant in 2010. In 2013, an agreement was made with Japan to establish a nuclear power plant in Sinop (Güngör & Buldurur, 2017, p. 301). It was decided that the Akkuyu nuclear power plant would be financed with Russian capital and be owned by Russia. In addition, Russian engineers were held responsible for everything of the reactor to the last stage (Erdoğan, 2016, p. 65).

1.2. Turkey's Renewable Energy Resources

Looking at the development of renewable energy in Turkey, it can be seen that there has been an improvement since the 2000s. The share of renewable energy, which was 0.1% of the electricity consumed in 2000, has now increased to 24% (Elektrik Üretim Anonim Şirketi, 2018, p. 17). Renewable energy, which has increased its share in the production of electricity, can also meet energy needs in different fields. Together, Turkey has a 0.8% share in terms of global renewable energy consumption (Tiftikçigil & Yesevi, 2015, p. 80). Inspecting Turkey's renewable energy resources, we shall first examine solar energy. The solar potential of Turkey, which ranks second after Spain, which has the largest number of sunny days per year in European countries, is described as 56 GW (WWF, 2017). Within this framework, Turkey receives 977 x 10^{12} kWh of solar energy in one year within its borders. This solar energy is equivalent to 111,5 x 10^{6} MW power, and it has more than 5,000 times the power of Turkey's installed power stations (Dinçer, 2011, p. 10). Despite the existing solar energy potential, Turkey effectively turned to generating electricity in this sense only after the 2000s. As of 2017, it has been able to increase its installed power to 823,000 tonnes of oil equivalent (TOE) heat energy (T.C. Enerji ve Tabii Kaynaklar Bakanlığı, n.d.-d). In addition, Turkey has 564 installed power plants, 15 of which are licensed and 549 of which are unlicensed (T.C. Enerji ve Tabii Kaynaklar Bakanlığı, n.d.-d).

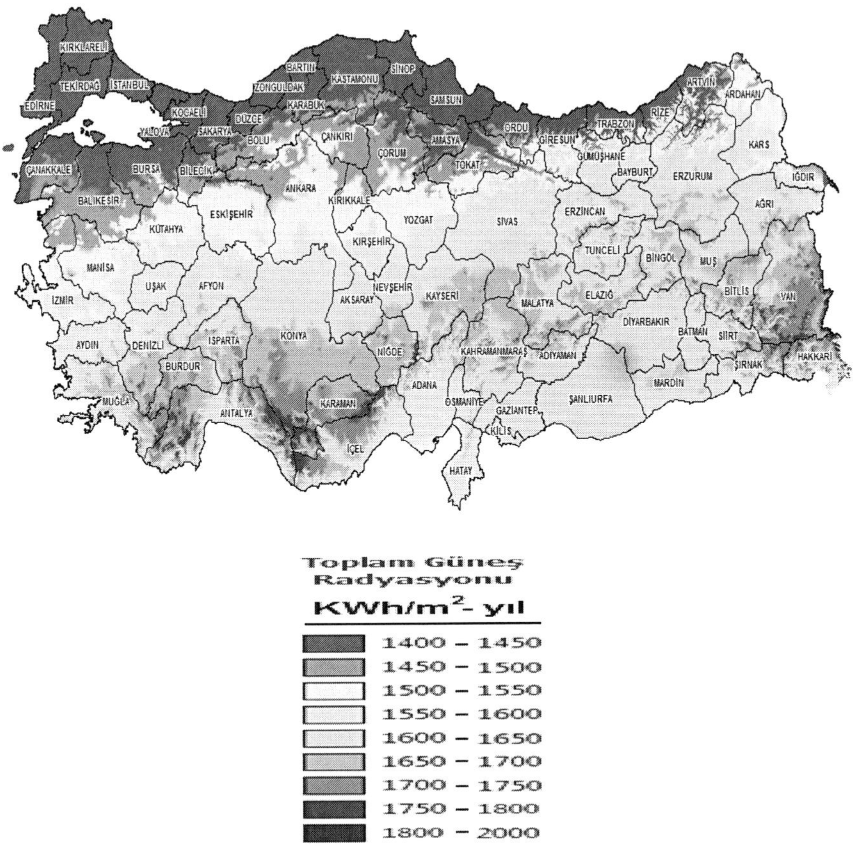

Figure 3: Turkey's Solar Energy Potential Atlas. Source: Yenilenebilir Enerji Genel Müdürlüğü, n.d.

When the wind energy of Turkey is analyzed, it is seen as a country with existing conditions that can be considered rich in this respect. In this context, Turkey is a suitable country for wind energy production in all areas, and Turkey's measured wind energy potential is described as around 120 billion kWh. The first wind power plant, which was founded in 1996, became active in Izmir in 1998. In this context, the Çeşme Germiyan wind power plant, which started production in 1998, has a power of 1.5 MW (Hayli, 2001, pp. 24-26). Today, there are 192 installed wind power plants (WPPs) in Turkey, of which 175 are licensed and 17 are unlicensed. (Enerji Atlası, n.d.-b). The existing power plants in Turkey produce an average of 15 million kWh of electricity annually. This production covers 6.10% of Turkey (Elektrik Üretim Anonim Şirketi, 2018, p.17). Today, China has the highest installed capacity and potential in terms of wind energy, followed by the United States and Germany in terms of installed power. In this context, 320 billion euros is expected to be invested in the wind energy sector in Europe by 2030 (Bayraç, 2011, p. 55). These expected goals are manifest in concrete terms. While data and projects related to wind energy in the world are being created within this framework, investment and production information in Turkey is seen to be lagging behind global examples. It can be observed that Turkey, which has approximately 7 times more potential than Germany, has 8.5 times fewer installed WPPs than Germany (Karagöl & Kavaz, 2017, p. 23).

When the hydroelectric power potential of Turkey is examined, it can be seen that the establishment of the first hydroelectric dams in Anatolia occurred during the Hittite period. Such dams, which were established in the first place for drinking water and irrigation purposes, were used for electricity generation in Turkey after the 1900s. The first hydroelectric power plant (HPP) was established in Tarsus in 1902 with low energy production, then in 1913, a second power plant was established in Istanbul with more production power (Gökdemir et al., 2012, p. 20). Today, large and small HPPs have been established in almost every area of Turkey. The number of registered power plants has reached 640 (Enerji Atlası, n.d.-a). Hydroelectric generation for Turkey in terms of energy production and consumption is of great importance because Turkey holds a theoretical total of 433 billion kWh of hydroelectric power. However, Turkey is able to convert 216 billion kWh of this existing power into electrical energy within the technical framework (Maden Tetkik ve Arama Genel Müdürlüğü, n.d.). Thus, with these conditions, Turkey has 1% of the hydroelectric potential in the world, but within Europe it has a share of 15% (Devlet Su İşleri Genel Müdürlüğü, n.d.). In addition to all this, two important issues in hydroelectric power generation should not be forgotten. The first of these issues is that as a result of urbanization, demographic change, and climate change, Turkey has become a country with problems in terms of water resources (Gökdemir et al., 2012, p. 19). The other issue is that the plants that are being built pose big problems that need to be dıscussed because the HPPs have a variety of negative consequences on nature and the climate.

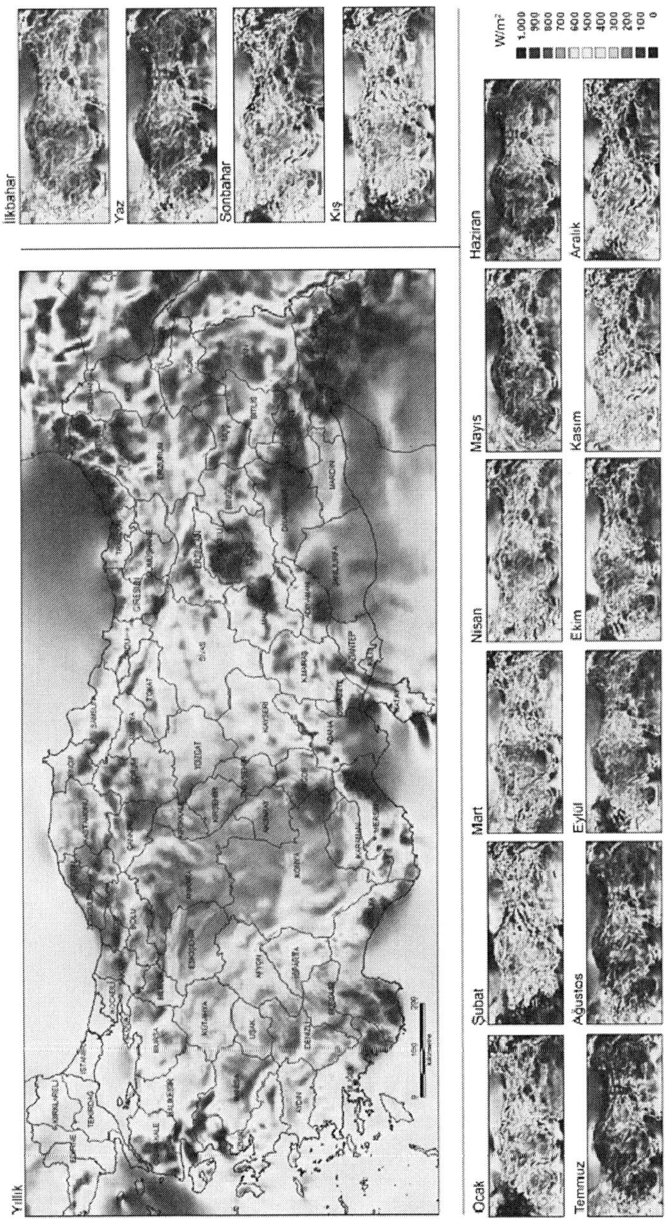

Figure 4: Turkey's Wind Energy Potential Atlas. Source: Wind Atlas, n.d.

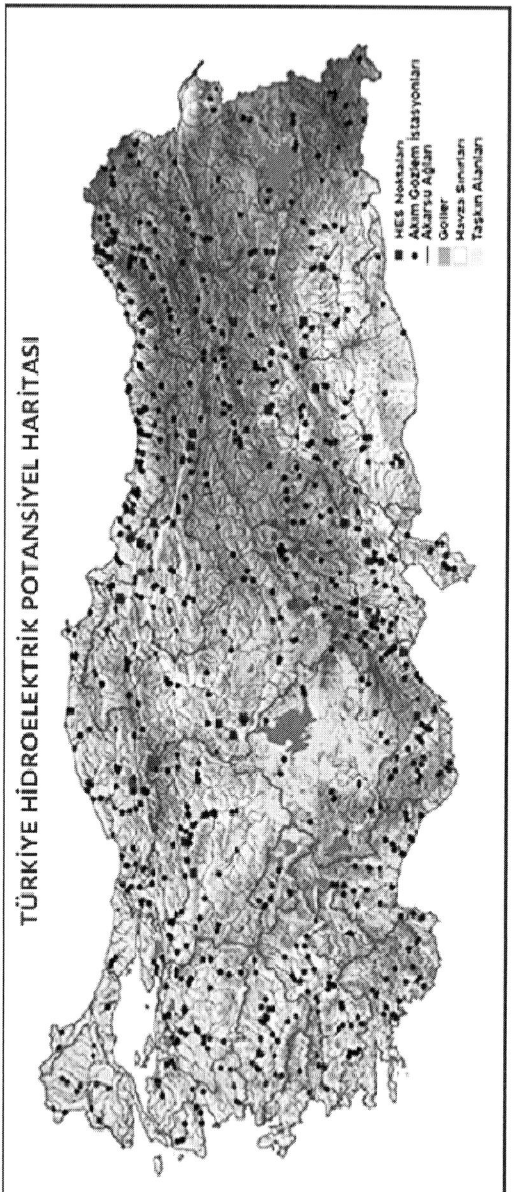

Figure 5: Turkey's Hydroelectric Potential Map. Source: Gooenergy.com, n.d.

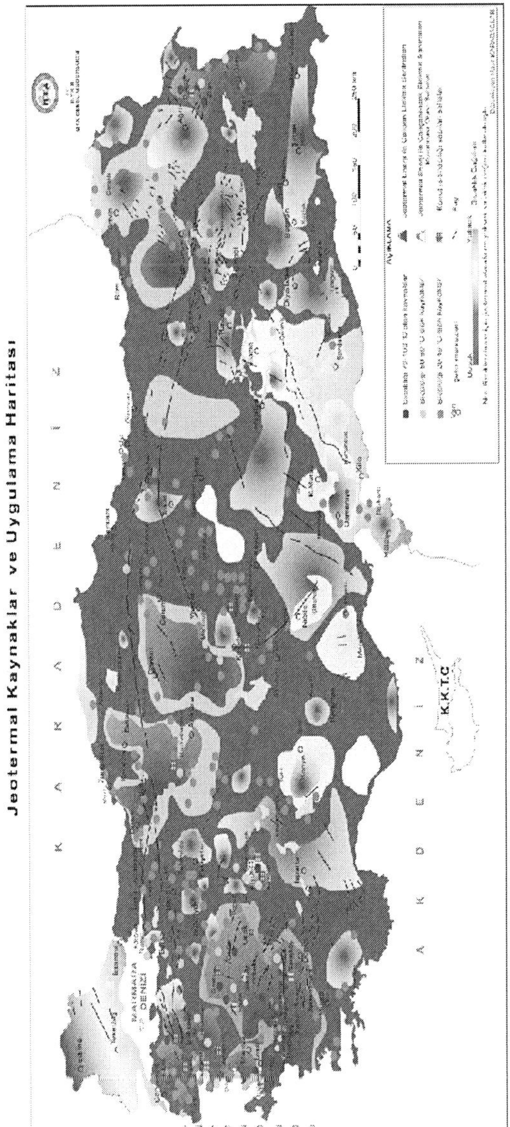

Figure 6: Geothermal Resources and Application Map. Source: T.C. Enerji ve Tabii Kaynaklar Bakanlığı, n.d.-f.

Geothermal energy is a form of energy that is commonly found in Turkey. Turkey ranks fourth after the USA, Philippines, and Indonesia in the world's production of geothermal energy (T.C. Enerji ve Tabii Kaynaklar Bakanlığı, n.d.-f). Turkey's geothermal energy potential is 31,500 MW. But not all of this potential is conducive to electricity generation. In this context, non-favorable sources are also used in various areas such as greenhouses and individual and central heating. Thus, the energy that exists is converted into a useful form. Turkey can convert this useful production into an average of 4 million kWh of electrical energy per year (Enerji Atlası, n.d.-c). Accordingly, geothermal energy has a share of 0.67% in electricity production (Elektrik Üretim Anonim Şirketi, 2018, p. 17).

1.3. Turkey's Energy Resources Renewed in Certain Conditions

Energy resources that can renew themselves under certain conditions are "biomass energy" and "wave energy". Examining biomass energy, we can say that it is described as a type of energy that has gained importance in Turkey in recent years. However, this energy has great disadvantages in terms of agricultural area and agricultural products. In parallel, it is suggested that Turkey's biofuel waste potential is 8.6 million tonnes of oil equivalent (MTOE) on average. Furthermore, the amount of biogas that Turkey can produce is suggested as 1.5-2 MTOE. However, it is not possible to convert this current state of potential energy into fully usable electrical energy. However, Turkey was able to convert this potential into 3,216 GWh of electrical energy in 2018 with its installed power of 811 MW (T.C. Enerji ve Tabii Kaynaklar Bakanlığı, n.d.-e).

Another source of energy to be discussed is wave energy. Due to its geographical conditions, Turkey has a lot of wave energy potential due to its coastal winds and the fact that three of its four sides are surrounded by seas. However, the acceptance of fossil fuels as primary energy sources and the high cost of generation of wave energy pose major obstacles to this energy production. However, after 2020, it is suggested that the seas will also be a major energy production area. In this context, it is said that the Black Sea coastline, the north of the Bosphorus, and the Marmaris and Finike regions have great potential in terms of wave energy (Sağlam & Uyar, 2005, p. 5).

2. Turkey's Natural Gas Pıpelıne Projects

When Turkey's energy production and consumption are investigated, it can be observed that these have developed in direct proportion to both economic and technological developments in recent years. Turkey often tries to meet its energy needs from fossil fuels. Moreover, it produces electricity from hydroelectric and fossil sources.

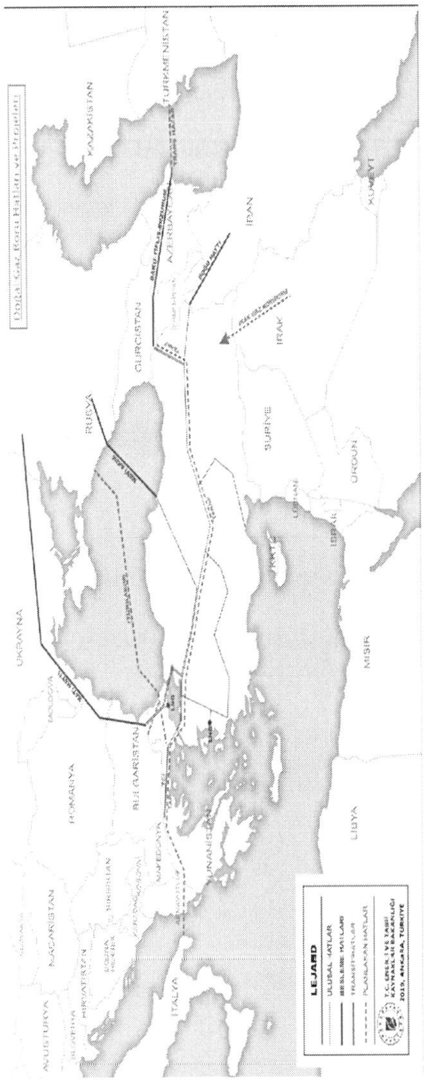

Figure 7: Natural Gas Pipelines and Projects. Source: T.C. Enerji ve Tabii Kaynaklar Bakanlığı, n.d.-a.

2.1. Russian-Turkey Natural Gas Pipeline (West Line)

The construction works started on October 26, 1986, and the line reached Ankara in 1988. The foundations of this line were established by a 25-year agreement with the Soviet Union. The length of this pipeline, which entered Turkey through Bulgaria, is 845 km, and its highest capacity is 14 billion m^3/year (Yılmaz, 2005, p. 8).

2.2. Blue Stream Gas Pipeline

As provided for by the 25-year Natural Gas Purchase-Sale Agreement signed between BOTAŞ and Gazexport on December 15, 1997, natural gas is transported from the Russian Federation to Turkey. According to the agreement, 16 billion m^3 of natural gas per year is supplied to Turkey (T.C. Enerji ve Tabii Kaynaklar Bakanlığı, 2015: p. 84). The characteristics of this pipeline are extremely important. It was constructed in three main parts. The first part is in Russian territory; with a total length of 370 km, the pipeline system consists of 308 km of 56" pipeline and 62 km of 48" pipeline. The second part is under the Black Sea, between Djubga and Samsun, where there are two parallel lines of 24" diameter, each about 390 km in length. The third part is in the territory of Turkey; this system is 501 km of 48" pipeline (Gazel, 2004, p. 17). This line was completed in 2002, and the pipeline was put into operation in 2003.

2.3. Eastern Anatolian Natural Gas Main Transmission Pipeline (Iran-Turkey)

A Natural Gas Purchase-Sale Agreement was signed between Iran and Turkey in 1996 in Tehran for the purpose of supplying natural gas to Turkey to meet the energy needs of Eastern Anatolia via a pipeline. This line, which started to be used in December 2001, has a length of approximately 1,491 km and a diameter ranging between 48" and 16". This line started with a carrying capacity of 3 billion m^3 per year and has a capacity of 10 billion m^3 today (Yılmaz, 2005, p. 8). The Eastern Anatolian Natural Gas Main Transmission Line extends from Doğubayazıt to Ankara via Erzurum, Sivas, and Kayseri to Seydişehir and Konya (T.C. Enerji ve Tabii Kaynaklar Bakanlığı, 2015, p. 83).

2.4. Baku-Tbilisi-Erzurum Natural Gas Pipeline

This pipeline carries the gas produced in the Shah Deniz area of the Caspian Sea of Azerbaijan to Turkey and has a length of 690 km and a capacity of up to 20 billion m^3. At the end of the negotiations for the purchase of gas from Azerbaijan, an agreement was signed between Turkey and Azerbaijan on March 12, 2001 for the shipment of Azerbaijan's natural gas to Turkey (T.C. Enerji ve Tabii Kaynaklar Bakanlığı, 2015, p. 84). Created to transport 6.6 billion m^3 of Azerbaijani natural gas per year to Turkey, this line is approximately 690 km long and 42" in diameter. The construction of this pipeline, which enters Turkey through Georgia, started in October 2004, and the gas flow through the pipeline started in July 2007. Turkey will purchase natural gas to be supplied through this line for 15 years (T.C. Enerji ve Tabii Kaynaklar Bakanlığı, n.d.-a).

2.5. Turkey–Greece Natural Gas Interconnection (ITG)

This agreement is the first phase of the "South European Gas Ring", which was signed between the Republic of Turkey and the Hellenic Republic on February 23, 2003. The use of this line for exportation rather than importation is extremely important for Turkey. The natural gas supply started in 2007 (T.C. Enerji ve Tabii Kaynaklar Bakanlığı, n.d.-a).

2.6. Trans–Anatolia Natural Gas Pipeline Project (TANAP)

In order to meet the rising natural gas demand of Turkey, negotiations were conducted with the Azerbaijani government and Shah Deniz Consortium that developed the Shah Deniz field in Azerbaijan. An agreement concerning the annual supply of 6 billion m^3 of Azerbaijani gas to Turkey was signed on October 25, 2011. In addition, for the transit of 10 billion m^3 of Azerbaijani gas to Europe through Turkey via a newly constructed pipeline, an Intergovernmental Agreement concerning the Trans-Anatolian Natural Gas Pipeline (TANAP) system between Turkey and Azerbaijan and a Host Governmental Agreement, which is an annex to the Intergovernmental Agreement, between Turkey and the Project Company were signed on June 26, 2012. With these agreements, the legal framework was established to ensure the realization of the TANAP project. The final investment decisions of the Shah Deniz Phase II development, the Southern Caucasus Pipeline Expansion (SCPX) project, TANAP, and the Trans-Adriatic Pipeline were taken at a ceremony held in Baku in December 2013. On September 20, 2014, the groundbreaking ceremony for SCPX, which will supply gas to TANAP, took place. Regarding the TANAP project, the plan is to build a nearly 2,000 km-long pipeline that will run from Turkey's border with Georgia to the border with Greece and/or Bulgaria, with a maximum annual capacity of 32 billion m^3. Engineering activities for the project are performed by the TANAP Natural Gas Transmission Corporation based in Turkey. The route studies of the project have been completed, and the route has been established as a result of the engineering studies carried out. The EIA Report for the TANAP project was approved in July 2014 (T.C. Enerji ve Tabii Kaynaklar Bakanlığı, 2015, p. 81).

2.7. TurkStream Gas Pipeline

This project, which is of great significance for Turkey and Russia, is considered as important for both the political and economic interests of the two countries. The foremost part of this project is the 900 km-long section that passes under the Black Sea, which is the first phase that was realized by the trade agreement signed between Turkey and Russia on October 10, 2016. There are two pipes in this line, which are each planned to carry 15.75 billion m^3 per year. In this context, with a total capacity of 31.5 billion m^3 per year, natural gas will be released from Russia and transported to Europe via Turkey (Özalp, 2018, p. 152).

3. Turkey's Oıl Pıpelıne Projects

3.1. Iraq–Turkey Crude Oil Pipeline

This crude oil line started to operate in 1976. The first time a tanker was loaded with oil from this pipeline, which is 986 km long, was on May 25, 1977. The annual crude oil-carrying capacity of the first pipeline was analyzed as 35 million tons. In addition to this first line, a second pipeline was added in 1987. Thus, the annual oil-carrying capacity of the two established pipelines is seen as 70.9 million tons (Kuleyin & Cerit, 2011, p. 21). The BOTAŞ Petroleum Pipeline Corporation (BOTAŞ) is the owner of the part of the pipeline that is in the territory of the Republic of Turkey, and it is also the operator of that part of the pipeline. The amount of crude oil transported from these lines is heavily affected by global policies and terrorist incidents. Therefore, the oil line may not continue to operate at full capacity. An amendment concerning the renewal of the Kirkuk-Yumurtalık Crude Oil Pipeline Agreement and its protocols, and the extension of these agreements for 15 years was signed between the Republic of Turkey and the

Republic of Iraq on September 19, 2010 (T.C. Enerji ve Tabii Kaynaklar Bakanlığı, n.d.-b).

3.2. Baku–Tbilisi–Ceyhan Crude Oil Main Export Pipeline

Energy resources in the Caspian region are of great importance in this junction of the world, but the unresolved status of this region and regional power balances cause difficulties in reaching resources here. The line created for this area, which is of great importance for Turkey, provided an opportunity for these resources to move both to the Turkish domestic market and to the global market by exiting Azerbaijan. However, Russia opposed this crude oil pipeline both in terms of energy policies in the domestic market and because of its goal of achieving energy leadership in the region. Nonetheless, this 1,776 km-long oil line opened for operation in July 2006 (Kuleyin & Cerit, 2011, p. 22).

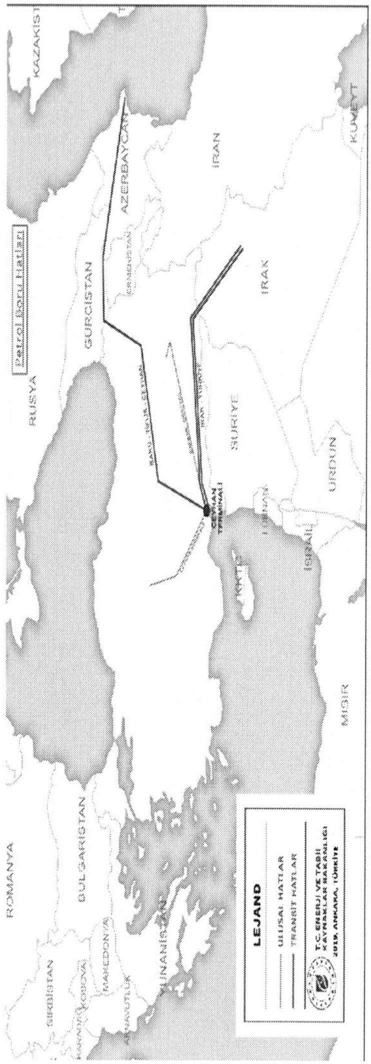

Figure 8: Oil Pipelines. Source: T.C. Enerji ve Tabii Kaynaklar Bakanlığı, n.d.-b.

4. Turkey's Nuclear Power Plant Projects

4.1. Akkuyu Nuclear Power Plant Project

On January 13, 2010, an agreement was signed between Russia and Turkey called the "Joint Declaration of Cooperation on Nuclear Power Plant Facility". A joint commission was formed by this agreement. In this context, works were initiated on the text of the international agreement to be signed for the Akkuyu project. As a result of these studies, the Intergovernmental Agreement on "Cooperation on the Establishment and Operation of a Nuclear Power Plant on Akkuyu Site" was signed between the government of the Turkish Republic and the Russian Federation on May 12, 2010. According to the signed agreement, the power plant will have 4 VVER-1200 type units (AES-2006) and a total installed power of 4,800 MW. In addition, the total operating life of the power plant will be 60 years (T.C. Enerji ve Tabii Kaynaklar Bakanlığı, 2015, p. 64).

4.2. Sinop Nuclear Power Plant Project

On May 3, 2013, an Intergovernmental Agreement on "Cooperation on the Development of Nuclear Power Plants and Nuclear Power Industry" was signed with Japan. Under this agreement, a nuclear power plant to be established in Sinop is envisaged to have 4 ATMEA-1 type units and a total installed power of 4,480 MW. The total working time of the NPP was determined as 60 years. In addition, according to the agreement, the first two units of the plant are expected to start operating in 2023 and 2024 and the other units in 2027 and 2028 (T.C. Enerji ve Tabii Kaynaklar Bakanlığı, 2015, p. 68).

5. Turkey's Energy Relations with Neıghborıng Countrıes

5.1. Energy Relations with Greece

The European Union, Greece, and Turkey have signed a gas pipeline agreement between Turkey and Greece. The agreement infrastructure of this line was established during a meeting between the parties on July 7, 2000 within the framework of the INOGATE program (İşcan, 2002, pp. 87-117). Turkey's existing energy companies signed the "Intergovernmental Agreement on Turkey-Greece Natural Gas Interconnection" during the integration phase with the European Union in 2003. In parallel with these developments, a trade agreement was reached between BOTAŞ and DEPA.

In addition, the Prime Ministers of Turkey and Greece met and signed the joint gas pipeline project on July 3, 2005. In line with this agreement, the Turkey-Greece gas pipeline started operating on November 18, 2007. The text of this agreement has two important consequences for Turkey. The first one is, due to the Blue Stream project, thanks to Russian natural gas, which Russia has the option to sell, it has a chance to meet the needs of its domestic market. Secondly, Turkey has played an important role in the transportation of natural gas from Azerbaijan and Iran to Europe. Thus, in terms of both commercial and foreign policy development, it has taken on the role of a member of the European Union. Turkey should also be able to transmit the energy it receives from Central Asia and the Middle East to European countries, as well as to provide its energy supply. The "South European Gas Ring" project was created with a view to the development of the energy supply that may occur. As part of this project, the Intergovernmental Agreement on the "Development of the Turkey-Greece-Italy Natural Gas Transport Corridor" was signed on July 26, 2007 on behalf of the energy activities of Europe. Thus, it is envisaged that energy will be delivered to European countries through natural gas and oil pipelines. But at this stage, Russia's blocking of an alternative route to its own lines, and therefore its orientation to European countries, has caused countries such as Greece, which need energy, to turn toward Russia.

5.2. Energy Relations with Iraq

Iraq, which has an estimated 11% of the world's oil energy resources, has an important place in Turkey's energy policies. The first oil pipeline project between Turkey and Iraq, the Kirkuk-Yumurtalık pipeline, started on August 27, 1973 and was completed in 1977. Turkey also declared its neutrality in the Iran-Iraq War. An agreement was signed in 1981 to increase the capacity of the Kirkuk-Yumurtalık pipeline and to prevent Turkey from having an oil problem in a process where Iraq and Iran found Turkey's neutrality sincere. Turkey warned Iran about the pipeline, which was attacked during the war years, and Iran gave Turkey a positive response in that sense. The capacity of the pipeline was enlarged in 1984 and 1987, and this line became an important source of revenue for the two countries. This line was closed during the first Gulf War, and this caused Turkey to experience economic problems. With regard to Iraq, Turkey stands out as the safest economic route when we consider the straining of the political situation in Syria and other regional situations. Turkey's regional policies, terror struggles, and other reasons for the negative developments in its policies with Iraq reached their highest level.

Turkey's ethnic, religious, and economic structure, historical development, and access to water resources create significant advantages for new policies on behalf of the region. The fact that Turkey did not approve the March 1 resolution during the US invasion of Iraq caused the relationship between the two countries to be strained and produced different results in the new post-war order in Turkey-Iraq relations. In this context, the actions in the areas of Mosul and Kirkuk and the current changes in terms of the terror problem that Turkey has been dealing with for many years are of great importance.

5.3. Energy Relations with Azerbaijan

Azerbaijan is of great importance for Turkey in terms of global political relations on behalf of the Central Asian region. After Azerbaijan gained independence, Turkey's supportive political policy prepared an environment for the formation of trust and cooperation between the two countries. The most important cooperation between Turkey and Azerbaijan is over energy. Central Asian countries and Azerbaijan are well-equipped in terms of oil and gas reserves. However, following the dissolution of the USSR, Azerbaijan and other Central Asian countries were forced to pursue a global policy under the yoke of Russia. The oil resources of the region are available in the north, and Azerbaijan's oil reached Russia via the Baku-Novorossiysk Oil Pipeline and then the world by sea transport. In an effort to get rid of Russia's existing influence, Azerbaijan has sought to increase its existing energy routes. Against all pressure from Russia, Azerbaijan signed the "Treaty of the Century" with Georgia on March 8, 1996, and thus the first step was taken for the realization of the Baku-Supsa oil pipeline. With this agreement, Azerbaijan's first goal was to create an energy center and energy corridor. For this reason, reaching energy sources in the Middle East and Central Asia became the most important issue.

Turkey has created reliable and cheap energy for itself by creating energy projects such as Baku-Tbilisi-Erzurum and Baku-Tbilisi-Ceyhan. Thus, it is envisaged that relations with other countries will be strengthened through Azerbaijan and an energy trade will take place, with the energy going to Europe. Natural gas from the Baku-Tbilisi-Erzurum line is taken to Europe by the Turkey-Greece ITG. Following the tension between Azerbaijan and Armenia, Turkey aligned itself alongside Azerbaijan and imposed an embargo, halting its relations with Armenia (Cafersoy, 2001). Turkey's attempt to carry out smooth policies in global politics led to a change in relations with Armenia, and Azerbaijan's reaction to this situation led to a return to the old form of relations. Although the shortest pipeline to be created for the transportation of energy resources from the countries of the region goes through Armenia, the fact that Azerbaijan and Turkey are acting as strategic partners prevents the formation of this line from being viewed positively. As a result of these developments, the Baku-Tbilisi-Ceyhan pipeline has made progress, and the route has been extended by 300 km (Yüce, 2006, p. 290). Moreover, this line is of great importance for Azerbaijan in terms of its full independence (Pamir, 2005, p. 81).

5.4. Energy Relations with Georgia

Although Georgia is not a rich country in terms of energy resources, it is of regional strategic importance. Georgia, which is the only country in Central Asia with a coast on the Black Sea, is the only gateway to reach the countries of Central Asia. Iran, Armenia, and the Nagorno-Karabakh issue are seen as major problems in Turkey's foreign relations. Turkey's good relations in this area with trade and energy agreements regarding the East-West energy corridor that consists of the Baku-Tbilisi-Erzurum, Baku-Tbilisi-Ceyhan, and Baku-Tbilisi-Kars lines, where Georgia is highly active, has solved its resource problem. In addition, in the early stages of the Baku-Tbilisi-Ceyhan line, US companies opposed its construction from Azerbaijan through Iran and Nakhichevan to Turkey, meaning the Turkish line would pass through Iran. Given this negative stance of the United States, the line was instead proposed to pass through Armenia. However, due to the Nagorno-Karabakh issue between Azerbaijan and Armenia, this line instead moved in the direction of Georgia. After this, the line was finally named Baku-Tbilisi-Ceyhan, and thus reconciliation was achieved (Aras, 2001, p. 101). As a result, this project strengthened bilateral relations with Georgia and affected the countries of the region de facto, and Azerbaijan and Georgia's commitment to Russia gradually began to decline (Yüce, 2006, p. 319).

Conclusion

The Republic of Turkey is considered as an energy-dependent country. It has been analyzed that the need for energy will increase each day within the framework of the sustainable development of the fossil resource structure and insufficient energy efficiency. In order to meet its increasing energy needs and to establish energy supply security, Turkey has carried out a number of activities in line with the goals and objectives that have been set in its local and global political plans. In this regard, the energy potential of Turkey was first analyzed in this chapter. As a result, its fossil and renewable energy resource potential were evaluated, and studies have been initiated within the framework of the law in order to eliminate Turkey's insufficient fossil resources and energy efficiency. It is planned for foreign investors to make various investments in this field in areas such as build-operate and build-operate-transfer projects and to achieve high-level yields from the resources and internal dynamics. With this aim, the search for fossil sources has increased, and different sources have been found. The majority of these resources did not meet the expected yield due to insufficient reserves and the resource structure not being suitable for production, but the work continued. In addition, a variety of energy has been created in the domestic market for the interest of domestic and foreign investors, with various laws adopted at these stages. Turkey's renewable energy potential is also quite high. Based on the Kyoto Protocol, energy diversity was intended to be realized by increasing clean energy as well. Turkey has huge energy potential from hydroelectric power plants, wind power plants, and solar power plants. In order to make accurate use of this existing potential, research such as environmental impact assessments carried out by corporations should be evaluated in the most accurate way.

In addition to this, it should be noted that one of the most important steps to minimize energy dependence is nuclear power plants. Within the framework of Turkey's 2023 vision, it is planned that the targeted nuclear power plant projects will draw up to 50% of Turkey's energy dependence, which is 75% in the process of energy production. In the present world order, the countries that hold the power of energy benefit more from nuclear energy, and Turkey needs to benefit from nuclear energy and technology in every sense by reducing its dependence on energy in order to be able to progress as a country in this direction. Thus, it is not only about energy potential, but also employment, technology, and the ability to obtain domestic nuclear weapons are also great possibilities provided by nuclear power. All these will likely be important reasons for more moderate and peaceful perspectives both in the world and regionally, creating an environment of energy supply security and deterrent power. On the other hand, it is very important for Turkey to establish a close relationship with both global and regional actors in the energy wars around the world. Turkey has already had an active role in the energy wars of major global powers such as the United States, Russia, and the EU due to its geopolitical characteristics. Turkey has also taken strong steps to become a central country in the East-West and North-South energy corridors, especially with projects on a significant scale that have been brought about by its relations with neighboring countries. On the one hand, Turkey is the source country for producers, and, on the other, it is realizing its win-win policy by assimilating its projects created by enabling its geographical position. Turkey should not ignore the existing problems of the energy system in order to implement the policies and projects that are followed within the framework of this target. Turkey's need for imported energy sources, its energy consumption being predominantly fossil fuel, and having very low energy efficiency compared to the countries it competes with are its biggest issues. Therefore, in order to achieve energy policy objectives and solve existing problems, energy policies must be developed. Turkey's successful reforms for its own fossil and renewable energy sources and its desire to increase energy production will be important steps for strengthening its foreign policy. These would be important and big steps, despite the risks that they could pose, especially in the name of capturing the countries it competes with in the energy diversity and technology market by dominating both global and regional power. As a matter of fact, for Turkey, which is dependent on imported energy, such activities bring advantageous situations in foreign policy.

References

Aras, O. N. (2001). *Azerbaycan'ın Hazar Ekonomisi ve Stratejisi*, İstanbul: Der Yayınları.

Bayraç, H. N. (2011). "Küresel Rüzgâr Enerjisi Politikaları ve Uygulamaları", *Uludağ Üniversitesi İktisadi ve İdari Bilimler Fakültesi Dergisi,* Cilt XXX, Sayı 1, s. 55.

Cafersoy, N. (2001). *Azerbaycan Türkiye İlişkileri*, TÜRKSAM.

Dinçer, F. (2011). "Türkiye'de Güneş Enerjisinden Elektrik Üretimi Potansiyeli – Ekonomik Analizi ve AB Ülkeleri ile Karşılaştırmalı Değerlendirme", *KSU Mühendislik Dergisi*, 14(1), s.10.

Doster, B. (2017). *Türkiye Kime Kalacak*, 2. Baskı, İstanbul: Asi Kitap.

Dünya ve Ülkemiz Enerji ve Tabii Kaynaklar Görünümü, (2015). Enerji ve Tabii Kaynaklar Bakanlığı, Strateji Geliştirme Başkanlığı.

Elektrik Üretim Anonim Şirketi, *"Elektrik Üretim Sektör Raporu"*, (2018). Strateji Geliştirme Daire Başkanlığı Stratejik Planlama Müdürlüğü.

Erdoğan, S. (2016). *Arz Güvenliği Bakışı ile Türkiye'de Enerji Politikaları*, 1. Basım, Ankara: Orion Kitabevi.

Ergün, S. & Polat, M. A. (2012). "Nükleer Enerji ve Türkiye'ye Yansımaları", *İnönü Üniversitesi Uluslararası Sosyal Bilimler Dergisi İdari Bilimler*, Vol. 1, No. 2, s. 48.

Gazel, F. (2004,). *Mavi Akım*, İstanbul: Siyah Beyaz Metis Güncel Yayınları.

Gökdemir, M., Kömürcü, M. İ. & Evcimen, T. U. (2018). "Türkiye'de Hidroelektrik Enerji ve HES Uygulamalarına Genel Bakış", TMMOB

İnşaat Mühendisleri Odası Su Yapıları Kurulu, TMH-471, 2012-1.
Güngör, M. K. & Buldurur, M. A. (2017). Türkiye'de Enerji Potansiyelinin Doğru Kullanımı: Nükleer Enerji Yatırım Projelerinin Doğru Değerlendirilmesi", *İdeal Kent Dergisi,* Sayı 21, Cilt 8, s. 301.
Hayli, S. (2001). "Rüzgâr Enerjisinin Önemi, Dünya'da ve Türkiye'deki Durumu", *Fırat Üniversitesi Sosyal Bilimler Dergisi,* Cilt 11, Sayı 1, s. 24.
İşcan, İ. H. (2002). *Küresel Değişimin Getirdiği Yeni Stratejilerle Enerji Güvenliği Sorunu ve Türkiye*, Avrasya Etütleri.
Karagöl, E. T. & Kavaz, İ. (2017). "Dünyada ve Türkiye'de Yenilenebilir Enerji", *SETA Analiz,* Sayı 197, s. 23.
Kuleyin, B. & Cerit, A. G. (2011). "Ham Petrolün Dünya Pazarlarına Ulaştırılmasında Ceyhan Terminali'nin Rolü", *Dokuz Eylül Üniversitesi Denizcilik Fakültesi Dergisi*, Cilt: 3, Sayı: 2, s. 21.
Özalp, M. (2018). *Küresel Enerji Denkleminde Merkez Ülke: Türkiye*, 1. Baskı, Ankara: Seçkin Yayınları.
Pamir, N. (2005). *AB'nin Enerji Sorunsalı ve Türkiye*, Stratejik Analiz Dergisi, Cilt 6, Sayı 67.
Sağlam, M. & Uyar, T. S. (2005). "Dalga Enerjisi ve Türkiye'nin Dalga Enerjisi Teknik Potansiyeli", *III. Yenilenebilir Kaynakları Sempozyumu Sonuç Bildirileri*, s. 5.
T.C. Enerji ve Tabii Kaynaklar Bakanlığı, (2018). "2017 Yılı Taşkömürü Sektör Raporu", Türkiye Taşkömürü Kurumu.
Tamzok, N. (2016). Dünya'da ve Türkiye'de Kömür, *"Türkiye'nin Enerji Görünümü Raporu",* TMMOB Makine Mühendisleri Odası, s. 41.
Tiftikçigil, B. Y.& Yesevi, Ç. G. (2015). *Türkiye'nin Enerji Görünümü Stratejiler ve İlişkiler,* 1. Baskı, İstanbul: Derin Yayınları.
Yılmaz, M. (2012). "Türkiye'nin Enerji Potansiyeli ve Yenilenebilir Enerji Kaynaklarının Elektrik Enerjisi Üretimi Açısından Önemi", *Ankara Üniversitesi Çevrebilimleri Dergisi*, 4(2), s.35.
Yılmaz, N. F. (2005). "Petrol ve Doğal Gaz Boru Hatları Üzerine Genel Bir Değerlendirme", *Tesisat Mühendisliği Dergisi*, sayı 87, s. 8.
Yüce, Ç. K. (2006). *Kafkasya ve Orta Asya Enerji Kaynakları Üzerinde Mücadele*, İstanbul: Ötüken Nesriyat.

Internet Sites

Devlet Su İşleri Genel Müdürlüğü. (n.d.). *Sunumlar.* Retrieved April 16, 2019, from http://www.dsi.gov.tr/faaliyetler/sunumlar
Enerji Atlası. (n.d.-a). *Hidroelektrik Santralleri.* Retrieved April 16, 2019, from https://www.enerjiatlasi.com/hidroelektrik/

Enerji Atlası. (n.d.-b). *Rüzgâr Enerji Santralleri*. Retrieved April 16, 2019, from https://www.enerjiatlasi.com/ruzgar/
Enerji Atlası. (n.d.-c). *Jeotermal Enerji Santralleri*. Retrieved April 16, 2019, from https://www.enerjiatlasi.com/jeotermal/
Maden Tetkik ve Arama Genel Müdürlüğü. (n.d.). *Kömür Arama Araştırmaları*. Retrieved April 23, 2019, from, http://www.mta.gov.tr/v3.0/arastirmalar/komur-arama-arastirmalari
Ministry of Foreign Affairs of the Republic of Turkey. (n.d.). *Turkey's International Energy Strategy*. Retrieved April 22, 2019, from https://www.mfa.gov.tr/turkeys-energy-strategy.en.mfa
T.C. Enerji ve Tabii Kaynaklar Bakanlığı. (n.d.-a). *Doğal Gaz Boru Hatları ve Projeleri*. Retrieved April 16, 2019, from https://enerji.gov.tr/bilgi-merkezi-dogal-gaz-boru-hatlari-ve-projeleri
T.C. Enerji ve Tabii Kaynaklar Bakanlığı. (n.d.-b). *Petrol Boru Hatları*. Retrieved April 16, 2019, from https://enerji.gov.tr/bilgi-merkezi-petrol-boru-hatlari.
T.C. Enerji ve Tabii Kaynaklar Bakanlığı. (n.d.-c). *Doğal Gaz*. Retrieved April 16, 2019, from http://www.enerji.gov.tr/tr-TR/Sayfalar/Dogal-Gaz
T.C. Enerji ve Tabii Kaynaklar Bakanlığı. (n.d.-d). *Güneş*. Retrieved April 16, 2019, from https://www.enerji.gov.tr/tr-TR/Sayfalar/Gunes
T.C. Enerji ve Tabii Kaynaklar Bakanlığı. (n.d.-e). *Biyokütle*. Retrieved April 16, 2019, from https://www.enerji.gov.tr/tr-TR/Sayfalar/Biyokutle
T.C. Enerji ve Tabii Kaynaklar Bakanlığı. (n.d.-f). *Jeotermal*. Retrieved April 16, 2019, from https://www.enerji.gov.tr/tr-TR/Sayfalar/Jeotermal
Türkiye Petrolleri Anonim Ortaklığı. (n.d.). *Türkiye Petrolleri Anonim Ortaklığı*. Retrieved April 16, 2019, from http://www.tpao.gov.tr
Wind Atlas. (n.d.). Retrieved April 23, 2019, from, http://www.yegm.gov.tr/YEKrepa/REPA-duyuru_01.html
WWF. (2017, October 11). Düşük Karbon Ekonomisi: Enerji Verimliliği ve Yenilenebilir Kaynaklar Enerji Politikalarına İlişkin Riskleri Nasıl Azaltabilir? https://www.wwf.org.tr/basin_bultenleri/raporlar/?7160/dusuk-karbon-ekonomisi
Yenilenebilir Enerji Genel Müdürlüğü. (n.d.). *Güneş Enerjisi Potansiyeli Atlası (GEPA)*. Retrieved April 23, 2019, from http://www.yegm.gov.tr/MyCalculator/

CHAPTER FOUR

RUSSIA AND ENERGY

ARZU AL[*] & HAYRI KAYA[**]

Introduction

Energy has been more effectively involved in human life since the Industrial Revolution, especially with the advent of steam engines. Of course, the energy we mean here is non-renewable energy sources. People have previously used wind energy in sailing ships and mills, benefited from the kinetic energy of humans and animals, and obtained heat and light with wood, which is a forest product. In fact, people have used petroleum as gas oil for lighting purposes. Thus, they realized their production and kept their economies alive. However, with the steam boilers and internal combustion engines that emerged after the Industrial Revolution, mechanization was started in production, and the energy demand and energy consumption of the world economy and world industry increased.

With the Industrial Revolution that began in the 1700s, the emergence of steam engines, and, in later years, the use of internal combustion engines, both the usage areas of energy improved and the consumption of energy started to accelerate. Furthermore, it can be seen that countries with energy resources increased their incomes by exporting their existing resources even if they do not produce anything else. The active use of non-renewable energy sources compared to a hundred years ago has reached a level that can cause environmental disasters and adversely affect the environment. In general, the increase in carbon emissions due to the

[*] Assoc. Prof. Arzu Al, Head of the Department of International Political Economy, Department of International Relations, Marmara University. E-mail: arzu.al@marmara.edu.tr.

[**] Hayri Kaya, M.A. student, Department of International Political Economy, Marmara University. E-mail: m.hayrikaya.hk@gmail.com.

formation of renewable energy sources from fossil fuels and the destruction of green nature cause the emergence of diseases affecting the health of many people. On the other hand, countries are obliged to develop their industries in order to increase their levels of development and prosperity. Therefore, they are dependent on energy. Energy demand is a factor that is considered an indicator of development.

Russia is one of the countries with the highest reserves in terms of non-renewable resources. The vast majority of the economy is dependent on the energy resources it owns. Russian President Vladimir Putin's recent statement is remarkable. According to his statement, "Renewable energy sources are not actually as friendly as thought. Each time the wind turbines turn, they affect the movements under the soil and destroy the life of the worms. This is a carnage of the environment that cannot be underestimated" (Sputnik, 2019). It is clear that Russia, whose economy depends heavily on gas exports and which also has a large resource in terms of reserves, made these comments because it does not want renewable energy to be put in front of natural gas, which it uses as a weapon to avoid its political-economic interests being overshadowed.

1. Energy

Energy is the simplest form of motion and the ability to do work. Substances need energy to change their state. For example, while the state of wood in nature does not emit heat and light, when its physical form changes by burning, it begins to emit heat and light around it. Today, the movement of cars, the warming of our house, production in industry and factories, the sprouting of seeds in nature and the light and heat emission of the Sun are all directly related to energy. There are eight main types of energy scientifically. These are kinetic, electrical, nuclear, chemical, potential, heat, light and sound. Potential energy is the energy of a substance or body due to its position or physical state, for example, a stretched bow. Kinetic energy is the energy of bodies or substances with velocity. A spinning wheel, a falling ball or a running child can be cited as examples. Heat energy, on the other hand, is the energy of a substance or body due to its current temperature. All substances have heat energy. An example is geothermal energy (the ascent of hot water or steam as a result of the heating of underground water by magma). Electrical energy is the kind of energy that objects or substances have due to the electrical charges they carry. The energy of light is the energy that provides illumination. It turns energy from burning wood, the Sun or a lamp into light. Chemical energy is the result of chemical reactions. Nuclear energy occurs when the atomic nucleus is broken down by fission or fusion reactions. In this way, energy is obtained from nuclear power plants. Sound energy is the type of energy that emerges with the vibration and oscillation of matter (T.C. Enerji ve Tabii Kaynaklar Bakanlığı, 2015).

1.1. Energy Resources

In order to obtain or use the energy types described in the above section, we need energy sources. Energy sources can be studied in five main groups: sustainable, convertible, organic/inorganic, physical and underground/aboveground sources. Sustainable energy resources are examined in two groups according to the renewability of the resource.

We can explain renewable energy as the energy source being able to replenish itself faster than the speed of its depletion. For example, wind, hydropower, biomass, wave, solar, hydrogen, tides and piezoelectricity are renewable energy sources. Another group, non-renewable resources, is often called fossil, traditional or conventional energy. Although many new resource areas have been discovered by scientists today, there is a possibility of depletion due to their fossil origin. For example, petroleum, natural gas, uranium, coal, thorium and bituminous schists are energy sources that are likely to be depleted (Küçükkaya, 2018).

Convertible energy sources vary depending on whether the source is used directly or indirectly to release energy. Direct energy sources are called primary energy sources: for example, coal, biomass, nuclear, hydraulic and wave energy. Indirect energy sources are called secondary energy sources. Electricity, diesel, gasoline and LPG energy are included in this group as examples of energies obtained by converting substances according to their status in nature (Küçükkaya, 2018).

Organic/inorganic energy sources are formed by grouping energy sources as organic or inorganic according to their genetic characteristics. Sources of organic origin have been formed as a result of fossilization, and examples of sources of inorganic origin are nuclear (radioactive) energy sources such as uranium and thorium.

Resources are allocated their physical state according to their physical condition at room temperature. Solid energy sources include wood, coal and uranium; liquid energy sources include LPG, diesel, petroleum and biodiesel; and gas energy resources consist of methane gas, biogas and natural gas (Küçükkaya, 2018).

Sources of energy are also separated according to their origin; those of underground origin are obtained from under the Earth's crust, such as coal, oil and natural gas, and are also known as fossil resources. Aboveground energy sources include wind, solar and biomass sources, which are of great importance because they are sustainable (Küçükkaya, 2018).

1.1.1. Energy Reserves and Their Usage

In this section, we will explain in detail the role of energy sources, which were discussed in general terms in the previous section, in international relations with regard to their use and reserves in the world using two main groups: non-renewable and renewable energy resources.

1.1.1.1. Non-Renewable Energy Resources

1.1.1.1.1. Coal

It can be observed that the use of coal, which constitutes one-third of the energy used in the world and 38% of the produced electricity, has increased since the 1600s and now plays an important role, especially for the iron and steel industry. It has maintained its popularity for many years, especially because it is easier to access than other energy sources, is economically cheap, and is the main element of the iron and steel industry (Eniscuola Energy and Environment, 2019). The fact that coal is a cheap and easily accessible energy source has played an important role in the emergence of European industry. With the start of the Industrial Revolution in Europe and the burning of coal into heat energy, steam machines were brought to life, and all developed countries used coal as their primary energy source. Today, it can be seen that it continues to be consumed as an important energy source in less developed and developing countries. The fact that this cheap energy source causes air and environmental pollution and even global warming by increasing the amount of carbon emissions has been criticized, especially in recent years. Many developed countries are aiming to combat global climate change by replacing coal-based energy production with other energy sources.

According to 2018 data, the USA has the leading coal reserves in the world with 250,219 million tons, Russia is in second with 160,364 million tons, Australia is in third with 147,435 million tons, and China is in fourth with 138,819 million tons (Statistical Review of World Energy-BP (2019:42) (see Figure 1).

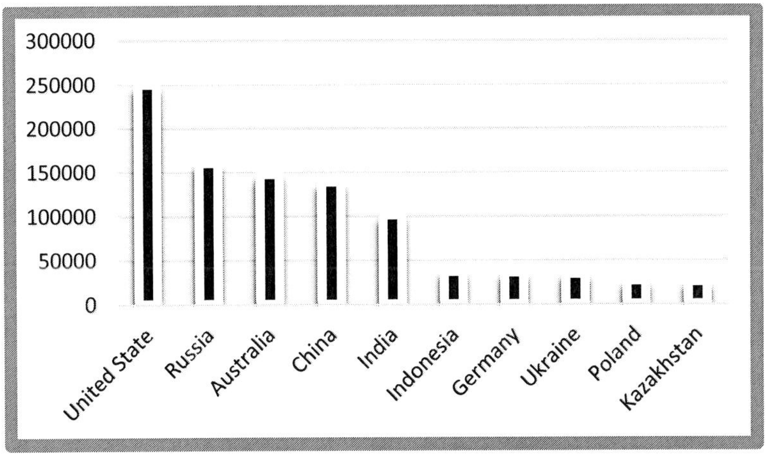

Figure 1: Word Coal Reserve (Mt), Source: (Bp, 2019: 42)

In the world coal production list, China is the leader with a production of 3,545 million tons of coal, five times that of its closest follower. Behind China, India produced 741 million tons, the US 685 million tons, Indonesia 548 million tons, Australia 483 million tons, and Russia 432 million tons (US Energy Information Administration, 2019a) (see Figure 2).

China also leads the world's coal consumption list with 3,770 million tons. India consumed 982 million tons, the USA consumed 624 million tons, Russia consumed 234 million tons, Germany consumed 217 million tons, and Australia consumed 113 million tons (Enerdata, 2019).

It is clear that developing countries benefit the most from cheap and easy to obtain coal. Contrary to the climate policies of developed countries, Asian countries such as China and India ignore global climate policies in the way of development. The main reason why Russia is in the middle of the list is the large share of natural gas reserves in the country. Due to global climate policies, coal production and consumption in the USA have been decreasing in recent years. Instead, the United States has begun to pay more attention to renewable energy sources and nuclear energy.

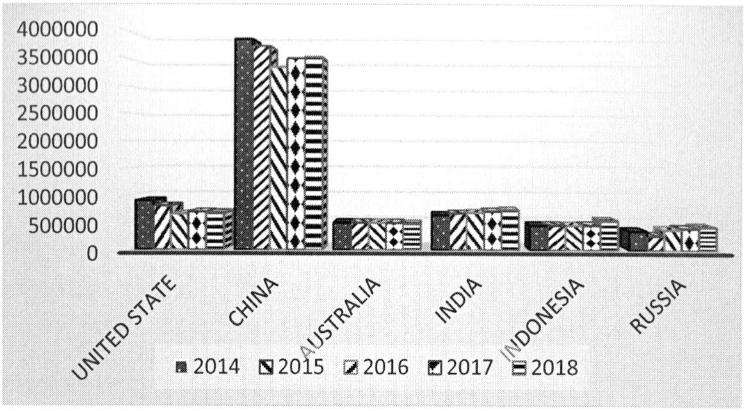

Figure 2: World Coal Production (Mt)
Source: US Energy Information Administration 2019a

1.1.1.1.2. Oil

Oil is one of the non-renewable underground energy sources based on fossilization, just like coal and natural gas. In addition to the most common energy fuels (gasoline, petroleum, diesel) in the world, it is the main raw material of the petrochemical industry and the plastics industry. Especially with oil's use as a commercial commodity in the USA, it has started to meet the increasing raw material and energy needs since the Industrial Revolution. The invention of internal combustion engines, the development of the automobile industry, and the war industry (tanks, airplanes, ships) have led to increasing demand for energy in the world based on countries' production and industrial development, and the consumption of oil has increased. The development of the petroleum-based petrochemical industry has been directly proportional to the advancement of technology and science. Today, the multinational corporations that are leading the oil industry have reached a size and level of power to shape the world political economy.

Looking at the world crude oil reserves list, Venezuela is the leader with 300,878 million barrels. Saudi Arabia has 266,455 million barrels, Canada has 169,709 million barrels, Iran has 158,400 million barrels, Iraq has 142,503 million barrels, Kuwait has 101,500 million barrels, the United Arab Emirates has 97,800 million barrels, Russia has 80,000 million barrels, Libya has 48,363 million barrels, and the US has 39,230 million barrels (The World Factbook 2018, 2019a) (see Figure 3).

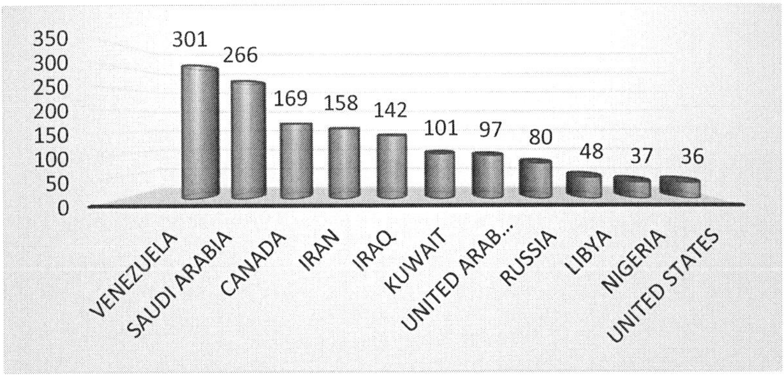

Figure 3: World Crude Oil Reserves (BBL).
Source: The World Factbook 2018, 2019a

In terms of the world's production, the USA ranks first with 10,9 million barrels per day (Bbl/D) of oil produced. The USA is followed by Saudi Arabia with 10,4 million Bbl/D, Russia with 10,7 million Bbl/D, Canada with 4,2 million Bbl/D, Iran with 4,2 million Bbl/D, China with 3,7 million Bbl/D, and Venezuela with 1,4 million Bbl/D (*The World Factbook 2018, 2019*b) (see Figure 4). In terms of oil consumption, the USA is at the top of the list with 20 million Bbl/D of oil consumed, while China consumed 13,5 million Bbl/D, India 4,3 million Bbl/D, Russia 3,6 million Bbl/D, Canada 2,4 million Bbl/D, Saudi Arabia 3,3 million Bbl/D, and Iran consumed 1,8 million Bbl/D (U.S. Energy Information Administration, 2019c).

From the last century to the present day, the importance of oil has been increasing day by day, and oil-based industries in particular are developing. In addition to being a resource that meets energy needs, it continues to be used as a raw material. Together with the technological developments in our age, the main actors in the global field are increasing oil production day by day. Although the United States ranks tenth in its reserve capacity, its top ranks in production and consumption show that, like other developed countries, its economy and industry are oil-based.

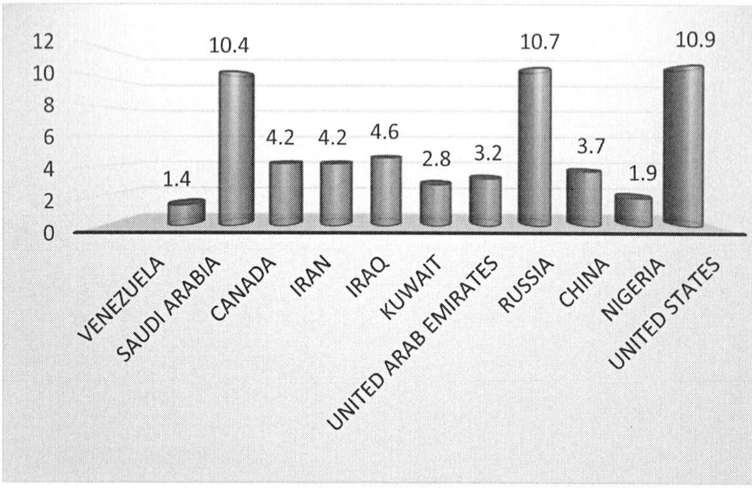

Figure 4: World Crude Oil Production (Bbl/D)
Source: The World Factbook 2018, 2019b

1.1.1.1.3. Natural Gas

Natural gas, which is a fossil fuel like oil and coal, has not been used for many years due to a lack of exploration. Natural gas, which entered into our daily lives with the use of gas lamps for lighting purposes in the late 1800s, turned into an active energy source especially after the 1960s. Russia, Qatar and Iran, which own more than half of the world's reserves, are exporting this energy through pipelines today. The fact that natural gas is a climate-friendly and environmentally friendly energy source strengthens the hand of the exporting countries, especially in recent years when climate policies have been on the agenda, and provides them with economic development and enrichment. According to *The World Factbook 2018 prepared by the CIA*, Russia has 47.8 trillion cubic meters of natural gas reserves, Iran has 33.5 trillion cubic meters, Qatar has 24.3 trillion cubic meters, and the US and Saudi Arabia each have 8.6 trillion cubic meters (The World Factbook 2018, 2019c) (see Figure 5).

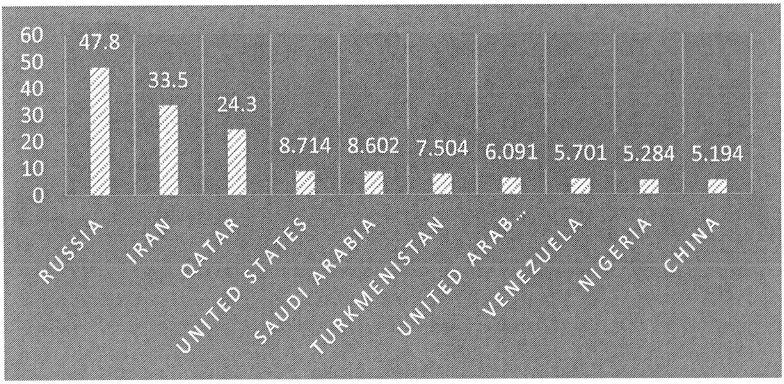

Figure 5: World Natural Gas Reserve (tcm)
Source: The World Factbook 2018, 2019c

In terms of production, the USA is at the top of the list with 831 billion cubic meters; Russia follows with 669 billion cubic meters, Iran with 239 billion cubic meters, Canada with 184 billion cubic meters, Qatar with 175 billion cubic meters, China with 161 billion cubic meters, and Saudi Arabia with 112 billion cubic meters (BP, 2019: 32) (see Figure 6).

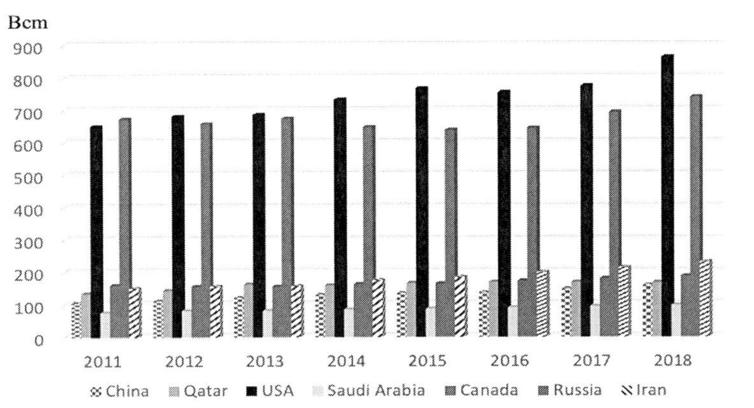

Figure 6: World Natural Gas Production
Source: BP, Statistical Review of World Energy 2019: 32

The USA also ranks first in natural gas consumption with 817 billion cubic meters, followed by Russia with 454 billion cubic meters, China with 283 billion cubic meters, Iran with 225 billion cubic meters, Canada with 115 billion cubic meters, and Saudi Arabia with 112 billion cubic meters (BP, 2019: 34).

As can be seen, the USA's production and consumption figures are higher than other countries when natural gas reserves are taken into consideration. We can say that this situation was created by the USA especially to meet its energy needs and to reduce its dependence on foreign sources. Considering the current production figures, it can be seen that if the production trends of the USA and Russia do not decrease compared to their reserve rates, they will be deprived of resources in the near future. However, it can be understood that the high production figures of Russia, where energy exports occupy an important place in its economy, are in order to respond to exports to Europe. Another issue is the emergence of liquefied natural gas, known as LNG, with the development of technology. This situation allows countries such as Qatar and Nigeria to export their existing natural gas by ship without the need for a pipeline and to further their economic development.

1.1.1.1.4. Nuclear

Nuclear energy is the energy produced in nuclear reactions by separating atomic nuclei from each other (fission) or by combining them with each other (fusion). The heat generated by the nuclear reaction and the evaporation of the water in the nuclear reactors by heating are used to generate electrical energy. Nuclear power plants are more advantageous for countries that are deprived of resources or want to reduce their external dependence, as well as to provide more energy with less resources. Reliable, sustainable and inexpensive, the fact that the power plants have active and passive security systems and advanced technological equipment reinforces the reason why they are preferred among other energy sources. In addition to these advantages, however, there are disadvantages. For example, nuclear power plants emit hazardous chemical waste and have destructive effects on nature and human beings in any accident that may occur. While the safe and careful use of nuclear energy benefits countries, the accidents at the Chernobyl and Fukuyama nuclear power plants in the past remind us to be very careful in the use of today's power plants. Australia ranks first in the world's proven net uranium reserves with 1.8 million tons, followed by Kazakhstan with 842,000 tons, Canada with

514,000 tons, Russia with 485,000 tons, and the USA with 47,000 tons (World Nuclear Association, 2019a) (see Figure 7).

Country	tonnes U	percentage of world
Australia	1,818,300	30%
Kazakhstan	842,2	14%
Canada	514,4	8%
Russia	485,6	8%
Namibia	442,1	7%
South Africa	322,4	5%
China	290,4	5%
Niger	280	5%
Brazil	276,8	5%
Uzbekistan	139,2	2%
Ukraine	114,1	2%
Mongolia	113,5	2%
Botswana	73,5	1%
Tanzania	58,2	1%
USA	47,2	1%
Jordan	43,5	1%
Other	280,6	4%
World total	**6,142,600**	
WORLD NUCLEAR ASSOCIATION	www.world-nuclear.org	

Figure 7: World Uranium Reserve
Source: World Nuclear Association, 2019a

In production, Kazakhstan is at the top of the list with 23,321 tons, followed by Canada with 13,000 tons, Australia with 6,000 tons, Russia with 3,000 tons, China with 1,800 tons, and the USA with 940 tons (World Nuclear Association, 2019b) (see Figure 8). Considering the consumption amounts, the USA ranks first with 19,000 tons, followed by France with 9,500 tons, China with 8,000 tons, Russia with 5,000 tons, and Canada with 1,500 tons (Zararsız, 2005;9). When we look at the number of nuclear plants in the world, the USA has 95 active plants, while France has 56, China 49, Japan 33, and Russia 38 (IAEA, 2019) (see Figure 9).

Country	2010	2011	2012	2013	2014	2015	2016	2017	2018
Kazakhstan	17,803	19,451	21,317	22,451	23,127	23,607	24,586	23,321	21,705
Canada	9783	9145	8999	9331	9134	13,325	14,039	13,116	7001
Australia	5900	5983	6991	6350	5001	5654	6315	5882	6517
Namibia	4496	3258	4495	4323	3255	2993	3654	4224	5525
Niger	4198	4351	4667	4518	4057	4116	3479	3449	2911
Russia	3562	2993	2872	3135	2990	3055	3004	2917	2904
Uzbekistan (est.)	2400	2500	2400	2400	2400	2385	2404	2404	2404
China (est.)	827	885	1500	1500	1500	1616	1616	1885	1885
Ukraine	850	890	960	922	926	1200	1005	550	1180
USA	1660	1537	1596	1792	1919	1256	1125	940	582
India (est.)	400	400	385	385	385	385	385	421	423
South Africa (est.)	583	582	465	531	573	393	490	308	346
Iran (est.)	0	0	0	0	0	38	0	40	71
Pakistan (est.)	45	45	45	45	45	45	45	45	45
Czech Republic	254	229	228	215	193	155	138	0	0
Romania	77	77	90	77	77	77	50	0	0
Brazil	148	265	326	192	55	40	44	0	0
France	7	6	3	5	3	2	0	0	0
Germany	8	51	50	27	33	0	0	0	0
Malawi	670	846	1101	1132	369	0	0	0	0
Total world	**53,671**	**53,493**	**58,493**	**59,331**	**56,041**	**60,304**	**62,379**	**59,462**	**53,498**
tonnes U_3O_8	63,291	63,082	68,974	69,966	66,087	71,113	73,56	70,12	63,087
% of world deman	84%	87%	94%	91%	85%	98%	96%	93%	80%

WORLD NUCLEAR ASSOCIATION www.world-nuclear.org

Figure 8: World Uranium Production
Source: World Nuclear Association, 2019b

Based on the information given so far, we can easily say that the US is a leader in the field of global energy. When we examine the production and consumption values of coal, oil, natural gas and nuclear energy sources, it can be seen that the USA is in first place and China, which is its closest competitor, follows the USA at the same speed. Nuclear energy has been subject to intense criticism from the world public, especially given the past disasters. However, the fact that the United States, which has the most power plants, and China, which has caught the trend of economic upswing, have policies to increase their number of power plants and the fact that there are a remarkable number of nuclear plants in Europe, especially in France, contrasts these criticisms. Undoubtedly, energy resources have a significant impact on the development and growth figures of countries.

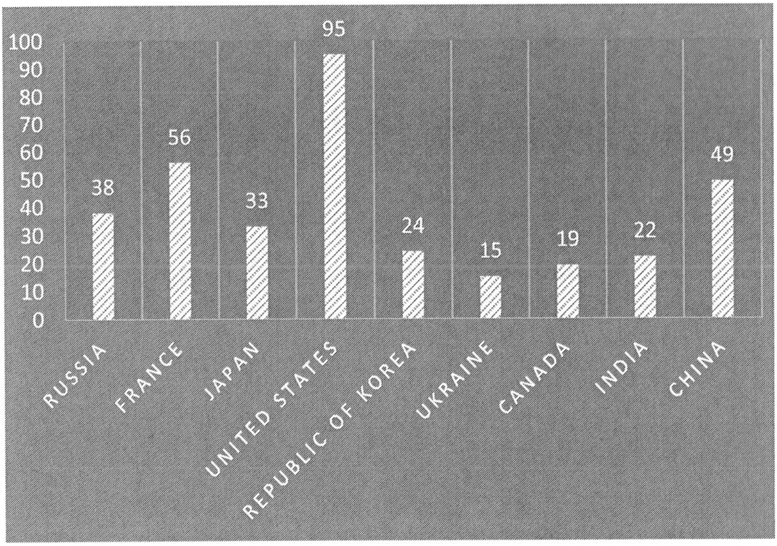

Figure 9: Ranking of Nuclear Power Plants in Use
Source: IAEA-PRIS Database, 2019

1.1.1.2. Renewable Energy Resources

Unlike non-renewable energy with its fossil origins and the possibility of depletion, solar, hydraulic, geothermal, wave and bioenergy are renewable energy sources. As a result of increasing carbon emissions and climate change policies in recent years, interest in renewable resources has increased globally. The indirect use of resources and the ability to generate energy without the problem of exhaustion emerges as essential issues, especially for countries that will devote significant resources to energy imports in the coming years. Solar energy is a renewable resource that can be used by both countries and individuals in this field, and it can be used for electricity generation or converted into hot water and lighting. According to 2016 data, 333 GWh of solar energy is obtained in the world. This increased to over 700 GWh by 2020. Ranked by installed solar power, China is at the top of the list with 78 GW, while Germany and the USA have 40 GW and the UK has 11 GW (Statistical Review of World Energy-BP, 2021) (see Figure 10). According to solar energy consumption figures, China leads the way with 66 GWh, followed by the USA with 56 GWh, Germany with 38 GWh, and the UK with 10 GWh (Ritchie & Roser, 2019).

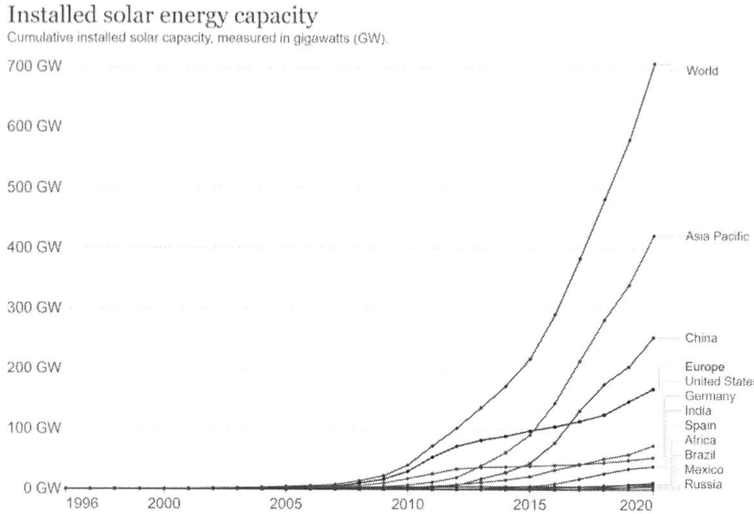

Figure 10: Installed Solar Power Capacity
Source: Statistical Review of World Energy-BP (2021)

Bioenergy, which is another renewable energy source, is the transformation of plant-origin organisms that store solar energy by photosynthesis into biological energy sources thanks to advanced technology. Energy derived from traditional biomass sources like burning charcoal and organic wastes were important for a long time in the human history. However, in today's World energy produced by this way doesn't carry much importance as it is roughly estimated to be 1 TWh. Biofuel energy obtained mainly from bioethanol and biodiesel are taken more into account while considering the bioenergy. In 2020, a total of 1043 TWh of biofuel energy is produced in the World and the US alone produces approximately 400 TWh of this figure. What is noteworthy is that Brazil produces over 200 TWh of biofuel energy which is more than the whole Europe or the Asia-Pacific region (Statistical Review of World Energy-BP, 2021) (see Figure 11).

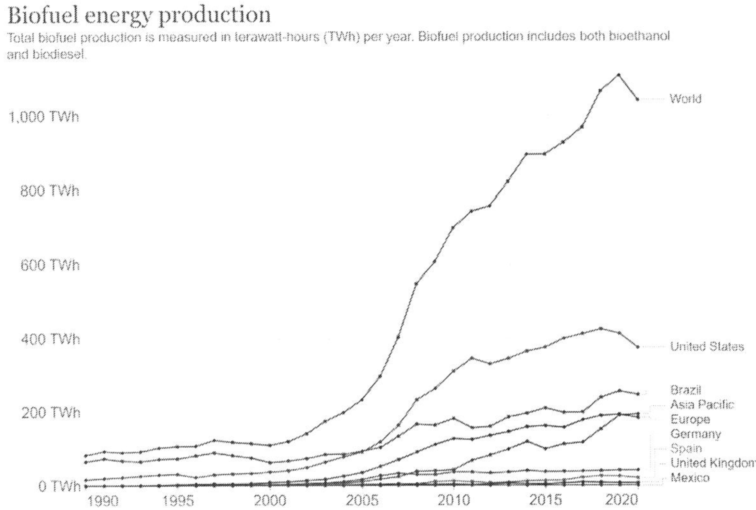

Figure 11: Annual Biofuel Energy Production
Source: Statistical Review of World Energy-BP (2021)

Wind energy, on the other hand, emerges as the storage of energy generated by the wind, which is a natural phenomenon, by turning wind turbines. With 282 GW installed capacity in the world, China ranks first in this field, while the USA has a capacity of 118 GW and Germany with 62 GW (Statistical Review of World Energy-BP, 2021) (see Figure 12). In terms of consumption figures, a total of 960 TWh produced wind energy is consumed in the world, and China is the leader again with 241 TWh, while the USA consumes 228 TWh and Germany consumes 77 TWh (Ritchie & Roser, 2019).

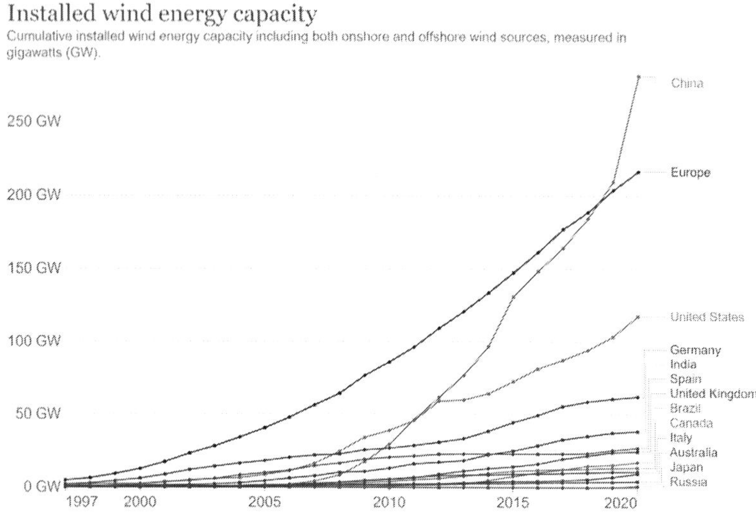

Figure 12: Installed Wind Energy Power
Source: Statistical Review of World Energy-BP (2021)

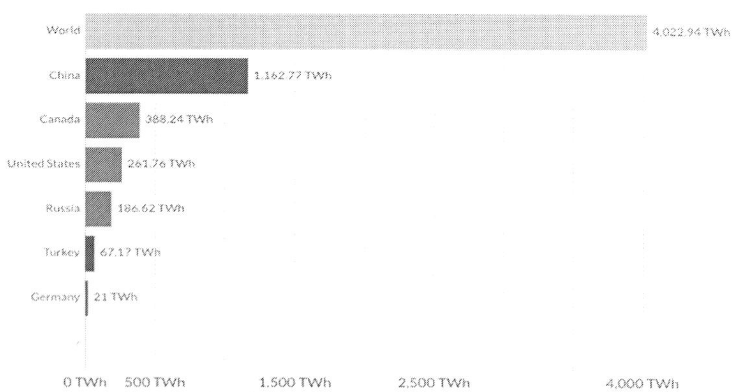

Figure 13: World Hydroelectric Power Consumption
Source: Ritchie & Roser, 2019.

Hydroelectric power is the type of energy obtained by damming rivers or water sources and turning turbines to generate electricity through water power. As of 2018 approximately 4,000 TWh of hydroelectric power is generated in the world. Of this figure, 1,100 TWh is consumed by China,

388 TWh by Canada, and 261 TWh by the United States (Ritchie & Roser, 2019) (see Figure 13).

Geothermal energy is generated by hot water steam coming out of the ground, and the world has a geothermal energy capacity of 13,000 MW. While the US produces 2,500 MW of this amount, Turkey and Iceland take their place on the list with their approximate production levels of 700 MW each in 2016 (Ritchie & Roser, 2019).

1.2. Energy and International Relations

The energy resources that we explained in the previous section are directly related to countries' development and prosperity, especially since the Industrial Revolution. The mechanization initiated by the Industrial Revolution has caused energy consumption to increase more than ever before. In order to meet the consumption demands, the production of existing reserves with the development of energy-oriented technology has started, and new reserves and new types of energy resources have been discovered. Energy competition, which started with the commercial use of oil in the USA, has been going on for many years all over the world through multinational corporations crossing the boundaries of states. Energy demand in the industrial production of countries is progressing in direct proportion with their development. Today, countries that are deprived of energy resources or fail to respond to domestic demand meet their energy needs by importing from other countries. Interdependence arises from the fact that energy-importing countries are dependent on foreign sources and energy-exporting countries obtain commercial income. In the context of the international relations discipline, another area that can affect the relations of countries with each other is the energy trade between them. It has been seen that this process of interdependence created by globalization and the energy trade relationships between countries has caused a series of crises that have deeply affected the world economy in recent history (Sevim, 2012, pp. 4379-4381).

Before the Industrial Revolution, countries fought each other for land, competition and power, and we can say that after the Industrial Revolution, there were wars based on raw materials. The formation of the oil-based industry has allowed oil to be an important raw material not only as an energy source but also for the petrochemical and plastic industries. On the other hand, the fact that coal is the main instrument of the iron and steel industry and that natural gas is an environmentally friendly type of energy that does not emit as much carbon as other fossil-based sources show that the world economy is developing on the basis of energy (Sevim, 2012, p. 4382).

The following events in our recent history can be given as examples: Germany and France waged war against each other for coal mines in Alsace-Lorraine; as a response to oil prices, energy prices increased during the energy crisis that began in 1973 when OPEC countries stopped producing oil; and the fact that Russia, which exports energy to Europe today, derives the main source of its economy from this export.

Globalization has increased the economic interdependence of countries, and since crises can affect all countries, efforts are being made to prevent energy-based crises. For example, when Russia cut off its natural gas pipelines to Ukraine in the course of an economic and political crisis, Europe's natural gas supply was cut off, so Europe needed to overcome the crisis with alternative routes due to its natural gas dependence on Russia. On the other hand, in 2015, when Turkey shot down a Russian military jet on the grounds that it had carried out a border breach, Russia did not cut off the flow of gas, even though there were political reactions to the crisis. There is no doubt that about $50 billion of natural gas exports to Turkey played an important role in this attitude of Russia.

2. Russia

With the collapse of the Soviet Union, the Russian Federation began to adapt to the globalization process and entered a series of reforms in line with neoliberal policies within the country (Babaoğlu & Çobanoğlu, 2017, p. 288). While the Soviet Union adopted a closed economic system, the post-1991 Russian Federation used a lot of privatization to increase its economic gains and achieve its development goals. It adopted an export-oriented development strategy through these privatization initiatives that enabled it to be integrated into globalization processes. The natural resources of the Russian Federation have an important place in its economy (Baysoy, 2009, pp. 62-63). When Vladimir Putin came to power in 1999, taking his "Mineral and Raw Materials Resources and the Development Strategy for the Russian Economy" thesis into consideration as well, it can be said that the Russian economy determined an economic strategy for the export of natural resources. With this strategy, it can be seen that the Russian Federation wants to rebuild its international image and the development level lost by the Soviet Union and rebuild it strongly by exporting the energy it derives from its natural resources. The Russian Federation, which has a large part of its economy shaped by this energy and natural resource export income, clearly wants to benefit from interdependence (Şahin, 2005).

Today, Russia's GDP has reached $1.65 trillion, a nearly threefold increase since 1991. Per capita income is around $11,000. After twenty years of Putin, exports in Russia reached 30% of GDP, 48% of which was supplied by crude oil, natural gas and petroleum products, while iron and steel, precious minerals and metals accounted for 10%. Russia's exports to Europe account for around 60% of its total exports, while countries in the Asian continent account for 35%. The total export figure was $411 billion in 2017 (The Global Economy, 2019).

When considered on a country-by-country basis, Russia reached a total figure of $39 billion in exports to China, while exports totaled $35 billion with the Netherlands, $25 billion with Germany, $19 billion with Belarus, and $18 billion with Turkey. Total imports amounted to $320 billion, but they are generally composed of machinery, electrical and electronic equipment, and chemical products. In line with the data obtained from the import and export figures, the net trade surplus was $91 billion in 2017. Thus, when the country's income and development moves are taken into consideration, it can be seen that energy exports constitute the basis for the national economy (Trading Economics, 2019).

2.1. Energy in Russia

Russia has reserves of 80 million barrels of oil, 1.7 trillion cubic meters of natural gas, 160,364 million tons of coal, and 485,000 tons of nuclear material (uranium, thorium). With these resources, it can be said that it holds 10% of the world's energy (Baysoy, 2009, p. 62). According to the figures stated in the energy section above, Russia's energy production figures are as follows: 276 million barrels of oil, 741 billion cubic meters of natural gas, 412 million tons of coal, 3,000 tons of nuclear energy. Its consumption figures are as follows: 147 million tons of oil, 505 billion cubic meters of natural gas, 234 million tons of coal, and 5,000 tons of nuclear energy.

In the Russian Federation, energy often refers to electricity. As of 2018, the total energy produced is equivalent to 1,492 million tons of oil. 37% of this figure was obtained from oil, 16% from coal, 41% from natural gas, 5% from electricity, and 1% from biofuels (Enerdata, 2019). 1,128 TWh of electricity was produced during the year, accounting for 5% of total energy production, while 929 TWh was consumed and 200 TWh of electric power was exported. 17% of total electricity production was obtained from renewable energy sources. While wind and solar energy, which are two of the renewable energy types, are almost never used in the country, a total of 0.73 TWh of electricity is generated annually from biofuels, geothermal and wave energy. However, despite the low rate of renewable energy use, 186 TWh of electrical energy is obtained from hydraulic energy (Ritchie & Roser, 2019). At the 36 nuclear facilities in operation, 29 GWe of electricity is generated. There are currently 24 new nuclear facilities under construction which are planned to generate a total of 25 GWe of electricity (World Nuclear Association, 2019a).

Oil production takes place in Western Siberia, the Urals-Volga region, Eastern Siberia and the Far East, Arkhangelsk, the Komi Republic, the Caspian and the Arctic. Natural gas is obtained from Western Siberia, the Far East and Eastern Siberia and the Urals-Volga region. Russian coal is mainly supplied from the Russian Kuzbass Basin. Russia's largest oil companies are Rosneft, Lukoil, Surgetneftegaz, Gazprom, Tafneft, Slavneft, Bashneft and Novatek. Russia's natural gas companies are Gazprom, Novatek, Rosneft, Lukoil and Surgetneftegaz (U.S. Energy Information Administration, 2017).

2.1.1. Energy Exportation

Energy exportation is a commercial activity carried out by selling natural resources owned by countries to contribute to the national economy. This exportation occurs when natural resources are sent to another country, with which trade relations are established according to the nature of the resources. In addition to transportation options such as road and maritime routes, energy exports can also be realized through oil and gas pipelines. It can be said that Russia is trying to create interdependence by using the existing energy resources in order to increase both its income and international influence (Kakışım, 2019, p. 83). While creating a market by exporting oil and natural gas to many countries through pipelines that cross borders, it also achieves political gains in the country where the line is located (see Figures 14 and 15).

In 2018, Russia exported 260 million tons of crude oil, 150 million tons of petroleum products and 220,000 million cubic meters of natural gas (Central Bank of the Russian Federation, 2019).

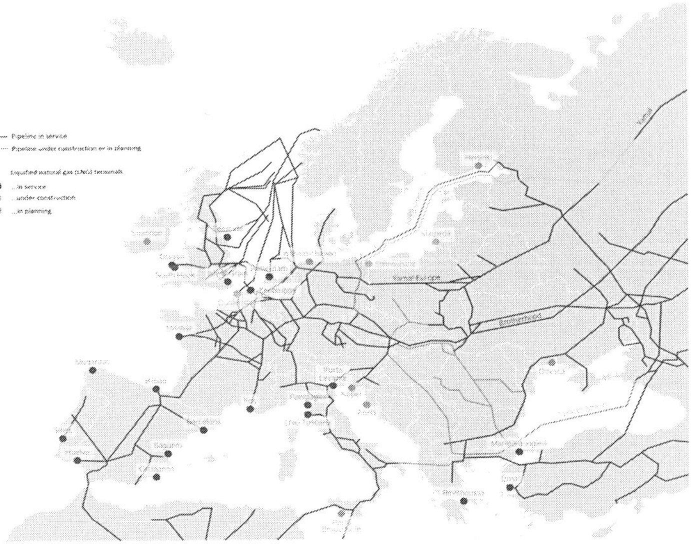

Figure 14: Russian Oil and Gas Pipelines to Europe.
Source: Sherman & Wettengel, 2018.

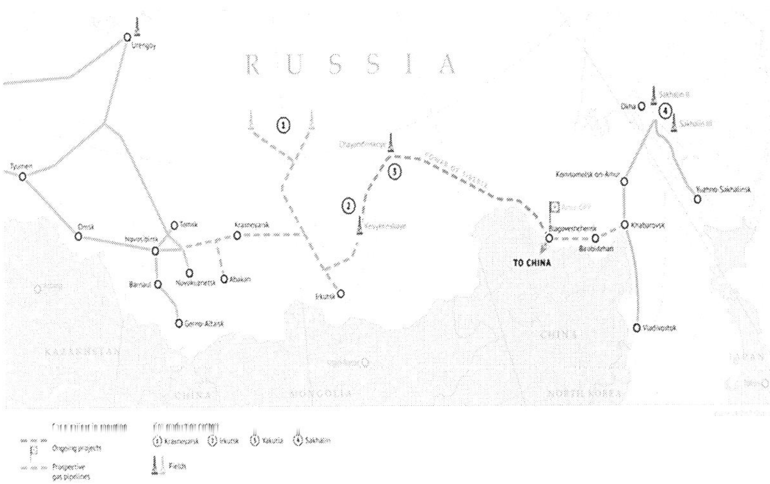

Figure 15: Russian Oil and Gas Pipelines to Asia. Source: Gazprom, 2019b.

2.1.1.1. Oil Exportation

While the continent of Europe, which is the region that imports the most Russian oil, is dependent on Russia for its energy, Russia is dependent on the income that it receives as a result of this consumption. The continents of Asia and Oceania use Russian oil resources as an alternative to Middle East energy sources due to Russia's geographical proximity. According to the 2016 data of the American Energy Information Administration, crude oil exports from Russian ports were equivalent to 4,355 million barrels of oil. Of this total, 1,407 million barrels were exported from Novorossiysk's port, 978 million barrels from Primorsk, 669 million barrels from Ust-Luga, and 594 million barrels from Kozmino (U.S. Energy Information Administration, 2017) (see Figure 16). Outside the ports, Russia exports energy through oil and natural gas pipelines.

Port	Thousand b/d
Novorossiysk	1,407
Primorsk	978
Ust-Luga	669
Kozmino	594
De Kastri	230
Murmansk	185
Prigorodnoye	112
Others	180
Total	**4,355**

Figure 16: Crude Oil from Russian Ports
Source: U.S. Energy Information Administration, 2017

2.1.1.2. Oil Pipelines

The pipelines that are managed by Transneft, a state-owned company with a wide distribution and export line, dominate Russia. Some of the major pipelines have the following capacities: Druzhba – 2 million barrels, Baltic Pipeline I – 1.5 million barrels, Baltic Pipeline II – 0.6 million barrels, and the Caspian Pipeline Consortium – 1.3 million barrels (U.S. Energy Information Administration, 2017) (see Figure 17)

Facility	Status	Capacity (million b/d)	Total length (miles)	Supply regions	Destination	Details
Western pipelines						
Druzhba	operating	2	2,500	West Siberia and Urals-Volga regions	Europe	completed in 1964
Baltic Pipeline System 1	operating	1.5	730	connects to Druzhba	Primorsk Port on the Gulf of Finland	completed in 2001
Baltic Pipeline System 2	operating	0.6	620	connects to Druzhba	Ust-Luga Port on the Gulf of Finland	completed in 2012
North-West Pipeline System	inactive	0.3	500	connects to Druzhba	Butinge, Lithuania and Ventspils, Latvia on the Baltic Sea	completed in 1968; inactive since 2006
Caspian Pipeline Consortium (CPC)	operating	1.3 by end 2017	940	Tengiz and Kazakhstan fields in Kazakhstan and Russian Caspian fields	Novorossiysk, Russia on the Black Sea	completed in 2001
Baku-Novorossiysk Pipeline	operating	0.1	830	Caspian and central Asia, via Sangachal Port, Azerbaijan on the Caspian Sea	Novorossiysk, Russia on the Black Sea	completed in 1996
Omsk-Pavlodar-Atasu Pipeline	operating	0.2	650	West Siberia and Urals-Volga regions	Pavlodar refinery in Kazakhstan and China via the Kazakhstan-China Pipeline	part of a series of pipelines originally completed in the 1980s
Eastern pipelines						
TransSakhalin	operating	0.2	500	Sakhalin fields (offshore northern Sakhalin)	Pacific seaport of Prigorodnoye (Southern Sakhalin Island)	completed in 2006
Eastern Siberia-Pacific Ocean (ESPO) Pipeline	operating	ESPO-1 – 1.2 currently, 1.6 by 2020 ESPO-2 – 0.6 currently, 1.0 by 2020 China spur – 0.4 currently, 0.6 by 2018	ESPO-1 – 1,700 ESPO-2 – 1,300 Daqing spur – 660	East Siberian fields and, via connecting pipelines, West Siberian fields and Yamal-Nenets region	Pacific seaport of Kozmino with a spur to Daqing, China	ESPO-1 (Taishet-Skovorodino) completed in 2009 ESPO-2 (Skovorodino-Kozmino) completed in 2012 Skovorodino-Daqing, China spur completed in 2010
Purpe-Samotlor Pipeline	operating	0.5	270	Yamal-Nenets and Ob Basins	connects to ESPO Pipeline	completed in 2011
Zapolyarye-Purpe Pipeline	operating	0.6 (expandable to 0.9)	300	Zapolyarye and Yamal-Nenets region	connects to ESPO pipeline via the Purpe-Samotlor pipeline	completed in 2017; initially expected to operate below capacity as development at connected oil fields has been delayed
Kuyumba-Taishet	operating	0.16 expandable to 0.3	440	Yurubcheno-Tokhomskoye field and Kuyumba field (startup delayed until 2018)	connects to ESPO Pipeline	completed in 2017; initially expected to operate below capacity as development at connected oil fields has been delayed

Figure 17: Russian Crude Oil Pipelines
Source: U.S. Energy Information Administration, 2017

2.1.1.3. Natural Gas Exportation

Most of Russia's natural gas pipelines date back to the Soviet era, and Gazprom, a state-owned enterprise in the natural gas pipeline industry, is in a monopoly position. In total, Russia exported 220,000 million cubic meters of natural gas in 2018. Close to 200,000 million cubic meters of this figure were exported to Europe, while more than 20,000 million cubic meters were exported to the Asian continent, mainly to China (Gazprom, 2019a). As such, Russia, which has a mutual dependence on Europe's gas consumption, sends most of its gas exports to Europe. As a result of the political tensions we have seen in recent years, Russia has started to diversify its natural gas exports and develop the LNG sector and search for markets in the Asian continent. There are currently two LNG facilities (Sakhalin and Yamal), but another eight new LNG facilities are planned in the country (U.S. Energy Information Administration, 2017).

2.1.1.4. Natural Gas Pipelines

The limited and costly transfer process of natural gas increases the need for natural gas pipelines, which allow for political pressure and economic bargains. There are now 14 different natural gas pipelines for the European continent, over which Russia fought in the past (see Figure 18).

Facility	Status	Capacity (trillion cubic feet per year)	Total length (miles)	Supply regions	Markets	Details
Western pipelines						
Yamal-Europe	operating	1.2	more than 1,000	West Siberian fields including Urengoy area	Poland, Germany, and northern Europe via Belarus	first section started operations in 1996
Blue stream	operating	0.6	750	West Siberian fields including Urengoy area	Turkey via the Black Sea	started operations in 2003
Nord stream	operating	1.9	760	West Siberian fields including Urengoy area	Germany and northern Europe via the Baltic Sea	started operations in 2011
Nord stream 2	planning	1.9	760	West Siberian fields including Urengoy area	Germany and northern Europe via the Baltic Sea	planned start in 2011
Urengoy-Ukhta, Bovanenkovo-Ukhta, and Ukhta-Torzhok	operating and under construction	more than 5.0	more than 1,300	Bovanenkovo field on the Yamal peninsula and Urengoy area fields	Western Russia and Europe via Yamal-Europe, Nord Stream, and other routes	Urengoy-Ukhta-Torzhok started operations in 2006; the 1st Bovanenkovo-Ukhta line started operations in 2012
Soyuz and Brotherhood (Urengoy-Pomary-Uzhgorod)	operating	more than 3.5	more than 2,800	West Siberian fields including Urengoy area, Russian Urals fields, and Central Asia	Western Russia and Europe via Ukraine	first major natural gas export lines to Europe, built and brought online during the Soviet era; first section started operations in 1967
Southern Corridor pipelines	construction	2.2	Western route - 550 Eastern route - 1,010	West Siberian fields including Urengoy area	Southern Russia, Turkey, and Europe via Turkish stream pipeline	construction on the Western route is due to be completed in 2017
Turkish stream	construction	up to 1.1	more than 500	West Siberian fields including Urengoy area	Turkey and Southeast Europe via the Black Sea	scheduled to start in late 2019

Eastern pipelines						
TransSakhalin	operating	0.3	500	Sakhalin fields (offshore northern Sakhalin)	Sakhalin LNG plant, Prigorodnoye, southern Sakhalin Island	started operations in 2008
Sakhalin-Khabarovsk-Vladivostok	operating	0.2	1,100	Sakhalin fields (offshore northern Sakhalin)	Eastern Russia with potential exports to Asia via proposed Vladivostok LNG or new pipelines	started operations in 2011; expandable to 1.1 Tcf per year with additional compression.
Power of Siberia 1 (Eastern route for exports to China)	construction	mainline – up to 2.2 China spur - 1.3	more than 1,200	East Siberian fields including Chayadinskoye in Yakutia region and Kovytka in Irkutsk region	Northeast China with a later extension to connect with the Sakhalin-Khabarovsk-Vladivostok pipeline	deliveries to China scheduled to begin by the end of 2019
Power of Siberia 2 (Altai/Western route)	planning	initial - 1.1	1,620	West Siberian fields including Urengoy area	China	2020 or later; could lay parallel lines in the future, doubling or tripling the initial capacity

Figure 18: Russian Natural Gas Pipelines
Source: U.S. Energy Information Administration, 2017

The Nord Stream pipeline, which has an annual capacity of 55 billion cubic meters and started operations in 2011, enables Russia to export natural gas directly to central Europe. The Nordeuropaische Erdgasleitung (NEL) pipeline has an annual capacity of 20 billion cubic meters and connects Nord Stream to Germany. The German-made Opal pipeline, with an annual capacity of 35 billion cubic meters, connects Nord Stream to eastern Germany and Central Europe. Northern Lights and Yamal Europe, with an annual capacity of 84 billion cubic meters of natural gas, are two main systems that transport Russian gas to Eastern Europe. The Soyuz and Brotherhood pipelines are the natural gas lines with which Russia sends gas to Europe via Ukraine with a total capacity of 158 billion cubic meters. For present political reasons, Russia has embarked on new projects in which it will not use Ukraine as a transit country. Blue Stream is a natural gas pipeline that sends gas to Turkey with an annual capacity of 19 billion cubic meters. The Russian Gas-West Pipeline is another pipeline that exports gas to Turkey via Ukraine, Romania and Bulgaria. Nord Stream 2 will be added to the other pipeline of the same name with its planned capacity of 55 billion cubic meters per year. TurkStream is a gas transport line to Southern Europe as an alternative to Ukraine with an annual capacity of 63 billion cubic meters. The Eastring Pipeline is a planned pipeline with an annual capacity of 20 to 40 billion cubic meters with the aim of connecting the TurkStream via Bulgaria and Romania with Slovakia and sending gas to Europe. The Trans-Adriatic Pipeline is a pipeline, known as TAP, that transmits the resources of the Caspian Basin to Europe via Turkey through the TANAP project with an annual capacity of 10 billion cubic meters. TANAP is a pipeline that transmits the resources of the Caspian Basin to Europe with an annual capacity of 16 billion cubic meters and is articulated with the TAP project. South Stream, with a natural gas capacity of 63 billion cubic meters, was the planned pipeline representing the line connecting Russia to Bulgaria and then to Europe via Serbia. However, this project was canceled as a result of the Ukrainian crisis and the TurkStream project (Front, 2015).

Russia has four natural gas pipeline projects for Asia. TransSakhalin, which commenced operations in 2008, connects Sakhalin with LNG factories with a capacity of 0.3 trillion cubic feet. The Sakhalin-Khabarovsk-Vladivostok line, with a capacity of 0.2 trillion cubic feet, connects Sakhalin to the Vladivostok LNG line and lines to Asia in eastern Russia. The Power of Siberia I and II lines are pipelines intended to export natural gas to China with a capacity of 3.3 trillion cubic feet.

2.2. Russia's Energy Policy

Russia, which holds more than a quarter of the world's energy resources, began to use the energy card as an instrument in foreign policy after the disintegration of the Soviet Union. Putin is actively using energy exports in foreign policy in order to reassert Russia politically, militarily and economically, to become a superpower as in the Cold War period, and to gain influence again in the geography of the dispersed Soviet Union (Erbil, 2010, p. 91). Today, it can be seen that Russia is trying to produce more than any other reserve-owning country in the world, but it consumes less energy and makes political-economic gains by exporting the energy it does not consume (Güneş & Arslan, 2018, p. 36).

We can say that Russian energy exports take place generally in the axis of Europe and Asia. According to Eurostat data, it can be seen that Europe, which is particularly dependent on foreign energy, is dependent for 36% of its energy on Russia (oil, natural gas and coal). Europe, Russia's largest market for natural gas, undoubtedly gives Russia absolute power. For Russia, which supplies more than 50% of government revenues from net energy exports, it is essential to find new markets, but its primary goal is to protect its existing markets and increase its export revenues. With this interdependence, Russia wants to re-establish the image of the country that it lost with the dissolution of the Soviet Union both diplomatically and politically (Güneş & Arslan, 2018, p. 44).

Russia, which has a large energy transfer line, transports its natural gas resources to Europe via transit countries such as Ukraine and Slovakia. There are also pipelines that provide energy flow directly without using transit countries, such as Blue Stream (Turkey) and Nord Stream (Germany). Russia also acts as an intermediary for countries that want to import energy. The Soyuz natural gas line transports Kazakhstan's, Turkmenistan's and Uzbekistan's natural gas to Europe, the Caucasus oil line transports Kazakhstan's oil to Europe, and the Novorossiysk oil line transports Azerbaijan's oil to Europe via Russia (Kakışım, 2019, p. 74).

As we discussed in the previous section, the pipelines used for the export of energy resources through many countries have led Russia to expand its political sphere of influence, but sometimes it can be seen that the opposite occurs. The fact that nearly 90% of the energy Russia exports to Europe passes through the territory of Ukraine has made Ukraine a transit country. As a result of Ukraine's policies against Russia, Russia did not delay in its intervention and reaction, causing the energy flow to Ukraine to stop during the crisis with Ukraine in recent years, and as a result of this, European energy imports were endangered (Al & Özdil, 2017, p. 161).

Although the current energy security problem allows Europe to turn to new energy supply sources, the construction of alternative pipelines to those crossing Ukraine has come onto the agenda due to Europe's dependence on Russia (Dal & Kurşun, 2017, pp. 27-29). Reactions to Russia's intervention in Ukraine and the occupation of Crimea have also been insufficient due to Europe's existing energy dependence. Despite Europe turning to transit countries in which Russia is experiencing problems, Russia has embarked on building new lines to ensure and increase the continuity of energy exports to the European market and has developed projects such as Nord Stream II under the Baltic Sea and TurkStream I and II across Turkey (Kakışım, 2019, p. 75).

The fact that Europe has turned to the Caspian Basin and Middle East resources in order to reduce its dependence on Russia has not escaped the attention of Russia. In particular, Russia has tried to respond to the transportation of the Caspian Basin's energy resources to Europe via Turkey through the TANAP project by activating the TurkStream project. Another project in which Turkey stands out as an energy corridor, but which has been shelved, is the Nabucco pipeline. With this line, the energy resources of the Middle East were intended to be delivered to Europe. But the Ukraine crisis and the Middle East tensions have been key factors in shelving this project. On the other hand, while Russia and Turkey are two competing states in terms of regional interests, Turkey's dependence on Russian natural gas and Russia's orientation to Turkey as an energy corridor to reach Europe enables cooperation in the direction of mutual interests (Güneş & Arslan, 2018, pp. 44-47).

Russia, which has turned to the Asian market in order to reduce its interdependence with Europe, is also making new energy agreements with countries such as China, Japan, and North and South Korea and is thus diversifying its export market. Russia's economic interest-based relations with China, its global and regional rival, are particularly notable. It can be seen that Russia, which is dependent on the energy demanded by Europe for its economic outlook, is trying to eliminate this interdependence with the Chinese and Far Eastern markets. Thus, it aims to strengthen its hand in order to conduct more effective negotiations on energy export prices with Europe. The oil and gas lines that are under construction for energy exportation to China will also allow Russia's energy network to reach the East Asia region (Kakışım, 2019, p. 76; Ozsağlam, 2019, pp.78-80).

Conclusion

We have seen, using the case of Russia, that the unequal distribution of energy resources provides countries with political-economic opportunities. First of all, the fact that energy prices are constantly moving up and down, and that most of its GDP is based on the export of consumable energy sources, causes Russia to have a very fragile economy. Russia, which exports oil, coal, natural gas and nuclear energy (uranium, thorium), also wants to increase the variety of products it exports and markets it exports to by investing in the LNG sector. The fact that Qatar and Nigeria are active actors in the LNG market and therefore create alternatives to Russian natural gas is causing Russia to try to be more active in the LNG sector to export energy to non-pipeline areas.

With its energy revenues, Russia is advancing rapidly on the path of development and is trying to respond to the USA, European states, and Asian rivals in the global context with its energy trump card. When we examine it on a global scale, we can see that Russia, which is trying to counter the US activity in Asia by strengthening its past ties, is also involved in the Syrian crisis in the Middle East. When we evaluate the US pressure on Europe in the context of energy dependence on Russia together, Russia seems to be reaching the goal of being a global power under the leadership of Putin. Although Russia's pipeline and transcontinental expansion relieve the European states and China on the issue of energy supply, it can be seen that Russia's global goals and the steps toward becoming a political pole concern these states.

It is thought that the overproduction figures of Russia compared to its existing reserves will lead to the rapid depletion of its reserves. Due to global climate change, Russia has started to look for new resources in the Arctic Circle and the Arctic Ocean and is thus trying to increase its resources. Lastly, it can be said that today, when renewable energy investments are increasing all over the world, Russia's investment in this issue is almost nonexistent, and when its resources are exhausted, its energy-based economy will face an irreversible crisis. However, although it is unlikely that renewable energy will be used as the primary energy source in the world in the coming years, it is foreseen, when the existing resources and future policies of countries around the world are examined, that it will be highly popular in the near future.

References

Al, A., & Özdil, B. (2017). Karadeniz'in Uluslararası Politik Ekonomisi: Rusya ve Ukrayna İlişkilerinin Yeniden Analizi. *Marmara Üniversitesi Siyasal Bilimler Dergisi, 5*(2), 151-167.

Babaoğlu, C., & Çobanoğlu, S. (2017, October). Rusya Federasyonu Başkanlık Sistemi ve Türkiye'ye Yansımaları. *Ömer Halisdemir Üniversitesi İktisadi ve İdari Bilimler Fakültesi Dergisi, 10*(4), 285-297.

Baysoy, E. (2009). Rusya, Ab, Abd İlişkileri Bağlamında Enerjinin Ekonomi Politiği Ve Küreselleşmenin Jeopolitiği. *Güvenlik Stratejileri Dergisi, 5*(10), 59-82.

Central Bank of the Russian Federation. (2019, July 8). *Main Commodities' Export of the Russian Federation Seasonally Adjusted.* Retrieved July 10, 2019, from http://www.cbr.ru/eng/statistics/?prtid=dfo_table#highlight=exports

CIA. (2018, January 1). *The World Factbook.* Retrieved June 30, 2019, from https://www.cia.gov/library/publications/the-world-factbook/rank order/2253rank.html

Dal, E. P., & Kurşun, A. M. (2017). Hazar Bölgesinde Rusya ve AB Ekonomi-Politik Çekişmesi ve Ukrayna Faktörü. *Marmara Üniversitesi Siyasal BİlimIer Dergisi, 5* (Special Issue), 17-31.

Dillinger, J. (2019, January 8). *The World's Largest Oil Reserves By Country.* World Atlas. Retrieved June 30, 2019, from https://www.worldatlas.com/articles/the-world-s-largest-oil-reserves-by-country.html

Enerdata. (2019). *Global Energy Statistical Yearbook 2019.* Retrieved June 30, 2019, from https://yearbook.enerdata.net/

Eniscuola Energy and Environment. (2019). *Coal.* Retrieved June 30, 2019, from http://www.eniscuola.net/en/argomento/coal/coal-knowledge/what-it-is1/

Erbil, Y. (2010). *Rusya-Ukrayna Doğalgaz Krizi ve Enerji Güvenliği.* Kadir Has Üniversitesi Sosyal Bilimler Enstitüsü.

Front, S. (2015, August 22). *A Network of Geopolitical Power: Gas Pipeline of the European Continent*. Global Research. https://www.globalresearch.ca/a-network-of-power-gas-pipelines-of-the-european-continent/5470824

Garside, M. (2019a, April 8). *Leading countries based on uranium consumption worldwide in 2016*. Statista. Retrieved June 30, 2019, from https://www.statista.com/statistics/264796/uranium-consumption-leading-countries

Garside, M. (2019b, June 14). *Proven coal reserves of the leading countries worldwide in 2018*. Statista. Retrieved June 30, 2019, from https://www.statista.com/statistics/237096/proven-coal-reserves-of-the-top-ten-countries/

Gazprom. (2019a). *Delivery Statistics.* Gazprom Export. Retrieved July 10, 2019, from http://www.gazpromexport.ru/en/statistics/

Gazprom. (2019b). *East Gas Program.* Gazprom. Retrieved July 25, 2019, from https://www.gazprom.com/projects/east-program/

Güneş, M., & Arslan, T. (2018). Enerji Bağımlılığında Avrupa Birliği, Rusya, Türkiye Üçgeni ve Doğu Akdeniz Alanı. *Uluslararası Beşeri Bilimler ve Eğitim Dergisi, 4*(7), 32-60.

Küçükkaya, E. (2018, October 30). *Enerji Nedir? Enerji Kaynakları Nelerdir.* Enerji Portalı. Retrieved July 9, 2019, from https://www.enerjiportali.com/enerji-nedir-enerji-kaynaklari-nelerdir/

Kakışım, C. (2019, March). Karşılıklı Bağımlılık Kapsamında Türkiye-Rusya Enerji İlişkilerinin Analizi. *Uluslararası Siyaset Bilimi ve Kentsel Araştırmalar Dergisi, 7*(1), 67-89.

Ozsağlam, M. T. (2019). Sınırlı Stratejik Ortaklık: Rusya-Çin İlişkileri. *LAÜ Sosyal Bilimler Dergisi, 10*(1), 70-90.

Ritchie, H., & Roser, M. (2019). *Renewable Energy*. Our World in Data. Retrieved June 30, 2019, from https://ourworldindata.org/renewable-energy

Sevim, C. (2012). Küresel Enerji Jeopolitiği Ve Enerji Güvenliği. *Journal of Yasar University, 7*(26), 4378-4391.

Sherman, L., & Wettengel, J. (2018, August 16). *Gas pipeline Nord Stream 2 links Germany to Russia, but splits Europe.* Clean Energy Wire. Retrieved July 27, 2019, from, https://www.cleanenergywire.org/factsheets/gas-pipeline-nord-stream-2-links-germany-russia-splits-europe

Sputnik. (2019, July 10). *Rüzgâr enerjisi kuşlara ve solucanlara zarar veriyor, bu işin şakası yok.* SputnikNews. https://tr.sputniknews.com/rusya/201907101039629586-putin-ruzgr-enerjisi-kuslara-ve-solucanlara-zarar-veriyor-bu-isin-sakasi-yok/

Statistical Review of World Energy-BP (2019).
Statistical Review of World Energy-BP (2021).
Şahin, K. (2005). *Rusya Federasyonu Enerji Sektörünün Yapısı, Sektörde Yaşanan Gelişmeler Ve Rusya Federasyonu'nun G-8 Başkanlığı.* T.C. Dışişleri Bakanlığı. Retrieved July 7, 2019, from http://www.mfa.gov.tr/rusya-federasyonu-enerji-sektorunun-yapisi_-sektorde-yasanan-gelismeler-ve-rusya-federasyonu_nun-g-8-baskanligi-.tr.mfa
T.C. Enerji ve Tabii Kaynaklar Bakanlığı. (2015). *Enerji Nedir?* Yenilenebilir Enerji Genel Müdürlüğü. Retrieved July 7, 2019, from http://www.yegm.gov.tr/genc_cocuk/Enerji_Nedir.aspx
The Global Economy. (2019). *Russia*. Retrieved July 7, 2019, from https://www.theglobaleconomy.com/Russia
Trading Economics. (2019). *Russia*. Retrieved July 7, 2019, from https://tradingeconomics.com/russia
U.S. Energy Information Administration. (2017, October 31). *Russia.* Retrieved July 7, 2019, from https://www.eia.gov/beta/international/analysis.php?iso=RUS#note
Wang, T. (2019, June 26). *Number of operable nuclear reactors as of June 2019*. Statista. Retrieved June 30, 2019, from https://www.statista.com/statistics/267158/number-of-nuclear-reactors-in-operation-by-country/
World Nuclear Association. (2019a). *Nuclear Power in Russia.* Retrieved July 10, 2019, from https://www.world-nuclear.org/information-library/country-profiles/countries-o-s/russia-nuclear-power.aspx
World Nuclear Association. (2019b). *World Uranium Mining Production.* Retrieved June 30, 2019, from https://www.world-nuclear.org/information-library/nuclear-fuel-cycle/mining-of-uranium/world-uranium-mining-production.aspx

CHAPTER FIVE

UNDERSTANDING THE FUNDAMENTAL PRACTICES OF RUSSIA'S NEW ENERGY POLICY IN THE WAKE OF THE 2014 CRIMEAN CRISIS

SINA KISACIK*

Introduction

In the aftermath of the official dissolution of the Soviet Union in 1991, several states gained their independence. One of the most important new nations that emerged out of the former Soviet Union was the Russian Federation. From its foundation to the beginning of the 2000s, the Russian Federation would experience several domestic and external crises caused by the effects of disintegration. But the March 2000 presidential elections would be a milestone development for the country: the ex-KGB agent and ex-President of the Russian Federal Service (FSB) Vladimir Putin would surprisingly win the elections and become the President of Russia. Thanks to the centralist and strong policies followed by Putin and with the help of the increasing prices of hydrocarbons at that time, the Russian Federation recovered itself from a deep crisis and then turned out to be one of the most prominent actors in world politics once again.

Regarding the importance of natural resources to the economic system of the Russian Federation, it first has to be mentioned that the country is mostly at the top of the lists of possession of raw materials, namely oil, natural gas and coal, in today's world. It is expected the country will keep its top positions in terms of natural resources in the mid-term and longer term. Within the context of this paper, the natural gas export dimension of

---

* Sina Kısacık, Ph.D. (Political Science and International Relations), Lecturer in the Energy Law Programme of the Department of Public Law, Social Sciences Institute, Özyeğin University, Istanbul. E-mail: sina1979@hotmail.com/sina.kisacik@ozyegin.edu.tr.

the Russian Federation's energy policy will be elaborated. When it is considered from the perspective of natural gas in the current circumstances, the Russian Federation has been ranking in first place for several years and will continue to preserve its position in terms of drilling and exportation within the forthcoming years. It should also be kept in mind that more than 50% of the Russian Federation's federal budget is comprised of the sale of natural resources.

When we come to Ukraine in relation to the Russian Federation, the former has always been of great significance for the latter due to geostrategic, geopolitical, geoeconomic and geocultural factors for many centuries. After the dissolution of the Soviet Union, one of the states that gained its independence was Ukraine. Due to the political preferences of the ruling elites in Ukraine, this country has been stuck between the Euro-Atlantic bloc and Russia. Also, one should remember that almost 70% of Russian natural gas going to Europe passes through Ukraine. In November 2013, the then Ukraine President Viktor Yanukovych refused to sign the Association Agreement with the European Union (EU) for national security reasons, which ended up with mass protests in Ukraine. This crisis would then spread into Crimea and Eastern Ukraine in the first months of 2014, which resulted in Russian intervention in these regions. Especially since the occupation of Crimea by Russia in March 2014, the Euro-Atlantic bloc has been implementing a wide range of sanctions toward Moscow. Among them, for instance, is the termination of the Russian-originated South Stream pipeline, which came to the forefront in late 2014 when Brussels used legal impediments.

In response to the sanctioning policies of the Euro-Atlantic bloc against Russia, the latter has been prioritizing putting forward new natural gas transportation pipeline projects with Turkey, China and Germany since 2014. In this way, Moscow has been aiming to show that it holds and will hold the capacity to find new natural gas export markets even if it is under the Euro-Atlantic bloc's sanctions in the present and in future.

By taking into consideration the aforementioned parameters, this paper will try to examine the central practices of the new Russian energy policy being implemented since the 2014 Crimean crisis by focusing on the TurkStream, Power of Siberia and Nord Stream 2 natural gas pipelines as case studies. Firstly, the paper will discuss the central components of the Russian energy strategy in the 1990s and 2000s. Secondly, it will briefly discuss the main parameters of the November 2013 Ukraine crisis. Thirdly, in the first case study, this paper will elaborate the significance of the TurkStream natural gas pipeline for the Russian energy export strategy in the post-2014 period. In the second case study, this paper will elaborate the importance of the Power of Siberia natural gas pipeline project for Russia and China. In the third case study, it will examine Nord Stream II's prominence in the Russian energy export strategy in the post-2014 period. In the conclusion, the current and possible future developments on the researched topic will be analyzed.

The Central Components of the Russian Energy Strategy in the 1990s and 2000s

In the aftermath of the fall of the Soviet Union, the Russian economy experienced difficulties and, as a solution, preferred to establish a free market via privatizations and therefore integrate itself with the world markets. Together with the effects of the oil crisis in the 1970s, this condition caused an economic crisis in the Russian economy as a result of the low oil prices. Thus, in the short term, Russian energy policies aimed to close this gap in the economy in the easiest way, in other words, to benefit from its energy resources. It was thought that Rosneftegaz, established by the transformation of the Fuel and Oil Ministry into a firm, could play an effective role in this process, and it initiated the operationalization of new fields such as Sakhalin Island and Northern Siberia for the use of Western firms. However, given the disagreements between the Duma and the government, the signed deals would not come into effect and nor would new deals be made. The 1998 economic depression would not end up with the experiencing of declines in oil exportation. Together with this, there would have been an increase in the foreign trade deficit as a result of production in those fields being negatively affected. The loss in the value of the rouble as the Russian Federation tried to recover after the economic crisis ended up with an increase in exports and oil prices. Therefore, in this way, the Russian economic system became revitalized. A similar process would be seen within the context of natural gas, and gas prices would follow an increasing trend until the sanctions in the period after the 2014 Ukraine crisis. The energy sector, seriously affected by the privatization tendency, would be taken under the control of the state by expropriation due to Putin's evaluation of energy resources within the framework of the national security of the country. This policy was outlined in a study named "Strategic Planning and Politics" written by two academics in 1978 (Kısacık, 2017, pp. 151-154). Putin quoted from 6 pages of this study in his Ph.D. dissertation titled "Minerals and Raw Materials Resources and the Development Strategy for the Russian Economy" in 1997. In this dissertation and some other articles written by Putin, he mentioned that, at that time, other developed countries would have an average growth rate of 2-3%; in order for Russia to close this gap, its growth rate had to be between 4% and 6%. Putin also underscored that Russia could achieve this thanks to the natural resources of the country. In his dissertation, he stated that the Russian economy will be dependent on raw materials until at least the first half of the 21st century. Within this context, according to the dissertation, the energy sector has to be managed by the state through the use of market methods for the country to become an economic power. Here, Putin also addressed the fact that Russia has the world's largest natural gas reserves (33% of the global total), ranks in second place after Saudi Arabia in terms of oil, and third place after the US and China in coal Putin mentions that half of the Russian budget revenues comes from the energy sector in order to emphasize the importance of minerals and raw material resources. He also highlighted that, at that time, 70% of Russian export income was formed by the sale of natural resources (later, these rates decreased to 40% and 50%, respectively) (Başlamış & Deprem, 2018, pp. 184-185). In view of this point, the logic behind the fact that more than 50% of Gazprom's shares are under the control of the government and other oil firms following the formation of Rosneft can easily be understood. This policy, defined as the government taking on a superpower role over its energy resources, was enacted with moves such as the resignation of Viktor Chernomyrdin from Gazprom, a change of nomenclature in 2000, and the exclusion of oligarchs – principally Vladimir Gusindky, Boris Berezovsky and Mikhail Khodorkovsky – from the energy sector through accusations and arrests (Caşın & Kısacık, 2018, pp. 90-91).

The year 2000 was a significant year because of the beginning of Putin's presidency and his energetic contribution in dynamically designing the country's foreign policy and energy strategy (Caşın, 2015, pp. 363-365). Russia has seen very wide-ranging alterations within the framework of its domestic and foreign politics, especially in the aftermath of the start of Putin's era in 2000. Putin has underscored that "*Unless Russia is socially and economically developed, one cannot mention the possibility of being a superpower again and if this is not done, it will be wiped out*". Putin's establishment of domestic order thanks to a centralist policy has resulted in positively shifting Moscow's vision to the international arena. As the Kremlin can pursue an independent foreign policy, it can straightforwardly employ numerous tools in its foreign policy with much more proficiency. Due to this factor, Putin has been successful in integrating Russian foreign policy with its energy strategy. Nevertheless, it should be kept in mind that Putin's Russia is indebted to the constructive international atmosphere for its revival. In the first term of Putin's presidency, the Russian economy surely saw the positive effects of high hydrocarbon prices. The promptly rising energy demands of countries like China and India and the uncertainties going on in countries enjoying plentiful energy resources ended up with an upturn in energy prices. Russia holds one of the world's main hydrocarbon reserves and embraces its location within the milieu of the energy sector in current conditions (Kryukov, 2014, pp. 61-63). Moscow currently holds just about 25% of the world's gas reserves and 10% of oil resources. When we come to oil production, the Kremlin is the leader in that regard. In terms of existing reserves, as of 2011, it is anticipated that its oil production will continue for possibly 22 years. Within the context of gas as of 2011, this period is estimated as 80 years. The Russian hydrocarbon sector has one dominant thing in common: in spite of the reform initiatives instigated for the last 25 years, its structure and decisions relating to it are still principally regulated by the central planning mechanism and staff of the former USSR (Kısacık, 2017, p. 156).

Moscow is positioned in first place with regard to the world's proven gas reserves. It represents the second-largest oil producer in the world and the third principal energy consumer as well. Energy resources compose 65% of Russian exports. Over time, the prominence of energy resources in Russian foreign policy has upturned steadily. When one wants to discuss Moscow's energy policy, the most vital issue that needs to be concentrated on is Gazprom. The company holds 17% of the world's gas reserves, and this share represents 60% in the country. Gazprom intends to retain its leading position among the global energy firms by increasing new markets, differentiating its business activities and ensuring the security of its supplies. The Kremlin arranges 22.5% of the world's gas production (Örmeci & Kısacık, 2018, pp. 134-136). Gazprom, which oversees 65% of Russian gas production at present, obtains more than half of the gas that it drills from vast gas basins, namely Urengoy, Yamburg and Medvejye. On the other hand, owing to the decreasing reserves in these basins, Gazprom has highlighted the innovation of technologies to be utilized in the operationalization of new basins (Kryukov, 2014, p. 78). While Gazprom is vital for the world's energy security, it is not wrong to assume that, as time has passed, it has been viewed that this company is a political tool for the Kremlin. Primarily, Gazprom manages Russian exports to Europe, regarded as its highest profitable market, through Gazprom Export, a subsidiary company that functions relatively independently from the main body and is highly specialized in foreign markets. To exemplify this, unlike the main company, Gazprom Export moved its administrative centre from Moscow to St. Petersburg in 2015 (Özdemir, 2019, p. 165). The main priorities of Gazprom in foreign economic relations can be listed as follows:

- To compete for the operational rights in upstream fields outside of Russia,
- To get international sponsorships for the implementation of midstream projects that are developed for the transportation of Russian natural gas, and
- To acquire foreign assets in different fields within the context of downstream operations that are taking place outside the Russian Federation as far as possible and also to expand and diversify its external sale markets (Özdemir, 2019, pp. 164-165).

The Ukraine Crisis (November 2013 to Present)

Following the downfall of the Soviet Union in December 1991, one of the states that gained its independence was Ukraine. In the post-independence era, Ukraine has been an arena of struggle between Russia and the Euro-Atlantic bloc due to its geopolitical, geostrategic, geoeconomic and geocultural prominence (Kısacık & Kaya, 2016, pp. 174-180). Correspondingly, in consequence of the numerous fluctuations in the governmental staff of Ukraine since independence, the country has been sandwiched between Moscow and the West. In November 2013, the then President of Ukraine, Viktor Yanukovych, refused to sign the Association Agreement with the EU and put off the preparation committee dealing with this agreement by presenting national security concerns as the crucial cause. After that, he would negotiate and sign an agreement encompassing $15 billion in financial aid and discounts on gas prices with Moscow. The pro-Westerners protested against this decision of Yanukovych and organized rallies against him. At that point, on account of several events, Yanukovych was forced to resign from the presidency. On top of this, the crisis spread to other regions of Ukraine, especially Crimea and Eastern Ukraine. At the same time, the tensions between the Kremlin and the Western bloc were intensifying in consequence of the mutual restrictions and continual declarations. Russian President Vladimir Putin paid an official visit to Crimea in order to participate in the remembrance ceremonies of the Soviets' victory against the Nazis (Victory Day) on May 9, 2014. Putin talked about the reintegration of Crimea with the Russian Federation as a historical actuality and underscored that the year 2014 would be remembered in forthcoming years as the year that the local population determined it would reunite with Russia in a validation of a pledge to historical legitimacy (Hubar, 2018, pp. 305-318; Şöhret, 2018, pp. 319-333; Derman, 2018, pp. 1223-1238). On May 11, 2014, a referendum for the formation of the Lugansk and Donetsk People's Republics and these two republics' confirmation of independence from Ukraine was organized by pro-Russian groups in Donetsk and Lugansk. Following this referendum, the newly formed People's Republic of Donetsk accepted its unification with Russia. On May 24, 2014, the People's Republics of Donetsk and Lugansk would unite in a ceremony attended by numerous Russian officials, who started to label them as Novorossiya (New Russia). As a reaction to this, the EU, USA and Turkey made it known that this statement would be held null and void owing to the illegitimacy of the plebiscite, and Brussels and Washington continued to declare further sanctions against Moscow (Örmeci & Kısacık, pp. 425-426).

Important Pipeline Projects of Moscow in the Post-Crimean Crisis Period

After the Crimean referendum in March 2014 and the announcement of Crimea's occupation by Russia, Western states started to apply diplomatic isolation and economic sanctions in response to Crimea's invasion by Moscow and Moscow's Ukraine policy (Özdal, 2016, pp. 258-261). The EU also took part in the implementation of sanctions introduced by Washington soon after. In those sanctions, the financial resources of the people acting together with Putin in his Crimea policy, secessionist leaders and top-level Russian executives with roles in the organization of the Crimean referendum were initially frozen, and then travel restrictions were applied on them. When the White House, which has a considerable amount of financial dealings with Moscow, instantly initiated sanctions, EU member countries, themselves in significant economic relations with the Kremlin, moved to put those sanctions into place by admitting the forthcoming damages after a short assessment. Banks (predominantly Bank Rossiya, Sberbank, Gazprom Bank, VTB and Rosselhozbank), energy companies (Rosneft, Gazpromneft and Transneft), and industrial companies (Kalashnikov Concern and Dobrolet), as well as such military industry enterprises as Uralvagonzavod, United Aviation Group and Oboronpromde, were put onto sanction lists in Brussels and Washington.[1]

---

[1] For the detailed analysis on this issue please see Mesut Hakkı Caşın & Sina Kısacık, "Understanding The New Russian Energy Policy After The Crimean

Within the framework of the sanctions, those banks and companies would not access credit and would be unable to make any stockholding contracts in European stock markets. Additionally, the industrial companies would not import high technology products from the US and Europe. Together with the corporations, Putin's political staff and the people who were supposed to have been prevailing in the foreign policy followed in Kyiv came upon the fact that they were prevented from entering the US and EU and encountered the freezing of their property in the US and EU member states (Kısacık, 2017, pp. 291-292).

In addition to these sanctions, the economic considerations of the politically driven Ukrainian crisis have been an important issue. Moreover, with the sanctions, the Russian economy experienced a severe halt due to the removal of foreign investments from Russia and the implications of speculations. These sanctions overwhelmingly impacted Russia-EU relations since the most powerful component of these two foreign policy actors' two-sided economic connection is their energy-intensive commercial activities (Rettman, 2016). While the trade volume between Germany and Russia in 2012 remained more than €76 billion, the trade volume between Moscow and the EU would reach a level of $335 billion. As of 2013, Russia would be enlisted as the foremost energy supplier of Germany, 71% of the imports of which is energy. 35% of Germany's oil, 38% of its gas and 25% of its coal is supplied by Moscow. Russia, as one of the largest gas suppliers in the world, supplies one-third of Europe's gas demands, 40% of Germany's requirements – the leading economy of Europe – and 100% of the Baltic states' gas consumption. The reason why the ongoing Ukrainian crisis involves an energy feature that includes Russia, Ukraine and the EU and contains the likelihood of an energy crisis rests in the fact that 66% of Russian gas goes to Europe via Ukraine (Özdal, 2016, pp. 260-262). When the former gas crises that happened between Moscow and Kyiv in 2006 and 2009 are remembered, it is not surprising that the Ukrainian crisis has impacts on the energy scenario as well. According to 2013 energy reports, in 2013, 39% of the EU's gas imports, 29.95% of its oil imports and 27% of its coal imports were supplied by Russia. Therefore, the Union is dependent on Moscow by an average of 30% for its energy. On the other hand, when the shipping network of Russian gas to Europe is taken into account, it is clearly apparent that Ukraine retains a very significant location as a transit country.

Crisis: A Case Study on Turkstream, Power of Siberia, and Nord Stream 2 Natural Gas Projects", *UPA Strategic Affairs,* Vol. 2, No.1, March 2021, pp. 206-255.

TurkStream Natural Gas Pipeline between Russia and Turkey

The institution of the EU's Third Energy Package (TEP) in 2011 has damagingly obstructed Gazprom. This TEP has organized the third party access to the pipeline capacity grounded on declared tariffs or the methods of them approved by national regulatory authorities and also unbundling of transmission possessions and the classification of transmission network operators – nevertheless an exception from these provisions is granted by the National Regulatory Authority which too has to be ratified by European Commission (EC) (Kısacık, 2017, p.298). Consequently, this by-law has caused fundamental difficulties within the framework of Moscow's gas exportations to the EU for abiding with the varying regulatory sphere in terms of current and new pipeline capacities. Gazprom has not yet managed to employ the full capacity of the Nord Stream pipelines' onshore additions (OPAL and NEL). Despite the fact that the German partner of the project arranged an exclusion allowing Gazprom exclusively to operate OPAL, the EC Competition Authority fixed it at 50%; after that, Gazprom and the EC discussed the issue for just over a year and reached an agreement relating to the operation of 100% of OPEL's capacity by Gazprom, otherwise the demands over access would be established by independent parties to be determined by means of auctions (Stern et al., 2015, pp. 3-4). It was expected that the EC would support this release as of March 2014; nevertheless, it broke with that decision, citing technical matters and the issue of the worsening of Brussels-Moscow relations over Kyiv. However, the OPAL exception assessment procedure would be dismissed by the European Commission in December 2014 due to Gazprom's fiasco for the postponement of deadline in its settlement deal over the guarantee with the German part interpretation cancelled the considerable changes in the exception that the European Commission was going over. Aleksandr Novak, the Energy Minister of the Russian Federation and a member of Gazprom's Board of Directors, has the intention of submitting for a new exception, and the operation of 100% of OPAL's capacity will be asked for by the Kremlin. But when it is deliberated within the present-day atmosphere, this would possibly be unproductive (Kısacık, 2017, pp. 298-299).

As a result of the adverse developments as regards OPAL, Gazprom preferred not to file an exception for South Stream; conversely, it openly favoured depending on the project with a set of intergovernmental deals that were signed with host countries. Nevertheless, these agreements were judged by the EC as being in violation of the TEP, and it requested their negotiation or rejection if the connected member countries were subject to breach procedures (Yafimava, 2013, pp. 17-18). It would also claim these discussions to be under the rules of the World Trade Organization, despite the TEP's discriminatory feature. In the same vein, the countries supposed to host South Stream would come across a great test: the refusal of intergovernmental settlements, thereby making these countries accountable to punishments applied by Moscow or the detainment of these settlements for that reason, making the concerned countries lawfully liable to the fines applied by the EC (Stern et al., 2015, p. 4). Within that background, for instance, the EC commenced breach processes against Sofia – one related to the contravention of the TEP and another associated with the legality of the pipeline's procurement – that ended up with the pipeline's construction being halted in August 2014 by Sofia (Caşın & Kısacık, 2018, p. 225). On the other hand, after the Ukraine crisis and the takeover of Crimea, the connection between the EU and the Russian Federation was interrupted, creating a great problem, even with organizing dialogues between Brussels and Moscow. This caused the faltering of the Moscow-Brussels working group regarding South Stream and a deferral within the setting of EU decision-making processes as regards numerous other gas-linked matters with the Kremlin, including DG COMP Procedures. The lack of even a discussion between the two sides and also the lack of agreement on regulatory matters ended up with the invalidation of South Stream (Stern et al., 2015, p. 5).

Given the ongoing political situation between Russia and Ukraine, the EU suspended the authorization process for South Stream and, as an alternative, intended to uphold the pipeline projects transporting gas from Baku. On December 1, 2014, Russian President Vladimir Putin, together with ten ministers, paid a visit to Ankara, Turkey. Very significant decisions regarding energy issues would be made by Moscow and Ankara during this official visit of Putin. Among those decisions, the top one was the annulment of the South Stream gas pipeline project by the Kremlin, with the announcement of the European Union's discontentment given as the central cause (Grigas, 2017, pp. 112-114; Özdemir, 2019, pp. 252-258). Vladimir Putin described the decision to terminate South Stream as follows:

> We believe that in the current conditions Russia cannot continue with the realisation of this project. ... Bearing in mind that you need to construct the pipeline under the Black Sea, we cannot begin construction so long as we do not have permission from Bulgaria. To begin construction in the sea, get to the Bulgarian beach, then stop – it would be ridiculous. ... The position of the European Commission was not constructive ... If Europe does not want to realise it, well, then, it won't be realised. (Rettman, 2014)

On November 24, 2015, a Russian SU-24 warplane flying over the Turkish-Syrian border violated Turkish airspace for 17 seconds. Although it was warned by Turkish jets ten times in five minutes, the Russian plane endlessly violated Turkish airspace and was then downed by Turkish warplanes. This would fuel a great tension between Ankara and Moscow. Ankara claimed that the Russian aircraft was violating Turkish airspace and was shot down by Turkish warplanes in line with rules of engagement. After that, the Kremlin blamed Ankara for this incident and pursued policies against Turkey, encompassing embargoes in numerous fields and the postponement of energy projects, to be exact, TurkStream and the Akkuyu power plant. When the crisis between Ankara and Moscow was ongoing with the reciprocal harsh assertions and Russian embargoes toward Turkey, a key initiative came from Turkey to resolve this problem on June 24, 2016. Turkish President Recep Tayyip Erdoğan expressed regret to Russia for the downing of the jet on November 24, 2015 and pronounced Turkey's enthusiasm for the restoration of its relationship with Russia, which was recognized by the Kremlin (Özden-Cankara, 2019, pp. 498-513; Kısacık, 2018, pp. 185-190).

After Gazprom got authorization from Ankara for the construction of TurkStream, a significant development regarding this subject would occur during the 23rd World Energy Congress held in İstanbul, Turkey, between October 9 and October 13, 2016. On October 10, the energy ministers of Turkey and the Russian Federation, Berat Albayrak and Aleksandr Novak, signed the agreement regarding the operationalization of TurkStream. This project envisions more Russian gas transference to Turkey under the Black Sea. The project having a combined delivery of 31.5 bcm per annum through its two lines signifies that it will offer practically two times more than Blue Stream's capacity. Since then, as of late December 2019, both parties have been emphasizing their willingness for the operationalization of this natural gas pipeline. In parallel with this decisiveness, both parties have been intensively working toward reaching that goal. By November 2018, the sub-sea section of this pipeline project had been completed and the construction of its land section was due to start (Kısacık, 2018, pp. 188-197). By October 2019, more than 80% of this construction had been completed, and when the statements of the high-level officials from Turkey and the Russian Federation are closely examined, it can be clearly understood that the anticipated operational date of this natural gas pipeline is December 31, 2019. It should also be pointed out that such European countries as Bulgaria, Romania, Hungary, Serbia and Italy are closely interested in this project, which aims to bypass the Ukraine option for the transportation of natural gas to European markets, as of late December

2019. On January 8, 2020, TurkStream became operative with the participation of high-level officials from Turkey, Russia, Bulgaria and Serbia. The importance of this pipeline was put forward by Alexey Miller, Gazprom's management committee chairman, as follows: "*The launch of TurkStream is a history-making event. Firstly, taking into account exports via Blue Stream, we have paved the way for direct transit-free supplies to fully meet Turkey's needs for Gazprom's gas. Secondly, Europe now has a new and reliable route to receive Russian pipeline gas*" (NS Energy, 2020).

At this opening ceremony, Turkish President Erdoğan set forth the significance of this pipeline project as follows:

> In the past 33 years, we have procured approximately 400 billion cubic meters of natural gas from Russian Federation. This picture is the best example of a win-win based cooperation built on the mutual interest of our countries. Our cooperation in the field of energy, as in other fields, has successfully passed all kinds of tests. As Turkey and Russia, we will continue with news projects and new successes on the ground of this cooperation. We see that European countries show great interest in Russian gas coming from the second line within the scope of the project. (BOTAŞ, 2020)

The noteworthiness of the TurkStream natural gas pipeline was highlighted by Russian President Putin at this opening ceremony as follows:

> "The cooperation between Russia and Turkey is developing step by step in all fields. Despite the extremely difficult situation in the world, and despite the fact that some international players are trying to hinder our cooperation developing in the direction mutual benefit, these efforts are continuing. The implementation of this large-scale joint project and the successful laying of the natural gas pipeline from the bottom of the Black Sea is an indication that Russian-Turkish strategic partnership bears significant and concrete fruits, he also pointed out that TurkStream is an extremely special and unique gas transportation system. The Russian President said that With TurkStream, natural gas from Western Siberian fields will come with the first line, and with the second line the gas will be transported over Turkey to the Balkans, Bulgaria, Greece and Serbia. Putin also noted that TurkStream Natural Gas Pipeline is environment-friendly and it will be operated reliably"(BOTAŞ, 2020).

After the operationalization of this pipeline, it was announced by Gazprom that, as of January 27, 2020, it had successfully supplied its first billion cubic metres of gas through the TurkStream gas pipeline. Of that volume, nearly 54% went into the Turkish gas market, and around 46% was transported to the Turkey-Bulgaria border (Gazprom, 2020).

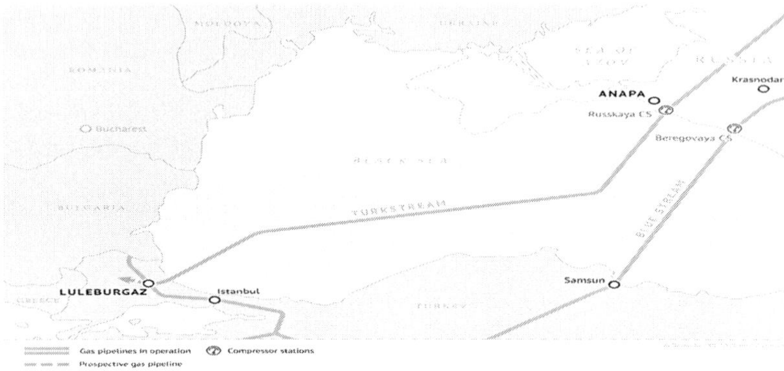

Figure 1: TurkStream Natural Gas Pipeline Project. Source: TurkStream, 2020.

The Power of Siberia Natural Gas Pipeline Project between Russia and China

As the world's greatest carbon dioxide emitter encountering dual international and domestic pressures, China is increasingly seeking natural gas and renewables to meet its internal energy demand. In 2014, China and the US signed an important deal. In that context, the US would decrease its emissions and China would stopping the increase in its emissions by 2030. Also in 2014, China's National Development and Reform Commission (NDRC) declared Beijing's formal plan to deal with climate change between 2015 and 2020, confirming again that it would support cleaner fossil fuels, specifically natural gas, and constrain coal consumption nationwide. For this plan, natural gas will account for 10% of the country's fundamental energy consumption (approximately 360 billion cubic metres) as of 2020. Xie Xinhua, China's special representative regarding climate change, further confirmed this transformation towards low-carbon gas and renewable energies at the 2015 Paris Climate Conference, even though he did fall short of presenting more promises that would compromise China's economic growth and development. In order to meet its energy demand and sustainable development targets, China has been attaching its sui generis interest to natural gas markets for importation and a unique emphasis regarding the differentiation of natural gas sources and routes (Grigas, 2017, p. 236).

When looked at from a Russian point of view, while the Western European markets are 6,000 kilometres away, the Chinese market is situated 2,000-3,000 kilometres away from Moscow's Eastern Siberia resources. For the Kremlin, energy exportations to China remain very central. The new markets have become much more essential to Moscow in consequence of the structure and problematical situations of the European market and Europe's initiatives to decrease the volume of energy coming from Russia within the context of energy security. When it is deliberated from Beijing's point of view, the country's energy demand in its emerging economy is upturning day by day. For Beijing, Moscow will remain the utmost supplier for this growth and energy demand. Owing to the problematic relations with the world faced by Iran, one of the central suppliers of China's oil demand, it is important for Beijing to orient itself towards Moscow, so this is a noteworthy factor for the continuance of Russian-Chinese collaboration. Russia has started to pursue an "Eastern Oriented Policy" in order to better its market and downsize its risks. *"The Russian Energy Policy till 2020"* published in 2003 and *"The Russian Energy Policy till 2030"* published in 2009 (see Ministry of Energy of the Russian Federation, 2010; Mastepanov, 2014) set forth significant modifications in that manner. These alterations focused on the collaboration of Russia with Asia-Pacific countries in the area of energy exports, and in this way, the Kremlin has endeavoured to advance the regional energy partnership. Beijing, Tokyo, Seoul and New Delhi are viewed by Moscow as important partners in the energy field. Consequently, Moscow wishes to offset its reliance on the European market. In that sense, it has been developing its eastern energy policy. Moscow plans to make energy exportation to the region tangible by creating a comprehensive oil and gas refinery and a supply mechanism between Eastern Siberia and Far East countries. Russia's eastern energy policy backs up the foreign direct investments of Chinese state energy companies. The success of similar energy policies in China and Russia facilitates these two countries' collaboration (Kısacık, 2017, pp. 320-324; Grigas, 2017, pp. 257-263).

On May 21, 2014, Gazprom and CNPC finalized the agreement to build a pipeline that would convey 38 bcm of Russian gas annually to China. The importance of this agreement was assessed by Alexey Miller as "*This deal is the greatest deal in the history of the Russian Federation and Gazprom. During the 25-year period of this deal, more than 1 trillion cubic meters of natural gas will be exported. Russian gas will have been transported to a completely new market. Within the Russian Federation, an investment of $55 billion will be made, ranging from production to transportation.*" On the other hand, China, which uses a very high percentage of coal in its energy mix (67.5%), attempted to balance this situation with its growing use of gas. In that regard, the Chinese government has stated that it foresees the country's gas demand will rise from 170 bcm in 2013 to 400-420 bcm in 2020. Russia has long worked on the conclusion of this project. Nonetheless, the parties would not decide on economic issues, principally the gas price. Moscow did not wish to trade gas to China below the price at which it exported to Europe (Kısacık, 2017, pp. 325-326). As of 2013, when Gazprom insisted on the average European sale price ($380/million cubic metres), China would demand see the price of $320/mcm that it pays for Turkmen gas as the market value level. Even if it seems that the parties had agreed, when it is considered that China's most important import is LNG and, most significantly, that China's national currency, the Yuan, was accepted, it can be understood that a historical step had been realized by Beijing (Özdemir, 2019, pp. 177-178). But Moscow, which has been in severe conflict with Europe, specifically owing to the fight between Ukraine and Russia along with the takeover of Crimea, admitted to giving concessions to Beijing. This was because, when the Kremlin overcame the European bans with a new option, it set up an additional affiliation with China in which Moscow obtains the essential financial support that its energy sector necessitates (Pamir, 2017, pp. 302-303; Örmeci & Kısacık, 2018, pp. 185-189).

For this project, a combined complex production system was established by pooling the production systems in the Chayandinskoye gas field in Yakutistan, which holds 1.2 tcm reserves, and the Kovyktinskoye gas field in Irkutsk, which holds 1.5 tcm reserves. This incorporated structure will supply gas both to the Far East region of Russia and to China through the 61 bcm-capacity Power of Siberia, the first pipes of which were integrated on September 1, 2014. In May 2014, Alexey Miller and Zhou Jiping, the President of the CNPC, would conclude the deal concerning sales of 38 bcm of gas each year for a 30-year duration. This agreement has been greatly significant for both sides and was completed in the aftermath of long discussions on account of Russia's aspiration to reduce its reliance on the European continent as its foremost trade market up to now and China's endeavours to differentiate its resources due to the country's increasing energy demands (Kısacık, 2017, pp. 326-327).

It is anticipated that the price of gas to be transported through this pipeline will remain lower than the price of gas to be conveyed from the eastern route (Pamir, 2017, p. 305). In the final analysis, by developing such a project for the Asian market, and primarily for China, Moscow aims to send the message to Europe and its sanctions against it that it has another huge export market aside from Europe at proper prices. Other advantages in terms of Moscow's orientation to China remain the relative proximity of Chinese markets compared to European markets and the inexistence of third countries, explicitly Ukraine and Poland, on the route. During the Asia-Pacific Economic Cooperation Summit in Beijing held in November 2014, numerous mutual contracts were made among member states. The most important among these agreements were the Russian-Chinese deal and the Memorandum of Understanding (MoU) concerning the 30-bcm gas export to China. Despite the fact that this MoU is not a mandatory one, when it is assessed together with the agreement covering the conveyance of 38 bcm of Russian gas yearly to Beijing from 2018 that was settled during Putin's Shanghai visit in May 2014, it is clear that Russia and China have taken conclusive steps for energy collaboration. Those agreements constitute milestones of a term that can be well-defined as "win-win" by the formation of significant benefits in terms of both countries. When it is observed within the agenda of Moscow, it is clear that it wishes to vary its hydrocarbons trade markets. At the start of 2016, Gazprom announced that it might possibly cut the volumes of gas that it envisaged to transport China owing to the declining of global energy prices and continuing vagueness in the Chinese economy. Sources correspondingly expressed that the project will still be operational, however in the preliminary phase, the gas volumes to be directed to China in 2019 would remain lower than the projected volumes. It was also underscored that the price of crude oil stood at more than $100 per barrel when the gas agreement between Moscow and Beijing was contracted; however, this later fell to $30. Along with this, the Chinese economy has also endured severe unproductivity because of the deterioration in its currency and havoc in its stock market (Kısacık & Denizelli, 2018, pp. 875-877). On July 4, 2017, Gazprom president Aleksey Miller declared that as of late 2019, natural gas would be supplied to China with a new pipeline as part of a $400 billion energy deal between Moscow and Beijing. Moreover, Miller also underlined that the natural gas stream from the pipeline named Power of Siberia would begin on December 20, 2019, and there have been ongoing negotiations between Russia and China on the construction of a second Far East Pipeline. By September 7, 2018, according to the Russian broadcaster RT, Gazprom had manufactured 93% of the Power of Siberia for the transportation of Russian natural gas to China. According to RT, Gazprom verified that 119 operational natural gas wells were complete at the Chayandinskoye field in Yakutia. Gazprom also added that more than 2,000 kilometres of pipelines had been connected and positioned from Yakutia to the Russian-Chinese border (Temizer, 2018). In order to better understand the significance of the

Power of Siberia natural gas pipeline for Russia and China, two analyses will be provided here. One is from Dimitriy Abzalov, a Russian political analyst. Cited by the China Global Television Network, Abhazalov underscored that *"If tomorrow, the U.S. 'colleagues' want to pressure, for instance, Huawei again, or gas prices in Europe are more attractive to them, then their LNG ships will turn away from China"*. The other is from Ling Xiao, vice-president of the energy colossus PetroChina and head of its gas and pipeline division, who underlined that *"the pipeline construction is right on track and we think we can hit the target to get the supply by December 20, 2019"*. It should also be mentioned here that Xi Jinping defines Vladimir Putin as his best friend (Aneja, 2019). On December 2, 2019, this pipeline project became operational, and the official inauguration ceremony was attended by high-level officials from Russia and China. Putin and his Chinese counterpart Xi directed the official opening of the pipeline. At this ceremony, Putin evaluated this situation as a "genuinely historic event" for the two countries. In parallel with this statement of Putin, Xi assessed the newly launched gas pipeline as *"a landmark project of bilateral energy cooperation"* and an *"example of deep integration and mutually beneficial cooperation"* (Hurst, 2019).

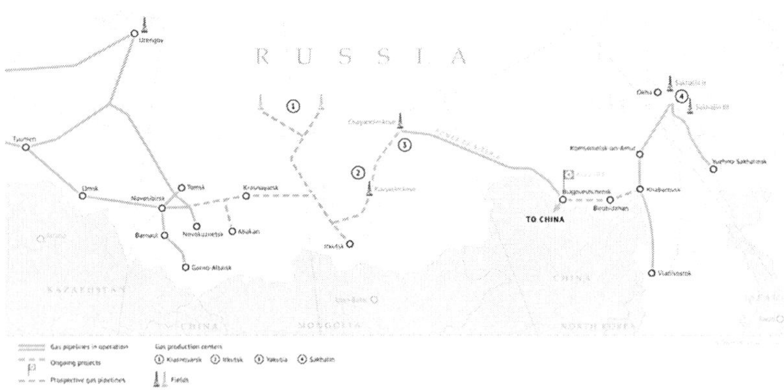

Figure 2: Natural Gas Reserves and Gas Transportation Network in Eastern Russia. Source: Gazprom, n.d.

The Nord Stream 2 Natural Gas Pipeline Project between Russia and Germany

Nord Stream is a project that will transport natural gas through a pipeline assembled underneath the Baltic Sea between Russia's Vyborg province and Germany's Lubmin province (Nord Stream AG, 2016). When the twin pipelines, each of them 1,224 kilometres long, are completely operative, a gas flow will be realized between Germany and Russia, depriving them of the necessity for any transit country. This makes the project a sui generis one. This project is foreseen to carry 55 bcm of gas annually. While Gazprom stands as the principal shareholder in this project with 51%, the German BASF Wintershall and E.ON Ruhrgas possess 15.5% shares each. Of the remaining shares, 9% belong to the Dutch N.V. Nederlandse Gasunie, and another partner in the project, specifically the French company GDF Suez, holds 9% shares as well. In this way, the Russian-German control in the project is equivalent to 91%. The Baltic countries and Poland have countered this project with plausible reasons (Kamalov, 2008, pp. 288-291). Gazprom selected the former German Chancellor Gerhard Schroeder as the head of the project with the expectation of breaking Northern European countries' opposition. It was planned that when the project would become functional in the last quarter of 2015, these two pipelines would be capable of providing 55 bcm of Russian gas to the EU for at least 50 years. The first line of Nord Stream became operative in November 2011 and stretched to its project volume of 27.5 bcm. The second line, planned to have the same capacity as the first line, was finished in April 2012 and turned out to be functional as of October 2012. Studies on the realization of third and fourth lines continued. Subsequently, Gazprom, E.ON, Shell and OMV reached an MoU/Good Will Protocol for Nord Stream 3 and 4, adding another 55 bcm to the total capacity on top of the previous 55 bcm, on June 18, 2015. After this signing ceremony, the top executives of Gazprom, BASF, E.ON, ENGIE, OMV and Royal Dutch Shell reached a deal on a Shareholding Agreement for the enactment of the Nord Stream 2 project, which planned to upturn gas supply to the EU market, at the Eastern Economic Forum held in Vladivostok on September 4, 2015. The project would be advanced by a new project company entitled New European Pipeline AG. For the contracted document, Gazprom would possess 51% shares in the project company. E.ON, Shell, OMV and BASF/Wintershall would have 10% shares each. The remaining 9% of shares would be controlled by ENGIE. The extension of one of these pipelines to England remains under discussion. With this line, it is aimed to convey gas to England, the Netherlands, France, Denmark and other EU members (Caşın & Kısacık, 2018, pp. 242-244).

It is clear that this project is certainly a very significant one within the framework of the Kremlin's economic and strategic interests. One noteworthy fact has to be revealed in that regard. When the EC approves countless decisions in the dynamic topics explicitly lessening the reliance on Russia, differentiating resources and ensuring security of supply, the project which will upsurge the dependency of Europe on Moscow in natural gas is being implemented under Berlin's leadership (Pamir, 2017, p. 301). When the EC recommends to the European Parliament that, in terms of energy resources' importation, a non-EU member country ought not to possess above 30% shares in view of the security of energy supply and resource diversification goals, it must be underscored that the prioritizing of this project over these recommendations remains a meaningful issue to be deliberated over. Principally Berlin, but other capitals as well, stand firm to consider only their interests after the determination of their particular circumstances. In such conditions, the interests of countries or companies far outweigh the Union's interests and policies (Kısacık, 2019, pp. 2-3).

On June 9, 2016, a Good Will Protocol was signed by Nord Stream 2 AG and Allseas Group for the laying of the first line of this pipeline in the Baltic Sea. Following this development, on April 24, 2017, this pipeline's financing agreement was signed between Nord Stream 2 AG and ENGIE, OMV, Royal Dutch Shell, Uniper and Wintershall. These five European companies committed to meet 50% of the pipeline's cost. A group of countries within the EU, led by Poland and the Czech Republic, opposed the Nord Stream 2 project owing to several reasons, including environmental issues and the further increasing of Gazprom's monopoly. The European Union has mentioned that it demands that its member countries make their own decisions and take initiatives. One of the discussed subjects was the suitability of this project to the European Union's Third Energy Package. The Nord Stream 2 AG underscored the unnecessity of this process and also underlined that this project is irrelevant to the Third Energy Package. On the other hand, EU officials claimed that the continental (land) part of this pipeline has to be evaluated within the context of the package. While the discussions were ongoing, due to this complex process, it was assessed that the project would be delayed until towards late 2020 (Caşın & Kısacık, 2018, pp. 246-257).

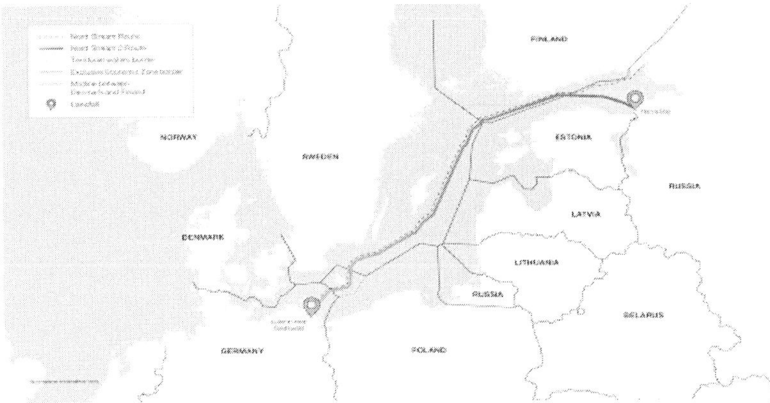

Figure 3: Nord Stream 2 Natural Gas Pipeline System. Source: nord-stream2.com.

Conclusion

To preserve its gainful place in the European natural gas supply and sidestep Ukraine as a transit state, Russia has preferred to develop different natural gas transportation projects to Europe since the eruption of natural gas crises between Ukraine and itself in 2006 and 2009. The most important projects coming onto the agenda have been the South Stream and Nord Stream projects. South Stream was settled by Russian and Italian energy monopolies in 2007 with an envisioned capacity of 63 bcm. However, numerous key developments slowed down the enactment of South Stream, explicitly the high cost of the project, which was projected to reach €29 billion, the non-allowance of the indemnity decision to Russia for the ownership of this project and the EU's pressure on such countries as Bulgaria not to give Russia permission regarding this issue due to the Ukraine policy followed by Moscow. After the outburst of the Ukraine crisis in November 2013, discussions concerning South Stream were halted, and as a response to this initiative by the EU, Moscow presented the TurkStream project with Ankara. The associated deals between them over this project have been concluded, and this pipeline was anticipated to be fully operative in late December 2019 in the form of twin pipelines possessing a total capacity of 31.5 bcm. In January 2020, this pipeline started to pump Russian natural gas to Turkey.

A significant new pipeline within that framework is Nord Stream. The first line has been in operation ever since 2012. Gazprom and its European partners have been increasingly concentrating their efforts on the extension of this pipeline in the form of Nord Stream 2, 3 and 4, which will similarly hold capacities of 55 bcm. This project is critically significant for Russia due to the direct transference of its natural gas to the European markets (Germany), bypassing Ukraine.

Within the perspective of Gazprom's alternate natural gas exportation market strategy, China has been enjoying an analytically significant place since the 2000s. There have been some dynamics regarding the expansion of close energy dealings between Russia and China. For China, the country's natural gas demand is envisioned to increase from 170 bcm in 2013 to 400-420 bcm in 2020. Also, when it is examined in terms of oil, due to the awkward relationships with the world faced by Tehran, one of the principal oil suppliers of Beijing, China is forced to orientate itself towards Moscow. The geographical closeness between Russian hydrocarbon resources in Eastern Siberia and China, which is 2,000-3,000 kilometres compared to the 6000-kilometre distance from the Western European markets, the main official energy papers of Moscow entitled "The Russian Energy Policy till 2020" and "The Russian Energy Policy till 2030", highlighting the improvement of Russia's energy dealings with Asia-Pacific countries and the sponsoring of Chinese energy companies' investments in the Russian energy sector according to the eastern energy policy of Moscow, ought to be considered as quickening and easing aspects within the context of this affiliation.

For Russia, after facing the sanctioning policy of the West owing to its Ukrainian policy since November 2013 and especially in March 2014, it was a sensible move to set up closer relations with China. In accordance with this assumption, the talks over the transference of Russian natural gas to China were completed in May 2014, following the resolution of the price issue. Both parties settled on the assembly of the Power of Siberia, which foresees the shipping of 38 bcm of natural gas from Russian gas fields in Siberia to China annually from 2018 for a 30-year period, and the valuation of this deal is $400 billion. For most Russian officials, such as Alexey Miller, this agreement signifies the largest contract in the Russian Federation's and Gazprom's history and will embrace the transportation of more than 1 tcm of natural gas into the Chinese market and the realization of a $55 billion investment ranging from production to transportation. Nonetheless, at the start of 2016, Russia proclaimed that it may perhaps think about lessening the natural gas volumes that it envisages to transport to China as a result of the falling oil prices harshly disturbing the Russian economy and also due to the continuing ambiguity in the Chinese economy. But in December 2019, natural gas pumping from Russia to

China officially began, considered by the leaders of these two countries as a historically significant moment.

In the aftermath of the invasion of Crimea along with the Moscow-sponsored independence plebiscites of Donetsk and Luhansk, the Euro-Atlantic bloc and Russia have been competing to counter-sanction each other ever since 2014. This reciprocal sanctioning policy remains unproductive owing to the fact that Moscow has not retreated from its present standpoint. Decision-makers in Moscow persistently put emphasis on the fact that the state of affairs in Crimea and in Eastern Ukraine will be unchangeable in the forthcoming years. When the high level of economic connections between the EU and Russia is taken into account, the existence of reciprocal sanctioning policies will continue to adversely affect and distress this multifaceted and mutually dependent relationship. The Russians' interference in Ukraine constitutes a very good instance of a new kind of war termed "hybrid war".

Based on the fact that the reciprocal sanctioning policy between Brussels and Moscow vis-à-vis Ukraine endured, Moscow increasingly preferred to establish new natural gas export routes with different buyers, explicitly China (Power of Siberia) and Turkey (TurkStream), compliant with its policy of diversifying its energy export routes. Furthermore, one should not forget that the unsteady economic conditions of China and Russia, along with the diversity of strategies between Ankara and Moscow over the handling of the continuing Syria and Ukraine crises, will remain the essential and decisive dynamics in the persistence of energy-centered dealings between Russia-China and Russia-Turkey in the forthcoming years. The Russian Federation also ascribes unique importance to the completion of the prolongation of the Nord Stream natural gas pipeline projects, sponsored primarily by Germany, the countries on the route of this pipeline and major European energy companies, that aim to transfer its natural gas to Europe while avoiding Ukraine in the coming years.

To conclude, Moscow, despite facing the comprehensive sanctioning policies of the Euro-Atlantic bloc due to its Crimea policy since 2014, has not been reversing its proactive energy export projects to Europe and Asia. Moscow has been successfully implementing this policy with Turkey, China and Germany via TurkStream, the Power of Siberia and the Nord Stream 2 natural gas pipeline projects. In the final analysis, it can be stated that these three natural gas projects developed by Russia illustrate the best practices of this country's unchallengeable effectiveness and dominance in terms of energy transportation within the context of Eurasian energy security in the 21st century. When the abundant natural gas reserves of Russia are considered, this country will continue to hold the first ranking in the transportation of this asset to the world markets by pipelines in the near and longer terms.

References

Aneja, A. (2019, October 12). *'Power of Siberia' warms China-Russia ties*. The Hindu. https://www.thehindu.com/news/international/power-of-siberia-warms-china-russia-ties/article29668009.ece

Başlamış, C., & Deprem, O. (2018). *Vladimir Vladimiroviç Putin: Rusya'yı Ayağa Kaldıran Lider.* Doğan Kitap.

BOTAŞ (2020, January 15). *TurkStream Project Launched.* https://www.botas.gov.tr/Icerik/turkstream-project-launched/234.

Caşın, M.H. Caşın & Kısacık, S. (2021). "Understanding The New Russian Energy Policy After The Crimean Crisis: A Case Study on Turkstream, Power of Siberia, and Nord Stream 2 Natural Gas Projects. *UPA Strategic Affairs*, *2*(1), 206-255.

Caşın, M. H. (2015). *Novgorod Knezliği'nden XXI. Yüzyıla Rus İmparatorluk Stratejisi.* Atlas Kitap.

Caşın, M. H., & Kısacık, S. (2018). *Avrupa Birliği Enerji Hukuku ve Güvenlik Algılamaları.* Çağlayan Kitap & Yayıncılık & Eğitim.

Derman, G. S. (2018). Rusya'nın Kırım'ı İşgal ve İlhakı Bağlamında Türkiye'nin Ukrayna ve Rusya Federasyonu ile İlişkileri. In H. Çomak, C. Sancaktar, V. Tatar, & B. Ş. Şeker (Eds.), *Karadeniz Jeopolitiği* (pp. 1223-1238). Beta Basım Yayım Dağıtım.

Gazprom (2020, January 27). *First billion cubic meters of gas supplied via TurkStream*. https://www.gazprom.com/press/news/2020/january/article498525/

Gazprom. (n.d.). *Power of Siberia.* Retrieved May 8, 2020, from https://www.gazprom.com/projects/power-of-siberia/

Grigas, A. (2017). *The New Geopolitics of Natural Gas.* Harvard University Press.

Hubar, G. (2018). Rusya'nın Kırım'ı İlhakı ve Kırım Referandumunun Uluslararası Hukuka Aykırılığı. In H. Çomak, C. Sancaktar, V. Tatar, & B. Ş. Şeker (Eds.), *Karadeniz Jeopolitiği* (pp. 305-318). Beta Basım Yayım Dağıtım.

Hurst, L. (2019, December 3). *Russia opens Power of Siberia gas pipeline to China*. Euronews. https://www.euronews.com/2019/12/03/russia-opens-power-of-siberia-gas-pipeline-to-china

Kamalov, İ. (2008). *Putin Dönemi Rus Dış Politikası: Moskova'nın Rövanşı.* Yeditepe Yayınevi.

Kısacık, S. ve Kaya, F. (2016). Russian Eurasianism versus American Eurasianism within the Perspectives of Brzezinski and Dugin: A Case Study on the Recent Ukrainian Crisis. *International Journal of Arts & Sciences*, *9*(2), 161-185.

Kısacık, S. (2017). *The Ukraine Policy of the Russian Federation and The Paradigms in European Energy Security* [Unpublished doctoral dissertation]. Yeditepe University, İstanbul.

Kısacık, S. (2018). Türkiye-Rusya Federasyonu İlişkileri. In G. Tüysüzoğlu & A. Özkan (Eds.), *Soğuk Savaş Sonrası Türkiye'nin Kafkasya ve Orta Asya Siyaseti* (pp. 133-222). Detay Yayıncılık.

Kısacık, S. (2019, March 15). Kuzey Akım 2 Doğalgaz Boru Hattı Projesi'nin Rusya-AB-ABD Rekabetindeki Konumunu Anlamlandırmak. *İstanbul Gelişim Üniversitesi Siyaset Bilimi ve Uluslararası İlişkiler Bölümü E-Bülten, 16.* https://panel.gelisim.edu.tr/assets/2019/dokumanlar//SBU%C4%B0%20E-B%C3%BClten-16_71d7b0e9cdb7446499a8b98e74e19310.pdf

Kısacık, S., & Denizelli, Ş. (2018). Yüzyılda Karadeniz Jeopolitiği Bağlamında Jeostratejik Bir Yapılanma Olarak Şanghay İşbirliği Örgütü (ŞİÖ). In H. Çomak, C. Sancaktar, V. Tatar, & B. Ş. Şeker (Eds.), *Karadeniz Jeopolitiği* (pp. 857-888). Beta Basım Yayım Dağıtım.

Kryukov, V. (2014). Mix of Russian Liquid Hydrocarbons: Reasons/Sources for Change and Further Prospects. *Perceptions*, *19*(3), 61-80.

Mastepanov, A. M. (2014, October 30). *On the development of the new Energy Strategy of Russia (ESR-2035).* http://www.energystrategy.ru/ab_ins/source/Mastepanov_30.10.14.pdf.

Ministry of Energy of the Russian Federation (2010). *Energy Strategy of Russia for the Period up to 2030.* http://www.energystrategy.ru/projects/docs/ES-2030_(Eng).pdf

Nord Stream AG. (2016). *Nord Stream – Operations*. Retrieved September 15, 2016, from http://www.nord-stream.com/operations/

Nord-stream2.com. (n.d.). Nord Stream 2 Route. Retrieved May 8, 2020, from https://www.nord-stream2.com/en/pdf/document/125/

NS Energy (2020, January 9). *Russia, Turkey officially launch TurkStream gas pipeline.* https://www.nsenergybusiness.com/news/turkstream-gas-pipeline-launch/

Örmeci, O., & Kısacık, S. (2018). *Rusya Siyaseti ve Rus Dış Politikası: Teorik Çerçeve-Tarihsel Arka Plan-Örnek Olaylar.* Seçkin Yayıncılık.

Özdal, H. (2016). *Sovyetler Birliği'nin Dağılmasından Kırım'ın İlhakına Rus Dış Politikasında Ukrayna.* USAK Yayınları.

Özdemir, V. (2019). *Rusya'nın Kodları: Türkiye'de Rusya'yı Ararken, Rusya'da Türkiye'yi Bulmak.* Destek Yayınları.

Özden-Cankara, p. (2019). 2000'li Yıllarda Türkiye-Rusya İlişkileri. In S. Kekevi & Ö. Kurtbağ (Eds.), *Türk Dış Politikası (2000'li Yıllar)* (pp. 483-520). Berikan Yayınevi.

Pamir, N. (2017). *Enerjinin İktidarı: Enerji Kaynaklarını Elinde Tutan, Dünyayı Elinde Tutar!* Hayykitap.

Rettman, A. (December 2, 2014). *Putin says will not build South Stream gas pipeline*. EU Observer. https://euobserver.com/foreign/126749

Rettman, A. (January 13, 2016). *Sanctions to have little impact on Russia in 2016, US says*. EU Observer. https://euobserver.com/foreign/131812

Stern, J., Pirani, S., & Yafimava, K. (2015, January). *Does the cancellation of South Stream signal a fundamental reorientation of Russian gas export policy?* The Oxford Institute for Energy Studies. https://www.oxfordenergy.org/wpcms/wp-content/uploads/2015/01/Does-cancellation-of-South-Stream-signal-a-fundamental-reorientation-of-Russian-gas-export-policy-GPC-5.pdf

Şöhret, M. (2018). Kırım Sorunu ve Soruna Müdahil olan Devletlerin Savundukları Tezler. In H. Çomak, C. Sancaktar, V. Tatar, & B. Ş. Şeker (Eds.), *Karadeniz Jeopolitiği* (pp. 319-333). Beta Basım Yayım Dağıtım.

Temizer, M. (2018, September 7). *Power of Siberia gas pipeline almost complete*. AA Energy. https://www.aa.com.tr/en/energy/energy-security/power-of-siberia-gas-pipeline-almost-complete/21510

TurkStream. (2020, January 8). *Launch ceremony for the TurkStream Pipeline held in Istanbul*. https://turkstream.info/press/news/2020/211/

Yafimava, K. (2013, December 4). *European Regulatory Challenges for South Stream: The Way Forward.* The Oxford Institute for Energy Studies. https://www.oxfordenergy.org/wpcms/wp-content/uploads/2014/06/European-Regulatory-Challenges-for-South-stream-A-Way-Forward.pdf

CHAPTER SIX

JAPAN AND ENERGY

MERT GÜL[*] AND EMRAH CEYLAN[**]

"Don't be afraid of the black rock in the rice. Be afraid of the white ones."
—A Japanese Proverb

The Third-Largest Economy in the World

Japan is a G7 member with the third-ranked economy in the world, a highly educated population of 125 million,[1] and an advanced position in industry, science and technological production. Japanese culture contains a refined social life and has an important position among countries in the world as a soft power regarding its counterparts. The economic development of modern Japan transformed its production base to export-oriented industrialization, and it became a pioneer in modern technology during the economic history of Asian countries. Today, Japan's commercial relations with China, which rose after 1978, remain important for both countries despite political problems which have escalated in the recent decade. Japan's long-standing economic relations with South Korea, Taiwan and Australia are also deepening and multi-layered as a factor that reinforces the regionalizing transformation of this part of the world.

Contrarily from the beginning of official relations between Japan and the People's Republic of China and unilateral transfers of capital and

[*] Assist. Prof. Mert Gül, Economics Department, Beykent University. E-mail: mertgul@beykent.edu.tr.
[**] Dr. Emrah Ceylan, The Economists' Platform. E-mail: emrah.ceylan@ekonomistler.org.tr.

[1] In Japan, the population has continued to increase in the last 50 years but the demographic expansion has started to slow down in recent years. It can be observed that the population structure changed significantly in the 2000s. As of today, those between 0-14 years of age constitute only 16.7% of the population and the proportion of those aged 65 and over has increased to 28.9%.

technology, China has modernized and expanded its economic performance since 1978 through rapid growth rates. As of 2015, Japan's foreign direct investment in China had reached 8-10 billion dollars annually. In the same period, Japan's investment in the US was around 39-40 billion dollars annually, and the Japanese economy constituted the largest share of US foreign investments. Again, in 2017-2018, Japan's investment in the ASEAN countries also increased. Today, China and the US are the two most important countries in terms of Japan's bilateral trade activities.

The Japanese Miracle

Despite its substantial losses in World War II, the rapid development of Japan in a short period and its transformation into one of the world's leading economic powers has been regarded as the "Japanese miracle" and has been shown as an example for many developing countries for many years. By the end of the 1980s, the economic development of Japan became so significant that, under the slogan "Japan as Number One", various policies for Japan to become the world's largest economic power began to be made.

The factors behind the economic success of Japan after World War II were the main reasons behind the economic recession. In the post-World War II period, Japan was ruled by a trio of pillars of stable political power (the Liberal Democratic Party was almost alone by the mid-1990s), several Keiretsu[2] and strong bureaucracy. The cooperation between these three power groups allowed Japan to take strong and bold decisions and enable it to construct a strong industrial structure. In particular, every Keiretsu could obtain the financing they needed through very favorable conditions through the giant banks they formed within their groups and rapidly developed under the direction and protection of the government. The additional bureaucratic aid by officials transformed these domestic conglomerates into leading business actors in many industrial sectors in the world. Further state guarantees on the banks' legislation and the concept of lifetime employment, which allows workers in every Keiretsu to work safely in the same company from the first day of their employment until their retirement, provided the necessary trust for the system within society.

[2] A Keiretsu is a financial term in Japanese for a set of companies with interlinked shareholdings such as conglomerates.

Foreign Trade Relations

Japan is a member of the World Intellectual Property Organization (WIPO) and follows the agenda of the World Trade Organization (WTO). It has established distribution networks, especially in the automotive, electrical appliances and cosmetics industries. Ordering, archiving, inventory and other daily activities are linked to automation. Almost all stores have online connections with their wholesalers, head offices and banks. The company or the person who will export the product should inform the General Directorate of Customs about the quality, quantity, value, price and other important features of the product, and an export license may be obtained after the checks are completed.

Although there are a limited number of official restraints regarding commerce in Japan, various associations operating in the country occasionally carry out activities for the imports of products. Also, rent prices in both the airports and the important seaports are quite high in the country, and this leads to significant cost increases in the entry process of the products. The Japanese Industrial Standards (JIS) [3] and Japanese Agricultural Standards (JAS) are the two most widely used sets of quality standards in Japan.

Japan applies protective policies to its agricultural sector, and there are quota practices for some agricultural products. Since the government has developed strategies to reduce food waste, it is impossible to achieve liberalization in the agricultural sector in the short or medium period.

Japan is the global actor in the manufacturing of electronics, automobiles and machines, and these products are at the basis of the country's international trade success. Both sectors have experienced difficulties in recent years due to the overvaluation of the Japanese yen.

Foreign trade is of great importance to become an economic "superpower" for a country with limited resources, like Japan. Yet, the country is the most important iron and steel producer in the world. Japan is one of the largest importers in the world of basic raw materials such as foodstuffs, timber, textile materials, metals, and crude oil and other fuel sources. On the other hand, Japan is the world leader in the export of high-precision optical and electronic products such as color television sets, other electrical appliances, automobiles, vessels, cameras and watches.

[3] JIS applies to the standard, quality, size and other characteristics of a wide range of products such as textiles, heaters, electrical appliances, shoes, kitchenware, sports equipment and musical instruments. Japan developed JIS to promote the creation of a certain quality of export products.

Japan, as a capital-abundant country, imports raw materials and exports final products to the rest of the world.

Even though Japan has such a successful export performance due to the emergence of changes in brand and design after-sales services with developing consumer preferences as factors that affect trade and international reactions, there has also been an increase in Japan's imports of finished goods since the mid-1980s.

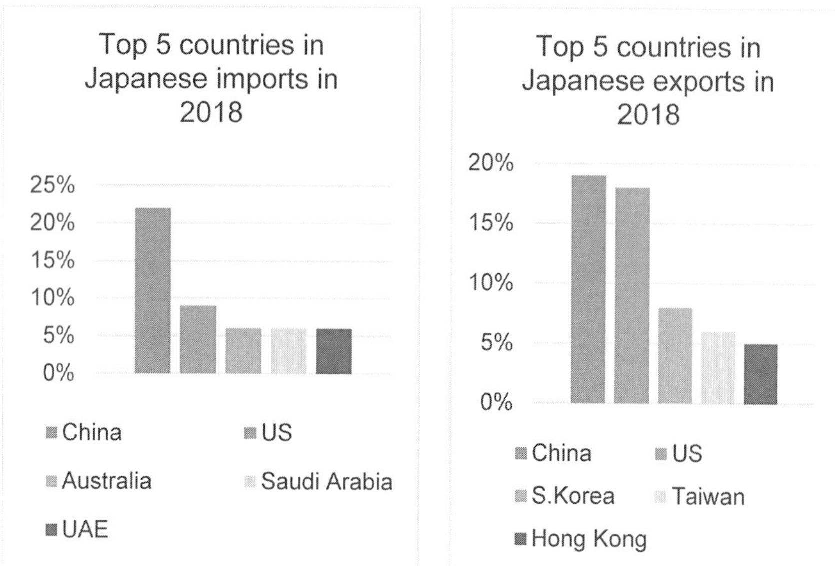

Figure 1: Japan's Biggest Trade Partners by Exports and Imports in 2018. Source: UNCTAD, n.d.

Foreign Trade Objectives

For Japan, the most important objective in foreign trade is to develop a strong export economy based on advanced technology and to consistently ensure the importation of the natural resources it lacks. The main objective of large private companies such as Mitsubishi and Mitsui, which carry out industrial production and foreign trade in Japan, is to produce in this direction and create the necessary funds for the import of the natural resources that Japan needs. Japan's foreign economic relations are also based on this, and its foreign policy requires it to concentrate on the USA and China.

Japan, the third-largest economy in the world, had a gross domestic product in 2018 of 5 trillion dollars, exports of 688 billion dollars, imports of 575 billion dollars, and per capita income of 43,000 dollars. In Japan's economic relations, the USA and China have the highest share of exports. Japan's total exports in 2018 amounted to 688 billion dollars; 19% of these exports were sent to China and 18% of them to the US. Again, in 2018, Japan's import volume was 575 billion dollars, of which China's share was 22% and the USA's was 9%. South Korea, Taiwan, Hong Kong, other Southeast Asian countries and EU countries followed China and the USA in Japanese import volume.

Comprehensive Economic Diplomacy

After World War II, Japan started to follow a path of being a superpower. Meanwhile, almost all Japanese governments have supported a free trade approach for international organizations such as the WTO, APEC and OECD to maintain the economic order. Japan is concerned about the protectionist policies of recent years and aims to develop its import capacity and export value through international markets by various free trade zone agreements. Another aspect of Japan's economic diplomacy is to provide large direct investments in the global economy. Since the 2000s, Japanese investments have been increasing, especially in Asia, competing with Chinese investments (Casanova, 2018).

The Trans-Pacific Partnership Agreement (TPP) and the Trans-Pacific Partnership (TPP-11)

On the initiative of Japan, the USA and Australia, negotiations between the countries on the coast of the Pacific Ocean began. On October 6, 2015, the Trans-Pacific Partnership Agreement (TPP) was drafted between Australia, Brunei, Canada, Chile, Japan, Malaysia, Mexico, Peru, New Zealand, Singapore, the USA and Vietnam that would promote free trade within the region, representing 40% of the world's economy. The TPP was then signed on February 4, 2016. In response to the USA's withdrawal from the TPP in 2017, with the strong support of Japan and Australia, 11 countries revised the agreement on March 8, 2018 in Chile and signed the Comprehensive and Progressive Agreement for the Trans-Pacific Partnership (TPP-11). The agreement, which left the door open for the future re-entry of the USA, is considered important for Japanese foreign policy, although it has not yet been ratified by the member states (Goodman, 2018).

Japan-EU Association Agreement

The most important of Japan's interregional free economic cooperation and trade partnership agreements is the free trade agreement signed with the EU. On July 17, 2018, Japan and the EU signed the Japan-EU Association Agreement, seen as the basis of Prime Minister Shinzo Abe's strategy called Abenomics.[4] After the ratification of the agreement in the European Parliament and the Japanese Diet, it is expected to enter into force in 2019. This agreement, by removing most of the customs duties in the Japanese and EU trade markets, will create a large market that will cover 30% of the world's economy and 40% of the world's trade revenue. According to the perspective of the Japanese Ministry of Foreign Affairs, this market will be an exemplary model of free trade and fair exchange rates in the 21st century. This agreement, which covers automotive industry products, chemical products, agricultural products and electronic goods, is expected to provide jobs for 290,000 people by increasing Japan's gross domestic product by 1% (5 trillion yen) annually (Japan Ministry of Foreign Affairs, 2018).

Energy Policies

Over the past two decades, Japan has applied several energy policies to manage its energy supplies. The governments indisputably changed the direction of energy policies by attempting to compensate for all costs for their soft power[5] superpower country. To substantiate this, energy policies in renewables, fossil fuels, and nuclear power had to be reorganized by the needs of their conjuncture.

Given the position of Japan, the country will never fully power its national economy with the cleanest premium fossil fuels. Therefore, alternative energy sources are needed, such as wind, solar, hydrogen and even nuclear power. It is believed that every country follows its own

---

[4] For more detailed information on this, see the subsection "Abenomics (2012 to Current Day)" below.

[5] Japan uses economic power to stimulate its position among both regional and global players. Japanese governments use both hard practices in economic issues by blockading ports of rival countries and soft practices such as forcing favorable terms in trade agreements or stopping foreign direct investment flows into other countries.

agenda depending on the extent of its economic linkages with other regional and global players. The positive relationship between the weight of economic dependence and diplomatic weight in international politics is supported by asymmetrical dyads theory, in which the higher-placed partner designates the rules of specific political interactions with others (Aremu, 2010).

The South China Sea is the main sea route for the global crude oil trade (30% of total trade), and in 2016, after Japan had announced its Fourth Strategic Energy Plan in 2014, 15 million barrels of crude oil passed through the same route per day. Furthermore, 90% of all crude oil that flows into the South China Sea flows through the Strait of Malacca, which is the shortest route between oil suppliers in the Middle East and Africa with Southeast Asian countries. Nine crude oil barrels out of every ten for Japanese oil importers used this trade route to obtain their energy supply products.

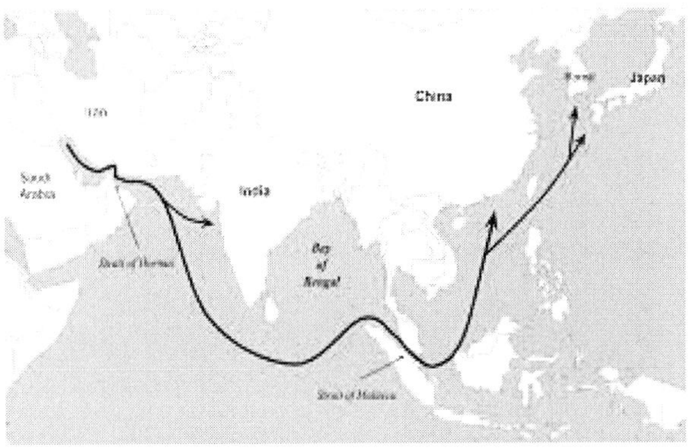

Figure 2: Sea routes from the Middle East to Japan and Southeast Asia. Source: Calder, 2018.

As a political issue, the security of foreign fossil fuel transportation to Japan's islands is a high-priority one for the country. Disruptions to energy supplies are more likely to happen on the high seas.[6] In the last two decades, the relative decline in Japan's control over Asia has turned the political situation into a multipolar arena due to China's rise, the North

[6] The most vital maritime chokepoints for Japanese imports are the Strait of Malacca and the South China Sea. While Beijing improves its naval capabilities every day to achieve its energy policies, Tokyo needs to rely more on its alliance with the United States due to its naval deficiencies.

Korea threat, and the power shift in Central Asia. The "game changers" like Chinese economic growth, North Korean military provocations and other Asian countries' militarization are crucial issues for Japan in its environment (Oros, 2017).

Energy Policies at a Critical Juncture

Following the two consecutive oil crises in the 1970s, Japan's response was that of a pioneer as it decided to diversify its energy supplies to various sources such as renewable energy sources, nuclear energy and fossil fuels. In spite of this diversification, oil is still the lead source with 40% of total energy production, and more than 80% is imported from the politically unstable Middle East region.

Despite importing oil from countries with unstable political conditions, the lack of electricity produced in neighboring countries on the Asian mainland, issues of transportation to Japanese islands and the urgent need for global warming strategies render Japan helpless in its current situation.

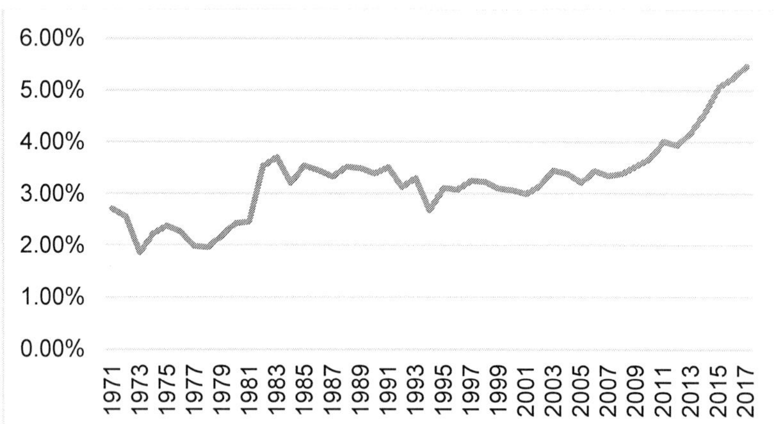

Figure 3: Renewable Energy Sources as Primary Energy Supply (%) for Japan. Source: IEA, n.d.

The Beginning of the 21st Century after the IT Crisis in 2001

In the aftermath of the IT Bubble in 2001,[7] a global economic recovery took place, and this was a suitable environment for global players in international markets. In terms of GDP, the Japanese economy, as the world's third-biggest economy, experienced a recovery to reach its former levels. Since the reconstruction period between 1945 to 1954 for Japan, the expansionary phase for Japanese businesses lasted for seven years from 2001 at the very beginning of the 21st century.

The government, led by Prime Minister Junichiro Koizumi, favored audacious structural reforms to follow long-term economic growth during the expansionary phase. The core of these reforms aimed to ensure the prosperity and economic independence of the nation. The various Japanese governments have been fully aware of the fact that Japan is the third-largest oil importer country and the largest natural gas importer in the world. Therefore, the main problem for these reforms and policies is to overcome such a dependency on foreign energy from fossil sources.

During the recovery period, direct investments to the Asian mainland continued mostly in faster-growing large economies such as China and India to seize strategic cornerstones. Besides direct Japanese investments, the government aimed to collaborate with developing countries in the same region with regional trade agreements under GATT and WTO frameworks. But the difficulty in compromising the trade agreements between advanced and developing countries led Japan to sign Economic Partnership Agreements (EPAs) with several countries, starting with Singapore in 2002. Koizumi's speech in Singapore underlined the importance of EPAs between Southeast Asian countries and the pursuing of East Asian Community ideals under ASEAN trade as counterparts to international trade activities, but mostly for energy security in the region.

Financial Crisis (2008)

The subprime mortgage crisis of 2008 ended the advancement of the Japanese expansionary process in its economy, as in the rest of the world. Although the Japanese financial sector had not invested too heavily in subprime mortgage-related financial derivatives, the sharp drop in

---

[7] The 2001 IT Bubble, also known as the Dot-com Bubble, caused the downfall of financial investments on internet start-up business by ignoring traditional financial statements of companies such as cash flow statements. The bubble lasted for a period from 1995 to 2000, and it started to collapse in 1999.

international demand for Japanese products made the domestic economy vulnerable to negative GDP growth and unemployment issues.

This exposure of the economy created a dilemma. The economic dilemma is set up by the traditional high saving rates on the personal income of households for economic growth policies while it results in weak demand for household consumption. For the first time since 1980, in 2011, the retrogressive economy caused Japan to have a foreign trade deficit. As a result of this dilemma and deepening deflation, Japan surrendered its position as the world's second-largest economy to China in 2010. General price decreases and low economic growth where the original crisis happened, the US, crippled the Japanese economy further.

Fukushima Daiichi Incident (2011)

The Fukushima Daiichi incident played a crucial role in the energy policies of Japan. Before the Fukushima incident in 2011, the Japanese government had aimed to increase the capacity and usage of nuclear energy for public consumption and mass production over the next 20 years.[8] But after Fukushima, the Japanese public lost its faith in nuclear power facilities and reliance on nuclear energy.[9]

In the months following the incident, 50 intact reactors in the country were shut down by the government. At that time, PM Yoshikiko Noda announced the plan "to phase out all nuclear power by 2040". Spur-of-the-moment corrections were also made, such as separating power transmission and distribution and liberalizing the regional energy monopolies.

However, even if the residents of the Fukushima region have not come back to their former living areas, the general public is substantially aware of the importance of decarbonization. The fact that Shinzo Abe, who came into office at the end of 2012, says that "Japan cannot do without its nuclear power plants" is an important sign of the public's opinion. Along with his statement, almost half of the "shut down" power plants (24 of them) have restarted their operations. The government did also aim to decrease nuclear energy dependency and enacted several policies on this

---

[8] 33% of Japan's total energy consumption was met by 54 nuclear power facilities before the Fukushima Daiichi incident in 2011.

[9] The damaged nuclear facility was decommissioned, 100,000 residents in the area were evacuated, and only 14% of residents resettled in their former residences by July 2019. The devastating impact of the incident cost over 188 billion dollars, the payment of which has been undertaken by the public through increased taxes, electric bills, etc.

line. The process of moving responsibility for moving power generation away from large energy companies has been revised by energy reforms.

Abenomics (2012 to Current Day)

In the last decade, the relationship with China has become more crucial to Japanese energy policies. The volatile relationship of "cooperation and coexistence" and "competition and friction" with China endangers the situation of Japan's power in the international arena. The modernization of the Chinese army and militarization in North Korea jeopardize energy security. Apart from these ongoing issues, the tension between Japan and China is also increased due to the recurring debates over Taiwan, which need a long period of normalization in international politics for these countries to resolve them.

In December 2012, Shinzo Abe came into office and explained his economic policy packages. Overcoming deflation, strengthening economic growth and ensuring energy sources were the main objectives of his policy packages. These three objectives are supported by three main economic policies: flexible fiscal policies, audacious monetary policies and promoting private investments for economic growth.

The Japan Revitalization Strategy was published in 2013, and two years after that announcement, with the renewed Abenomics II policy packages, the Trans-Pacific Partnership negotiations were successfully concluded. Another remarkable result of Abenomics II for Japanese energy sources was the liberalization of the retail of electricity in April 2016, which improved efficiency in energy consumption.

The aftermath of Fukushima

The Fukushima Daiichi incident is a very important case for energy security and supply. Overnight, the Japanese public changed their perspective on nuclear energy from "strategic power" to "fatal domestic weakness". In the several months following the incident, the lack of coordination and the late response to the crisis management of regional energy monopolies were observed.

In April 2014, the Japanese government released the first post-Fukushima strategic energy plan, which identifies some nuclear plants as baseload central power sources. The energy plan was fully supported by the Ministry of Economy, Trade and Industry's (METI) long-term program. The program focuses on reasserting the country's energy policies to secure homegrown energy supplies. In addition to that, some inevitable social changes after Fukushima, such as targeting renewable energy sources and wind and solar energy production, were promoted in higher levels due to the lack of domestic fossil fuels. Nonetheless, Japan also became more reliant on foreign fossil fuel imports than before Fukushima.

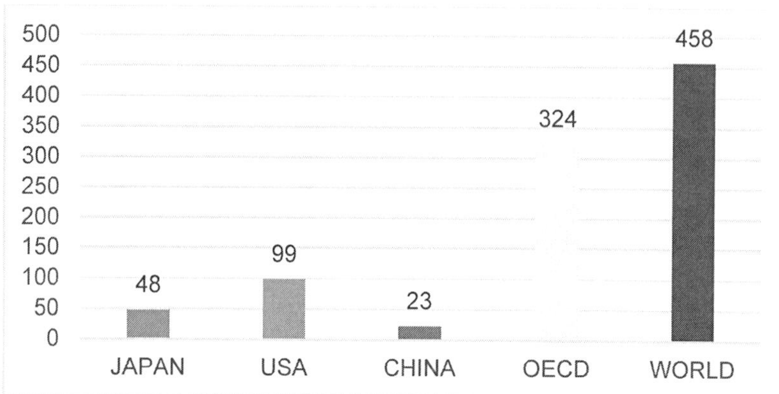

Figure 4: Total Nuclear Power Plants (2014). Source: OECD, n.d.

Fourth Strategic Energy Plan for Japan (2014)

The plan for the conversion of Japan to a low-carbon society by around 2050 contains technical difficulties within its structure. The latest (4th) edition of the basic policy was announced in April 2014 to present the main targets of Japanese energy policies on renewable and other sources for the next fifteen years. For instance, it targeted an increase in self-sufficiency in energy production at a rate of 25% after the rate reached its lowest level of 6% in 2013 due to the nuclear plant shutdowns following the Fukushima incident.

The Present Day (2018-2019)

The Basic Act on Energy Policy in Japan is set every three years to draw a new line for the mid- and long-term energy policies of the country. Japan's fifth installment of the Basic Act on Energy Policy was applied in 2018. The current energy policy focuses on alternative energy sources to reduce greenhouse emissions to zero by the year 2030. The desired objective of reducing greenhouse emissions was announced with three simultaneous headlines:

1. Create a self-sufficient energy supply at a rate of at least 25% after this decreased to 6% following the shutdowns of nuclear power plants in 2013,
2. Regulate the possible energy price rises for the manufacturing sector,[10] and
3. Follow global warming mitigation protocols with the US and Europe.[11]

In summary, the government's 2030 vision heavily depends on renewable and nuclear sources as a steady supply of energy. Although nuclear energy is accepted as a self-sufficient supply due to the high capacity for stocking uranium resources, it is another story for renewables. In the second half of 2019 alone, the increasing capacity of renewable energy sources and the feed-in tariff system in energy production will cost the public and industrial sectors at least 2.4 trillion Japanese yen (equivalent to 22 billion dollars). Also, wind and solar energy make up less than 10% of total energy production (see Figure 2), which makes the public question the cost-efficiency of these renewable energy sources (Takeuchi, 2019).

In developed economies such Japan's, energy supplies are lifelines for industry-dominant markets. In addition, the lack of domestic fossil fuel resources means the Japanese government needs to promote energy-saving campaigns in public and increase renewable energy sources. When promoting such energy policies, it is essential to supervise the entire chain of supply, from the production stage and procurement to distribution and consumption in the mid- and long-term periods.

Meanwhile, Japanese automobile manufacturers are investing heavily in hydrogen and laying the groundwork for using it as a replacement for petroleum in the mid-21st century. Hydrogen-based electricity and transportation will crucially be improved as an alternative to current major energy sources. New technologies like hydrogen-based energy will alter the possible new energy sources for consumption with the changing definition of energy security in the modernization process.

Still, it is a tremendous challenge for the government to reduce the cost of renewable energy sources, pull down the almost 80% rate of energy production from fossil fuels to lower rates, overcome technical instability

---

[10] In 2014, the feed-in tariff system for renewable energy supplies and global price rises in fossil fuels elevated energy costs by around 40% for domestic industry owners.

[11] To achieve such a goal, on June 11, 2019, the Japanese cabinet approved a new energy policy to fight against climate change in the next decades.

challenges, and manage the public's concern about safety issues in nuclear energy.

Conclusion: Decarbonization vs. Recarbonization

Since the middle of the 19th century, the world energy system has been shifting toward a lower carbon content. The accessibility of resources and efficiency measures have shaped the main energy consumption sources from wood to coal, coal to oil, and oil to natural gas. The broadening of that transformation enables the energy source importers to be able to diversify their demands. By having the same goal on the agenda, over the last two decades, Japan has reduced its dependency on Middle Eastern oil step-by-step and improved its import capacity by diversifying with Russian, African and Caspian oil.

As a foreign energy supply side for Middle Eastern oil, Japan suits its soft power attitude and uses it as a negotiator rather than an enforcer on delicate international matters. For instance, on July 7, 2019, Iran announced that its uranium enrichment program would exceed the appointed level of 3.67% determined by the Joint Comprehensive Plan of Action (JCPOA). Just five days later, PM Abe visited Iran on this matter to ease the tensions and avoid further misunderstandings in the region. All the diplomatic threads between Japan and Iran are based on the objective of the Japanese benefit of ensuring the security of oil transportation from Gulf countries.

Even though Japan continues to depend on imported oil as a primary energy supply, the government still aims to shift to renewable or nuclear energy-based policies for several reasons: climate change, dependency on foreign fossil fuels, etc. To ensure such a transformation soon, Japan needs to combine an optimum strategy on three foundations: secure energy transportation, providing economic efficiency, and dispelling concerns about nuclear energy. A proactive series of energy policies will strengthen the energy supply situation of Japan for its 2030 goals.

References

Aremu, F. A. (2010). Trade, Asymmetrical Dependence and Foreign Policy Behavior: An Analysis of Japan and Korea's Relationship with East Asian Countries. *Ritsumeikan Journal of Asia Pacific Studies*, *27*, 15-29.

ASEAN. (2016). *Regional Comprehensive Economic Partnership*. https://asean.org/?static_post=rcep-regional-comprehensive-economic-partnership

Calder, K. E. (2018). *The Bay of Bengal: Political Economic Transition and Strategic Implications*. The Sasakawa Peace Foundation.

Casanova, C. (2018, January 22). *Japan outstrips China in investment in Asia*. Brink News. https://www.brinknews.com/japan-outstrips-china-in-investment-in-asia/

Esenbel S. (2018). *In the Light of Changing World Order, Geopolitical Visions and Policies of Japan and South Korea in the 21st Century.* Boğaziçi University-TÜSİAD Foreign Policy Forum Research Report.

Goodman, M. P. (2018, March 8). *From TPP to CPTPP.* Center for Strategic and International Studies. https://www.csis.org/analysis/tpp-cptpp

IEA. (n.d.). *Extended World Energy Balances.* IEA Data and Statistics. https://www.iea.org/data-and-statistics/data-products

Kaplan, R. D. (2014). *Asia's Cauldron: The South China Sea and the End of a Stable Pacific*. Random House.

Japan Ministry of Foreign Affairs. (2018). *Japan-EU Economic Partnership Agreement.* https://www.mofa.go.jp/erp/ep/page22e_000707.html

OECD. (n.d.). *Nuclear power plants.* https://data.oecd.org/energy/nuclear-power-plants.htm

Oros, A. L. (2017). *Japan's Security Renaissance: New Policies and Politics for the Twenty-First Century*. Columbia University Press.

Saito, J. (2016). *Japan's Economy and Policy in a Global Context: Postwar Experience and Prospects for the 21st Century.* Center for Strategic and International Studies.

Takeuchi, S. (2019, July 1). *Japan's Energy Policies at a Critical Juncture.* The Japan Times. https://www.japantimes.co.jp/news/2019/07/01/business/japans-energy-policies-critical-juncture

UNCTAD. (n.d.). *Statistics*. https://unctad.org/statistics

Part II:

Region-Based Analysis

CHAPTER ONE

ASIA-PACIFIC: ENERGY'S POLITICAL ECONOMY

DENİZ İSTİKBAL*

Introduction

Since the beginning of human life, economic and political formations have influenced the course of history. Today, energy sources for economic growth and development are in the same position, while economic sustainability is in a climacteric position for the long-standing of politically organized states. Sustainability in energy resources is crucial in terms of ensuring the economic security of states. While this made the transmission of energy sources to consumption centers a necessity, Asian countries began to gain significance in the world's political and economic structure. In particular, the economic rise of countries such as China, Japan, South Korea, India, Russia, Indonesia and Malaysia caused the emergence of alternatives to the Western-based political and economic structure. Although there are some exceptions, the lack of energy resources in Asian countries places relations with the source countries in an essential position. The regions from which Asian countries import energy include the Middle East, Africa and the Americas. The fact is though that instability in energy import areas could affect Asian countries in both cost and stability. The relationship between stability, energy and the economy is prominent, considering the damaging effects of conflict areas in the region in terms of economic development and growth. The Asia-Pacific region, which is the world's manufacturing industrial production base, has insufficient resource diversity in terms of energy resources. Other Asian countries, excluding Russia and Central Asian countries, do not have energy sources that can affect the world energy economy. This requires energy to be supplied from

* Deniz İstikbal, Ph.D. Candidate, Political Science and International Relations, İstanbul University. E-mail: den.istikbal@gmail.com.

outside countries. The location of regional organizations specific to the Asian region, such as the Shanghai Cooperation Organization and ASEAN, is of great significance to the transportation of energy resources of the countries in the region. Still developing, Asian countries, which are developing countries, need energy sources more and more every day. Trade wars have created new threat areas for Asian countries. The downward acceleration of economic growth among the emerging threat areas has the potential to cause internal conflict for the countries of the region and to undermine the perception of political legitimacy.

There are many problems in the Asian region, including North Korea's nuclear tests, Myanmar refugees, the South China Sea continental shelf problem, the Pakistan-Indian conflict, Russian sanctions, the issue of the Uighurs, and the Afghanistan war, as well as economic issues. Unlike past years, the region's countries are collaborating with different regional organizations to solve the problems. The Shanghai Cooperation Organization and ASEAN are two important organizations established for stability, economic development and the solution of political issues in the region (Becker, 2011, p. 9). Economic development needs to be taken to an advanced level in order to solve the problems between the countries of the region through dialogue and reconciliation. In order to advance economic development, a secure and continuous supply of energy resources must be provided (Suter, 2015, p. 120). In this study, the Shanghai Cooperation Organization for the Asia-Pacific region will be analyzed with regard to ASEAN, South Korea and Japan with an energy-oriented economic-political perspective. The relationship between economy and energy will be evaluated for the countries of the region, and the last 15 years will be taken into account. In addition, the current issue of trade and exchange rate wars is important for a good analysis of economic prosperity shifting from Western countries to Asian countries.

Asian Century: The Shanghai Cooperation Organization, ASEAN, Japan and South Korea

Established in 2001 with Beijing as its center, the Shanghai Cooperation Organisation (SCO) is formed of eight member states, comprising China, Russia, Kazakhstan, Uzbekistan, Tajikistan, Kyrgyzstan, India and Pakistan. Aiming to cooperate in areas such as mutual good neighborliness, border security, regional peace, stability protection, terrorism, fighting separatism, migration, science, culture, education, politics and economics, the SCO undertakes a NATO-like mission in the Asia region (Becker, 2011, p. 8; Suter, 2015, p. 13). The organization was founded in 2001 to resolve border disputes that occurred following the dissolution of the Soviets, and it has played an important role in the face of regional conflicts. It is a critical body in the world political arena that operates in many fields, from the sharing of direction in the fight against terrorist organizations to releasing publications on the economic development of the countries of the region. Counting state organizations such as India and Pakistan that have historically fought a number of times as two of its members, it also has an important function in resolving regional conflicts (eng.sects.org, 2019).

Established in 1967 in Bangkok, the capital of Thailand, ASEAN was established within the framework of basic objectives such as economic development and growth, social improvement, cultural development, the health of revenue justice and peace among the region's countries. Indonesia, Malaysia, Myanmar, Cambodia, Thailand, the Philippines, Singapore, Brunei and Vietnam are members of ASEAN, which was established for the purpose of regional integration and is currently moving toward a European Union-like construction (ASEAN, 2019).

Japan and South Korea are not members of either organization. If it does not involve Japan or South Korea, works on Asia-Pacific studies are missing the level of regional analysis . The economic size of Japan and South Korea, which are significant in the world economy, is close to $6.3 trillion. Japan and South Korea, which have a 7.78 percent share in the volume of the $80.9 trillion world economy, are also home to two of the world's high-level energy consumption countries (World Bank, 2019; BP, 2018). Notably, Japan and South Korea, which lack energy sources, import energy from different countries of the world in high quantities. It is critical for national security that energy from the opening of these two countries, which have economically export-based development models, is delivered to the regions where energy is demanded continuously and safely. A shift to an Asia-based world economy is clearly seen in future-oriented economic projections (PWC, 2017). The issue of opening global production centers of large-volume economies such as China, Japan and South Korea is important for the manufacturing industry. Together with the shift of current prosperity, the world's energy demands have also moved from the West to Asian countries.

Asia-Pacific Energy Economy Policy

The Asia-Pacific region, where the world's largest energy-consuming countries are located, has an orientation toward renewable energy consumption. Renewable energy investments led especially by China, Japan and South Korea cover the bulk of renewable energy investments in the world (Houlihan Lokey, 2015). More than 35 percent of China's investments between 2005 and 2018 cover the energy sector, which stands out more in terms of energy investments than Japan and South Korea. It appears that China, which is in a weak position in terms of energy resources, is trying to compensate for its current vulnerability through its strategic investments (Istikbal, 2019, pp. 63-64). Looking at other economically developing Asian countries, it can be seen that more than half a billion people across the continent are unable to reach basic consumer products such as electricity. It seems that India, Pakistan, Myanmar and other emerging economies are failing to provide the necessary amounts of energy, which have reached high levels. Asian countries are in a better position than African countries and can replace Western states in terms of economic size (Varathan, 2018). But in an environment where regional conflicts are intensifying and trade wars are emerging, economic development is becoming more difficult to sustain (Akhtar, 2017).

As developing countries, over the past years, SCO and ASEAN countries have not been careful in their energy consumption. Unconscious energy consumption, one of the main causes of environmental pollution and climate change, has become a national security issue in Asian countries. Air pollution due to the consumption of energy sources that are non-renewable and environmentally damaging has made diseases a major problem in the countries of the region, while Western countries have continued to shift their industrial investments to Asian countries due to cheap costs. In addition to current regional conflicts, Asia, the world's manufacturing industrial production base, is exposed to problems that threaten the entire world, such as air pollution and climate change. The ASEAN and SCO countries that signed the Paris climate change treaty have made significant investments in a field that concerns all the world's states (Akhtar, 2017). However, when we look at the industrialization histories of Western countries, it can be seen that they have had a more important role in changing the world's climate compared to Asian countries. Industrialized Western countries make some criticisms of Asian countries because of their energy consumption. Current criticisms focus on the use of energy sources that damage the environment. Being newly industrialized, Asian countries have a failed history of diversifying their energy consumption in order to continue their production lines due to their current position. The energy resource diversification required by large investments and the construction of an environmentally sensitive economic model point to a challenging path for Asian countries that lack adequate economic resources.

With emerging technology, lower costs in renewable energy sources have opened up new opportunities for Asian countries. Wind and solar power generation, which has reduced in cost by 58 percent since 2010, is aimed at reaching a further 59 percent cost reduction in solar power and 12 percent in wind power production over the next 10 years, according to the International Renewable Energy Agency (IEA, 2019). Asian countries, which use energy sources such as coal, oil and natural gas, will reduce costs if they turn to renewable energy. The fact that Asian countries' plans had invested $160 billion in renewable energy resources as of 2015 indicates the existence of strategic energy policies (Akhtar, 2017).

East Asia's Energy Economy Policy (SCO)

Established in 2001 to solve the border problems in the countries of the region through peace and dialogue, the SCO has evolved into an international organization of which the major countries of the continent are now members. The fact that member states have 25 percent of the world's oil resources, 50 percent of its natural gas reserves and 35 percent of its coal resources indicates that the organization can influence the world energy market in the field of supply as well as by its economic size (Infoshos, 2015). In 2006, a proposal was made to establish the Russian-led "SCO Energy Club". In this proposal, which was made by Russian President Vladimir Putin and accepted by Kazakhstan on many points, it was emphasized that an energy club should be established and natural gas should be given weight under it (Becker, 2011, p. 152; Suter, 2015, pp. 120-121). The goals of this energy club included the construction of a natural gas line stretching as far as Iran, Pakistan and India. It was also extremely remarkable that Russia offered technology and unlimited economic resources to implement its goals within the scope of the energy club (Becker, 2011, p. 154). Although some important steps have been taken by Russia and Kazakhstan for the implementation of energy projects, no significant steps have been taken for the development of these energy cooperation projects. Economic impossibilities are not the reason why there has been no significant progress in this regard. Russia wants to break China's power in the region's energy field based on the principle of the free movement of goods and services, and the fact that Kazakhstan and Russia have the same ideas about energy affects China's energy policies. Energy targets are not fully implemented because of the policies developed by both China and Western countries. China prefers to determine its energy policies with multilateral agreements within the scope of the SCO (Becker, 2011, p. 154; Suter, 2015, p. 120).

China and Russia's special positions within the organization, which undertakes projects around the world for the installation of nuclear power reactors, offer billions of dollars of investment and profits to these two countries (China Hands, 2018). However, economic sanctions against Russia and commercial tariff practices are driving down Russia's income revenues in an environment where energy prices are gaining downward momentum, while China's export markets are shrinking. The chaotic environment in which the United States implements aggressive policies makes new areas of cooperation mandatory in the international arena (Ünay & Dilek, 2018, pp. 7-12). In an environment where economic sanctions are being used as a damaging weapon, Russia and China are trying not to stand up to the United States as one. The United States, which has put forward policies that harm Russia's energy sector and China's exports, also does not hesitate to confront its Western allies (Istikbal & Dilek, 2019, pp. 56-58).

While China's growing energy needs following its economic rise have forced energy to be imported from different countries, Central Asian energy sources have come to prominence as a stable transmission line. The Central Asian countries provide important opportunities for the transmission of their energy resources to the consumption centers. Being the most energy-consuming country in the world, China's presence in the region has created opportunities for the surrounding countries, making the region a competition area for the great powers (BP, 2018; Suter, 2015, p. 119). China serves an important function for the economic and political balancing of the United States and Russia in the Central Asian region (Suter, 2015, p. 120; Kavalski, 2010, p. 135; Chung, 2004, p. 1000). But while China, which directs its economic investments to Central Asian countries, has a good perception of the current governments, it does not have a positive outlook for the people of the region. The fact that Chinese workers are employed in direct investments and that Chinese companies are making significant investments makes the people of the region uneasy. China's acquisition of the right to operate infrastructure centers of African and Asian countries for periods such as 49 or 99 years after its investments and loans justifies the unrest of Central Asian societies (Hashimova, 2018). However, China, which is considered as an alternative to Russia in the transportation of energy sources to consumption centers, is in an indispensable position for the countries of the region (Kalu, 2012). The Central Asian countries that are members of the SCO need cooperation in the fields of economic, political, social and security as a strategic policy regarding energy sources. This assessment contributes to energy security for both China and Central Asian countries while positively affecting regional stability (Rahman, 2011).

Country	Oil	Gas	Coal	Nuc-lear	Hydro-electric	Renew-able	Total
Uzbekistan	3.3	35.8	1.2	-	2.7	-	43.0
Kazakhstan	14.6	14.0	36.2	-	2.5	0.1	67.8
Pakistan	29.2	35.0	7.1	1.8	7.0	0.8	80.9
India	222.1	46.6	424.0	8.5	30.7	31.8	465.4
Russia	153.0	365.2	92.3	46.0	41.5	0.3	698.3
China	608.4	206.7	1892.6	56.2	261.5	106.7	3132.2

Table 1: Energy Consumption of SCO Countries (2017 – Million Tons Equivalent to Oil). Source: BP, 2018.

Table 1 shows the total energy consumption of six of the member states of the SCO. According to the information in the table, China, which borders the supply countries with energy resources, is the most energy-consuming country in the SCO. This position, on the one hand, contributes to energy supply security while also providing demand security for the source countries. China offers alternative investment and loan opportunities to other supply countries except for Russia due to their difficulties in financing the necessary energy investments (Istikbal, 2019, p. 55). The fact that the internal political instability of countries such as Afghanistan, Pakistan and Myanmar could trigger serious terrorist activities for the member states of the SCO also puts the countries of the region at a clear risk of external interventions and prepares the ground for the intervention of the United States in the region.

The possibility that North Korea's development of nuclear weapons could trigger a regional war and give legitimacy to the US position in the region poses a threat to the founding purpose of the SCO (Scott, 2019). Russia's attempts to fill the vacuum of authority in the region after the fall of the Soviet Union not only bother the SCO member states but also and especially the United States. The border conflicts between Pakistan and India caused by the Kashmir problem present themselves as other factors that pose a threat to the region's economy and political and energy security (Seiwert, 2019). As a result, energy is an important tool for moving economic development to an advanced level, while regional stability and cooperation are factors of great importance (Grace, 2018). Russian President Putin's speeches in 2008 and 2009 show that he is no longer involved in the SCO energy club (Becker, 2011, p. 154). This has been seen as a fundamental policy to ensure the energy security of the member states of the SCO. Accordingly, aims such as "renewable energy" and "eco-friendly energy" that form the basis of energy policies have ceased to be political and economic targets (Becker, 2011, p. 155).

Southeast Asia's Energy Economy Policy (ASEAN)

With a population of 630 million and an economic size of $3 trillion, ASEAN is thought to be the fifth-largest economy in the world as of 2020 and a regional organization with a 60 percent increase in its energy needs over the last 15 years. As a result of economic growth, the rise in urbanization rates has increased the need for energy. With an economic size of $1 trillion, Indonesia is the largest energy-consuming country in the organization, followed by Malaysia, Thailand and Vietnam. ASEAN countries, which are expected to have a $300 billion energy trading base by 2040, will also be dependent on the outside for 78 percent of their oil resources. The countries in the region, where electricity, oil, natural gas and coal demands increase every day, need high levels of foreign direct investment due to having economies in developing countries. The main sources of foreign direct investment are China, Japan and South Korea. The countries of the region, which recovered rapidly economically after the financial crisis in 1997, have not achieved enough success on issues such as inequality and corruption. Military interventions also sometimes occur in the region, where democratic culture is not fully settled (Ariffin, 2018).

	2016		**2040**	
Resources	**Production (Mtoe)**	**Demand (Mtoe)**	**Production (Mtoe)**	**Demand (Mtoe)**
Oil	118.0	220.0	79.0	308.0
Natural Gas	188.0	141.0	185.0	225.0
Coal	278.0	112.0	262.0	271.0
Hydroelectric	11.0	-	30.0	-
Bioenergy	129.0	-	136.0	-
Other Energy Resources	28.0	-	88.0	-
Total	753.0	708.0	783.0	1186.0

Table 2: Energy Production and Demand of ASEAN Countries (2016-2040). Source: IEA, 2019.

Table 2 shows energy production and demand quantities, energy consumption resource types, and total energy consumption for 2016 and 2040 for ASEAN countries. In general, it can be observed that there will be a decline in all types of energy production resources except for bioenergy and renewable energy sources. It is clear that energy supply security will be important for ASEAN countries, which are calculated to import more energy from the outsourcing countries due to the increase in demand. When looking at ASEAN countries, Indonesia is known to be the first-ranked of the countries in the region for exporting coal and LNG. Thailand's position, dependent on energy imports, is similar to that of Malaysia. But the types of natural resources such as oil that Malaysia owns suggest that it is less dependent on energy imports than other ASEAN countries. Singapore's energy profile is largely dependent on foreign countries. Vietnam's self-sufficient energy consumption is mainly provided by coal, natural gas, nuclear, oil and renewable energy sources (Senderov & Vorobev, 2018, pp. 7-8). Vietnam, which is less dependent on foreign countries for energy, is among the countries that will become more in need of energy due to its developing economic structure. The Philippines is in a self-sufficient position in natural gas but imports oil entirely from foreign countries. Laos's economically weak position makes it mandatory for it to make more use of hydroelectricity sources, causing problems with neighboring countries over water. While Cambodia has low rates of energy consumption, it has great potential in terms of natural gas resources. Brunei, as a net energy-exporting country among ASEAN countries, obtains 60 percent of its national income from energy exports (Senderov & Vorobev, 2018, pp. 7-8).

Moving to alternative energy sources, which have gained more importance with the economic development of ASEAN countries, is an issue of concern for the countries of the region in terms of production-demand balance. In particular, oil production is expected to decrease among ASEAN countries over the next 15 years, but demand is expected to increase. While there is no such situation for other sources of energy, the problems with oil are more important due to the relations with the oil source countries. The repercussions of internal instability in petroleum-exporting countries on ASEAN countries have the potential to restrict the economic potential of governments. While ASEAN countries, except Brunei, are in an outward-dependent position on oil, Malaysia, Indonesia, Vietnam and Brunei will also reach a foreign-dependent position on natural gas. ASEAN countries are investing in renewable energy sources but will have an important problem in terms of energy supply security in the following years (Senderov & Vorobev, 2018, pp. 8-13). Consequently, the ASEAN countries formed the ASEAN Energy Cooperation Action Plan for the years 2016-2025. The plan aims to ensure 23 percent of energy consumption is provided by renewable energy sources by 2025. Under this plan, ASEAN countries must also make savings in energy usage. Accordingly, these countries are obliged to save up to 20 percent of the energy they currently use by 2020 and up to 30 percent by 2025. In order to meet these targets, the countries in question must develop their policies on energy, especially renewable energy (Giz, 2019). ASEAN countries want to use renewable energy sources such as solar and wind power more effectively. Countries such as Thailand, Vietnam and Indonesia, for example, want to benefit more from wind power in the future. It is also known that ASEAN countries are conducting studies to further exploit renewable energy sources between 2020 and 2030 and are seeking to diversify their energy consumption sources. The provision of renewable energy, an indispensable input for economic development without harming the environment, is important for the lives of future generations (Wu, 2016, pp. 120-122).

Coastal Asia's Energy Economy Policy (Japan and South Korea)

Today, Japan, which turned to nuclear energy after the oil crises of the 1970s, meets its need for energy from liquefied natural gas, also known as LNG. As Japan is heavily dependent on source countries for energy, it is among the countries that will be most affected by changing price costs in the event of any instability in the source countries. It has turned from nuclear energy to other sources of energy since the nuclear reactor accident in 2011 and now needs a high amount of energy as the world's third-largest economy. Despite its low growth rates in recent years, its energy needs are increasing, and it is seen to be more interested in energy supply security. It invests large amounts in renewable energy and is sensitive to energy price fluctuations. Its strong economic structure, which allows it to buy liquefied gas from countries such as Australia, Indonesia, Qatar and the US, has the potential to deliver the current energy flow. Due to North Korea's attempts to test long-range ballistic missiles off the coast of Japan, its nuclear program is pushing its local environment toward a regional crisis. Increasing the possibility of regional conflict poses a danger to the energy resources provided by the sea. However, the United States-North Korea talks are promising with a view to eliminating this threat (Butler, 2018).

Table 3 shows the types of sources used by Japan in its energy consumption. As mentioned above, Japan has reduced its use of nuclear energy due to the nuclear reactor accident in 2011. After the accident, natural gas became more prominent, and Japan began to attach importance to energy resource diversity through investments in renewable energy (Zhihai, 2019).

With 96 percent of its energy dependent on foreign countries, South Korea is the tenth-largest energy consumer in the world. South Korea is among the top six countries in energy consumption worldwide. South Korea, which needed more energy due to its growing economy since the 1970s, has leaned on nuclear energy under the threat of the communist North (Istikbal, 2017). South Korea's Energy Ministry's aim to reduce energy demand in line with its 2030 targets shows that energy security is critical for the country. But North Korea, which has conducted nuclear weapons and long-range ballistic missile tests, is among the biggest problems that pose a threat to South Korea's economy, political and energy security. Table 4 shows the types of energy sources in South Korea's energy consumption. It can be seen that the country leans on nuclear energy and makes high amounts of use of other types of sources (Ahn Hyun, 2015). Iran, which is one of South Korea's largest energy providers, has been subject to US sanctions, leading to the suspension of oil and gas imports. But South Korea has begun importing more energy from other energy source countries (Reuters, 2019).

Energy Resources	Consumption (Equivalent to Million Tons of Petroleum)
Nuclear	6.6
Hydroelectric	17.9
Renewable Energy	22.4
Natural Gas	100.7
Coal	120.5
Oil	188.3
Total	456.4

Table 3. Japan's Energy Consumption Resources (2017). Source: BP, 2018.

Energy Resources	Consumption (Equivalent to Million Tons of Petroleum)
Hydroelectric	0.7
Renewable Energy	3.6
Nuclear	33.6
Natural Gas	42.4
Coal	86.3
Oil	129.3
Total	295.9

Table 4: South Korean Energy Consumption Resources (2017). Source: BP, 2018.

Following Donald Trump's election as US president, the impact of trade wars on the world economy emerged as the most important factor affecting Japan and South Korea. Sanctions imposed on Iran and Russia and trade tariffs imposed on China's exports are not positive moves for countries with an export-centric development model, such as South Korea and Japan. The trade relations with China of Japan and South Korea, which are among the major Asian allies of the United States, are bringing the two Asian countries closer to China than the United States (Moos, 2019). Moreover, the upward acceleration of energy prices has the potential to drive up production costs for energy-dependent countries such as Japan and South Korea. In the event that energy sources that pose a threat to climate security, such as coal, are preferred, an energy policy output that will be harmful to the health of communities such as through air pollution will emerge. The least costly solution for both Japan and South Korea would be to increase investment in renewable energy sources.

Conclusion

It is clear that Asia-based economic development, which has begun to be felt more and more since the early 2000s, has contributed to the increase of energy needs. In addition to renewable energy sources, Asian countries have been coming together in organizations such as the SCO and ASEAN and are also investing in nuclear energy to ensure their energy supply security. As a result of these investments, Asian countries' dependence on source countries has decreased, though they have not yet achieved success in displacing natural resource types such as oil, natural gas and coal. The start of trade wars, the North Korean nuclear tests, the continuation of the civil war in Afghanistan, the India-Pakistan tensions, and fluctuations in energy prices are seen as the most important threats to energy security for the countries of the region. Energy resources, which are critical in sustaining economic development, are important in the political and social stability of the countries in the region. Asian countries with a more unfair distribution of income compared to South Korea and Japan are not yet in a strong enough position to form an alternative to the Western-based economic structure. This current situation will bring about an increase in energy needs, which in turn will put the relations between the energy source countries and Asian countries in a more special position.

Asian countries are turning to renewable energy sources, and educating societies in this direction is an important issue for climate security. The use of environmentally friendly energy sources will be critical for the living standards of future generations. In this respect, the mission and objectives of the organizations and cooperation platforms established in the Asia-Pacific region are crucial. Choosing methods that are both environmentally friendly and independent of other countries is extremely important in providing the needed energy. Therefore, it is essential for Asian countries to take care of renewable energy. Although ASEAN countries put an emphasis on renewable energy sources in some of their action plans, these are extremely inadequate compared to Western countries. It is very important for Asian countries to address their energy needs with the participation of their citizens and make serious plans for renewable energy. In the education to be given to citizens, progress should be made on issues such as the separation of garbage from landfill and obtaining energy from landfill, as reflected by the need to obtain energy from natural sources such as wind and solar power.

References

Ahn Hyun, S. (2015). Republic of Korea's Energy Security Conundrum: The Problems of Energy Mix and Energy Diplomacy Deadlock. *Journal of International and Area Studies, 22*(2), 67-87.

Akhtar, S. (2017, January 16). *Asian-Pacific's Energy Change: Regional Solutions Key To Sustainable Energy Transition*. APPS Policy Forum. https://www.policyforum.net/asia-pacifics-energy-change/

Ariffin, E. (2018, April 30). *Keeping Southeast Asia's energy secure. The ASEAN Post.* https://theaseanpost.com/article/keeping-southeast-asias-energy-secure

ASEAN. (2019). *About ASEAN*. Retrieved May 7, 2019, from https://asean.org/asean/about-asean/

Becker, C. (2011). *Die Shanghaier Organisation für Zusammenarbeit. Grenzen und Möglichkeiten der Kooperation autoritärer politischer Systeme.* Peter Lang.

BP. (2018). *BP Energy Outlook 2018 Edition*. https://www.bp.com/content/dam/bp/business-sites/en/global/corporate/pdfs/energy-economics/energy-outlook/bp-energy-outlook-2018.pdf

Butler, N. (2018, July 8). *Japan is nervous about its energy security*. Financial Times. https://www.ft.com/content/66c37158-801a-11e8-bc55-50daf11b720d

China Hands. (2018, May 30). *The Shanghai Cooperation Organization Energy Club: A Collaborative Future for Nuclear Energy*. China Hands. https://chinahandsmagazine.org/2018/05/30/the-shanghai-cooperation-organization-energy-club-a-collaborative-future-for-nuclear-energy/

Chung, C.-P. (2004). The Shanghai Co-operation Organization – China's Changing Influence in Central Asia. *China Quarterly, 180*(240), 989-1009.

Eng.sects.org. (2019). *The Shanghai Cooperation Organisation*. Retrieved May 7, 2019, from http://eng.sectsco.org/about_sco/

Giz. (2019). *Förderung Nachhaltiger Energielösungen in Der ASEAN-Region.* https://www.giz.de/de/weltweit/16395.html

Grace, A. (2018). The Lessons China Taught Itself: Why the Shanghai Cooperation Organization Matters. *The Jamestown Foundation China Brief*, *18*(11), 1-17.

Hashimova, U. (2018). *Why Central Asia is Betting on China's Belt and Road.* The Diplomat. https://thediplomat.com/2018/08/why-central-asia-is-betting-on-chinas-belt-and-road/

Houlihan Lokey. (2015). *Investing in Emerging Asia's Renewable Energy Future.* https://www.mergermarket.com/assets/Houlihan_Newsletter_No7_FINAL.pdf

IEA. (2019). *Sustainable Development Goal 7.* Retrieved June 25, 2019, from https://www.iea.org/sdg/renewables/

Infoshos. (2015). *SCO Energy Club: Structure Ready for International Interaction, Not Shanghai Six's Elite Club.* http://infoshos.ru/en/?idn=13913

Istikbal, D. (2017). Comparison of 1st and 2nd Economic Development Plans of Brazil and South Korea. *Kırklareli Üniversitesi Sosyal Bilimler Dergisi*, *1*(1), 119-131.

İstikbal, D. (2019). Legitimacy of The Regime and Enerjy Security: Chinese Communist Party's Enerjy Policies. *Uluslararası Ekonomi, İşletme ve Politika Dergisi*, *3*(1), 49-68.

İstikbal, D., & Dilek, Ş. (2019). Brics in A Changing World Order and Its Effect On Turkey. *Uluslararası Afro-Avrasya Araştırmaları Dergisi*, *4*(7), 47-62.

Kalu, M. (2012). *Understanding Africa's China Policy: A Test of Dependency Theory and a Study of African Motivations in Increasing Engagement with China* [Unpublished doctoral dissertation]. University of Nebraska-Lincoln.

Kavalski, E. (2010). The Shanghai Cooperation – Framing China's Socialization of Central Asia. *Journal of Asian and African Studies*, *42*(2), 131-145.

Moos, D. (2019, May 23). *With Friends Like the US., Who Needs Economic Foes*. Bloomberg. https://www.bloomberg.com/opinion/articles/2019-05-23/japan-south-korea-get-reminder-of-how-powerful-china-s-economy-is

PWC. (2017). *The World in 2050. The long view: how will the global economic order change by 2050?* Retrieved May 9, 2019, from https://www.pwc.com/gx/en/issues/economy/the-world-in-2050.html

Rahman, K. (2011). Central Asia, Energy Security and Shanghai Cooperation Organization. *Pluto Journal*, *8*(1), 65-75.

Reuters. (2019, March 25). *South Korean Officials to Press for Iran Sanctions Waiver in United States*. https://www.reuters.com/article/us-iran-nuclear-usa-southkorea/south-korean-officials-to-press-for-iran-sanctions-waiver-in-united-states-idUSKCN1R61Z0

Scott, G. (2019, February 26). *How Effective Is the SCO as a Tool for Chinese Foreign Policy?* E-International Relations. https://www.e-ir.info/2019/02/26/how-effective-is-the-sco-as-a-tool-for-chinese-foreign-policy/

Seiwert, E. (2019, March 23). *India-Pakistan Tensions Test the Shanghai Cooperation Organization's Mettle*. The Diplomat. https://thediplomat.com/2019/03/india-pakistan-tensions-test-the-shanghai-cooperation-organizations-mettle/

Senderov, S., & Vorobev, S. (2018). Ensuring Energy Security in ASEAN Countries: Current Trends and Major Challenges. *E3S Web of Conferences*, *27*, 1-14.

Suter, D. (2015). *The Shanghai Cooperation Organisation, A Chinese Practice of International Law*. Schulthess.

Ünay, S., & Dilek, Ş. (2018). *Yeni Korumacılık ve Ticaret Savaşları. (Analiz No. 228)*. SETA.

Varathan, P. (2018, January 23). *The recent history of the global economy, in one chart*. Quartz. https://qz.com/1183308/the-economic-reversal-of-asia-and-africa-in-one-striking-chart/

World Bank. (2019). *GDP (current US$) – Korea, Rep., Japan*. Retrieved May 9, 2019, from https://data.worldbank.org/indicator/NY.GDP.MKTP.CD?locations=KR-JP

Wu, Y. (2016). Electricity Market Integration in ASEAN: Institutional and Political Barriers and Opportunities. In Y. Li & S. Kimura (Eds.). *Achieving an Integrated Electricity Market in Southeast Asia: Addressing the Economic, Technical, Institutional, and Geo-Political Barriers (ERIA Research Project Report 2015-2016)* (pp. 109-125). ERIA.

Zhihai, X. (2019, March 21). *Rethinking Japan's Energy Security 8 Years After Fukushima.* The Diplomat. https://thediplomat.com/2019/03/rethinking-japans-energy-security-8-years-after-fukushima/

CHAPTER TWO

THE WESTERN BALKANS: THE INTERPLAY BETWEEN ENERGY AND POLITICS

HASAN KORKUT,* ENDRİS MEKONNEN FARİS** AND HAMZA PRELJEVİC***

Introduction

This chapter examines the evolving interplay between energy and politics in the Western Balkans (WB) by considering the proactive involvement of the European Union (EU), Russia, China, and Turkey. The WB has been at the center of increased geopolitical attention from the leading world powers. These geopolitical interests have been greatly motivated by significant economic, security, and political advantages to the great powers, which skillfully use the WB as a tool to control international and regional affairs. In this regard, this work surveys the clash of energy interests among the EU, Russia, China, and Turkey for influence over and the eventual control of the WB. Actually, the interplay between energy and politics is the toughest manifestation of geopolitical rivalry between these states in the WB sphere of influence. By exploring this subject, we attempt to demonstrate why there is an increasing presence of these powers in the WB. In this regard, the WB certainly represents a single geopolitical region that naturally attracts the leading actors of world politics to compete for the WB sphere of influence and control. Thus, the WB is indeed a typical geopolitical region, especially

* Prof. Dr. Hasan Korkut, Faculty of Political Sciences, Marmara University. E-mail: hkorkut@hotmail.com.
** Endris Mekonnen Faris, Ph.D. Candidate, International University of Sarajevo. E-mail: edrismekonnen@hotmail.com.
*** Hamza Preljevic, Ph.D. Candidate, International University of Sarajevo. E-mail: hamzapreljevic@gmail.com.

with regards to its common history, language, religion, ethnicity, and culture. The WB is also a valuable geopolitical region that opens the door and access to the West, the Mediterranean, and Central Europe. This work attempts to explore this geopolitical uniqueness of the WB region by exploring the EU's, Russia's, China's, and Turkey's exercise of power that is aimed at both energy and politics. Therefore, Winston Churchill's definition of the Balkans as the "soft underbelly" of Europe is still relevant today because of the peninsula's energy, economic, security, and political aspects.

The Western Balkans and EU Energy Security

The EU, under its existing organizational structure and authority, directly deals with twenty-plus key topics, including energy (European Union, n.d.). Unlike other topics, it turns out that the EU member states commonly agree on the EU's energy policy and particularly with the WB's prospects for and challenges with energy. Putting it concisely, the EU has successfully developed a common concern among Europeans that energy security is their common interest and that the EU member states should work together in developing energy policies and regulations (Siddi, 2018). In this regard, the exponentially rising energy consumption and continuous import dependency (Eurostat, n.d.-b) further strengthened the EU's rationale to place energy security as its top priority. Thus, the EU's agenda always address the perennial insecurity of the continent's energy supply. An additional concern relates to foreign suppliers being relatively powerful actors (Bieri, 2015). These great powers use energy as a major foreign policy tool. In this regard, Russia, Turkey, and, more recently, China are often accused of using energy to influence the WB's politics (Energy Community Secretariat, 2018).

The EU's Approaches to the Rising Energy Demand

The EU still has energy-related concerns, which require a continuous strategic policy approach. Thus, over the past two decades, the EU has devised a number of regulations and instruments to tackle energy concerns more effectively. In the mid-2000s, numerous energy-focused documents asserted that Europe had entered a new energy era (European Commission, 2006). Therefore, this continuous energy focus contributed to the EU taking firm control and becoming a stirring leader of energy policies in Europe (Renner & Trauner, 2009). Consequently, the EU succeeded in bringing both its own member states and other regional countries into a so-called energy coalition that respects the common agenda, energy framework, energy regulations, energy security, and energy initiatives (Youngs, 2011).

Since the 1990s, Western European countries have made significant shifts from mere production to a service-based economy, finance, banking, telecommunications, pharmaceutical industry, research, high technology, and energy. Although this unprecedentedly aggressive economic shift contributed to economic growth and development, it also began to challenge European sustainability regarding the energy and labor supply. This economic growth and development significantly depended on the energy supply, which the existing energy supply chain could not provide even at maximum capacity. This chronic energy supply problem topped the EU policymakers' concerns. However, the EU's strategic energy approach and proper assessments, which were carefully carried out, opened the door for new opportunities. The opportunities included, besides energy, positive experiences in solving collective problems under institutionalized mechanisms. In this regard, the European Coal and Steel Community (ECSC) laid the foundation for European energy cooperation. This and similar institutions initially brought the founding member states into a purely economic union, and energy was thereby the primary cause of EU unification. Actually, since 1952, ECSC has enabled the significant pooling of the then major energy resources located in the six Western European countries. Consequently, due to the common interests of these six countries, overseeing the production and streaming of energy was assigned to the highest Community level. Most importantly, though, they also began to address their shared concerns of energy security (Petzina et al., 1981) and the ideal of Europeanizing the energy system (Kamlage & Nanz, 2016). The leaders transformed these energy concerns to a different level that consequently led to the birth of the Energy Community.

The Energy Community began to feature Europe's lofty aspiration to extend energy concerns across the EU nations as a common official policy in order to create an integrated and sustainable energy supply (EC, 2006). Accordingly, all member and non-member states are encouraged to pool their efforts to address the increasing energy demand from within, primarily through diversification and the common market. This viable ambition under the loose leadership of the EU continues to efficiently operate in bringing together over forty European states and a number of non-member states from the Balkans. In 2006, a Green Paper titled "A European Strategy for Sustainable, Competitive and Secure Energy" (ESSCSE) articulated the energy scheme as the second most innovative and also comprehensive mode of energy governance after the ECSC (Renner, 2009). Most importantly, though, the Community gave a well-calculated response to the existing energy security and supply challenge: it notably incorporated the Balkan states into the European regional market for gas and petroleum products. The platform came out as a highly institutionalized and 'top-down' instrument aimed predominantly at pre-accession countries (Tholens, 2014). The Energy Community turned out to be the best showcase and the first-ever legally binding instrument that has held the powerful EU and the WB countries together. Though the treaty apparently lacks supranational competency and is vulnerable, the Community is effective in drawing the Balkan region closer to the European Union in the energy area and beyond (Energy Community Secretariat, 2018). Actually, membership of the Energy Community is straightforwardly linked to EU membership (European Commission, n.d.-a). Thus, energy is like the transposition and implementation of *acquis communautaire* (Buschle & Lesjak, 2018) in the WB. Subsequently, its far-reaching impact is in keeping the contracting countries in a mutual partnership.

The EU thus secured, on the one hand, close ties with WB countries to further the continent's energy security. Then, on the other, the EU projects the ambition of self-reliance regarding both the source of sustainable supply and free energy transactions. The most important achievement, which is hard to overlook, is the EU's ability to emerge as a single and potentially unrivaled organization that regulates continental energy governance. This has become a powerful EU tool for influencing and shaping the interplay between energy and politics. Nevertheless, while significant progress has been made regarding effective dealings with energy, the EU has also been exposed to the hitherto numerous political and diplomatic challenges that are interrelated and interconnected with energy security. For example, Russia's natural gas supply and the signing of the intergovernmental agreement between Russia and Serbia in 2012 (Gazprom, n.d.-a) is an excellent example to demonstrate the inseparable interplay between energy and politics.

The agreement (Republic of Serbia, 2012) allows Russia to increase its gas supply volume to 5 billion cubic meters per year until 2021. Thus, starting from 2012, Russia increased its hold on Europe's energy supply. The EU, whose interest is apparently protected by the Energy Community agreement, loudly voiced its disagreement in both political and economic terms. Consequently, the Energy Community was legally obliged to protect its signatories' interest and triggered a compliant case against Serbia, citing its failure to comply with the Energy Community agreement (Energy Community, 2019). Serbia responded by asserting the significance of the Energy Community agreement and argued that the provisions of the contract with Russia did not breach any of the clauses of the Energy Community treaty because the gas was intended exclusively for sale in the territory of the Republic of Serbia (Antic, 2017). Eventually, in October 2018, the Republic of Serbia rectified the breach in parliament and bowed to the Energy Community. This example clearly illustrates the EU's grip on the WB countries as signatories of the Energy Community. The Secretariat of the Community openly articulated the increasing energy challenge from China, Russia, and Turkey. Arguably, these powers have interests in the WB, and their subsequent actions are profoundly affecting the energy landscape. The EU established a legally binding instrument that makes the contracting bodies (WB6) feel its influential presence via the Energy Community. The case that involved Serbia-Russia and the Community indicates that the EU uses the Energy Community as a very effective tool to counteract influences from China, Russia, and Turkey (Energy Community Secretariat, 2018).

The Dynamics of Energy Politics in the Western Balkans

The EU also uses energy-related, Europe-engulfing regimes as an equally powerful instrument to execute its dominant energy-oriented interest in the region (Önsoy & Udum, 2015). This is coupled with the EU's renewable energy concerns connected with climate change. In this regard, more than half of the EU's energy supplies continue to be imported (Eurostat, n.d.-a), which preclude the EU from having energy *per se* as direct leverage and compel it to adopt different strategies (Siddi, 2018). Therefore, the EU's energy regulatory power at times could be seen in isolation and as self-sufficient, but, at the same time, it is often tied to the prospect of the EU's enlargement. The deployment of the EU's energy regulatory power can be seen in two related frameworks. The EU uses it, on the one hand, to persuade the WB countries to observe the EU's energy policy and, on the other, to prepare the WB countries to follow strategic energy developments in the future. Put concisely, the EU has equipped itself with a powerful tool to monitor and control the WB's present and future energy policies. Thus, the EU-WB countries' energy engagements oscillate and rest on the extreme poles of politico-economic foundations.

The EU's energy security strategy has been aimed at both energy price diversification and broader regional stability (Leal-Arcas et al., 2015). Emboldened by liberal free-market practices, the EU swiftly took the leadership role in rallying unconditional support for the free market energy trade. In addition, the economic opportunity within the integrated energy market was the main reason for the WB countries to straightforwardly accept the EU energy strategy and specific terms and conditions. In this regard, the WB countries have secured limited economic benefits from the EU at the expense of political influence and control. Actually, the EU has been using energy to exercise broader political dominance and to draw the region into its grip. The EU has maintained the consequent sustainable effects in the WB by merging together the need for political reforms and the EU's enlargement with energy security and the energy strategy. These evolving trends specifically over the last decade indicate that the EU's energy-grounded political influence continues to influence the WB region.

Similarly, Russia, China, and Turkey have been using energy-grounded political influence in the WB region, which again affirms the strong interplay between energy and politics, especially in the last decade. The magnitude of their involvement and the subsequent international uproar as a result of these influences entail significant political dynamism in the WB by Russia, China, and Turkey. The disparity that the individual actors display in terms of timeframe, specific area of energy, and infrastructure have been determined by the influence they expect to pursue in shaping the energy-colored political landscape. Accordingly, this approach explains the EU's subsequent reactions to Russian, Chinese, and Turkish influence as part of the energy-politics dynamics unfolding in the WB region.

The Russian, Chinese, and Turkish energy-targeted presence in the WB takes the form of engagement through investments in energy infrastructure, energy assets ownership, and provision of loans. Russia has long been taking the lead in efficiently implementing all these engagements at once. In the field of investing in energy infrastructures, Russia adopted an alternative strategy to supply its energy product to Europe via the WB. The existing efficient engagement in energy infrastructure investments has also been paired with penetrating property ownership to scale up the measure of influence. Starting from the late 1990s, Russian energy firms have made inroads into the WB region. In the earlier scramble to acquire energy assets, LUKoil was able to penetrate the WB and purchased 79.5 percent of Serbia's Beopetrol with 92.4m US dollars committed investment (Vatansever, 2005). Since 2003, the company has grown efficiently, comprising more than 138 retail chain of gas stations in its possession, which has positioned the company as the second-largest retail chain owner in the region (LUKOIL, 2019). The acquisition interest has been extended to Bosnia and Herzegovina (BiH), where Zarubenhneft – the Russian state oil company – bought Brod oil refinery and the lubricant producer Modriča in 2007 (Mulalic & Karic, 2014). In 2008, Gazprom Neft, a subsidiary of Gazprom, secured a majority stake in the oil and gas company NIS j.s.c. Novi Sad (NIS) – a significant contributor to the Serbian budget, standing currently at 56.15 percent, a 5.15 percent rise from 2009 (Gazprom, 2019). These particular investments show remarkable advancements through adding more subsidiary assets and privileges, including petrol retailers, storage tanks, and more convenient energy resource drilling and exploratory rights in Serbia.

Russia used energy investments for building leverage and major political influence in the WB region (Secrieru, 2019). Actually, Russia's energy policy and strategy in Europe clearly represent the structural power manifestation that is explicitly exercised through energy politics (Proedrou, 2018). However, Russian energy interests in the WB, besides political influence, have firm trade and economic elements. Thus, it is overwhelmingly subjective to label Russian energy companies as Trojan horses whose prime existence and function is to pursue the state's political objectives. Thus, Russian energy companies, such as Gazprom and LUKoil, among others, could be critically perceived as instrumental in Russian foreign policy and diplomacy (Tynkkynen, 2016). They enable Russia to acquire a dominant position to maintain its reemerging influence in the WB (Bieri, 2015). However, Russia's recent grip on gas pricing and gas delivery in Ukraine shows signs of greater political leverage.

Turkey's involvement in the WB energy and politics interplay has evolved because of historical and political developments. Turkey pursues an independent engagement in the WB on the basis of historically entrenched multifaceted influence. Furthermore, Turkey has been exerting conditional alignment and cooperation with Russia by using a balanced and realistic diplomatic strategy. By using smart power, Turkey is outweighing what Moscow can generally offer. Being energy dependent, Turkey's pragmatic and dynamic engagements in the WB turn out to be strong enough to markedly alarm the EU (European Community Secretariat, 2018). Turkey's energy influence in the WB constitutes a growing concern of the EU, primarily because Turkey often follows Russian energy undertakings in the WB. Consequently, the EU turned to a containment strategy by articulating the position of Turkey as a full member of the Energy Community. Therefore, Turkey does not openly act against Brussels and keeps an observant position towards the Energy Community.

The TurkStream project forms the major backdrop of the energy-politics dynamics that involve Turkey and the EU in the WB region. For Turkey, this project increases its own ever-increasing energy security while the infrastructure will strengthen the country's geostrategic position as the pipeline goes through its sovereign territory. The pipeline is outside the EU's supranational regulatory power, and Turkey will thereby primarily benefit from it. Moreover, the project will enable energy transfers that cross Ukraine, which will position Turkey as a key energy actor in the future. This will probably strengthen Turkey's bargaining position and subsequently its influence over the WB region, which will in effect complicate European energy supply security. These developments will certainly increase tensions in the future because the EU has built leverage in the WB region, and the Energy Community will exercise pressure and influence on the contracting parties to stay committed to the treaty. Therefore, TurkStream, similarly to South Stream, is a clear example of the interplay between politics and energy (Koch, 2015).

Proactive Chinese engagement in WB energy politics accelerated the EU's strategic engagement too. The EU pursues a committed far-reaching energy strategy, whereby its long-term plan is to transform its energy security in terms of using an environmentally friendly energy supply (European Commission, 2011). For instance, according to the latest research studies, Europe has reduced its use of coal significantly for the fifth successive year. Coal's share of Europe's total power generation fell to 20 percent in 2016 alone, while the share from renewable energy sources showed a 30 percent increase (The Economist Intelligence Unit, 2018). In this regard, China's recent involvement in the energy sector in the WB could play a reversing role because China specifically targets investing in coal. Coal accounts for 50 percent of the WB's primary energy production, primarily because it is more affordable than other imported energy sources and it is abundantly available in the WB (World Bank, 2018). In addition, the WB's coal industry has continued its operation uninterruptedly for several decades, and now it relies on old technology and infrastructure. These gaps have enabled Beijing to find a way into the WB energy market. Chinese companies and investment banks have since been showing a growing interest in several fresh coal projects in the WB, particularly in Serbia and BiH (Mileusnić, 2015). For instance, coal mines located near the power plants of Tuzla, Kakanj, Gacko, Ugljevik, and Stanari in BiH continue to supply its domestic energy sector. China pledged to provide loans to construct five more power utilities. The China Exim Bank and the Industrial Bank pledged to build power utilities in Tuzla and Banovići, respectively. In an apparent sign of strong support from BiH, the federal government approved a loan issuance from China for the construction of the 450 MW Tuzla 7 coal-fired power plant (Lachert & Kamiński, 2019).

Priority Energy Projects in the Western Balkans

The WB region is becoming an increasingly important energy-efficient corridor and hub because of its geostrategic location. This region is at the crossroads of energy corridors that link the East (the producers) and the

West (the consumers). Although the WB corridor and proposed pipelines could lead to an uninterrupted flow of gas to the WB countries and EU member states, it significantly depends on intra-state cooperation within the region (Önsoy & Udum, 2014). Furthermore, energy corridors and pipelines that will eventually pass through the WB countries are at the same time strategically important to Russia, the EU, and the United States and their geostrategic interests. Therefore, politics will determine the future of these investment projects in the WB region, which can bring different benefits in terms of economic growth and development, renting the corridor for the pipeline, and access to energy sources. In addition, the construction of pipelines will create price stability and energy security.

The EU's energy "hunger," combined with its fear of supply disruption, led to the promotion of an energy-diverse supply system. Thus, the EU's growing energy deficit contributed to new projects to tackle more effective energy demand and supply. Some of the European and Russian energy-related mega-projects are *Nabucco*, *Nord Stream*, *South Stream*, and *TurkStream*.[1] However, because of the Russia-Ukraine gas disputes, the EU decided to suspend the planned energy projects. Moreover, the EU supported Ukraine to ensure a stable and prosperous future; as Angela Merkel said, "it is important that Ukraine remains a transit country for Russian gas because this represents a security component for Ukraine" (Donceel, 2018). Stated differently, these are clear examples of the interplay between energy and politics.

The European-Russian energy trade has been significantly affected by US-Russia disputes over various issues. However, this interplay between energy and politics has contributed to more serious consequences for the European energy supply (Lohmann & Wesphal, 2019). Russia seeks to undermine the US-led unipolar model by using energy policy and economic means. Additionally, Russia's "conventional forces are now capable of imposing high costs on even a technologically superior adversary such as NATO" (Marcus, 2017), but Russia's regional impact in terms of the geopolitics of energy is much greater. Russia uses energy as a primary and cheap statecraft and foreign policy tool to achieve geopolitical goals. Such an approach has affected energy security, particularly in the EU and the WB countries. Therefore, the EU decided not to sit idly by and watch Russia's

[1] Although some of the planned pipelines do not pass through the Western Balkan countries, they can serve as examples of EU efforts to secure the transmission, distribution, storage, and supply of energy sources. More importantly, these examples are an indication that decisions regarding energy supply are not purely economic but political as well, as can be seen in the EU's decision to suspend the planned energy projects due to the Russia-Ukraine dispute.

investment in lucrative energy infrastructure in the WB. Therefore, in addition to military and political security, the economic component, accompanied by energy security, has become part of the broader national and international security question.

Despite the diversification of energy, reliance on renewable energy sources (wind and solar photovoltaics), and the environmentally unsafe coal-fired power plants,[2] gas remains the fastest-growing source of energy. Therefore, Russia seeks to exert its pressure through the gas supply, China is investing in coal power plants, while the EU is opting for renewable energy sources in the WB countries. The WB countries are being encouraged to develop renewable energy, which should reduce WB countries' dependency on gas imports from Russia. In addition, business cooperation in the energy sector between China and the WB countries has been rising under the *Belt and Road Initiative* (BRI). Mostly, China is funding the expansion of coal-based energy initiatives in WB investment-hungry countries (Warsaw Institute, 2019).

The Balkans has become a spot for the construction of gas and oil pipelines, primarily aimed at the European energy market. Although the Balkan countries have the highest possibility of becoming geostrategic partners for Europe as a transit route, the majority of the planned energy-related corridors have not been completed. From 1993 until 2018, the construction of eight major energy – oil and gas – corridors were planned, namely: *AMBO* (Albanian-Macedonian-Bulgarian Oil), *CPOT* (Constanta-Pančevo-Omišalj-Trieste), *Nabucco*, *TAP* (Trans-Adriatic Pipeline), *AGRI* (Azerbaijan-Georgia-Romania Interconnector), *Eastring*, *South Stream*, and *TurkStream*. Five of them – AMBO, CPOT, TAP, South Stream, and TurkStream – were planned to pass through some of the WB countries, but none of them have been fully realized.

Proposed back in the 1990s, AMBO is a planned oil pipeline that would carry oil from the Caspian to the Mediterranean. The pipeline would run for nearly 900 kilometers from the Bulgarian Black Sea port of Burgas via the Republic of North Macedonia to the Albanian Adriatic port of Vlore. ABMO, by its structure, would be "the first Western energy route from Eurasia that isn't under the direct control of either Russia or Turkey" (Korybko, 2015). This project had direct support from the EU (BBC News, 2004), which can be understood as an early effort made by the EU to

[2] The Energy Community states "propped up coal mining and electricity generation with direct and indirect public subsidies totaling at least 2.4 billion annually." See Bankwatch Network, 2019. The subsidies for coal-fired power plants are three times higher than for renewables support in Bosnia and Herzegovina, Kosovo, and Serbia. See Energy Community, 2019.

diversify its oil suppliers. In addition, AMBO's plans were in line with American foreign policy objectives.[3] It was an attempt to avoid the implementation of the Russian-led *Burgas-Alexandroupolis* pipeline project. The AMBO pipeline was designed to transfer 750,000 barrels of crude per day or around 40 million tons per year (Papaspanos, 2010). This project has faced many challenges, "including the physical existence of adequate crude oil in the Caspian Region, intense competition with other infrastructural projects on the Balkan Peninsula, funding for construction…, and, of course, geopolitics in the region" (Vlcek & Jirusek, 2019, p. 93).

CPOT is an abbreviation of the initial letters of the city names through which the oil pipeline would pass: Constanta, Pančevo, Omišalj, and Trieste. This project, which started in 2007, is known within the EU as the *Pan-European Oil Pipeline* (PEOP) project. The CPOT pipeline was intended to transfer Caspian and Russian oil from the Black Sea port Constanta in Bulgaria through Romania, Serbia, Croatia, and Slovenia to its final destination in Italy (EVS, 2013). This means that CPOT would create a Euro-Asian energy corridor and a stable crude oil supply for the European consumer markets. Furthermore, the CPOT pipeline would increase "revenue from transit tariffs and revenue for companies participating in the construction and operation of the pipeline" (Karasalihović Sedlar et al., 2009). The construction challenges to CPOT emerged when the Slovenian authorities stepped back and refused to support the project because a 30 kilometer-long stretch (the total length of the pipeline being 1,320 km) may have potential risks upon the safety of the *karst* environment (Alexander's Gas & Oil Connections, 2006). Then, in 2010, Croatia also decided to withdraw its participation from the building of the CPOT pipeline. "Slovenia's refusal to take part would mean higher costs, as the pipeline would have to be laid under the sea in the northern Adriatic to bypass Slovenia," and this was among the reasons why the Croatian government decided to step back (Reuters, 2009). However, the CPOT pipeline was purposefully stopped so as to decrease energy dependence on Russia and to diversify energy imports from other suppliers. The CPOT pipeline would have prevented the disruption of the supply of crude oil and petroleum

---

[3] US Trade and Development Agency (TDA) director Joseph Grandmaison said: "The competition is fierce to tap energy resources in the Caspian region. Over the last year, TDA has been actively promoting the development of multiple pipelines to connect these vast resources with Western markets. This grant represents a significant step forward for this policy and for U.S. business interests in the Caspian region. The TDA further stressed that American companies stood a good chance of winning contracts for work on AMBO's pipeline." See Alexander's Gas & Oil Connections, 1999.

derivates, but at the same time, it would have increased the EU's energy dependence on Russia.

In 2003, TAP was announced – a mega pipeline project that was planned to bring gas from the Greece-Turkey border via Albania and the Adriatic Sea to Italy and further to Western Europe. TAP offers the simplest route to Europe, unlike the Nabucco pipeline, which was more ambitious, complex, and costly. TAP is planned to run for 879 kilometers in total across northern Greece (545 km), Albania (215 km), and the Adriatic Sea (105 km) (Banktrack, 2017), with estimated construction costs of €5 billion. It will deliver the natural gas produced at Azerbaijan's *Shah Deniz II* gas development to the Western European market via the South Caucasus Pipeline (SCP) extension and through the *Trans-Anatolian Pipeline* (TANAP). Since it will enhance energy security and diversify gas supplies for the EU market, "the European Commission, Parliament and Council have given TAP *Project of Common Interest (PCI)* status under the new guidelines for Trans-European energy infrastructure (TEN-E)" (Trans Adriatic Pipeline, n.d.). PCIs are key cross-border infrastructure projects intended to help the EU achieve its energy policy (European Commission, n.d.-b). More than 95% of the construction of the TAP project has been completed successfully in Greece, Albania, and Italy. TAP is intended to lower the consumption of Russian gas by the European market, achieve significant CO_2 reductions, and demonstrate that energy security in the EU could be solved by relying on other – non-Russian-related – projects. The initial capacity of TAP will be 10 billion cubic meters (bcm) a year, with a possibility to double the capacity of the pipeline to 20 bcm a year. The same concern arises in the case of TAP as in the case of the Nabucco pipeline: does Azerbaijan have sufficient reserves of natural gas to supply the EU market through the TAP project? Given that Italy alone imports about 25 bcm of natural gas via pipelines from Russia a year, the TAP project will lead to a partial reduction in the consumption of Russian gas (BP, 2019, p. 41). The first delivery of gas by TAP is expected to be in the second quarter of 2020. This new route, however, could add a number of different sources, not only from Azerbaijan but also from Turkmenistan, Kazakhstan, and Uzbekistan, as well as from Iran, Iraq, and Egypt.

In 2007, the South Stream pipeline was proposed to transport natural gas from Russia across the Black Sea to Bulgaria through Serbia, Hungary, and Slovenia to Austria. Some branches would pass through Croatia and Bosnia and Herzegovina. South Stream has been presented as an important project that would contribute to the energy security of the EU, which would thereby reduce gas supply disruptions. The initial capacity was 31 bcm a year but, following the January 2009 Russia-Ukraine crisis, it was expanded to four lines and 63 bcm a year (Oxford Institute for Energy Studies, 2015). The South Stream project "was meant to supply 12 percent of the EU's natural gas demand in 2020" (Yesevi, 2018, p. 28). The total cost for the construction of South Stream was estimated at €17 million (Euractiv, 2014). Following the annexation of Crimea by Russia, however, the European Commission opposed Russia's South Stream pipeline (Lehane, 2014). The primary objective of the South Stream project for Russia was to bypass Ukraine as an energy transit country. By using this approach, Russia was planning to strengthen its energy policy (Yesevi, 2018, p. 29). In addition, some EU actors had long been skeptical of Russia's South Stream gas pipeline project, seeing it as a rival to the Nabucco project (Overland, 2016), as well as to TAP, for competitive supplies. However, Bulgaria suspended construction work on the South Stream pipeline following the demands of the European Commission. After the disputes with the EU, Russia abandoned the South Stream project in December 2014 and announced that they had instead agreed with Ankara to build *TurkStream* (Overland, 2016). President Putin named the European Commission as the main culprit for the failure of the South Stream project, "depriving Bulgaria of the possibility of behaving like a sovereign state" (DW, 2014). The EU "view of South Stream had been generally negative either because of the belief that the project would undermine diversification of gas supplies" (Oxford Institute for Energy Studies, 2015) and because the realization of the South Stream project would help Russia to achieve an even greater monopoly in the European – both the EU and non-EU/Western Balkans – energy market.

The TurkStream pipeline (TSP) project is planned to transport Russian gas to Europe under the Black Sea, helping Moscow limit the transit of gas through Ukraine. TSP has two lines, the first starting from Turkey and going through Bulgaria, Serbia, Hungary, and Austria, and the second through Greece and Italy. Some branches are planned to pass through Bosnia and Herzegovina and Croatia. The TSP project was agreed in 2014 after the Bulgarian government ordered the suspension of construction work on the South Stream pipeline. The initial project was supposed to consist of four parallel lines (each with a capacity of 15.75 bcm a year) with a total annual capacity of 63 bcm a year. The pipeline's capacity has been reduced to two parallel lines with a total of 31.5 bcm a year (Gazprom, n.d.-b). By way of comparison, all the gas transiting through Ukraine represents more than 80 bcm a year (De Micco, 2015, p. 9). Importantly, the TSP is less vulnerable to EU competition law than the previously planned South Stream (Gurbanov, 2017), and the realization of TSP is easier because Turkey is not bound by the EU's "Third Energy Package" (TEP) rules. The TSP has also experienced delays due to the crisis in Russia-Turkey relations following the shooting down of a Russian fighter jet by Turkish fighter jets in November 2015. However, following the normalization of bilateral relations, the intergovernmental agreement for TSP was signed in October 2016. The project's total cost is estimated at €11.4 billion (TASS, 2017). The TSP is a project worth investing in for Moscow because it aims to: (1) meet the needs for natural gas in northwestern Turkey and replace the gas transit via Ukraine, Romania, and Bulgaria for Turkey, (2) export natural gas to the European market through Turkey, and (3) diversify its gas transit routes in order to consolidate its energy security. However, any failure of the TSP project would be a major threat to the Russian economy. On the other hand, with the TSP project, the EU will diversify its supply routes but will be more dependent on Russian gas. The first gas delivery from Turkey to Bulgaria and Serbia is scheduled for 2020, while the first gas delivery to Hungary is supposed to take place in 2021 (Brokeš, 2019).

Conclusion

The Western Balkans (WB) has historically been the zone between West and East. The WB has always been a strategically important region for the EU because of its geographical location, which is particularly important for European energy policies. Stated differently, WB countries, because of their geographical location, can cover the transport of raw energy materials from alternative suppliers to the EU market adequately and safely. On the other hand, China, Russia, and Turkey are influencing these countries and have strong interests in the region. WB countries (especially Bosnia and Herzegovina and Serbia) are highly dependent on Russia for its energy supply, and this dependence could rise with new Russian investments in developing transport and energy infrastructure. Investment in energy projects in the WB is important for Russia in order to control the energy corridors that transit the region. China has taken a much more proactive role in the WB because of the rocky relations between the EU on one side and Russia and Turkey on the other. In addition, the extremely weak, skeptical, and indecisive role of the EU's engagement in the WB created the gap for greater Chinese exercise of smart power through investments in energy, bank loans, and infrastructural projects. Thus, Beijing continues to exploit geopolitical realities to strengthen and consolidate its presence in the WB countries. Although Chinese investments could strengthen WB countries' economic growth and development, loans given directly to governments could fuel more mismanagement and even corruption. Questions arise about the value of those projects and how the money from loans is spent. Chinese investments often disregard the promotion of a market economy, good governance, and regulatory standards, which in turn may increase the region's susceptibility to corruption.

Russia, Turkey, and China on one side and the EU on the other will continue to expand their sphere of influence in the WB. Energy and energy-related tools are key motivational factors that enable these powerful actors to compete against one another for influence (Stronski & Himes, 2019). They will pursue different strategies based on their strategic foreign policy capacity. The WB countries, on the other hand, will continue to play their individual roles and often side with these powers to implement their energy-based influence in the course of their multilayer engagements in the region. While the WB countries will maintain commitments to the clauses of the Energy Community, they will often be involved in activities that undermine the treaty. This might lead to the emergence of so-called attention-grabbing energy-politics dynamics in the WB, which will continue to evolve for the foreseeable period to come.

References

Alexander's Gas & Oil Connections. (1999, June 21). *TDA signs agreement with Bulgaria to finance extra work on AMBO pipeline.* http://www.gasandoil.com/news/1999/08/cne93297

Alexander's Gas & Oil Connections. (2006, April 13). *Romania halts construction of PanEuropean pipeline.* http://www.gasandoil.com/news/europe/4adda99838f5765746e521b34e70044e

Antic, A. (2017). Response to Reasoned Request in Case ECS - 18/16. Letter to Energy Community Secretariat Mr. Janez Kopac, Director. Belgrade, Serbia.

Banktrack. (2017, February 20). *Trans Adriatic Pipeline (TAP).* https://www.banktrack.org/project/transadriatic_pipeline

Bankwatch Network. (2019, March 25). *Energy Community: Western Balkan coal subsidies worth over 1.2 billion euros in 2017.* https://bankwatch.org/press_release/energy-community-western-balkan-coal-subsidies-worth-over-1-2-billion-euros-in-2017

BBC News. (2004, December 28). *Go-ahead for Balkan oil pipeline.* http://news.bbc.co.uk/2/hi/business/4130271.stm

Bieri, M. (2015). *The Western Balkans Between Europe and Russia (CSS Analyses in Security Policy 170).* ETH Zurich.

BP. (2019). *BP Statistical Review of World Energy 2019.* https://www.bp.com/content/dam/bp/business-sites/en/global/corporate/pdfs/energy-economics/statistical-review/bp-stats-review-2019-full-report.pdf
Brokeš, F. (2019, January 1). *Turkish stream and Europe.* Obserwator Finansowy. https://financialobserver.eu/cse-and-cis/turkish-stream-and-europe/
Buschle, D., & Lesjak, H. A. (2018). *The Energy Community Legal Framework*, 4th edn. Energy Community Secretariat.
De Micco, P. (2015, July). *Changing pipelines, shifting strategies: Gas in south-eastern Europe, and the implications for Ukraine.* Directorate-General for External Policies. http://www.europarl.europa.eu/RegData/etudes/IDAN/2015/549053/EXPO_IDA(2015)549053_EN.pdf p. 9
Donceel, H. (2018, December 6). *The Case With Nord Stream 2.* Euranet Plus News Agency. https://euranetplus-inside.eu/eu-us-the-case-with-nord-stream-2/
DW. (2014, December 2). *Russia axes South Stream project.* https://www.dw.com/en/russia-axes-south-stream-project/a-18104752
Energy Community. (2019, June 20). *Director unveils final results of study on coal subsidies and their impacts at EU Sustainable Energy Week.* https://www.energy-community.org/news/Energy-Community-News/2019/06/20.html
Energy Community Secretariat. (2018). *Knocking on the EU's Door through the Energy Community: Integration of Western Balkans into the Pan-European Energy Market.* Energy Community.
Euractiv. (2014, March 23). *South Stream victim of Crimea annexation.* https://www.euractiv.com/section/energy/news/south-stream-victim-of-crimea-annexation/
European Commission. (2006). *Green Paper – A European Strategy for Sustainable, Competitive and Secure Energy.* https://eur-lex.europa.eu/legal-content/EN/ALL/?uri=CELEX:52006DC0105
European Commission. (2011). *Energy Roadmap 2050.* https://www.kowi.de/Portaldata/2/Resources/fp7/coop/com-2011-Energy-Roadmap-2050-en.pdf
European Commission. (n.d.-a). *Chapters of the acquis.* https://ec.europa.eu/neighbourhood-enlargement/policy/conditions-membership/chapters-of-the-acquis_en

European Commission. (n.d.-b). *Projects of Common Interest.* https://ec.europa.eu/energy/en/topics/infrastructure/projects-common-interest

European Union. (n.d.). *Topics of the European Union.* Retrieved April 25, 2019, from https://europa.eu/european-union/topics_en

Eurostat. (n.d.-a). *Energy production and imports.* Retrieved 2019, from https://ec.europa.eu/eurostat/statistics-explained/index.php?title=Energy_production_and_imports#More_than_half_of_EU-28_energy_needs_are_covered_by_imports

Eurostat. (n.d.-b). *Energy Statistics – An Overview.* Retrieved June 2019, from https://ec.europa.eu/eurostat/statistics-explained/index.php?title=Energy_statistics_-_an_overview

EVS. (2013, January 7). *Shaking off old shackles: The Pan-European Oil Pipeline.* https://evs-translations.com/blog/pan-european-oil-pipeline/

Gazprom. (n.d.-a). *Serbia.* Retrieved 2019, from http://www.gazpromexport.ru/en/partners/serbia/

Gazprom. (n.d.-b). *TurkStream.* https://www.gazprom.com/projects/turk-stream/

Gurbanov, I. (2017, January 21). *Perspective for 'Turkish Stream' Project: Possible Scenarios and Challenges.* Natural Gas World. https://www.naturalgasworld.com/perspective-for-turkish-stream-project-possible-scenarios-and-challenges-35401

Kamlage, J., & Nanz, P. (2016). Crisis and Participation in the European Union: Energy Policy as a Test Bed for a New Politics of Citizen Participation. *Global Society, 31*(1), 65-82. doi:10.1080/13600826.2016.1235553

Karasalihović Sedlar, D., Dekanić, I., & Hrnčević, L. (2009). Oil Supply Security in Croatia. *Journal of Energy, 58*(1), 6-13.

Koch, F. (2015). *Turkish Stream and its implications for the EU.* EGMONT – The Royal Institute for International Relations.

Korybko, A. (2015, March 3). *The future of the Balkans runs through Macedonia (I).* https://orientalreview.org/2015/03/03/the-future-of-the-balkans-runs-through-macedonia-i/

Lachert, J., & Kamiński, K. (2019). *Western Balkans: Infrastructure and Energy, From a Geopolitical Perspective.* The Warsaw Institute Review.

Leal-Arcas, R., Ríos, J. A., & Grasso, C. (2015). The European Union and its Energy Security Challenges: Engagement Through and with Networks. *Contemporary Politics, 21*(3), 273-293. doi:10.1080/13569775.2015.1061242

Lehane, B. (2014, May 28). *EU calls for South Stream suspension.* Upstream Online. https://www.upstreamonline.com/live/1157072/eu-calls-for-south-stream-suspension

Lohmann, S., & Westphal, K. (2019). *US-Russia Policy Hits European Energy Supply: The Consequences of Unilateral Sanctions and Growing Market Competition.* SWP Comment 2019/C 06. https://www.swp-berlin.org/10.18449/2019C06/

LUKOIL. (2019). *LUKOIL in the Republic of Serbia.* http://www.lukoil.com/Company/BusinessOperation/GeographicReach/Europe/LUKOILinSerbia

Marcus, J. (2017, June 29). *How much of a threat does Russia pose, and to whom?* BBC News. https://www.bbc.com/news/world-europe-40428132

Mileusnić, D. (2015). *Beyond Borders: How Energy Union can turn the tide against coal in the Western Balkans.* CAN Europe.

Mulalic, M., & Karic, M. (2014). The Western Balkans Energy Politics and Russian Energy Politics. *Epiphany: Journal of Interdisciplinary Studies, 7*(1), 102-105.

Önsoy, M., & Udum, Ş. (2015). The role of Turkey in western Balkan energy security. *Asia Europe Journal, 13*(2), 175-192.

Overland, I. (2016). The Hunter Becomes the Hunted: Gazprom Encounters EU Regulation. In S. Andersen, A. Goldthau, & N. Sitter (Eds.), *Energy Union (International Political Economy Series)* (pp. 115-130). Palgrave Macmillan.

Oxford Institute for Energy Studies. (2015, January). *Does the cancellation of South Stream signal a fundamental reorientation of Russian gas export policy?* https://www.oxfordenergy.org/wpcms/wp-content/uploads/2015/01/Does-cancellation-of-South-Stream-signal-a-fundamental-reorientation-of-Russian-gas-export-policy-GPC-5.pdf

Papaspanos, J. (2010). *Caspian Energy Geopolitics: The Rise and Fall of Burgas-Alexandroupoli.* RIEAS Research Paper No. 148. https://www.files.ethz.ch/isn/125657/rieas148.pdf

Petzina, D., Stolper, W. F., & Hudson, M. (1981). The Origin of the European Coal and Steel Community: Economic Forces and Political Interests. *Journal of Institutional and Theoretical Economics*, 137, 450-468.

Proedrou, F. (2018). Russian Energy Policy and Structural Power in Europe. *Europe-Asia Studies, 70*(1), 75-89. doi:10.1080/09668136.2017.1419169

Renner, S. (2009). *The Energy Community of Southeast Europe: A neo-functionalist project of regional integration.* European Integration Online Papers (EIoP).

Renner, S., & Trauner, F. (2009). Creeping EU Membership in South-east Europe: The Dynamics of EU Rule Transfer to the Western Balkans. *Journal of European Integration, 31*(4), 449-465. Doi:10.1080/07036330902919988

Republic of Serbia. (2012). *O Potvrđivanju Sporazuma Između Vlade Republike Srbije I Vlade Ruske Federacije O Isporukama Prirodnog Gasa Iz Ruske Federacije U Republiku Srbiju.* http://www.parlament.gov.rs/upload/archive/files/lat/pdf/predlozi_zakona/623-13Lat.pdf

Reuters. (2009, September 28). *Croatia puts PEOP pipeline on hold, seeks new ways.* https://www.reuters.com/article/croatia-peop-idAFLS28073720090928

Secrieru, S. (2019, July 2). *Russia in the Western Balkans.* European Union Institute for Security Studies. https://www.iss.europa.eu/content/russia-western-balkans

Siddi, M. (2018). The Role of Power in EU-Russia Energy Relations: The Interplay between Markets and Geopolitics. *Europe-Asia Studies, 70*(10), 1552-1571. doi:10.1080/09668136.2018.1536925

Stronski, P., & Himes, A. (2019, February 6). *Russia's Game in the Balkans.* Carnegie Endowment for International Peace. https://carnegieendowment.org/2019/02/06/russia-s-game-in-balkans-pub-78235

TASS. (2017, January 27). *Turkey grants all permits required for work on Turkish Stream.* https://tass.com/economy/927665

The Economist Intelligence Unit. (2018, February 28). *Europe Energy.* https://www.eiu.com/industry/article/1846475768/coal-use-falls-again-in-europe-in-2017/2018-02-28

Tholens, S. (2014). An EU–South Mediterranean Energy Community: The Right Policy for the Right Region? *The International Spectator, 49*(2), 34-49. doi:10.1080/03932729.2014.906806

Trans Adriatic Pipeline. (n.d.). *EU status.* https://www.tap-ag.com/the-pipeline/the-big-picture/the-eu-status

Tynkkynen, V.-P. (2016). Energy as Power – Gazprom, Gas Infrastructure, and Geo-governmentality in Putin's Russia. *Slavic Review, 75*(2), 374-395. doi:10.5612/slavicreview.75.2.374

Vatansever, A. (2005). *Russian Involvement in Eastern Europe's Petroleum Industry: The Case of Bulgaria.* GMB.

Vlcek, T., & Jirusek, M. (2019). *Russian Oil Enterprises in Europe: Investments and Regional Influence.* Palgrave
Warsaw Institute. (2019, May 29). *Conference Report – Western Balkans: Infrastructure, Energy, Geopolitics.* https://warsawinstitute.org/western-balkans-infrastructure-energy-geopolitical-perspective/
World Bank. (2018). *Western Balkans: Directions for the Energy Sector.* World Bank.
Yesevi, Ç. G. (2018). Considering Pipeline Politics in Eurasia: South Stream, Turk Stream and TANAP. *Bilge Strateji, 10*(18), 11-52. https://dergipark.org.tr/download/article-file/677970
Youngs, R. (2011). *Energy Security: Europe's New Foreign Policy Challenge*. Routledge.

CHAPTER THREE

ENERGY POLITICS OF THE US AND CHINA IN LATIN AMERICA

GÖKHAN KATITAŞ*

Introduction

Along with the discovery of steam engines and the industrial revolution, the energy issue has been the main dimension in the political and economic development of states and empires. Because of that, energy has been playing a significant role in international politics for centuries, just like the determination of borders of states, the occurrence of regional and global struggles and the fulfilling of socio-economic and political needs. The main energy resources states compete for are oil, natural gas and coal, and those materials shape international relations in various ways, as mentioned above.

Until the 2010s, the MENA region was the main area for petrol reserves thanks to Saudi Arabia, which is the richest oil reserve country in the world; however, explorations in Venezuela changed this status and increased the importance of the Latin America region in terms of energy resources, and that led to geopolitical struggles in the area. Apart from Venezuela, other regional countries also have considerable energy reserves, such as Brazil in terms of oil, natural gas and renewable energy, and Argentina and Colombia in terms of oil and natural gas resources.

Following the Cold War era, the hegemonic status of the US, which was obtained by defeating the Soviet Union and resulted in the triumph of liberal capitalist thought, has been questioned due to false justifications of the invasion of Iraq after 9/11, the 2008 global financial crisis and the increasing visibility of Putin-led Russia. Other than these conditions, the

* Gökhan Katıtaş, Research Assistant, Department of International Relations, Faculty of Political Sciencess, Marmara University. E-mail: gokhan.katitas@marmara.edu.tr.

rising power of China is another factor in questioning the US' status in international politics. Since the millennium, by actualizing enormous economic development and widening its influence area, China has become a leading power in the world, and that has brought about challenges with the US, especially in economic terms.

The US and China have the biggest economies in the world, and that requires great energy reserves to meet the sustainability needs of their production chains. For this reason, these two countries try to exist in almost all countries that have rich energy resources. Latin American countries are some of those countries. While historically Latin America has been described as being backed by the US since the declaration of the Monroe Doctrine in 1826, China has been becoming more visible in the region year by year since the mid-2000s and strives to be influential there via commercial and political agreements.

These two superpowers of the international arena need energy resources to maintain their economic capabilities, and because of that, they pursue active geoeconomic policies in Latin America. Countries like Argentina, Brazil, Colombia and Venezuela have great energy sources; therefore, the US and China seek to create durable relations with those states by using their economic, political and military tools. Due to this fact, the value of the region has also increased politically as well as in an economic sense.

Consequently, this chapter will try to examine the bilateral relations of the US and China with regional countries within the perspective of geoeconomics and aims to consider the factors behind the energy relations of the actors, which are ideological convergence, economic dependency and strategic partnership. Within this scope, after the energy map of the region is introduced, the US and China's Latin American policies are examined, and later their bilateral relations with energy-rich countries, namely Argentina, Brazil, Colombia and Venezuela, are scrutinized. In the final part, the mutual relationships of the mentioned actors are assessed through the lens of political economy.

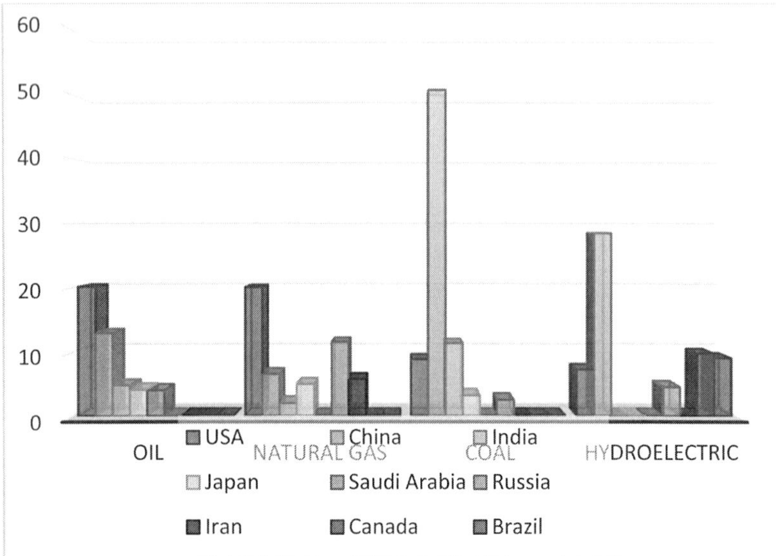

Figure 1: Energy Consumption Percentages of the Leading Countries in 2017. Source: BP, 2018b. Edited by author.

Energy Map of Latin America

As a consequence of prospecting activities in the area, it has been proved that Latin America has rich energy resources, and this makes the region attractive for leading countries of international politics. According to the obtained data, Latin America contains 19.5% of world oil reserves and 4.2% of world natural gas reserves, along with considerable levels of wind power and hydropower (BP, 2018a).

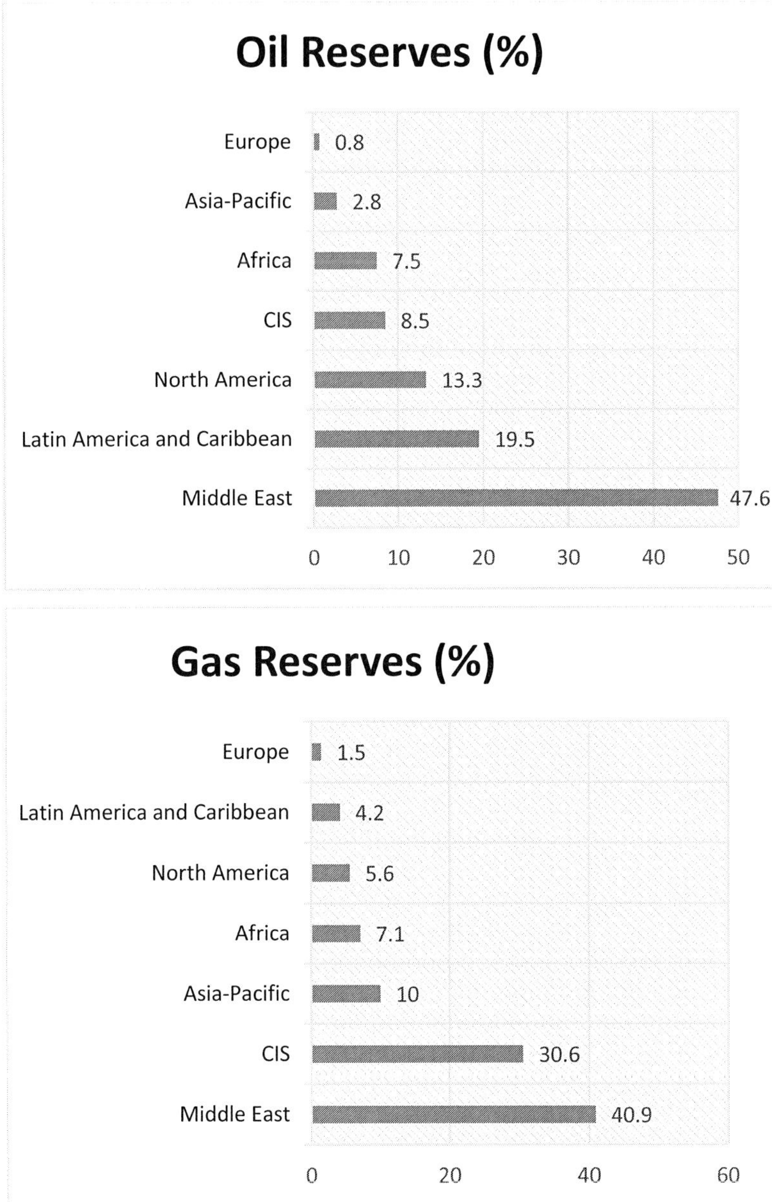

Figure 2: Global Oil and Gas Reserves. Source: BP, 2018b. Edited by author.

Latin American lands contain various energy types in their soils. This geography includes 329 billion barrels of oil, 7,331 bcm of gas, 15 gigatonnes of coal and 2,886 trillion watts/hour of hydroelectric capacity. Some countries in the region differ from others because of having rich energy sources, such as Venezuela in oil and gas reserves, Brazil in coal reserves and hydropower and Colombia in coal reserves.

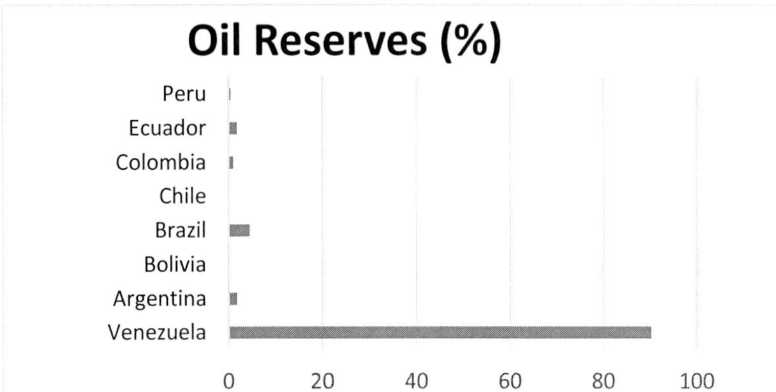

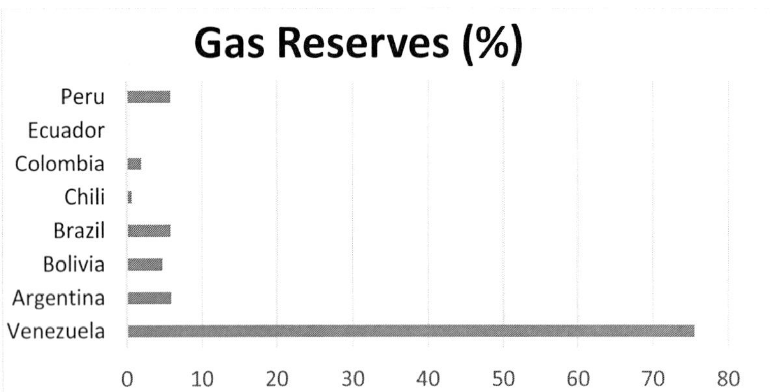

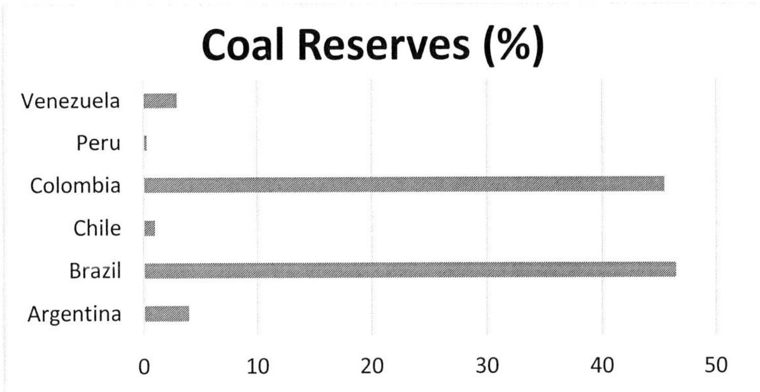

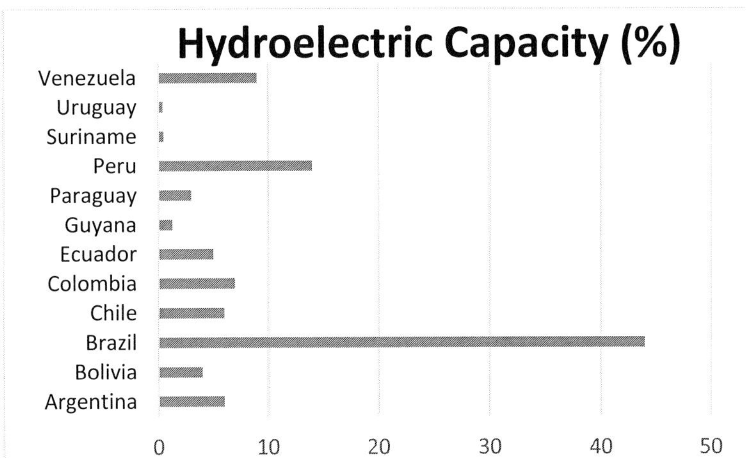

Figure 3: Energy Reserves of Latin America By Country. Source: BP, 2018b. Edited by author.

Latin American Policies of the USA

By virtue of the Great Wars that occurred in the early 20th century, Britain, which was the hegemonic power in the 18th century, began to lose its status to the US, which had adopted liberal capitalist norms, day by day. During the Cold War, the US had undertaken the leadership of the Western world against the Soviet Union and transformed itself into the only hegemonic power of the international arena by defeating the Soviets in that confrontation in the early 1990s. However, starting from the mid-

1990s, the US could not handle the critical cases that emerged in international politics, such as through its inability to prevent the Bosnian and Rwandan massacres, losing its credibility in the war on terror in Iraq and Afghanistan because of the proven fake justifications, and its role in triggering the 2008 global financial crisis. Moreover, in this process, other actors like China and Russia increased their power and visibility in the international arena that damaged the US-led international order, especially in the Eastern part of the world.

By dint of the reasons mentioned above, the supremacy of the US began to be questioned in the international arena, including in Latin America. Latin American countries started to obtain their sovereignties in the early 19th century, and this created critical national security and economic issues for the US, which was following isolationist policies at that time. As a result of discussions in the US Senate, in 1823, the Monroe Doctrine was declared and pronounced that Latin America was within its own geographic territory. Along with this doctrine, the US gave an ultimatum to European colonial powers about not intervening in Latin America in return for its own non-involvement in European issues (Monroe Doctrine, 1823). Thus, the US incorporated South America and the Caribbean into its own political-economic system and extended its sphere of influence to the whole continent of America. In consequence of this initiative, the US had great supremacy in the area. However, since the last decade, leftist politicians have taken charge of governments in regional states. In the early years of the 21st century, due to war on terror issues in Iraq and Afghanistan, US foreign policy focused on the Middle East in the George W. Bush era, tried to solve economic problems which occurred because of the global financial crisis in Barack Obama's first term, then the Arab crisis started in 2010, which dominated US foreign policies in Obama's second term. Therefore, Latin America kept a back seat in US policies. During these periods, on the one hand, Russia and China were increasing their international abilities at a global level, and on the other, anti-capitalist politicians were coming into power at a regional level, besides Cuba and Venezuela, like in Argentina and Brazil. Nevertheless, the US did not neglect Latin America completely. In the Bush era, in the country's national security document, the Western hemisphere was characterized as a frontline for US national security, and at this point, Latin America was labelled as an area that had to be supported by way of political and economic development (The White House, 2006). By defining the region like that, Latin America was specified as a tampon area for US security. In Obama's terms, the US, without preconditions, adopted a normalization process with countries that are on the opposite side to the US ideologically, notably Neo-Bolivarian states like Cuba and Venezuela. This policy was called the Obama Doctrine. Later, during the Trump administration, the US withdrew from the Obama Doctrine and began to pursue abstractivist and exclusionist policies towards Neo-Bolivarian countries.

US policies towards Latin America can be categorized into three areas, which are trade, governance and security (De La Fuente, 2017). From a commercial perspective, the US has great trade volumes with Latin American countries. While bilateral trade relations with Argentina, Brazil, Chile and Peru have been developed, commercial ties with Colombia have also progressed in recent years. The second area is governance. Democratic values and liberal capitalist norms have been integrated via trade relations and soft power tools, and USAID is the main institution in this manner. Through USAID, the country has been implementing aid and investment programmes and imposing a Western-based rule of law, governance methods and democratic values. Thus, the US is trying to widen its own values to the region at first, then to the whole world. The third category is security. Any possible chaos and instability would affect the US' national security, and for this reason, there is great significance to Latin America protecting itself from terrorist attacks, ideological confrontations, drug trafficking and political-economic weaknesses.

Due to these various dimensions, Latin America plays a critical role in US foreign policy. The US needs collaboration to overcome certain issues like climate change, health problems, cybersecurity, drug trafficking, the war on terror and food security. Apart from these issues, Latin America's geography, which is seen as part of the Western hemisphere from the US perspective, is crucial to prevent the incursion of any other great international power into the regional arena, like China and Russia. These two countries have increased their capacity and visibility in the region economically and politically, and this disturbs US officials. Another dimension that raises the importance of Latin America for the US is the energy reserves of those lands. One of the leading countries in energy consumption, the US requires these sources in order to sustain its economic production, meet social needs, pursue energy diversity and avert non-regional actors from obtaining this wealth of energy. In general US policy, the state aims to use its own resources as little as possible, and this is why they pursue aggressive or strategic policies in energy-rich lands, such as in the Middle East, Africa and Latin America: to generate resources for itself.

Latin American Policies of China

Chinese foreign policy is based on three principles, which are guaranteeing its own sovereignty, non-attendance of alliances and blocs, and non-intervention in other states' internal issues (Katıtaş, 2018a). Following the end of the Cold War, China adopted new concepts in its foreign policies: security, development, civilization and harmony in a new world. These shape China's relations on neighbourhood diplomacy that advocates a multi-dimensional and multi-polar world endowed with the harmony of societies and countries, instead of building a Western-type alliance and forming blocs. Along with its hyper-growing economy, China has a desire to spread its economic power into the whole world; this is called the Chinese Dream. According to this goal, China seeks to actualize national development by relying on a coherent society, to place a regional security mechanism within the framework of peaceful development, and to reform towards factors of production based on Chinese-type free-market principles.

China has become the second-biggest economy in the world through state-based initiatives, and in this process, the energy consumption of the state has increased enormously. Since 1990, the rise in the energy consumption of China has been approximately 356%, and the main resources used by the country are coal, oil, hydro and gas. Nearly 70% of this usage is realized in the industrial sector. It is expected that in 2040, China's energy consumption will have increased by 41% compared to 2016; as a result of this situation, its dependence level on foreign resources will rise from 63% to 72% for oil and from 34% to 72% for natural gas.

Because of its energy dependency, China aims to create links with source countries to meet its own energy needs, and Latin American states are some of these source countries for China. China-Latin America relations started in the 16th century within the scope of Pacific trade, and during the 18th and 19th centuries, Chinese people began to reside in the area as part of the slave and worker trade. Official relations between China and countries in Latin America began in the 1960s. China's first diplomatic relation in the region was actualized with Cuba, and these diplomatic ties increased after China gained membership of the United Nations in 1971. Following the end of the Cold War, thanks to its commercial ties, the interactions of China in the area increased, and these interactions widened with the adoption of the *Going Out Policy* in the 2000s. Thus, as part of its multilateral diplomacy, China's ties with regional states strengthened. The fact that most leading countries' governments in the area such as Brazil and Argentina come from a left-oriented political perspective facilitated China's entry into the region becomes understandable.

	Level		Rate (%)		Changing Amount		Changing Rate (%)		Changing Rate By Year (%)	
Term	2016	2040	2016	2040	1990-2016	2016-2040	1990-2016	2016-2040	1990-2016	2016-2040
Total	3,053	4,319	100	100	2,370	1,266	347	41	5.9	1.5
Oil (Mb/d)	12	16	19	17	10	3	436	28	6.7	1
Gas (Bcf/d)	20	60	6	13	19	39	>1,000	194	>10	8.3
Coal (Gigatonne)	1,888	1,552	62	36	1,360	-336	258	-18	5	-0.8
Nuclear	48	325	2	8	48	277	>1000	574	>10	8.3
Hydro	263	348	9	8	234	85	817	32	8.9	1.2
Renewable Resources	88	784	3	18	88	696	>1,000	789	>%10	9.5

Table 1: China's Energy Consumption Level. Source: BP, 2018a. Edited by author.

The main tools used by China on the ground are state-funded credit, its membership of the UN Security Council (UNSC), cheap products and international organizations led by its own people. Thanks to leftist politicians coming into power in various countries, the 2008 global financial crisis, demand for a new world order by rising powers, and the lack of interest of Western financial institutions towards Latin American states regarding credit and investments created an appropriate environment for China in the region. In order to expand its sphere of influence and to exist in new areas both for selling its products and for meeting its energy needs, China began to provide credit to Latin American states without preconditions like accountability and transparency. Moreover, this credit could be paid back as raw materials like oil and food. This kind of credit attracted regional actors, and bilateral relations with China started to increase. The convergence of relations between these actors relies on different interests for each one. From the perspective of China, besides obtaining energy and food sources, the country has taken the opportunity to invest in the area via Chinese investors, using its own raw materials and workers, and, following this, the country obtained a chance to affect local policies in those states by enhancing Chinese visibility. From Latin American countries' point of view, especially states ruled by leftist governments, apart from gaining suitable credit, they could utter their own demands via China's UNSC membership and could sell goods to new markets through China's global network. Thus, China could have a chance to be a leading country in the global political arena versus the US-led international order. Consequently, the country has been producing and implementing new projects and establishing new international institutions such as the Asia Infrastructure Investment Bank, the Belt and Road Project, the New Development Bank and so on.

Energy Politics of the USA in Latin America

The US is one of the leading countries for energy consumption in the world. According to the data, it takes first place in both oil and gas consumption with a 20% share of total consumption. Also, the US is the third-ranked country in the consumption of coal after China and India with 8.9% and fourth-ranked in hydroelectric usage with 7.3% behind China, Canada and Brazil, respectively.

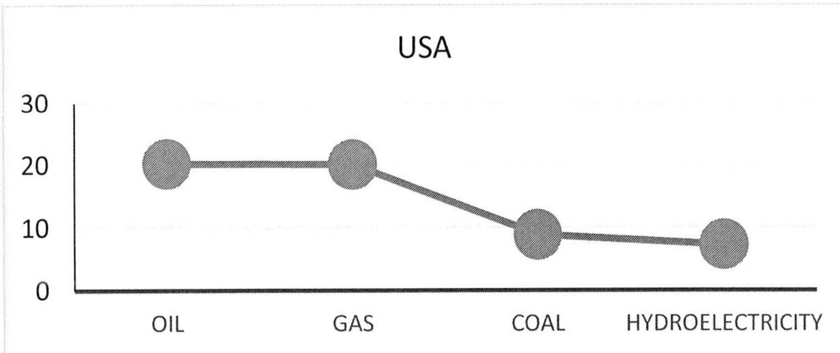

Figure 4. Global Share of Energy Consumption Rates of the USA. Source: BP, 2018b. Edited by author.

In order to provide sustainability for its own industrial, social and political supremacy in the world economy, the US aims to actualize resource diversity and has defined Latin America as one of its most important sources in this sense. In this section, the US' bilateral relations with regional countries, namely Argentina, Brazil, Colombia and Venezuela, are examined within the context of energy politics.

Argentina

After the Peso Crisis in 2001, Argentina remained incapable of investing in the energy sector due to unfavourable economic conditions. Following this negative period, in 2007, Peronist politician Cristina Fernandez de Kirshner came to power and pursued low-level bilateral relations with the US. In 2015, Mauricio Macri defeated Nestor Kirshner, who is the husband of the former president, in the presidential elections, and he preferred to follow close relations with the US administration. Thus, ties between the two countries grew and relations gained positive momentum.

Along with the new government in Argentina after eight years, the two countries started to pursue convergence politics. In March 2016, these two states signed the Trade and Investment Framework Agreement. This aims to deepen cooperation and increase trade volume. Also, the agreement led to a rise in mutual foreign direct investment (FDI). In 2017, the amount of FDI by the US in Argentina increased by 6% compared to the previous year and reached $14.9 billion. Also, Argentinian companies' FDI in the US increased by 16.8% in the same period and reached $1 billion (Census Bureau, n.d.-a). Moreover, in the last ten years, the US has provided nearly $50 billion in foreign aid (USAID, n.d.). Apart from that, in

September 2017, NASA and the Argentine Space Agency (CONAE) started to collaborate in space science, and in December of the same year, the two countries executed a drug trafficking operation named IceBridge through the use of military submarines.

US energy politics in Argentina became proactive with the change in political power in 2015. President Macri opened sectors to foreign investors, and this policy enured the energy sector, which had functioned only limitedly since the 2001 Peso Crisis, too. As a result of this policy, US-based investors began to be integrated into the energy area, and most US FDI, nearly 40%, was directed to this sector. On the one hand, Chevron signed an agreement worth $1.24 billion within the framework of search operations with Argentina's national oil company YPF; on the other hand, the same US company started feasibility studies in the Vaca Muerta region, seen as one of the biggest shale gas areas in the world, in order to invest nearly $15 billion (U.S. Department of Commerce, International Trade Administration, 2017). Also, Dow Chemical agreed to an investment worth $500 million with Shell Argentina, and ExxonMobil initiated a pilot project in the amount of $250 million for source search operations in the country (Foda, 2016).

Brazil

Along with having the most developed economy in the region, Brazil contains great energy resources. In terms of its oil and gas resources, the country takes second place in the area; Brazil also has 46% of coal reserves and 44% of hydroelectricity production in the ground that makes it the largest state of Latin America in this manner. According to BP data, Brazil outputs 2,734 million barrels in a day, which is equal to 3% of daily oil production in the world. The state also produced 27.5 bcm of gas, 3 million tonnes of coal and 590.9 terawatts/hour of electricity, which is equal to 2.3% of the whole world's output and puts it in eighth place.

Historically, the US was the first country that recognized Brazil's independence and was sensitive to the state's internal politics. However, this high sensitivity led to the divergence of Brazil from the US. Between 1962-1969, the US played a critical role in the military coup, and after this process, Brazil preferred to join the Third World and the Non-Aligned Movement during the Cold War. Following the Cold War, during the Cardoso administration, Brazil pursued close relations with the US, however the case changed again with the start of Lula da Silva's presidential term. In conjunction with structures like the Rising Powers phenomenon and BRICS, Lula, who was the leader of the left-oriented

Workers' Party, followed policies that challenged the US-led international order and created close ties with China, Cuba, Iran and Venezuela. After Lula's presidential term, Dilma Rousseff, who was the first female president in Brazilian history, took charge in the country and pursued similar policies to her predecessor. Incidentally, Rousseff was the head of the national petroleum company, Petrobras, between the years of 2003 and 2010. In 2012, there was a recession in Brazil, and therefore Rousseff got into a jam. After that, in 2013, she downgraded relations with the US that led to the CIA's secret operation against her, with wiretapping and accessing her e-mails and messages. In 2014, Rousseff was investigated by the police department because of Petrobras being involved in suspicious financial transactions worth nearly $22 billion, and she was suspended from the presidency in 2016. Michel Temer replaced her.

Thanks to the instability of the state administration and the change in Petrobras' management, the US benefited from these conditions and improved its relations with Brazil. The two countries had had a volume of trade of approximately $650 billion for the previous decade, and this rose after Rousseff's suspension; in 2017, it rose by more than 33% compared to the previous year. In the same period, the FDI amount of the US in Brazil in 2016 reached $64.4 billion, 24% of all the FDI in the country (U.S. Department of State, 2018a). Besides these developments, the two states established various platforms such as the Conference on Digital Economy, the Defense Industry Dialogue, and the Political-Military Dialogue. This rapprochement echoed in the energy sector, too.

Following the corruption scandal, President Temer removed a legal condition in November 2016 that stated that Petrobras must have a 30% share of any activities in the sector and cut content requirements in half to reduce FDI costs in the petroleum sector in February 2017. These policies created an energy-politics opportunity for the US in Brazil, and leading US-based energy companies, namely Anadarko, Chevron, ExxonMobil and Central Resource, turned into crucial players in the region (Agência Nacional do Petróleo, Gás Natural e Biocombustíveis do Brasil, 2016). Companies like Halliburton and Baker Hughes signed framework agreements with Petrobras worth multimillions of dollars that focus on energy technologies. Moreover, the US-based company AES executes electricity generation, commercialization and distribution in Brazil (AES Brazil, 2017). Additionally, General Electricity conducts activities in the electricity sector in Brazil. The company, which holds 30% of the industry, operates with gas and outputs it as electricity. In this direction, General Electricity won a tender for a 1500W natural gas power plant for an amount of $900 million in 2016. As part of this project, ExxonMobil would provide a liquid gas supplement to the area (Scott, 2017).

Colombia

Colombia is one of the most significant states when it comes to energy resources and mineral deposits in Latin America. The country's production in oil is 851,000 barrels a day that makes it the third-largest in the region; its natural gas production is 10.1 bcm; its coal production is 61.4 million tonnes, which puts it in eighth place in the world; and it generates 75 terawatts/hour of electricity (BP, 2018b).

Historically, the US and Colombia have had close relations. In the 1920s, Colombia's president Marco Fidel Suarez developed a policy named the "Follow the North Star Doctrine" and maintained convergence ties with the US. According to this doctrine, the US was symbolized as the North Star and Colombia as dependant on the US in terms of its geographical, democratic and commercial destiny (Countrystudies, n.d.). In the historical process, Colombia has experienced some deviations, but most of its presidents have adopted that doctrine. From a political perspective, Colombia supported the US in the Korean War by sending its military to support UN forces and in the Suez Canal Crisis. Thus, the country became the only Latin American state that is a member of NATO. In the 1980s, these two countries got closer, thanks to Nicaragua's claims on Colombia's islands with the support of Cuba. Following that, Colombia actualized military assistance for US-led UN forces in Israel-Egypt conflicts (Countrystudies, n.d.). From a geopolitical point of view, Colombia has a critical role for the US with its strategic location, as the country borders both Panama and the Caribbean and has access to the Atlantic and Pacific Oceans.

From an economic viewpoint, the USA is the largest trade partner of Colombia. The two countries initiated a trade development dialogue in 2006, and it transformed into an agreement that foresaw comprehensive free trade between the partners by 2012 (Census Bureau, n.d.-b). Commercial data between the US and Colombia affirms this progress and that their trade volume exceeded $300 billion in the last decade. The main products imported by the US are minerals, fuel and precious metals worth nearly $9 billion each year. Besides that, US-based investors have great enterprises in Colombia, and the FDI from US financiers in the country surpasses $7 billion. The main area invested in by these financiers is mining (U.S. Department of State, 2018b). This FDI constitutes one-fourth of all the FDI in the state. The main US-based companies that execute activities on the ground are ExxonMobil, Chevron and ConocoPhilips.

Chevron is the largest gas producer in Colombia and has a great storage capacity and distribution network.

Venezuela

Venezuela is a crucial country in terms of its energy resources, which include 303 billion barrels in oil reserves, which is equal to 17.9% of world petroleum, and 6.4 tcm in gas reserves, which corresponds to 3.3% of world gas reserves. The state also contains 731 million tonnes of coal reserves and 117 terawatts/hour power generation capacity in its own lands. However, because of the economic and political problems occurring in the last decade, the country's energy output capacity fell. Venezuela is dependent on its oil exports, which make up 95% of all its export income, and for this reason, all other sectors were negatively affected by this situation, and its inflation rate exceeded 1,000,000%.

US-Venezuela relations are affected by a complex set of circumstances. During the presidential term of Hugo Chavez, the country adopted Chavism and began to pursue socialist policies. In this perspective, Venezuela is against the existing international order and specifies the US as an imperialist country. On the other hand, the US has declared Venezuela as an authoritarian state (U.S. Department of State, 2018c). After the death of Hugo Chavez, Nicolas Maduro replaced him as president and adopted the same line as his predecessor. However, Maduro's presidential term has been turbulent due to the economic crisis, and this turned into a political crisis as well. His administration has been taking hard stances against US-led social protests, and this has created the pretext for the US to apply an embargo on the country. Moreover, the Trump administration supported opposition groups and declared their leader, Juan Guaido, as the new president of Venezuela by claiming Maduro's presidency to be invalid. Thus, the US has aimed to intervene in the internal politics of Venezuela and manage its large energy reserves.

In Chavez's presidential period, Venezuela adopted the nationalization of investment and projects in the country. Within this framework, the national petroleum company PdVSA was nationalized and tools and facilities belonging to ExxonMobil and ConocoPhilips were seized by the government. Thereupon, the US categorized Venezuela as similar to Cuba and pursued rigid policies towards the state. With the occurrence of instability in the country, the US sought to benefit from the circumstances and aimed to access Venezuela's energy sector. Within this process, US-based companies started to obtain Venezuelan resources. While Chevron became a partner in various projects, PdVSA signed a deal with the Y&V

Group, which is a sub-company of Baker Hughes, for drilling in 2016 (Crooks, 2016a). The Horizontal Drillers Company took a role in 191 drilling tasks in the Orinoco Belt, which is the largest energy ground in the country (Crooks, 2016b). Also, the FDI amount of the US in Venezuela surpassed $6.6 billion.

Energy Politics of China in Latin America

China has the second-largest economy in the world and is aiming to diversify its energy resources in order to maintain its economic growth and meet its social needs. As a result, Latin America is one of China's targets in its energy diversification policies, and the country is trying to create ties with regional energy-rich countries. In this part of the chapter, China's bilateral relations with energy-rich states in the region will be examined.

Argentina

Official relations between China and Argentina started in 1972, and these relations transformed into a comprehensive strategic partnership in 2014. From the perspective of Argentina, China offers many advantages for its own economic development. By getting closer with China, the country has a chance to develop its infrastructure, build nuclear reactors, and sell agricultural and energy goods to the international market; by doing so, the aim is to improve its economic capacity. Within this context, Argentina seeks to benefit from Chinese credit, investments and cheap labour; more than 25,000 Chinese workers live in Argentina and actualize nearly $6 billion in economic activities. From China's viewpoint, Argentina is an important state due to military and economic reasons. Along with the agreement signed in 2014, China has a space station in Patagonia, and thus it will have an advantage in supervising air traffic in the US' backyard for 50 years (Katıtaş, 2018b). Chinese FDI in Argentina exceeds $10 billion and executes various projects, from the construction of nuclear reactors to oil facilities. China also actualizes railway construction in the country and has provided approximately $12 billion in credit to Argentina (Paranga, 2014). Moreover, Argentina is the second-largest trade partner of China in the region; the main goods imported from China to Argentina are soybean and petroleum, which make up 96% of the total. The oil production of Argentina is approximately 626,000 barrels, and it exports 50% of this to China, which makes China the largest importer of Argentinian petroleum. Additionally, China has provided nearly $10 billion in foreign aid to Argentina since the 2008 financial crisis.

From an energy politics point of view, apart from oil, China plays active roles in Argentine wind power, hydropower and nuclear energy. The China Development Bank (CDB) became a Chinese entrepreneur in Argentina for the construction of wind turbines. In this direction, in 2012, the Beijing Civil Engineering Group signed an agreement with Generadora Eolica Argentina del Sur Safora worth $3.5 billion (Nielsen, 2012). Within the scope of this project, 1300W Chinese turbines were deployed over 45,000 hectares in the south of the country. Thanks to this project, Chinese turbine companies started to be integrated into the renewable energy market in Latin America. In the following years, other Chinese firms, namely XEMC Wind Power Company and HydroChina, took responsibility for the implementation of other projects. For example, while XECM signed an agreement with Groupo Isoluc Corsa for the construction and deployment of 100MW turbines (Nielsen, 2012), HydroChina agreed with the city of La Rioja to increase the wind power capacity of the Arauca wind farm from 50MW to 104MW (Yang, 2015). Chinese firms are active members of the hydroelectricity sector in the state as well. The Gecouba Group, with the support of $4.7 billion in CDB credit, won a tender from Electroingenieria for two dam-building projects in Patagonia (Shanghai Daily, 2014). Besides wind and hydropower, China is also effective in the nuclear sector in Argentina. After five years of negotiations, at the G-20 Antalya Summit in 2015, the two countries agreed on the construction of the fourth and fifth nuclear power stations in Argentina via the Argentine Heavy-WaterReactor Nuclear Station Commercial Contract and the Pressurized-Water-Reactor Nuclear Station Framework Contract. The cost of these two projects to Argentina is nearly $6 billion, and 85% of that amount was fulfilled by Chinese banks at a 6.5% per annum rate (Anderlini & Rathbone, 2015).

Brazil

China-Brazil relations can be traced back to the 19th century due to insufficient human capital in Brazil; following this issue, Chinese tea producers migrated to Latin America. Thereupon, relations between the two countries started officially, and they signed a treaty of amity in 1882. However, modern relations between the two states began in 1972 after the accession of China to UN membership. With Brazil's recognition of the One China policy, their ties increased enormously (Katıtaş, 2018b). These two countries initiated common programmes on science and spacc, then started to apply the China-Brazil Satellite Programme. In the aftermath of the Cold War, they declared a strategic partnership in 1993, and this transformed into a comprehensive strategic partnership in 2004. In the event of this kind of close relation, similar thoughts on international order become effective. The US-led, Western type of international order puts developing countries in a tight position and aims to prevent their rise; the WTO Doha Round is an important example of this. In time, China and Brazil got closer and have sought to build an alternative international order and governance mechanisms to the Western type. Having significant economic growth led to a desire for having more of a voice in international politics, and they started to establish new platforms and institutions with other rising powers, like BASIC, BRICS, the New Development Bank and the BRICS Development Bank.

Brazil is an important oil, gas and electricity producer, and this makes it critical for China in order for it to meet its own energy needs. Following the 2008 crisis, Chinese foreign aid to Brazil surpassed $20 billion. By 2009, China had become the largest trade partner of the country, constructing various railways and roads and improving its energy facilities. In 2008, China's share in Brazil petroleum was 11%, but this reached 42% in 2016. Moreover, in October 2013, China obtained the right to use oil in the territory of Rio for fifty years. In February 2014, Chinese State Grid firms won a tender from Eltrobras to construct the Belo Monte Dam electricity transmission line and transformation stations. This project became China's first overseas ultra-high-voltage electricity transmission technology project (U.S. Department of Commerce, International Trade Administration, 2017).

Colombia

Diplomatic relations between Colombia and China began in the 1980s, and these had improved by 2010. In this period, the two countries established the Chamber of Colombia-China Investment and Commerce at the Shanghai Expo. Colombia has signed various treaties with China to support and incentivize international trade. Thus, many Chinese firms started to exist in the country and vice versa – Colombia-based companies like Invest Pacific, Invest in Bogota, Probarranquilla, and ACI Medellin started to operate in China. As a result of these developments, relations between the two states deepened sociologically and economically. However, these close relations regressed due to the change in president from Juan Calderon to Ivan Duque, who has close ties with the US. As a result, Duque decided to withdraw from UNASUR and preferred to join OAS (Ojeda Vega & Delgado, 2018). This was a great signal of the transformation in Colombia's foreign policy.

The geographical location of Colombia attracts many countries, and China is one of them. The country is seen as the door to South America, and this promises great economic potential for the region. Besides that, because it has large energy resources and is located in the US' backyard, Colombia has strategic value for China. Within this scope, China attaches importance to Colombia and has improved its bilateral economic relations with the country to the extent that China has become the second-largest trade partner of Colombia, with a 19% import rate, after the US (Ojeda, 2017).

From an energy politics perspective, the main imported good to China from Colombia is oil. China's oil import rate from the country has increased consistently since 2008. In 2008, the rate of exported Colombian oil was 3.4%, which increased to 20% in 2014, but this then fell to 11% in 2018. The amounts of these rates in dollars were $333 million in 2008, $5.2 billion in 2014, and $878 million in 2018. The main factors in this fluctuation are the regression in relations under the Duque administration and the reduction in oil barrel prices.

Venezuela

Venezuela was the first strategic development partner of China in the region, and then, in time, it became a strategic partner. In this process, they mutually declared themselves to be brother countries. Sociologically and economically, the two countries have a common future and common development understanding. During the presidency of Hugo Chavez, Venezuela was criticized by the Western world and isolated from many activities. This situation created an opportunity for China to widen its sphere of influence, close to the US' backyard. The isolated Venezuelan government and ambitious China got closer in time and collaborated in several areas. Venezuela had a chance to develop via oil credits provided by China and found a way to defend itself by getting ammunition from China after the US embargos. Thereupon, apart from the energy trade, the ammunition trade between the two countries increased. After the US' prevention of sales of Israel's F-36 jetfighter to Venezuela in 2005, the country gravitated towards China for the purchasing of ammunition and military training. In 2011, its purchasing level was worth $1 billion, and this is increasing year by year (Nixon, 2016).

From an economic point of view, after the 2008 crisis and the isolation politics of the US, China supplied more than $65 billion in oil credits to Venezuela and became an executive in projects and the main buyer of the nation's petroleum. By getting closer with China, Venezuela and the

Maduro government have sought to reduce their dependence on the US, have a great power's support in the international arena, and find a purchaser for its own oil. For China, Venezuela means diversification in energy provision and access to the Latin American market. In this direction, China has provided more than $140 billion in credit to the region, and $65 billion of this has been given to Venezuela. Thanks to Chinese credit, Venezuela has constructed oil facilities, from drilling to distribution, with Chinese entrepreneurs. Also, the two countries' energy institutions, PdVSA and CNPC, signed a shareholding treaty whereby CNPC would have a 40% share in the Orinoco Belt for 25 years (Katıtaş, 2018b).

Venezuela had been producing 2 million barrels of oil before 2014, but the embargos applied by the US, decreasing oil barrel prices and the economic and political instability in the country led to reductions in its oil production. In parallel with that, the country could not pay back credit instalments to China; Venezuela has $4 billion overdue and is in $23 billion of general debt to China. China's oil imports from Venezuela increased over time, but these decreased after 2015; specifically, it was 59,000 barrels a day in 2005; 500,000 barrels in 2015, and 330,000 barrels in 2017. China benefits from Venezuela's trouble and provides it new credits in order to deepen Venezuela's dependency.

Partner	Argentina				Brazil				Colombia				Venezuela			
Origin Country	USA		China		USA		China		USA		China		USA		China	
Amount* Year	%	$	%	$	%	$	%	$	%	$	%	$	%	$	%	$
2008	31	1,780	11	730	24	6,620	42	6,920	71	10,600	17	76	95	41,700	98	5,390
2009	37	1,410	9	315	23	4,120	42	8,780	68	9,070	45	435	96	24,800	95	3,420
2010	31	1,190	12	696	27	5,650	57	17,800	70	12,000	68	1,410	97	29,100	94	5,430
2011	24	1,040	8	460	28	7,650	57	25,200	73	16,100	68	1,380	98	38,100	98	9,710
2012	23	948	13	642	26	7,140	40	20,300	71	15,900	77	2,610	97	33,700	99	12,400
2013	13	577	14	743	19	4,680	45	20,600	72	13,800	86	4,400	96	28,400	100	11,400
2014	24	1,070	4	144	18	4,970	40	16,500	65	9,530	92	5,310	96	27,200	99	10,100
2015	9	406	4	179	13	3,370	32	11,300	54	5,640	80	1,830	96	13,900	99	6,050
2016	7	295	9	393	8	2,210	31	12,000	53	5,600	78	895	95	9,870	98	4,830
2017	6	310	11	497	16	3,870	38	18,600	55	6,020	81	1,630	95	11,000	98	6,280

Table 2: Energy Trade Volumes of the USA and China in Latin America. Note: *%: per cent of total imports in that year; $: value of energy trade in million dollars. Source: The Observatory of Economic Complexity, n.d.-a-e. Edited by author.

Assessments

China and the US are the leading energy consumption states in the world and also have the two biggest economies in the international arena. Because of that, they are seeking to diversify their energy needs, and Latin America is one of the spheres of influence that both countries are competing for.

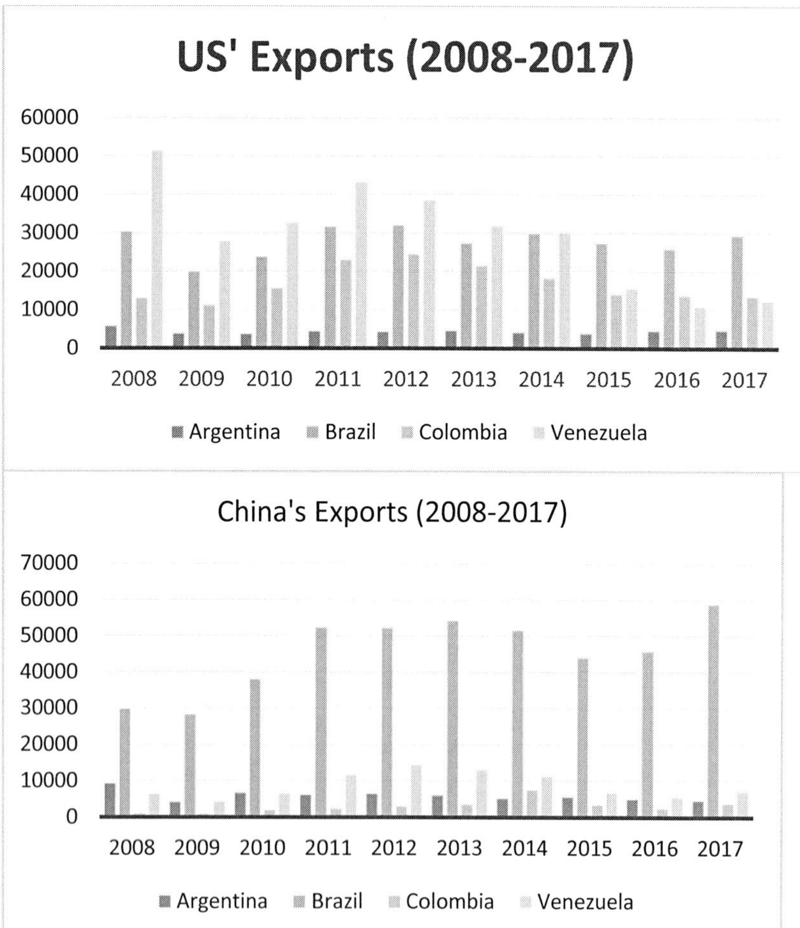

Figure 5. Exports of the US and China to Latin America ($ Million). Source: The Observatory of Economic Complexity, n.d.-a-e. Edited by author.

In the Argentinian case, the ideologies of the respective governments are effective for trade and energy politics. While China was more active in the country under Kirshner's regime, with the presidency of Macri, trade and energy cooperation with the US increased. This can be seen in the trade amounts and agreements signed during their presidential terms.

In the Brazilian case, on the one hand, China is a strategic partner of the country, but on the other, the US is as important a trade partner for the state as China. During the presidential terms of Lula and Rousseff, China's energy imports from Brazil were quite constant, but with the political instability in the state, this situation was shaken. However, this did not lead to a negative acceleration in relations and trade volume. According to the data, it can be said that China is more active and effective in the country's trade, especially in the energy sector, compared to the US. The main factor behind this situation is the ideological stance of the presidents of the country; China and Brazil are comprehensive strategic partners and against the US-led world order, which is not open to a free market.

In the Colombian case, while the US has great ties with the country historically, China has standard relations. These circumstances are reflected in their trade and energy import volumes. The US is the largest economic partner of Colombia, but China has a low level of trade volumes relative to its capacity. Moreover, with the presidency of Macri, who is a pro-US politician, China's energy imports from the state reduced to one-third compared to the previous presidential term. Like in the Argentinian case, the ideological stance of the country is important to importing energy from Colombia.

In the Venezuelan case, the state is seen as pure energy ore by both countries, and nearly 95% of both countries' imports from Venezuela consist of oil. No matter what ideological stance a country may have, Venezuela exports its oil to all actors. However, the US' embargo and support for the political opposition in the country in order to remove the Maduro government negatively affected trade and energy volumes as much as the reduction in oil barrel prices.

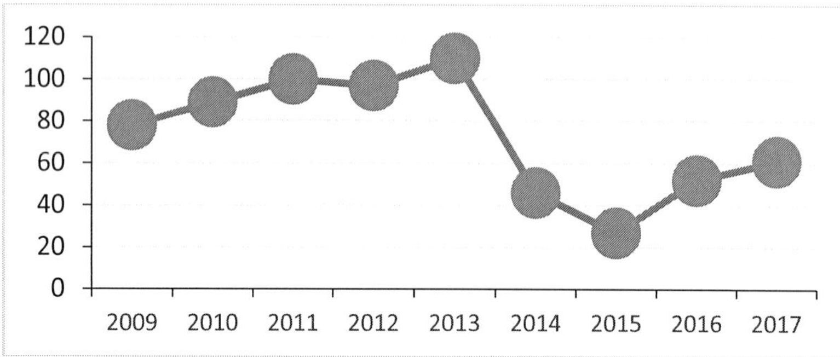

Figure 6. Barrel Price of Crude Oil ($).

Since 2008, China has benefited from the environment that has occurred due to the financial crisis and entered into the Latin American region with its easy credit. While the US is still effective on the ground, China is a decisive actor in the area, too, by creating dependency via its credit lines, investments and aid. Therefore, it can easily be said that China has become successful in diversifying its energy resources and in widening its international market network. In this kind of situation, ideological, economic and political ties play crucial roles. Both countries try to construct and strengthen their capacity in this sense across the region.

References

AES Brasil (2017). *Energy Generation.* http://www.aesbrasil.com.br/en/business-areas/conteudo/energy-generation

Agência Nacional do Petróleo, Gás Natural e Biocombustíveis do Brasil (2016). *Anuário estatístico brasileiro do petróleo, gás natural e biocombustíveis.*

Al, A., & Katıtaş, G. (2018). Geoeconomic Struggles in the Eastern Mediterranean Region. In H. Arıdemir (Ed.), *Turkish Republic of Northern Cyprus*. Flesh.

Alvaro, M. (2011, July 2). *Ecuador, China in big crude-oil deal.* Market Watch. http://www.marketwatch.com/story/ecuador-china-in-big-crude-oil-deal-2011-07-02

Anderlini, J., & Rathbone, J. (2015, November 17). *China to build two nuclear plants in Argentina in $15bn deal.* Financial Times. http://www.ft.com/intl/cms/s/0/2d264e78-8cf9-11e5-a549-b89a1dfede9b.html#axzz3yBoIScAg

BP. (2018a). *BP Energy Outlook 2018 Edition.* https://www.bp.com/content/dam/bp/en/corporate/pdf/energy-economics/energy-outlook/bp-energy-outlook-2018.pdf

BP. (2018b). *BP Statistical Review of World Energy.* https://www.bp.com/content/dam/bp/en/corporate/pdf/energy-economics/statistical-review/bp-stats-review-2018-full-report.pdf

Census Bureau (n.d.-a). *Trade in Goods with Argentina.* https://www.census.gov/foreign-trade/balance/c3570.html

Census Bureau (n.d.-b). *Trade in Goods with Brazil.* https://www.census.gov/foreign-trade/balance/c3510.html

Census Bureau (n.d.-c). *Trade in Goods with Colombia.* https://www.census.gov/foreign-trade/balance/c3010.html

Census Bureau (n.d.-d). *Trade in Goods with Venezuela.* https://www.census.gov/foreign-trade/balance/c3070.html

ChinaPower. (n.d.). *Does China dominate global investment?* https://chinapower.csis.org/china-foreign-direct-investment/

Countrystudies. (n.d.). *Colombia – Relations with the United States.* http://countrystudies.us/colombia/98.htm

Crooks, N. (2016a, September 27). *Venezuela's Y&V Teams Up With Baker Hughes to Tap Orinoco Belt*. Bloomberg. https://www.bloomberg.com/news/articles/2016-09-27/venezuela-s-y-v-teams-up-with-baker-hughes-to-tap-orinoco-belt

Crooks, N. (2016b, September 21). *PDVSA Readies One of 'World's Largest' Oil Drilling Projects*. Bloomberg. https://www.bloomberg.com/news/articles/2016-09-21/pdvsa-says-it-starts-one-of-world-s-largest-drilling-projects

De La Fuente, E. (2017). *U.S. Foreign Policy Towards Latin America Under Trump: Beyond Business as Usual*. d+i developing ideas, Llorente & Cuenca.

Foda, Q. (2016, July 28). *Next hot spot for shale drilling? Argentina*. CNN. http://money.cnn.com/2016/07/28/investing/argentina-shale-drilling/

Garzon, P. (2016, November 30). *Ecuador must re-invent its relationship with China*. China Dialogue. https://www.chinadialogue.net/blog/9446-Ecuador-must-re-invent-its-relationship-with-China/en

Katıtaş, G. (2018a). Avrasya'da Rusya'nın ve Çin'in Bölgeselcilik Anlayışı. In A. Al & M. Balcı (Eds.), *Uluslararası İlişkiler ve Yeni Dünya Düzeni*. Marmara Üniversitesi Yayınevi.

Katitaş, G. (2018b). *Bir Dış Politika Nüfuz Aracı Olarak Uluslararası Örgütler ve Dış Yardımların Politik Ekonomisi: ABD, Çin ve Rusya Üçgeni* [Unpublished Master's thesis]. Marmara Üniversitesi.

Krauss, C., & Bradsher, K. (2015, July 26). *China's global ambitions, cash and strings attached*. New York Times. https://www.nytimes.com/2015/07/26/business/international/chinas-global-ambitions-with-loans-and-strings-attached.html

Nielsen, S. (2012). *Argentina plans biggest wind project with $3 billion China loan*. Renewable Energy World. https://www.renewableenergyworld.com/wind-power/argentina-plans-biggest-wind-project-with-3-billion-china-loan/#gref

Nixon, A. (2016, August 24). *China's Growing Arms Sales to Latin America*. The Diplomat. https://thediplomat.com/2016/08/chinas-growing-arms-sales-to-latin-america/

Ojeda, G. (2017, June 5). *Commercial Relations between Colombia and China*. Farmfolio. https://farmfolio.net/articles/commercial-relations-colombia-china/

Ojeda Vega, G., & Delgado, G. P. (2018, July 18). *Meet Colombia's New President*. Fair Observer. https://www.fairobserver.com/region/latin_america/ivan-duque-colombia-presidency-politics-economics-farc-latin-america-news-18721/

Paranga, N. (2014, December 13). *Argentine railway project funded by China starts construction*. China Topix. http://www.chinatopix.com/articles/27660/20141213/argentine-railway-project-funded-china-starts-construction.htm

Scott, A. (2017). *Exclusive: General Electric wins $900 million Brazil power plant, grid contract*. Reuters. https://www.reuters.com/article/cbusiness-us-generalelectric-brazil-excl-idCAKCN12R0ME

Shanghai Daily. (2014, July 20). *China, Argentina agree US$7.5b loan*. http://www.shanghaidaily.com/national/China-Argentina-agree-US75b-loan/shdaily.shtml

Teng, C. (2017). The Pattern of China's Financial Initiative in Latin America: A Comparative Study. *Issues & Studies: A Social Science Quarterly on China, Taiwan, and East Asian Affairs*, *53*(1), 1740003.

The Observatory of Economic Complexity. (n.d.-a). *Argentina*. https://atlas.media.mit.edu/en/visualize/tree_map/hs92/export/arg/all/show/2016/

The Observatory of Economic Complexity (n.d.-b). *Brazil*. https://atlas.media.mit.edu/en/visualize/tree_map/hs92/export/bra/all/show/2016/

The Observatory of Economic Complexity (n.d.-c). *Colombia.* https://atlas.media.mit.edu/en/visualize/tree_map/hs92/export/col/all/show/2016/
The Observatory of Economic Complexity (n.d.-d). *Ecuador.* https://atlas.media.mit.edu/en/visualize/tree_map/hs92/export/ecu/all/show/2016/
The Observatory of Economic Complexity (n.d.-e). *Venezuela.* https://atlas.media.mit.edu/en/visualize/tree_map/hs92/export/ven/all/show/2016/
The White House. (2006). *The National Security Strategy.* https://georgewbush-whitehouse.archives.gov/nsc/nss/2006/
U.S. Department of Commerce, International Trade Administration. (2017). *Argentina – Shale Gas and Shale Oil Development Technologies*. Last published: February 22, 2017.
U.S. Department of State. (2018a). *US Relations With Brazil.* https://www.state.gov/r/pa/ei/bgn/35640.htm
U.S. Department of State. (2018b). *US Relations With Colombia.* https://www.state.gov/r/pa/ei/bgn/35754.htm
U.S. Department of State. (2018c). *US Relations With Venezuela.* https://www.state.gov/r/pa/ei/bgn/35766.htm
USAID (n.d.-a). *U.S. Foreign Aid by Country – Argentina.* https://explorer.usaid.gov/cd/ARG
USAID (n.d.-b). *U.S. Foreign Aid by Country – Brazil.* https://explorer.usaid.gov/cd/BRA
World Integrated Trade Solutions (n.d.). *Product Group.* https://wits.worldbank.org/CountryProfile/en/Country/
Yang, Y. (2015, February 2). *China to take on wind energy project in Argentina*. China Daily. http://usa.chinadaily.com.cn/world/2015-02/02/content_19461764.htm

CHAPTER FOUR

THE MIDDLE EAST'S ENERGY POLICIES

FERİT BELDER*

Introduction

Since its modern invention in the late 19th century in accordance with the perception of British imperial geopolitics, the term 'Middle East'[1] has usually been associated with energy sources thanks to the first industrial oil extraction in Persia, or today's Iran. It would not be wrong to argue that the international political history of the Middle East is also the history of the struggles over controlling, distributing or re-distributing energy resources between imperialist powers, nationalist forces and global energy companies. And all other conflicts or disagreements taking place in the region have often touched upon the energy issue in one way or another, directly or indirectly, because of the historically exclusive significance of the production and the transfer of oil.

The entangled history of post-colonialism, nation-building processes and nationalism in the region has enabled the observation of the embeddedness of energy politics in various crises like the military coup against the nationalist government of Mohammad Mosaddegh in Iran in the 1950s. The oil embargo launched by the oil-exporting Arab countries in 1973 as a reaction to the Western support of Israel in the Yom Kippur War is another case illustrating the inseparable linkage between energy and international politics. Even in the post-Cold War era, this embeddedness has

---

* Dr. Ferit Belder, Faculty of Political Science, Marmara University. E mail: ferit.belder@marmara.edu.tr.

[1] Middle East is not only a geographical term but also a political and social construction. The meaning and content of the term Middle East has changed over time and is still changing. It is currently popular to use the term MENA (Middle East and North Africa) instead of the Middle East. There are advantages and disadvantages to both terms but none are directly relevant to the content of this paper. So, the terms Middle East and MENA are used interchangeably here.

continued to be noticed, as in the case of the US-led coalition attacks on Iraq to force Saddam Hussein to withdraw from oil-rich Kuwait, which he invaded in 1990.

Alongside oil resources, natural gas is a comparatively new invention for the political economy of the region. However, it is also not free from disagreements, struggles or new sorts of alliances causing regional or global confrontations. As recently seen in disputes regarding the drilling rights for the East Mediterranean natural gas reserves, it has a strong potential to become a new cause for conflicts in the region alongside oil. The conflict-prone character of the current Middle East politics and the legacy of the foreign interventions (which still continue) have contributed to prioritizing the energy security of the region as it provides a significant proportion of the world's energy needs.

In this context, this chapter aims to understand the significance of the Middle East in global energy politics. In so doing, it firstly illustrates the current energy map of the Middle East in a comparative perspective to position the region in the world energy supply by sharing certain rates and numbers according to the data released by OPEC (Organization of Petroleum Exporting Countries) and the World Energy Council. Secondly, it discusses how important the Middle East's energy sources are for the global powers (both traditional and emerging) by emphasizing different types of dependencies on the Middle East's energy production as well as emerging disputes regarding energy sources. The main aim of this part is to show the significance of the energy security issue in the perceptions of the international actors in the Middle East. Lastly, it analyzes the current challenges to the energy security of the Middle East by dividing those into two categories: old and new threats. Conventional threats to energy security often derived from inter-state rivalries or conflicts throughout the 20th century. In contrast, new threats, including the activities of non-state actors, require a consideration of terrorist organizations' long-term strategies in the region as opposed to their traditional 'hit and run' tactics. This has become possible mainly since the outbreak of the Arab Uprisings because numerous small groups (and surely some are terror groups) have exploited the emerging situation of anarchy and claimed de facto sovereignty in various countries. In this part of the chapter, the issue of non-state actors' involvement in the energy politics of the region is analyzed using the case of ISIS[2] with respect to the dimension of foreign interventions. It is claimed that the great powers' prioritizing of energy security and repeated

[2] The Islamic State of Iraq and Syria (ISIS) is also known as the Islamic State of Iraq and the Levant (ISIL). In 2014, the group changed its name to the 'Islamic State'.

interventions in the region in this direction do not necessarily provide stability but, on the contrary, destabilize energy production and its safe transfer to the market. This chapter also asserts that the complexity of the relations regarding energy production or the distribution of resources are themselves creating crucial challenges to energy security because of the variety of participants that have different and sometimes controversial interests.

The Middle East in the Global Energy Production System

Middle Eastern countries, like their counterparts in the developed world, are trying to raise the relative ratio of renewable energy sources like solar, wind, or hydroelectricity in their overall annual energy production and consumption (Anderson, 2019; El Katiri, 2014; Margit, 2019; Nematollahi et al., 2016). However, the major reasons behind the increasing investments in renewable energy production vary on the country level. For instance, resource-rich countries want to lower the amount of oil and natural gas consumption in their domestic market to increase the share of oil export income, whereas it is resource-poor countries' desire to decrease their dependencies on expensive fuel imports (Anderson, 2019). However, despite this regional leap forward in recent years, the heavy dependency on fossil fuels is still the key variable to understand and analyze regional inter-state relations, global powers' positions towards the region as well as intra-state struggles with the participation of non-state groups that are controlling energy sources.

The Middle East has excessive fossil energy resources, which are the main ground for the functioning of the most developed countries' economies (Cirdei, 2017, p. 88). This position necessarily pushes Middle Eastern countries to play significant roles in global and regional energy politics. The interlinkage between the regional interactions and their global consequences makes the security and sustainability of the Middle East's energy more vulnerable and sensitive for both traditional and emerging powers. The comparative significance of hydrocarbons and the technical and economic limitations of replacing them with alternatives will likely keep the Middle East's energy at the centre of global energy politics in the long term (Cirdei, 2017, p. 90). In this regard, global crude exports are expected to rise in the future because of the steady rise of oil demands and the fall of supply in many regions (especially Asia-Pacific).

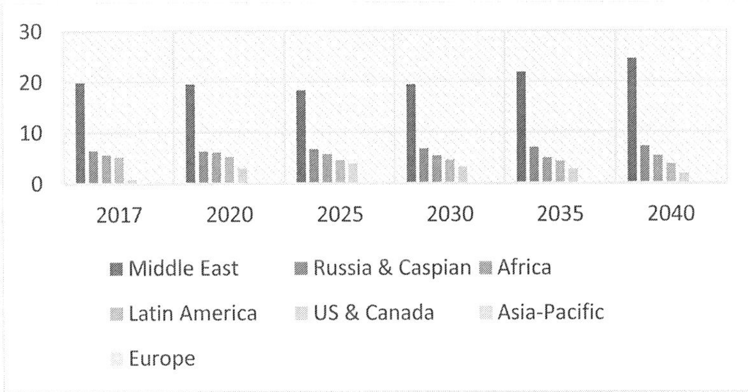

Figure 1: Global Crude Oil Exports by Origin (2017-2040). Source: OPEC, n.d.

The graph above (Figure 1) illustrates the long-term oil supplies from various regions and the outstanding position of the Middle East in sustainable oil exportation. According to OPEC statistics, it is predicted that crude oil exports from the Middle East will increase by 5% between 2017 and 2040, while Russian and Caspian, African and Latin American supplies are expected to be stable (which will make them unable to meet rising demands). The European and Asia-Pacific regions are unlikely to contribute to crude oil exportation in the long term despite their increasing oil dependencies.

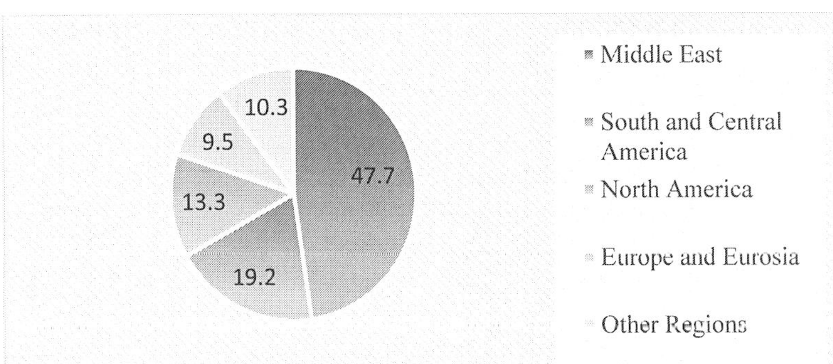

Figure 2. Proved Oil Reserves by Region (%). Source: BP Statistical Review of World Energy, 2017

In terms of proved oil reserves in the world as of 2016 (Figure 2), the Middle East region has the biggest portion (47,7%) compared to the recoverable reserves in South and Central America (19,2%), North America (13,3%), Europe and Eurasia (9,5%) and other regions (10,3%) according to the World Energy Council's statistics. Five out of the top ten oil-producing countries are also from the MENA region. In country-based results, Saudi Arabia and other Gulf countries, including Iran, have the biggest reserves. The proportion that North African countries have is comparatively lower than the Gulf reserves. In North Africa, Libya has the biggest recoverable oil reserves with 6.3 billion tonnes (Figure 3).

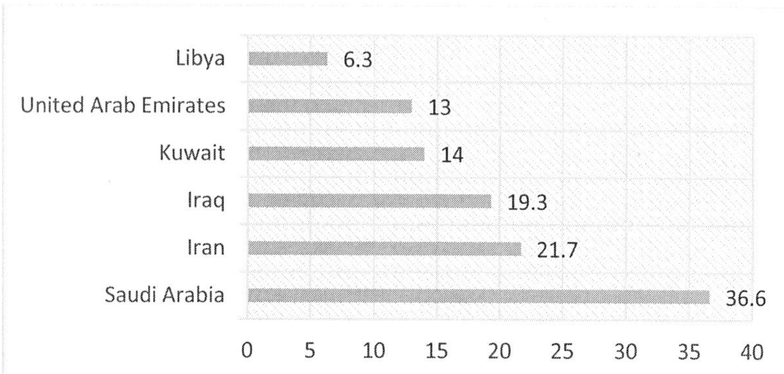

Figure 3. Recoverable Oil Reserves by Country (billion tonnes). Source: World Energy Council, n.d.

In addition to oil resources, natural gas has also been drawing attention thanks to the region's large gas reserves as well as its promising position as an alternative to the dominance of Russian natural gas for its immediate neighbours and, importantly, for the European market. From this side, unlike the global-scale impact of oil, the natural gas issue remains regional to a large extent. In terms of recoverable natural gas reserves, the MENA region is again at the top, with almost half of the total reserves in the world (Figure 4).

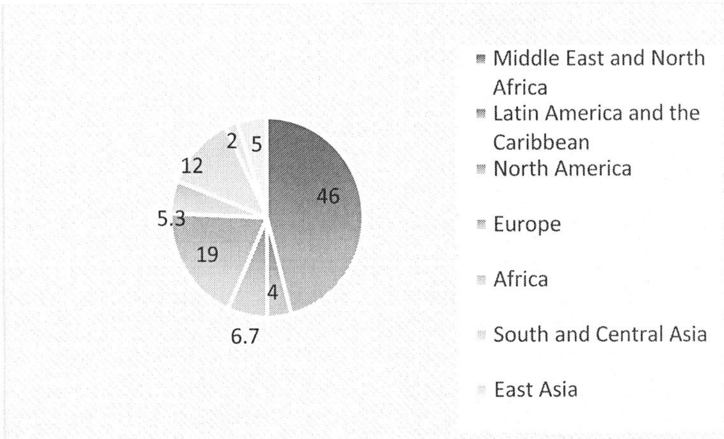

Figure 4. Recoverable Gas Reserves by Region. Source: World Energy Council, n.d.

In the country-based results, Iran can be noticed as having the biggest natural gas reserves in the Middle East. On a global scale, Iran is the third-biggest gas-producing country after the United States and Russia. Alongside Iran, other Gulf states like Qatar, Saudi Arabia and the United Arab Emirates also have remarkable reserves (Figure 5).

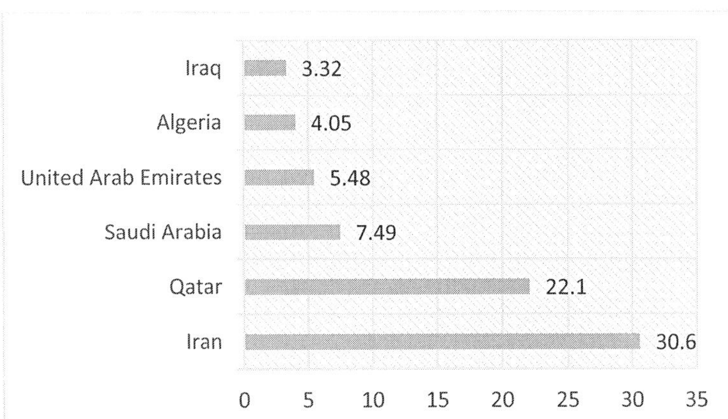

Figure 5. Recoverable Gas Reserves by Country (thousand Mtoe). Source: World Energy Council, n.d.

The enormous significance of the Middle Eastern energy reserves for the world energy market has historically drawn attention to the intra-national and inter-national developments taking place in the region as these are closely related to the security and stability of the world's energy supplies. In fact, the energy trade and the developed world's dependency on Middle Eastern energy are not unidirectional; energy-rich Middle Eastern countries have also rested on oil and natural gas incomes to fuel their economic and military developments as well as to get domestic consent because many of the energy-exporting countries are looking for non-democratic sources of accountability. For this reason, energy export revenues are the main source for the sustainability of state authorities or its adopted ideology. From the side of the global powers, the production and circulation of oil and natural gas have been the key engine for the global scale production process. These sorts of mutual dependencies continued throughout the 20th century, despite short-term deviations, and this is still the case for the 21st century with the participation of new actors in the energy politics of the Middle East.

Assessing Middle East Energy Politics through the Lenses of the Traditional and Emerging Powers

It is widely recognized that the core issues, centre of gravity, determinant dynamics as well as leading actors in international politics have been undergoing momentous transformations, which are repeatedly discussed in the emerging powers or non-West IR literature. Even though there is high stress on the term 'change', the strategic role of the Middle East regarding energy politics has barely been challenged in the last decades. In contrast, emerging powers like China and India have also begun to seek influence in the Middle East energy world in various ways and at various levels, most notably with the formulation of new ideological (anti-imperialist and South-South partnership discourse) and economic instruments in addition to those of the traditional powers like the US, Russia and the EU (and Great Britain), which have already been playing substantial roles in the creation and redesigning of Middle Eastern politics for some time. The continuity of this high focus on the region went hand in hand with the transformation of the great powers' interests in the region from a geostrategic orientation to a more energy-oriented perspective.

As a traditional great power, the US has a long history of Middle East engagement after the decrease of British hegemony, which is generally remembered with the 1956 Suez Crisis, and the subsequent Eisenhower Doctrine, which officially declared the significance of the US security and ideological interests in the region. Since then, Middle East politics has largely been shaped by the US-Soviet rivalry, and for a long time, energy security has been one of the key determinants behind the US' Middle East policies. Although recent surveys indicate that the US dependency on foreign petroleum (crude oil and petroleum products) is decreasing to its lowest percentage since the 1950s (EIA, 2018), it is still far from an independent energy position because it consumes more than it produces (O'Sullivan, 2018). In fact, the US' dependency on the Middle East's oil has historically never surpassed 15%, but keeping prices under control is one of the key motives which is itself the driving force that prioritizes the Middle East region for the US (Luft & Korin, 2013).

The link between the American perspective on energy security and price stability in the global market is still very close, and any disruption to oil supplies from the Middle East countries undermines US efforts to make itself more independent (Goldwyn et al., 2014). As Johnson correctly says, the rise of American oil production cannot be a total game-changer as long as Saudi Arabia holds the key to decide on crude oil prices (Johnson, 2018). This sort of indirect dependency pushes the US to continue its geopolitical interests in the region as it has for decades. In search of maintaining hegemonic stability in the region, the US has been challenged many times with various means. Recently, the increasing role of non-state actors in controlling the energy trade in the local market since the violent outbreak of civil wars in the region after the Arab Uprisings (and in Iraq after the 2003 US invasion) has become one of the major matters of concern for the US regarding the economic and security dimensions of its energy politics in the Middle East.

As one of the two Cold War superpowers, the role of the Middle East in Russia's energy outlook is no less important than in that of the US, as can be seen in the growing cooperation between Russia and energy-rich countries of MENA in two forms: (1) intensifying relations with oil- and gas-producing countries and (2) a nuclear energy partnership on the basis of a producer-consumer relationship (Nakhle, 2018). In the example of the Iranian nuclear issue, Russian President Vladimir Putin carried out nuclear cooperation with Iran as opposed to the international sanctions adopted against Iran (Li & Ma, 2010). Russia wants to make the energy industry one of the basic elements of its foreign policy strategy, and in this vein, it is searching for further cooperation with Gulf countries to make market conditions more predictable for itself (Barmin, 2017). One reason for this search is that the Russian economy is quite dependent on oil and gas exportation, which makes Russia more sensitive to any sort of instabilities in price fluctuations. Both oil and natural gas are important parts of this concern. In terms of oil, Russia is attempting to maintain close relations with OPEC countries, specifically with Saudi Arabia, to keep oil prices at around $60/barrel (Lund, 2019, p. 35).

Unlike oil and its global context, natural gas prices are less likely to be manipulated as they are often assessed at a regional level. Even though Russia adopts a similar cooperation strategy with energy-rich countries, it also faces some sorts of challenges, especially from alternative gas exportation sources and routes in the region, as can be seen in the example of Iran, which is willing to compete with Russia in the European market (Lund, 2019). In addition to market competition and price stabilization, Russian energy companies have also been engaging with MENA countries like Libya. The planning and investment activities of Gazprom, Lukoil Oversea, Tatneft, etc. in the country illustrates this trend (Kozhanov, 2018, pp. 11, 18). Russia's energy-led economy requires taking regional developments into account and being part of the complex play of energy relations in the region.

The EU is also an important part of Middle East energy politics, mostly as an energy market. Because of its lack of self-sufficiency, the EU is looking to find or maintain safe energy sources and routes to provide for its consumption needs. In fact, the Middle East is in a secondary position for the EU's energy imports compared to the decisive role of Russia. According to a report released by the European Commission, the main supplier for the EU's crude oil, natural gas and solid fossil fuels (accounting for more than 90% of the energy imports into the EU) is Russia. So, the priority of the EU regarding the Middle East's energy is largely related to its potential role of diversifying resources. The EU's strict dependence on Russian energy is seen as a potential threat to the energy supply of the EU in the event of any political crisis (European Commission, 2019b) because eleven members of the EU import more than 75% of their total imports of natural gas from Russia and four import more than 75% of their total oil imports from Russia (European Commission, 2019a). In this regard, the EU's search for alternative energy sources pushes it to act to stabilize the MENA region as a potential energy source rather than forcefully design it.

In recent years, the increasing tensions between Turkey, Greece and Cyprus over drilling rights in the East Mediterranean are also affecting the EU's regional energy outlook. As member states of the EU, both Greece and Cyprus put pressure on EU bodies to act against Turkey and stop its drilling activities in the territorial waters of Cyprus. Because the Turkish Republic of Northern Cyprus is not recognized by the EU, Turkey's efforts in the region in the name of supporting Northern Cyprus are interpreted as a violation of the rights of the Republic of Cyprus (or, from the Turkish side, the Greek Administration of Southern Cyprus). The complex picture of historical disagreements and energy competition is expected to lead to a direct political confrontation between Turkey and the EU, even if it is unlikely to be military (Mortimer, 2019). The potential consequences of this confrontation are twofold. First of all, as an energy-poor country, Turkey has geopolitical importance as the main bridge for the transfer of energy to Europe. Any kind of attempt towards the diversification of energy sources requires Turkey as the most appropriate place for a pipeline, but a lack of cooperation between Turkey and the EU would undermine the EU's search for alternative energy sources. Secondly, the natural gas resource issue in the East Mediterranean has other Middle Eastern participants like Egypt and Israel, whose further actions or initiatives could easily escalate disputes between parties and turn them into a regional gridlock. Therefore, the Mediterranean gas issue creates both opportunities and challenges for the EU, but, in any case, it keeps it within the sphere of Middle East energy politics.

Alongside the traditional great powers discussed above, some of the emerging powers like China and India have also started to expand their influences to the Middle East. Despite the fact that China holds the largest oil reserves in its region, it cannot satisfy its increasing domestic demand. For this reason, it is not surprising to see that Middle East energy is also seen as the lifeblood of the Chinese Belt and Road Initiative (Cohen, 2019). For instance, between 2002 and 2014, China's oil imports tripled from $2 billion to $6.2 billion per year (Daojiong & Meidan, 2015, p. 2). China also imports half of its oil from the MENA region, more specifically from Saudi Arabia and Iran. China's position as a growing energy investor in the Middle East prioritizes the protection of these energy investments (and trade investments) in its approach to the region. In the long term, China's oil demand is expected to evolve, and by 2035, the proportion of China's oil imports from the Middle East is likely to double (Kamel, 2018, p. 79), and the oil pipeline that was built by China through Myanmar will require large and reliable suppliers like Saudi Arabia (Daojiong & Meidan, 2015, p. 7). However, developing cooperation with countries that are bitter rivals in the region like Saudi Arabia and Iran will be a challenge for China's long-term regional strategies (Wormuth, 2019, p. 5).

Similarly to China, India is also one of the world's biggest energy consumers with its more than one billion population. 60% of its crude oil imports come from the Middle East, and this large dependency is unlikely to decrease when the huge energy needs of the country are taken into account (Khan, 2013). India's increasing energy needs for military and civilian purposes has made the Middle East even more crucial for national development. Another East Asian nation focusing on the Middle East's energy is Japan. It imports 80% of its crude oil from Middle East countries, and after the Fukushima nuclear accident, its energy import rates increased across various types, like natural gas, coal, crude and fuel oil (Klug, 2019). Energy is also the major driver for South Korean engagement with the Middle East as it is one of the biggest consumers of Gulf oil and natural gas. However, one has to emphasize that these increasing desires for cooperation are not unidirectional. In addition to the growing interests of the East Asian countries towards the Middle East's energy, the Middle Eastern actors, especially the Gulf countries, are also looking for increasing technological cooperation with East Asian countries like China, Japan and South Korea in order to diversify their energy sources (nuclear and renewable energy) (IIAS, 2018). That is to say, the recognition of mutual gains by East Asian countries and their Middle Eastern counterparts has evoked the intensification of an energy-centric relationship.

Middle East Energy Security and Current Challenges

The complex picture of these energy relations in the Middle East shows that any kind of instability deriving from domestic or regional developments can easily affect the global supply and demand chain and the security of the energy market. The consequences could be global or regional according to the intensity of the instability. The Middle East is still positioned at the centre of global energy production. This is mostly the case for oil. It is not only that a large proportion of oil reserves are located in the Middle East, but also that 80% of the world's spare oil capacity that can be brought to the market in the event of any disruption is also found in the region. And despite strong efforts to replace oil with alternative sources, it is still not clear how and to what extent these alternatives could meet the world's energy demands. For that reason, the security of the Middle East's energy (production, price and transfer) is the main concern shared by both the traditional great powers and emerging powers. The current challenges can be divided into two parts in accordance with the character of the threats. Conventional threats are mainly state-originated in the form of inter-state conflicts or the failure of the state mechanism, whereas new threats vary in the form of non-state actors like quasi-states or terrorist organizations.

Traditional Challenges to the Middle East's Energy Security

Almost all states that are dependent on the Middle East's oil and natural gas sources prioritize the stability of prices and appropriate transfer conditions. The securitization of the Middle Eastern energy supply in the historical process has yet to be ended. For oil transfers, the presence of the OPEC cartel and other risks deriving from terrorism or regional conflicts have long been considered as the major sources of potential cut-offs (Wilson, 2019, p. 118). The multitude of interests, actors and processes are also multiplying the sources of threats as well. Yetiv emphasizes five major threats against the Middle Eastern oil supplies that could cause disruptions. These are military threats, terrorism, the rise of extremism in Saudi Arabia, Saudi regional orientation and the oil weapon (Yetiv, 2010, pp. 390–394). In terms of natural gas supplies, it can be argued that the threats are the same because they are mainly threats against the sustainability of the energy supply. These traditional challenges are largely related to inter-state conflicts, so even today, disputes between countries are threatening the energy supply of the region. From this side, Iran and Saudi Arabia and their activities in international politics as well as in the Gulf region are seen as the key determinants of the Middle East energy supply.

In terms of military threats, Yetiv underlines three situations: (1) the shutting down of the Strait of Hormuz (by Iran), (2) conflicts between regional states, and (3) the use of weapons of mass destruction. The first is quite relevant for the security of energy transfers if one bears in mind that much of the world's oil is transferred through the 34-mile-wide Strait of Hormuz (Yetiv, 2010, p. 390). Being located on the northern part of the strait, Iran has a crucial role in securing/threatening the transmission of oil to the world market (Koolaee, 2011, p. 100). In fact, this threat will become a matter of fact if international actors, led by the US, impose sanctions against Iran over the nuclear proliferation issue. Iranian officials often threaten to close the Strait of Hormuz if sanctions targeting the transfer of Iranian oil to the world market are imposed (Shahla & Nasseri, 2019). It is true that US-led sanctions on Iran have been deterring the previous buyers of Iranian energy, but when it comes to the transport of oil that is bought from other countries, the Strait of Hormuz comes into question again. As seen in the Japanese, South Korean and Chinese examples, importing oil from other Middle Eastern countries also requires the use of the Strait of Hormuz for transport (Klug, 2019). For this reason, the relations between Iran and the international community led by the US are an important variable to assess the current and future challenges to the security of the energy supplies of the region, even if these are not directly produced and exported by Iran. That is to say, Iran's regional activism and willingness to use its geostrategic advantage as a foreign policy bargaining tool could be a source of major peril for the global oil trade.

The fear of inter-state conflicts that Yetiv stresses is also about the legacy of Saddam Hussein and is largely derived from his invasion of Kuwait in 1990. According to Yetiv, the unclear future of Iraq will eventually pose risks to the security of oil routes. It is also correct that Iraq currently poses a challenge to regional politics due to the instabilities and ambiguities in its domestic politics. At this point, another question about the consequences of repeated foreign interventions in the countries in the region appears. The strategic goal of stabilizing energy production and transfer has driven global actors to intervene in the region in various ways, and the global energy companies are implicit participants in shaping the content, context and borders of this goal. Although all these interventions aimed at securing the production and controlling the flow of oil to the world market, the consequences of such interventions created new sorts of threats to the energy sources.

One good example of this is the rise of the early form of ISIS as an Iraqi branch of al-Qaeda by exploiting the power vacuum that emerged after the US invasion of Iraq in 2003. And the emerging situation of anarchy that appeared after the transformation of massive protests into a civil war in Syria has also paved the way for the spread of ISIS' territorial gains. It also increased the popularity of the group in its competition with al-Qaeda for the leadership of the global jihadist movement. But ISIS was profoundly rooted in the organization of anti-US resistance in the fallen cities of Iraq after the occupation. So, the desired goals of the interventionists have barely been achieved in the case of Iraq, and often they even resulted in the opposite outcome to the one desired.

Regarding the traditional challenges deriving from inter-state conflicts, one must notice the evolving natural gas crisis in the East Mediterranean. As one of the hottest topics in the region, the East Mediterranean natural gas reserves issue has various actors in a complex web of relationships. As members of the EU, both Greece and Cyprus view the dispute as a violation of the EU's territorial waters and a confrontation between Turkey and the EU while also intensifying relations with Israel and Egypt on the natural gas reserves issue, which will eventually create a kind of regional alliance aiming to exclude Turkey. The involvement of regional states in this dispute and the pursuit of their own agendas will likely make the issue more complicated for the EU, whose primary motivation is to diversify and stabilize energy imports rather than actively engage in regional conflicts.

As one of the natural gas importers of the region, the Egyptian government is aiming to launch several gas projects in order to position itself as the regional hub for the international gas trade (The Conversation, 2019). Israel's main concern is being shaped in the context of the exportation of the abundance of its natural gas, and its immediate customers are regional states like Egypt. However, with the newly discovered natural gas reserves in the East Mediterranean, there are other projects which also include Israel and are expected to be launched. In the context of new groupings in the Mediterranean region, these projects also have major obstacles. For instance, the EAST-MED pipeline project, which aims to transfer natural gas to Europe while avoiding Turkish soil, is still far from being materialized because of the high expected costs as well as geographical and technological limitations. For the Mediterranean natural gas reserves, the drilling rights are not settled and the production and transfer strategies are not clarified. From this perspective, new natural gas reserves in the region may decrease the EU's dependency on Russia on the one hand but also open up new controversial dimensions which could destabilize the region by encouraging states to seek further groupings against each other.

According to Yetiv, another important risk for the Middle East energy supply is terrorism because terror groups often target energy sources and routes. They may hit oil reservoirs, hijack ships as well as challenge domestic authorities and the legitimacy of certain resource-rich regimes like Gulf monarchies (Yetiv, 2010, p. 393). For example, one of the core strategies of ISIS is to attack the oil and gas sectors to draw attention to itself, increase its influence and popularity and punish enemies (Tichý, 2019, p. 255). Compared to other regions of oil or natural gas production, the Middle East is more prone to be affected by terrorist attacks due to the current turmoil in the region.

Saudi Arabia, which is depicted as the central pillar of the Middle East's energy stability, is at the heart of the Middle East's energy security. Any kind of internal or external challenge to its pro-Western regime may also mean a challenge to the system that Saudi Arabia maintains. This is particularly correct for oil supplies. The last risk that Yetiv emphasizes is the use of oil in the foreign policies of countries to restrain others over certain issues. The 'oil weapon', as Yetiv describes the risk, is a challenge to energy supplies due to the West's high dependence on the Middle East's oil and the complexity of the regional conflicts (Yetiv, 2010, p. 394). A well-known example of this issue is the 1973 Arab oil embargo over Western support for Israel. However, one can predict that the choice of using such a measure effectively is not as likely compared to its first use in the 1970s when Western states were caught unprepared to take actions against an organized boycott. Moreover, today's complex energy interactions also decrease the potential of such a unified struggle to a large extent.

The Arab Uprisings and the Emergence of New Challenges to Middle East Energy Security

Almost all the challenges discussed so far are seen as explicit threats to the stability of the global oil market, despite some of them also being defensive measures taken by oil-rich countries against foreign pressure and domination. The common characteristic of these threats is their state-centric nature, that is to say, they are crises derived from inter-state conflicts or disagreements. Only terror groups and domestic challenges to regimes may be interpreted as being beyond this categorization. However, both challenges are depicted as threats against the energy production and transfer system organized by states. Unlike these state-centric threat perceptions, the events that are known as the ‘Arab Uprisings’ or the ‘Arab Spring’ enabled the emergence of new sorts of challenges like terror groups’ control over oil reserves. Following the massive protests and the fall of state authorities in major countries of the MENA region, non-state actors and terror groups began to seize oil-rich territories and control the black market, which also backed the terrorists’ actions in the region and elsewhere. For this reason, unlike the previous terror threats, contemporary terrorist organizations are not only ruining the established energy production and distribution system in the region but also creating their own territorial dominions as well as a particular system of governance that they forcefully imposed on the people living in the seized territories.

It has been almost nine years since the inception of the events, and the literature on the Arab Uprisings, containing several dimensions of the events at national and regional levels, is already well-developed. Despite all these dimensions touching upon the energy politics of the region in one way or another, the non-state actors dimension has exclusive importance and deserves much more attention in terms of challenging the state actor issue in the energy politics of the Middle East. It is clear that the most significant development regarding the increasing role of non-state actors is the establishment of the so-called Islamic State, or ISIS.

ISIS is a terror organization that not only uses conventional terror methods like launching attacks in many Western countries as al-Qaeda did before but also claims territorial sovereignty and offers a distinct form of social contract. And as its name clearly shows, ISIS aims to build a state that is eager to possess any kind of revenues within its self-claimed territories to create a single authority for the distribution of wealth in exchange for loyalty. Unlike al-Qaeda, ISIS has also declared one of its missions as providing for the essential needs of people living in the territories under its de facto sovereignty. Consequently, gaining control over energy sources and designing energy policies have become issues for the leaders of ISIS, just like other policymakers of nation-states.

The key sources of revenue of ISIS are very dependent on the territories it conquered, like taxes and fees, looting, confiscations, fines and, of course, oil. The estimated income from oil ranged from one to three million dollars per day in the months following the capture of oil-rich cities of Iraq like Mosul in the summer of 2014 (Heißner et al., 2017, p. 5). In 2014, ISIS managed to control more than 60% of Syrian oil production and less than 10% of Iraqi oil production, and in the meantime, it also monopolized the energy industry in the seized territories by taking control of oil and gas fields in Syria that had previously been controlled by other non-state actors (Tichý & Eichler, 2018, pp. 457, 464).

ISIS' control over oil-rich territories not only affects the regional oil market activities but also makes the group more resilient domestically and militarily. Energy is an important component of ISIS' strategy in the long run, and oil and gas sources are identified as the key economic sources for the survival of ISIS' caliphate efforts (Tichý, 2019, p. 255). When ISIS began to lose territories across the region, its revenues also declined, which eventually undermined its statehood claim and the ambitions of the group. However, ISIS' control of energy resources is not the only way that energy security is threatened. Like al-Qaeda, ISIS also conducted terror attacks against the energy fields across the MENA region, which directly affected the sustainability of energy production and transfer to the market.

One other dimension regarding the role of ISIS' presence in the Middle East and energy security is largely about the post-ISIS period, which will likely pave the way for other struggles over the redistribution of energy resources, as seen in post-ISIS cities of Iraq between the Kurdistan Regional Government and the Federal Government of Iraq. ISIS' territorial losses in Syria are also currently being exploited by other non-state actors that are also recognized as terror organizations by the regional powers. For example, Turkey's current efforts targeting pro-PKK Kurdish groups in the north of Syria are justified in the name of the national security of Turkey. According to the present conflict map of the Middle East, it can be said that the new dynamics shaping the regional reconfiguration of power are not clear enough to launch multilateral cooperation for the security of the Middle East's energy. In addition to the post-ISIS period, there are still some intra-state conflicts in many countries that should be taken into account in terms of the future consequences of the emergence of new regional power centres, their stability and their position toward the energy market. Even if the current conflicts are over in the near future, there will be satisfied and unsatisfied actors having different and contrasting visions and policies towards the energy politics of the Middle East.

Conclusion

The significance of energy sources in the MENA region and the high dependency of the developed world on the Middle East's energy continue to draw attention to the energy politics of the Middle East. As indicated in this chapter, the Middle East's large amount of oil and gas reserves are likely to shape the new configuration of relations among actors. And the variety of actors – from great powers to emerging powers, from nation-states to non-state actors, from international organizations to energy companies – contributes to the establishment of a complex web of relationships. The interconnectedness of all these relations has a stabilizing role to some extent, whereas it also has the risk of turning a micro-level dispute into regional groupings or, more importantly, into a global crisis.

The Middle East's energy security has always been at the top of the global agenda, and this trend will continue unless alternative energy sources challenge the conventional significance of fossil fuels to meet the energy demands of the world. In terms of energy security, threats to the production and free transfer of oil and natural gas, which often emerge at an inter-state level, have been identified here. These sorts of threats are still significant, as can be seen in the Iran-Saudi Arabia rivalries in the Gulf or current disputes over natural gas reserves in the East Mediterranean. However, the emerging anarchy situation in the region in the last decade has also paved the way for the development of non-state actorness in many fields like military, politics and energy. More importantly, terror groups' control over energy fields in seized territories and their attacks on other neighbouring countries are contemporary challenges to energy security in the region.

In conclusion, the historical importance of the Middle East's energy remains unchallenged, but there are various risks to the energy security of the region deriving from inter-state disagreements as well as intra-state actors' or transnational groups' destabilizing activities. In the short term, new energy projects are going to add new dimensions to the conflicts, disputes and actorness in the region because of the need for safe energy routes, especially for the energy-dependent developed world.

References

Anderson, K. B. (2019, February 6). *Renewable energy on the rise in the Middle East*. Arab News. http://www.arabnews.com/node/1448021

Barmin, Y. (2017). Russian Energy Policy in the Middle East. *Insight Turkey*, *19*(4), 125–136.

BP Statistical Review of World Energy 2017, https://www.connaissancedesenergies.org/sites/default/files/pdf-actualites/bp-statistical-review-of-world-energy-2017-full-report.pdf

Cirdei, I. A. (2017). Aspects Regarding the Energy Security in the Middle East. *Land Forces Academy Review*, *22*(2), 85–93. https://doi.org/10.1515/raft-2017-0012

Cohen, A. (2019, February 14). *Will China Replace The U.S. As The Middle East Hegemon?* Forbes. https://www.forbes.com/sites/arielcohen/2019/02/14/will-china-replace-the-u-s-as-the-middle-east-hegemon/#76bb23225cd1

Daojiong, Z., & Meidan, M. (2015). *China and the Middle East in a New Energy Landscape*. Chatham House.

EIA. (2018). *How much oil consumed by the United States comes from foreign countries?* https://www.eia.gov/tools/faqs/faq.php?id=32&t=6

El Katiri, L. (2014). *A Roadmap for Renewable Energy in the Middle East and North Africa*. OIES Paper: MEP 6.

European Commission. (2019a). *EU imports of energy products - Recent developments*. https://ec.europa.eu/eurostat/statistics-explained/pdfscache/46126.pdf

European Commission. (2019b). *Shedding light on energy in the EU*. https://ec.europa.eu/eurostat/cache/infographs/energy/index.html

Goldwyn, D., Rosenberg, E., & Henderson, S. (2014). *America's Shifting Energy Landscape and Middle East Policy*. Paper presented at the Weinberg Founders Conference.

Heißner, S., Neumann, P. R., Holland-McCowan, J., & Basra, R. (2017). *Caliphate in Decline: An Estimate of Islamic State's Financial Fortunes*. https://icsr.info/wp-content/uploads/2017/02/ICSR-Report-Caliphate-in-Decline-An-Estimate-of-Islamic-States-Financial-Fortunes.pdf

IIAS. (2018). *Reinventing the Middle East? South Korea's engagements with the Gulf amid geopolitical conflicts*. https://www.iias.asia/the-newsletter/article/reinventing-middle-east-south-koreas-engagements-gulf-amid-geopolitical

Johnson, K. (2018, November 14). *Why American Oil Hasn't Been a Total Game-Changer*. Foreign Policy.

https://foreignpolicy.com/2018/11/14/why-american-oil-hasnt-been-a-total-game-changer/
Kamel, M. S. (2018). China's Belt and Road Initiative: Implications for the Middle East. *Cambridge Review of International Affairs*, *31*(1), 76–95. https://doi.org/10.1080/09557571.2018.1480592
Khan, Z. al-Islam. (2013). *India's Middle East Energy Strategy*. http://studies.aljazeera.net/en/reports/2013/05/201351211444789282 1.html
Klug, F. (2019, June 15). *Middle East attack jolts oil-import dependent Asia*. AP News. https://www.apnews.com/9c8ec796f4f54a9d80782f0963464cd7
Koolaee, E. (2011). Iran's Role In Energy Security At Regional And Global Levels. *Iranian Economic Review*, *15*(28), 95–115. https://doi.org/10.22059/ier.2011.32716
Kozhanov, N. (2018). *Russian Policy Across the Middle East: Motivations and Methods*. Chatham House.
Li, X., & Ma, Y. (2010). A Comparative Analysis of US-Russia Middle East Energy Strategy. *Journal of Middle Eastern and Islamic Studies (in Asia)*, *4*(3), 81–102. https://doi.org/10.1080/19370679.2010.12023163
Luft, G., & Korin, A. (2013, October 15). *The Myth of U.S. Energy Dependence*. Foreign Affairs. https://www.foreignaffairs.com/articles/middle-east/2013-10-15/myth-us-energy-dependence
Lund, A. (2019). *Russia in the Middle East*. The Swedish Institute of International Affairs.
Margit, M. (2019, January 17). *Shunning Oil: Middle East Countries Developing Renewable Energy Sources*. The Media Line. https://themedialine.org/by-region/uae-saudi-morocco-egypt-lead-renewable-energy-race-in-middle-east/
Mortimer, C. (2019, July 15). *Turkey-Cyprus dispute: Why are the two countries arguing over drilling rights?* Euronews. https://www.euronews.com/2019/06/24/turkey-cyprus-dispute-why-are-the-two-countries-arguing-over-drilling-rights
Nakhle, C. (2018). Russia's Energy Diplomacy in the Middle East. In N. Popescu & S. Secrieru (Eds.), *Russia's Return to the Middle East: Building Sandcastles?* (pp. 29–36). European Union Institute for Security Studies.
Nematollahi, O., Hoghooghi, H., Rasti, M., & Sedaghat, A. (2016). Energy demands and renewable energy resources in the Middle East. *Renewable and Sustainable Energy Reviews*, *54*, 1172–1181.

O'Sullivan, M. (2018, October 19). *U.S. Is Forced to See It Is Far From 'Energy Independent'*. Bloomberg. https://www.bloomberg.com/opinion/articles/2018-10-19/u-s-needs-saudi-oil-despite-talk-of-energy-independence

Organization of the Petroleum Exporting Countries (OPEC). (n.d.). *OPEC World Oil Outlook 2040*. https://woo.opec.org/pdf-download/index.php

Shahla, A., & Nasseri, L. (2019, April 22). *Iran Raises Stakes in U.S. Showdown With Threat to Close Hormuz*. Bloomberg. https://www.bloomberg.com/news/articles/2019-04-22/iran-will-close-strait-of-hormuz-if-it-can-t-use-it-fars

The Conversation. (2019, July 18). *Five countries in the eastern Mediterranean are shaking up Europe's energy map*. http://theconversation.com/five-countries-in-the-eastern-mediterranean-are-shaking-up-europes-energy-map-119619

Tichý, L. (2019). The Islamic State oil and gas strategy in North Africa. *Energy Strategy Reviews*, *24*, 254–260. https://doi.org/10.1016/j.esr.2019.04.001

Tichý, L., & Eichler, J. (2018). Terrorist Attacks on the Energy Sector: The Case of Al Qaeda and the Islamic State. *Studies in Conflict & Terrorism*, *41*(6), 450–473. https://doi.org/10.1080/1057610X.2017.1323469

Wilson, J. D. (2019). A securitisation approach to international energy politics. *Energy Research & Social Science*, *49*, 114–125. https://doi.org/10.1016/j.erss.2018.10.024

World Energy Council. (n.d.). *Oil*. https://www.worldenergy.org/data/resources/resource/oil/

Wormuth, C. (2019). *Russia and China in the Middle East: Implications for the United States in an Era of Strategic Competition*. RAND.

Yetiv, S. (2010). Global Energy and the Middle East. In D. Sorenson (Ed.), *Interpreting the Middle East: Essential Themes* (pp. 382–406). Routledge.

CHAPTER FIVE

THE CASPIAN BASIN'S ENERGY POLICY

ALAEDDİN YALÇINKAYA*

Introduction: The Caspian Basin

Although the issue of energy is extremely important for the Caspian region, this region also constitutes an important crossroads of global and regional policies. In this context, which issues direct energy relations or which Caspian region problems actually arise from oil or gas politics is a controversial topic. The status of the Caspian, South Caucasus corridor, gas or oil pipelines, Nagorno-Karabakh conflict, Azerbaijan-Armenia-Turkey relations, Azerbaijan-Iran relations and Georgia-Russia relations are some of these issues. This chapter will focus on problems directly related to Caspian oil and gas. Other issues could be addressed in relation to these resources.

After the disintegration of the Soviet Union, along with the other newly independent states, the Caspian coastal countries were the Russian Federation, Kazakhstan, Turkmenistan, Iran and Azerbaijan. Before 1992, however, there was only the Soviet Union and Iran as independent states. Although, according to the Soviet Constitution, Azerbaijan, Turkmenistan and Kazakhstan had a certain autonomy, their energy resources were directly under the control of Moscow.

During Soviet times, Baku oil could only reach the port of the Black Sea coastal city of Novorossiysk via Chechnya. In this case, the marketing of Azerbaijani oil was beyond the control of the Baku administration. For this reason, the war over the independence of Chechnya from the Russian Federation is also linked to the "economic independence" of Azerbaijan as a new independent republic. Therefore, the economic-political dimension of the Chechen struggle for independence is very deep. A similar situation

---

* Prof. Dr. Alaeddin Yalçınkaya, Faculty of Political Science, Marmara University. E-mail: alaeddinyalcinkaya@gmail.com.

exists for Turkmenistan on the other coast of the Caspian Sea and its natural gas because, after its independence, Turkmenistan also wanted to sell its natural gas to the world markets independently from Russia, but the pipeline only passed through Russia.

The Caspian Sea and its hinterland, which was situated between the Soviet Union and Iran before 1992, were significantly out of the competing field of global powers. As the "Iron Curtain" countries, the Caucasus and Central Asian republics could only be connected to the outside world through Moscow. Although this meant a period of oppression or anti-democratic conditions for the countries and peoples of the region, on the other hand, there was a certain stability compared to the post-Cold War era. Essentially, Baku's oil was one of the issues of conflict in World War II, just like World War I. Hitler's ultimate goal was to reach Baku from the Black Sea coast. However, as is known, the Battle of Stalingrad did not allow this.

Given the fact that the Caspian is located between the Caucasus and Central Asia, the strategies within this scope have dimensions related to both regions. However, especially when the transformation of Caspian resources is considered, the Caucasus becomes more important. The 1990s mostly regarded the struggles of Europe and the United States to reach Caspian resources. The TRACECA (Transport Corridor Europe-Caucasus-Asia) organization and the Baku-Tbilisi-Ceyhan oil pipeline are the results of the West gaining ground against Russia in this struggle. In the 2000s, China also participated in this competition.

The Caspian and its hinterland, which is located on the historical Silk Road route, today stands out for the richness of its oil and natural gas. As well as which country has which rights to these resources, one of the areas of competition relates to which route it will be marketed on. Supply and demand energy security is another problem linked to these resources' transportation. Controlling energy (supply and demand) also means being active in the international political economy. Therefore, the issue is not limited to how and where oil and gas are delivered.

The New Silk Road (TRACECA, n.d.) is based in the Caspian (South Caucasus), and the center of this organization is in Baku. Azerbaijan-Turkmenistan maritime transport on this route demarcated by TRACECA, which is a strategic transportation organization extending from Europe to China, passes through the Caspian Sea. After the disintegration of the Soviet Union, a new order was established not only politically but also economically and strategically in regional relations. The European Union, appreciative of the emptiness left by the fall of the USSR, started to establish cooperative relations with the newly independent Caucasus and

Central Asian republics. The cooperation which was initiated by the EU within the framework of Technical Aid to the Commonwealth of Independent States (TACIS) programs in 1998 resulted in the TRACECA project, which played the transport role between Europe and Asia. The main objective of this organization is to renew and develop the transportation systems of the Caucasus and Central Asian republics so as to follow a European model. In this context, the hesitation about the functionality of China's Belt and Road project that came onto the agenda in 2013 and the meaninglessness of TRACECA being called the New Silk Road are separate issues. On the other hand, the TACIS programs and TRACECA aim to promote democracy, human rights and the rule of law in the former Soviet republics on both sides of the Caspian.

In this chapter, firstly, the geopolitical characteristics and the recent history of the Caspian Sea are briefly explained. In this context, the Soviet era, the importance of Caspian resources, and the developments realized in the process of the disintegration of the USSR are analyzed. The discussion of the status of the Caspian was an important outcome of the disintegration of the Soviet Union. Thanks to the 2018 Aktau agreement, a significant compromise has been reached in the debates on the status of the Caspian, which began upon the independence of the new republics. In light of these facts, the importance of this agreement in the context of the competition between regional and global powers over Caspian resources is summarized. Finally, in this context, the economic-political importance of the Baku-Tbilisi-Ceyhan pipeline and the TANAP project is analyzed.

Status of the Caspian

The Caspian Sea is one of the largest closed water bodies in the world. It is located between the 37-47 northern parallels and 47-55 eastern meridians. The coastline, which is composed of five countries, is approximately 7,000 km (Akiner, 2005, p. 314). The Caspian Sea coastal countries and coastal lengths are as follows: Kazakhstan 2,320 km, Russian Federation 1,930 km, Turkmenistan 1,200 km, Azerbaijan 1,000 km, and Iran 950 km (Aras, 2008, p. 5). The north-south length of the Caspian is about 1,225 km. The widest part of the east-west line is 556 km. The average width is 330 km. The total water volume is around 77,000 km^3. The deepest point is 1,025 m, while the average depth is 184 m. Many rivers carry water to the Caspian Sea. The Volga, Ural and Terek rivers provide 88% of the Caspian's waters and come from Russia in the north. The Sulak, Samur, Kura and various small rivers from the west provide 7% of the Caspian's water. Other rivers carry water from Iran from the south (Aladin &

Plotnikov, 2004, pp. 4-5). Although the Caspian Sea does not have a natural connection with an ocean, it has a convenient connection with the Azov Sea for the navigation of ships. However, the Black Sea and the Atlantic can be reached from the Volga through the Volga-Don channel and the Don River (Janusz-Pawletta, 2015, p. 9).

During the Soviet period, the Caspian was only located between two countries, the USSR and Iran, and there was no problem with sharing resources and thus status. Apart from a small region dominated by Iran in the southern region, the majority of the Caspian was controlled by the USSR. There was no oil field problem between the two states due to Iran's resources in the Persian Gulf (Birsel, 2006, p. 77).

In the period of Tsarism, the Treaty of Resht was signed between Iran and Russia in 1729 (Gökay, 2001, p. 20). The Tsarist administration wanted to move south in line with the will of Peter the Great and fought many wars with Iran. After these wars, which generally resulted in the defeat of Iran, two important agreements were reached between the Russians and the Persians regarding shipping rights in the Caspian. The 1813 Treaty of Gulistan prohibited Iran's naval presence in the Caspian Sea. The 1828 Treaty of Turkmenchay reiterated these restrictions on the Persians' shipping.

After the Bolshevik Revolution, the Russo-Persian Treaty of Friendship of 1921 abolished these agreements. The Trade and Maritime Agreement, which was signed in 1935 and renewed in 1940, granted the two countries the right to fisheries within 10 miles and did not set any limits on mining rights in the seabed. With this agreement, the Caspian became a Soviet-Iranian sea. In a 1954 treaty, the territorial boundaries between the two countries were determined. The restrictions on the Caspian Sea disappeared, and no specific boundaries were identified (Mehdiyoun, 2000, p. 180).

The agreements signed between Iran and the USSR in 1921 and 1940 lost their validity after the collapse of the USSR and the increase in the number of littoral countries (Bayülgen, 2009, p. 164). However, Iran has been reluctant to accept the rights of the newly independent states in the Caspian Sea and has defended the validity of these agreements.

When the newly independent republics with oil and gas reserves in the Caspian wanted to agree on the status of the Caspian, Iran firstly argued, based on the old conventions, that the UN Convention on the Law of the Sea could not be valid for the Caspian because it was a lake. Until the agreement of 2018, the coastal states continued their research, drill and production activities from time to time through bilateral or tripartite agreements. Kazakhstan and Azerbaijan reached an agreement on the legal status of the Caspian Sea in 1997, based on the boundaries of the sectors along the midline. Kazakhstan and Turkmenistan also signed a declaration in 1997 that they agreed to divide the sectors along the midline based on the division of the Caspian, provided that it was valid until a new status on the Caspian Sea had been agreed. In 1998, Kazakhstan and Russia signed a bilateral agreement to divide the North Caspian seabed along the midline. Russia signed a similar agreement with Azerbaijan in 2001 (Bahgat, 2004, p. 123). In 2001, Azerbaijan and Kazakhstan signed a new agreement confirming the 1997 agreement on the sharing of the seabed (Haghayeghi, 2003, p. 35). However, Iran and Turkmenistan argued that these were invalid because not all littoral states had signed them. Similar bilateral and tripartite agreements and objections have continued between the Caspian coast states for years.

Even though Russia and Iran acted against Azerbaijan in particular due to projects for the transportation of Baku oil, Moscow and Baku agreed on certain issues as stated above. Turkmenistan and Iran entered into a bilateral alliance against the three states, and in 2003, the two countries signed an agreement on the division of the southern sector of the Caspian Sea. Accordingly, it reached a consensus on the sharing of the seabed in accordance with the UN Convention on the Law of the Sea. However, according to this agreement, it is emphasized that each state should have 20% of the Caspian's resources, which was the position Iran had defended from the beginning (Bardakçı, 2003, p.10).

Although the foreign ministers of the five coastal countries met in 2004, no reconciliation was achieved. Similarly, in January 2005, the draft contract on the legal status of the Caspian Sea at the 16th Special Working Group meeting failed. The second meeting of the leaders of the Caspian countries was held in 2007 in Iran. At the end of this meeting, five littoral states signed a declaration, but no consensus was reached on the status of the Caspian Sea. However, the following principles were included in the communiqué (Terzioğlu, 2008, p. 30):

- The Caspian's sovereignty only belongs to these five countries, and only these five countries can benefit from the resources there.
- None of the five littoral countries will use this land to attack the other side, nor will it allow any of the littoral countries to use their territory to attack another country with a coast on the Caspian Sea.
- Negotiations on the determination of the status of the Caspian will continue within the framework of international rules, legal equality and a peaceful method.
- They will hang their own flags on the ships of neighboring countries until the status of the Caspian Sea is determined.

Significantly, it should be noted that these principles were included in the 2018 Aktau agreement. Until 2018, the main axis of the debate between the coastal states was whether the Caspian was a sea or a lake. The issue, according to this view, was whether the provisions of the Exclusive Economic Zone of the UN Convention on the Law of the Sea or the provisions of the lake in the form of the joint use of resources should apply to the Caspian. With this in mind, it is possible to summarize the position of each littoral country.

Russia

First of all, it should be noted that each state's approach to whether the Caspian is a lake or a sea is actually based on the needs of their own interests. Therefore, the attitude of these states has changed as conditions have changed. In the first years, Russia argued that the 1921 and 1940 agreements signed between Iran and the USSR were valid. So, the Law of the Sea could not be applied to the Caspian since the Caspian is a closed water basin (Terzioğlu, 2008, p. 36). The initial attitude of Russia was that the water body outside the 10- or 20-mile coastline and the seabed would be shared (Amirbek, 2015, p. 31). Russia's approach to the Caspian Sea is mainly built on the exclusion of states other than the littoral countries, the monopoly of natural resources and the debates on the use of the Caspian Sea by the former USSR. Russia has long argued that the Caspian Sea is a lake, based on the fact that the Caspian does not have a natural exit. For Russia, the Don and Volga channels are not international waterways. As a result, Russia wanted to put the Caspian under joint management (Poyraz, 2011, p. 38). Like some other states, Russia has put forward different views on the Caspian Sea in various periods after 1991, and from time to time these have contradicted each other. For example, in the agreement signed by Azerbaijan, Lukoil, the oil company of the Russian state, took part in the unilateral transaction of Azerbaijan by taking a share in the consortium. However, the Russian Ministry of Foreign Affairs condemned Azerbaijan's move and declared that it did not recognize unilateral movements in the Caspian Sea. Therefore, the attitude of the Russian Ministry of Foreign Affairs and the policy of the Russian Energy Ministry are in conflict (Oğan, 2001, p. 156).

Russia, which had previously adopted the principle of common use, has changed its ideas over time. In 1996, at the conference in Ashgabat, 45-mile views were raised by Russia. Accordingly, all countries should have exclusive sovereign rights over mineral resources in the 45-mile coastal area of the sea. However, the central part of the sea should be left for common use and operated by a joint company that would be established by the five states. However, this view was not accepted by other states. After this conference, Russia, Iran and Turkmenistan signed a tripartite memorandum on the common use of Caspian resources. Kazakhstan and Azerbaijan did not accept this. As a result of these developments, it was decided by Russia, Iran and Turkmenistan to establish a tripartite company within the scope of the research and development of oil and natural gas resources. However, as in many other initiatives, this did not happen because of differences of opinion between the parties within a short period of time (Mamedov, 2001, pp. 237-238)

Azerbaijan

Azerbaijan argues that the 1921 and 1940 agreements are limited only to navigation and fisheries and that there are no provisions concerning the seabed. At the same time, Azerbaijan has been producing oil in the Caspian for quite some time, and Iran, which was another party in the 1921 and 1940 agreements, did not object to this situation based on the agreements (Diba, 2003, p. 34). At first, Azerbaijan claimed that the Caspian had the characteristics of a border lake, and then it began to argue that the Caspian was a high sea. However, the main idea of Azerbaijan is to divide the Caspian into national sectors. In this context, the concept of status in relation to the Caspian does not have any significance for Azerbaijan. As a matter of fact, when the USSR disintegrated, Azerbaijan was the first newly independent country that foreign oil companies invested in. Of the 32 oil and gas fields in the Caspian, 25 belong to Azerbaijan. Even Azerbaijan's offshore production areas are under shallow water. Accordingly, it is possible for it to produce oil more easily and cheaply than anywhere else in the Caspian Sea. Under the agreements signed with international oil companies, approximately 80% of its production is realized through "offshore" production sites. As a result of this, Azerbaijan adopted the most stringent attitude towards the division of the sea according to the midline method, which would make all the coastal states equally dominant over the Caspian Sea's biological resources, seabed, navigation, water column and water surface. In this regard, former Prime Minister Hasan Hasanov stated that the Caspian is a lake and that there is no provision regarding the status of lakes in international conventions (Amirbek, 2015, p. 30).

Iran

Iran's Caspian policies have generally been in line with Russia's. This similarity stems mainly from security and pipeline issues. The policies of Russia and Iran regarding the Baku-Tbilisi-Ceyhan and Trans-Caspian pipelines are similar because both countries did not want these projects to be realized. Iran had desired Central Asia's and the Caspian's resources to reach the world's markets from its territory (Özbay, 2007, p. 170). Iran, which holds 10% of the world's crude oil reserves and 17% of its natural gas reserves, has the second-largest natural gas reserve in the world after Russia. Approximately 70% of Iran's crude oil reserves are around the Persian Gulf. Like its oil reserves, Iran's natural gas reserves are also far from the Caspian region. It is not very economical for Iran to operate a small amount of energy resources in the Caspian (Coffey, 2015, p. 7). Iran did not want any new state in the Caspian territory, and argued that it was defined as the Russian-Iranian sea in the 1921 and 1940 agreements. It has insisted on the common use of Caspian resources. Iran proposed that the sovereign area be increased to 20 miles and that the rest be shared. It opposed the division of the Caspian Sea and argued that common use was necessary. However, Iran also stressed the necessity to divide it equally among all states if a division occurred. When Azerbaijan signed a contract with British Petroleum (BP) in 2001 upon the discovery of the Alov-Araz-Orient site 50 kilometers from the former border between the USSR and Iran, a debate began between the two countries (Behzadi, 2010, p. 89).

Kazakhstan

It is estimated that there are approximately 4.5 billion tons of oil reserves in the 160 regions of Kazakhstan. Since a certain number of them are on the Caspian coast, Kazakhstan is an important country in the discussions on the status of the Caspian Sea. At the conference held in Moscow in 1993, Azerbaijan defended the division into national sectors in line with the border lake status, while Kazakhstan defined the Caspian Sea as a closed sea (Mamedov, 2001, p. 226). Kazakhstan's approach, however, is generally close to that of Azerbaijan. In this context, while Azerbaijan is in favor of dividing the Caspian into national sectors, Kazakhstan has adopted the sharing of the seabed and the common use of Caspian waters outside of a specific jurisdiction (Çolakoğlu, 1998, p. 112). In 1997, two papers on the status of the Caspian were published between Kazakhstan and Turkmenistan. One of them is related to improving cooperation in general and the other concerns Caspian-related problems. They agreed to establish a working group on the mutual enjoyment of the Caspian Sea. Accordingly, the parties would protect the administrative-territorial border within the framework of the midline until the agreement that determines the legal status of the Caspian was signed (Terzioğlu, 2008, p. 39).

Turkmenistan

Turkmenistan is the fourth-largest country with natural gas reserves in the world, and its utilization depends on its access to world markets. Although the Chinese pipeline was constructed as an alternative to the Soviet-era pipeline to Russia, Turkmenistan is also striving to increase its market alternatives in terms of energy security. Access to new markets is through the Caspian Sea. Therefore, the Caspian is important for Turkmenistan. The Trans-Caspian pipeline project, which came onto the agenda in 1997, has been ineffective because the issues related to the status of the Caspian could not be solved. Turkmenistan advocated different theses for the status of the Caspian at different times. Although it defended the thesis of the division of Azerbaijan and Kazakhstan into national sectors, it later changed its view and found it appropriate to establish an area open to the common use of the littoral states outside the 45-mile exclusive jurisdiction (Aras, 2008, p. 190). Having signed a joint declaration with Iran and Russia at the 1996 Ashgabat conference, Turkmenistan supported the common use of the Caspian natural resources (Mamedov, 2001, p. 237). In 1997, the President of Turkmenistan, Turkmenbashi, changed the names of the Azeri and Chirag oil fields, which had been set by the Azerbaijanis, and gave them new names. Since these sites are located beyond the 45-mile border, Turkmenistan changed its view towards re-division into national sectors (Çolakoğlu, 1998, p. 13). In fact, Turkmenistan was the first country to adopt a law on coastal waters, including 12 miles of territorial waters and an exclusive economic zone. Turkmenistan has also had a border problem with Azerbaijan and Iran in the Caspian Sea (Coffey, 2015, p. 17).

In 2015, Turkmenistan reached a consensus on the border issue with Kazakhstan in the Caspian Sea. This consensus is not related to status but to sovereign rights, including the development and use of natural resources in their national sectors. It can be stated that the developments between Russia and the Western world had an impact on the emergence of this situation. Turkmenistan aimed to accelerate the Trans-Caspian project with this agreement. As a matter of fact, the EU recently decided on the use of Turkmen natural gas for the first time. Maros Sefcovic, Vice-

President of the European Commission, stated that "Europe expects supplies of Turkmen gas to begin by 2019" (Michel, 2015).

The Aktau Convention, August 12, 2018

The Aktau Convention is not only a text that solved the dispute over the status of the Caspian but a declaration of the unity and solidarity of the coastal states against third parties, especially the global powers. In a sense, it is a declaration to keep non-littoral forces away from the Caspian. In this regard, Russian President Vladimir Putin's words at the summit are extremely important (President of Russia, 2018b):

> I agree with those colleagues who have spoken before me: this summit is indeed extraordinary, if not historic. The Convention On the Legal Status of the Caspian Sea, a document that we have been negotiating for over 20 years, at last formalises our exclusive rights and the responsibility each of us carries to protect the future of the Caspian Sea, and it establishes clear guidelines for its collective use. … Based on consensus and consideration for our mutual interests, we have produced a modern and balanced international agreement. The convention will replace the Soviet-Iranian agreements of 1921 and 1940. It is important that the Convention regulates the issues of necessary delimitations, regimes of navigation and fishing, establishes the principles of political and military interaction of member states, and ensures the use of the Caspian Sea solely for peaceful purposes and the non-presence of the armed forces of non-regional states in the sea.

In light of Putin's abovementioned comments, the 2018 Aktau Convention is a development far beyond the use of the Caspian or the sharing of energy resources. In this sense, it is very important that non-Western countries have been able to solve a regional problem among themselves. While the consensus on the status of the Caspian is not provided in all matters, the statements in the diplomatic field and the texts of reconciliation are extremely important. It should be noted that the peace, prosperity and richness of the regional countries are related to the development of cooperation among themselves, and the compromises based on friendship and mutual interest with their neighbors are of paramount importance. Considering that there is a greater Turkish population in Iran than in Azerbaijan, the negativity on fundamental issues has negative effects on peoples and economies. The post-Soviet Russian Federation, after all, has a certain influence on the former Soviet republics. As a result, the success that the littoral countries have had in reaching a consensus on the key elements of the Caspian's status will have crucial consequences on the economic and social development of these countries (Yalçınkaya, 2019).

According to the essential clauses of the Aktau agreement (President of Russia, 2018a):

- Each littoral state will rule over areas up to 15 nautical miles from the Caspian Sea coast;
- Each littoral state will be able to engage in fishing activities by adding another 10 miles to the specified 15 nautical miles;
- The other marine space will be accepted as a neutral zone open to the common use of the states;
- The principles of the UN International Convention on the Law of the Sea will be the basis for the exploration and exploitation of Caspian seabed and subsoil resources; and
- The rights of sovereignty at the bottom of the Caspian Sea can be determined later between the littoral states facing each other.

The Convention is based on the principles and norms of the Charter of the United Nations and international law, taking into account the atmosphere of cooperation, good-neighborliness and mutual understandings among the littoral states (President of Russia, 2018a). However, according to Article 22, Kazakhstan was determined as the depositary. Let us point out that Aktau, where the agreement was concluded, is a city in Kazakhstan. In international conventions, it is generally decided that the General Secretariat of the UN is the depositary. Here, it is clear that trust in Kazakhstan, which is one of the contracting parties, is more prominent than in the UN. Nevertheless, for the internationalization of the Convention, the submission of the approved text to the UN is specified in Article 23.

Article 3 regulates the activities of the Caspian Sea in a sense of full sovereignty for littoral states. Accordingly, these states should comply with the following issues (President of Russia, 2018a):

- Respect for the sovereignty, territorial integrity, independence and sovereign equality of littoral states, the non-use of force or the threat of force, mutual respect, cooperation and non-interference into the internal affairs of each other;
- Using the Caspian Sea for peaceful purposes, making it a zone of peace, good-neighborliness, friendship and cooperation, and solving all issues related to the Caspian Sea through peaceful means;

- Ensuring security and stability in the Caspian Sea region;
- Ensuring a stable balance of armaments of the Parties in the Caspian Sea, developing military capabilities within the limits of reasonable sufficiency with due regard to the interests of all the Parties and without prejudice to the security of each other;
- Compliance with the agreed confidence-building measures in the military field in the spirit of predictability and transparency in line with general efforts to strengthen regional security and stability, including in accordance with international treaties concluded among all the Parties;
- Non-presence in the Caspian Sea of armed forces not belonging to the Parties;
- Non-provision by a Party of its territory to other States to commit aggression and undertake other military actions against any Party;
- Freedom of navigation outside the territorial waters of each Party subject to the respect for the sovereign and exclusive rights of the coastal States and to the compliance with relevant rules established by them with regard to the activities specified by the Parties;
- Ensuring safety of navigation;
- The right to free access from the Caspian Sea to other seas and the Ocean and back in accordance with the generally recognized principles and norms of international law and agreements between the relevant Parties, with due regard to the legitimate interests of the transit Party, with a view to promoting international trade and economic development;
- Navigation in, entry to and exit from the Caspian Sea exclusively by ships flying the flag of one of the Parties;
- Application of agreed norms and rules related to the reproduction and regulation of the use of shared aquatic biological resources;
- Liability of the polluting Party for damage caused to the ecological system of the Caspian Sea;
- Protection of the environment of the Caspian Sea, conservation, restoration and rational use of its biological resources;
- Facilitation of scientific research in the area of ecology and conservation and use of biological resources of the Caspian Sea;
- Freedom of overflight by civil aircraft in accordance with the rules of the International Civil Aviation Organization; and
- Conducting marine scientific research outside the territorial waters of each Party in accordance with the legal norms agreed upon by the Parties, subject to the respect for the sovereign and exclusive

rights of the coastal States and to the compliance with the relevant rules established by them with regard to certain types of research.

Energy Profiles of Caspian Countries

As in other parts of the world, energy resources are not equal in the sovereign or exclusive regions of the Caspian coastal states. On the other hand, the importance and amount of energy in each country's national income is different. Naturally, each littoral state wants to make the most of these resources. The desire to have more shares from these sources leads to discussions about the status of the Caspian, as discussed above.

Azerbaijan obtains 50% of its GDP from the energy field. 93% of its exports are based on oil and natural gas (Macit, 2014, p. 6). Its proven total oil reserves are 7 billion barrels, and 881,000 barrels of oil are produced daily. The country's natural gas reserves are 0.9 trillion m^3, and its daily production is 16.2 billion m^3. The amount produced in the Caspian Sea is 15 billion m^3 (EIA, 2013a, p. 14). Azerbaijan's largest oil and gas deposits are located in the Caspian Sea, especially in the Azeri-Chirag-Guneshli region. It supplies 75% of its oil from this region. It is estimated that there is a total reserve of 5 billion barrels (EIA, 2014, p. 3).

Kazakhstan, which has been an oil producer since 1911, has the second-largest oil reserve among the former USSR countries. Daily oil production in the country is 1.7 million barrels. 75.8% of its exports are from oil and natural gas. The most important production deposits in the country are in the Tengiz, Karaçanak and Kaşagan regions (EIA, 2013b, p. 1). The proven oil reserves of Kazakhstan are 31.2 billion barrels, while its natural gas reserves are 3 trillion m^3. It is stated that 15.7 billion barrels of oil and 1 trillion m^3 of natural gas are located in the Caspian Sea (EIA, 2013a, p. 14).

Turkmenistan has the sixth-largest natural gas reserve in the world. In Eurasia, it is the second-largest natural gas producer after Russia (EIA, 2016). Turkmenistan has proven oil reserves of 600 million barrels and a daily oil production of 231,000 barrels. Its natural gas reserves are 17.5 trillion m^3 and its daily natural gas production is 62.3 billion m^3. 57.8% of its oil and 12.8% of its natural gas are in the Caspian Sea (EIA, 2013a, p. 11).

Iran is among the countries with the largest oil and gas reserves in the world. It ranks first in the world in terms of natural gas reserves and fourth in terms of oil reserves. Its daily oil production is 3.5 million barrels. Iran provides the majority of its oil and natural gas production from the regions in the southwest of the country and the Persian Gulf, and it does not have a remarkable source of oil or gas in the Caspian Sea or on its shores. Of Iran's total petroleum reserves, 0.3% (0.5 billion barrels) is in the Caspian Sea, which also contains less than 0.1% (28.3 million m^3) of its total natural gas reserves. Today, Iran does not produce oil and gas in the Caspian Sea. However, it has rights to the production of the Sardar-e Jangal field, which was discovered in 2011 and has a reserve of 100 million barrels, and it plans to process the oil to be obtained from this area by installing a refinery on the Caspian Sea coast. However, since it does has not come to an agreement with the neighboring countries of Azerbaijan and Turkmenistan, production has not yet commenced (EIA, 2013a, pp. 12, 14). According to the 2018 Aktau agreement, this problem is also expected to be resolved.

Russia, on the other hand, is one of the leading oil and gas producers in the world, and its economy heavily depends on energy exports. Natural gas and oil constitute 52% of the country's budget. More than 70% of its total exports are covered by oil and gas (EIA, 2017). Most of Russia's oil production in the Caspian Sea is in Krasnodar, Stavropol and Chechnya in the North Caucasus region. Daily production in this region is around 65,000 barrels. In 2010, Russia's Lukoil company started oil production for the first time at the Yuri Korchagin production site in the Caspian Sea. Russia's daily oil supply from the Caspian Sea is only about 1% of its total production (EIA, 2013a, p. 14). Other oil deposits discovered by Russia in the northern Caspian region are at Khvalynsoye, Rakushechnoye, Sarmatskoye and Zapadno Rakushechnoye (EIA, 2017).

BTC, TANAP and Other Pipelines

The political-economic importance of the transit routes of oil or gas pipelines is critical in almost every region of the world. However, none of them can be as important as those of Azerbaijan. In this sense, the fact is that Georgia and Armenia are both on the Baku-Ceyhan pipeline transit route, but while Armenia closed its doors to this project, the acceptance of Georgia was a turning point in terms of Caucasus or Caspian policies. In the context of the importance of the transit route, the situation of Georgia is similar to Ukraine in a sense. Viewed in this way, the geopolitics of the pipelines are remarkable with regard to the Caspian's resources (Ceragioli & Martellini, 2003)

During the preparatory phase of the BTC project, many countries and companies were interviewed between 1992-1997 and a consortium was formed with the following shares: BP (UK) 30.10%, AZBTC (Azerbaijan) 25.00%, Chevron (USA) 8.90%, Equionor (Norway) 8.71%, TP (Turkey)

6.53%, ENI (Italy) 5.00%, TOTAL (France) 5.00%, ITOCHU (Japan) 3.40%, INPEX (Japan) 2.50%, ExxonMobil (USA) 2.50%, and ONGC Videsh (USA) 2.36%. The BTC pipeline became operational in June 2006. This pipeline carries oil from the Azeri-Chirag-Gunashli field and condensate from Shah Deniz to the Ceyhan marine terminal on the Turkish Mediterranean coast. It also links the Sangachal terminal on the shores of the Caspian to Ceyhan. On the other hand, oil from Turkmenistan is to be transported through this pipeline. Starting in 2013, BTC has resumed the transportation of Tengiz oil from Kazakhstan too. The pipeline, buried along its entire length, is 1,768 km long in total: 443 km in Azerbaijan, 249 km in Georgia, and 1,076 km in Turkey. In recent years, BTC has exported about 250 million barrels of crude oil loaded on 320 tankers at Ceyhan (BP, n.d.).

Due to problems in the relations between Ukraine and Russia, the EU launched the Nabucco project to diversify its gas supply. In the framework of this project, particularly the Caspian region's gas would be transported to Europe. However, as a result of the agreement between Germany and Russia on a new northern line, Nabucco failed. Thereupon, Turkey and Azerbaijan realized the TANAP (Trans-Anatolian Pipeline) and TAP (Trans-Adriatic Pipeline) projects. In the process of realizing TANAP, as outlined in the statement "one nation, two states", the proximity between Azerbaijan and Turkey is extremely important, which is also true for the BTC. The Azerbaijani people and government view Turkey's presence in the region as a crucial factor not only for their economic development but also for peace and security. Turkey's regional presence has increased and become more important in the light of energy transportation routes and issues related to the security of the region. The Baku-Tbilisi-Ceyhan and Baku-Tbilisi-Erzurum oil and gas transportation routes and the Baku-Tbilisi-Kars railway route were the cornerstones of this cooperation. TANAP is going to contribute to the strengthening of bilateral ties, and a huge amount is being invested in the Turkish economy (Mehtiyev, 2015, pp. 32-33).

Georgia's choice in accepting cooperation with Azerbaijan and Turkey is important not only for the South Caucasus but also in terms of global politics. Azerbaijan and Georgia have forged close economic cooperation, especially in the field of energy resources and transportation routes as all Caspian oil and gas routes are being run via Georgia, and the Baku-Tbilisi-Kars railway line is going to be another link connecting Azerbaijan with Georgia and Turkey. Azerbaijan has invested hugely in Georgia, and the second-highest number of visitors to Georgia (after Turkey) came from Azerbaijan (Mehtiyev, 2015, pp. 40-41).

There are approximately 1.2 trillion cubic meters of natural gas reserves in the Caspian Sea, especially in the Shah Deniz region. This reserve volume means that Azerbaijan has one of the largest natural gas reserves in the world. This resource has also made Azerbaijan one of the major natural gas suppliers due to the increasing demand for natural gas in Europe. In 2012, in line with increasing demand, Turkey and Azerbaijan signed an agreement for the construction of TANAP (World Bank, n.d.). There are 20 cities and 60 districts on the TANAP route. Along the pipeline, there are 7 compressor stations, 4 measuring stations, 11 pigging stations, and 49 block valve stations. In addition, 2 pumping stations ensure Turkey's natural gas network. With a length of 1,850 km, TANAP is one of the largest construction projects in the world (TANAP, n.d.-c).

As of June 2019, approximately 1.8 billion cubic meters (bcm) of gas had been transported from the TANAP line, which opened in June 2018. TANAP's starting capacity is 16 bcm of gas, 6 billion of which goes to Turkey, while 10 billion goes to Europe. Its capacity will increase to 22 bcm, based on demand, and to 31 bcm with additional investments. After crossing the Greek border, it will continue to Albania. The TANAP gas, which reaches Italy through Albania and the Adriatic (TAP), will thus make a significant contribution to the energy security of Europe (TANAP, n.d.-b).

An important point of TANAP is that the major shareholder of this project is SOCAR, Azerbaijan's state oil company. However, as mentioned above, BTC's major shareholder was the British company BP. This fact shows that Azerbaijan, as a Caspian littoral country, has reached the stage of implementing a major global project. The same is true for Kazakhstan and Turkmenistan. The distribution of TANAP shares is as follows: SOCAR (Azerbaijan) 58%, BOTAŞ (Turkey) 30%, and BP (UK) 12% (TANAP, n.d.-a).

The oil and gas pipelines of Kazakhstan and Turkmenistan, both Caspian littoral countries, that reach Russia and China are also very important. It is clear that especially the pipelines reaching China are an important tool for China to establish influence in the region as a rising power. Therefore, the Turkmenistan-China natural gas pipeline in particular, as one of the longest pipelines in the world, should be considered within the scope of China's increasing influence in Central Asia rather than with regard to Caspian energy policies.

Conclusion

In terms of the Caspian Basin's energy policies, the 2018 Aktau Convention is an extremely important development. The fact that Russia and Iran, after more than 20 years, have accepted the demands of such countries as Azerbaijan is linked to global developments. Russia's conditions after the Ukraine crisis and Iran's situation as of 2018 were noteworthy in this respect. In this context, the prohibition of a non-littoral state having power in the Caspian is remarkable. For example, even if Azerbaijan were to become a NATO member, this organization's ships would not be able to sail in the Caspian Sea. On the other hand, it is clear that both Russia and Iran need more cooperation and solidarity with neighboring countries due to current circumstances (as of 2018).

After the disintegration of the USSR, the BTC pipeline has attracted attention, primarily in relation to Caspian energy policies. Thus, Azerbaijan was liberated from its dependence on Russia in terms of oil supply security. Although Turkmenistan is bound to Russia by gas sales, the agreement with Iran and the natural gas pipeline extending to China played important roles in this policy. However, the fact that Turkmenistan and Uzbekistan as well as Kazakhstan have become dependent on China for their energy supply may cause concern for Caspian energy policies. Chinese expansion policies conducted through the Belt and Road project reinforce this concern.

Following TANAP, which became operational in 2018 after BTC's operationalization in 2006, the transportation of oil and natural gas from Azerbaijan, Kazakhstan and Turkmenistan has strengthened the energy demand security of these countries. The EU's dependence on Russia in terms of energy supply has tied it up politically as well as economically. Similarly, the increasing dependence of the Caspian countries on China has been mentioned above. In light of these facts, the EU evaluated all energy production and transportation routes that could be alternatives to Russia. The EU also gave a €5 million grant to the TANAP pipeline, which transports Azerbaijan's Shah Deniz natural gas through Georgia and Turkey to Greece (Enerji Günlüğü, 2018). This policy shows the importance of similar projects outside Russia for the EU's energy supply security.

As a result, the combination of the policies of many regional and non-regional countries draws attention to Caspian energy policies. According to their order of importance and chronological developments, the following complications are noteworthy: Azerbaijan's and Turkmenistan's dependence on Russia for their energy demand security in the 1990s; the

EU's dependence on Russia for its energy supply security; China's rising influence in the region; the policy of utilization of the geostrategic benefits that Turkey possesses; the prevention of the entry of a non-littoral navy into the Caspian Sea; and the prevention of the intervention of non-regional countries in solutions to the problems occurring among the countries in the region.

References

Akiner, S. (2005). Environmental Security in the Caspian Sea. In S. Akiner (Ed.), *The Caspian: Politics, Energy and Security* (pp. 314-331). Taylor and Francis.

Aladin, N., & Plotkinov, I. (2004). *The Caspian Sea*, http://www.worldlakes.org/uploads/caspian%20sea%2028jun04.pdf

Amirbek, A. (2015). Soğuk Savaş Sonrası Hazar'ın Statüsü ve Sınırlandırma Sorunu: Kıyıdaş Devletlerin Yaklaşımları Açısından Analizi. *Karadeniz Araştırmaları Dergisi*, *46*, 23-48

Aras, O. N. (2008). *Azerbaycan'ın Hazar Ekonomisi ve Stratejisi*. Derin Yayınları.

BP. (n.d.). *Baku-Tbilisi-Ceyhan Pipeline*. Retrieved August 17, 2019, from https://www.bp.com/en_az/caspian/operationsprojects/pipelines/BTC.html

Bahgat, G. (2004). The Caspian Sea: Potentials and Prospects. *Governance: An International Journal of Policy, Administration, and Institutions*, *17*(1), 115-126.

Bardakçı, M. (2003). Russian Interests in the Caspian Region and Turkey. *Sosyal Bilimler Dergisi (Dokuz Eylül Üniversitesi)*, *5*(2), 1-29.

Bayülgen, O. (2009). Caspian Energy Wealth, Social Impacts and Implications for Regional Stability. In A. E. Wooden & C. H. Stefes (Eds.), *The Politics of Transition in Central Asia and the Caucasus: Enduring Legacies and Emerging Challenges* (pp. 163-188). Routledge.

Behzadi, R. (2010). Iran's Foreign Policy. *The Caspian Sea Basin, Central Asia and The Caucasus*, *11*(3), 86-93.

Birsel, H. (2006). *Eski Dünyanın Karanlık Yüzü Orta Asya Jeopolitiği*. IQ Kültür-Sanat Yayıncılık.

Ceragioli, P., & Martellini, M. (2003, May 25). *The Geopolitics of Pipelines*. Asia Times. http://freerepublic.com/focus/f-news/920139/posts

Coffey, L. (2015, December 4). *A Secure and Stable Caspian Sea is in America's Interest*. The Heritage Foundation. http://www.heritage.org/research/reports/2015/12/a-secure-and-stable-caspian-sea-is-in-americas-interest

Çolakoğlu, S. (1998). Uluslararası Hukukta Hazar'ın Statüsü Sorunu. *Ankara Üniversitesi Siyasal Bilgiler Fakültesi Dergisi*, *53*, 108-122.

Diba, B. A. (2003). *The Law and Politics of the Caspian Sea in the Twenty-first Century*. Ibex.

EIA. (2013a). *Caspian Sea Region*. Retrieved July 15, 2019, from http://www.eia.gov/beta/international/regions-topics.cfm?RegionTopicID=CSR

EIA. (2013b). *Kazakhstan*. https://www.eia.gov/beta/international/analysis_includes/countries_long/Kazakhstan/archive/pdf/Kazakhstan_2013.pdf

EIA. (2014). *International Energy Data and Analysis: Azerbaijan*. https://www.eia.gov/beta/international/analysis_includes/countries_long/Azerbaijan/azerbaijan.pdf

EIA. (2016). *Turkmenistan*. Retrieved July 15, 2019, from https://www.eia.gov/beta/international/country.php?iso=TKM

EIA. (2017). *Russia*. Retrieved July 15, 2019, from https://www.eia.gov/beta/international/analysis.php?iso=RUS

Enerji Günlüğü (2018, August 1). *AB'den TANAP'a 5 Milyon Euro Hibe*. https://enerjigunlugu.net/icerik/28280/abden-tanapa-5-milyon-euro-hibe.html

Gökay, B. (2001). *The Politics of Caspian Oil*. Palgrave Macmillan.

Haghayeghi, M. (2003). The Coming of Conflict to the Caspian Sea. *Problems of Post Communism, 50*(3), 32-41.

Janusz-Pawletta, B. (2015). *The Legal Status of the Caspian Sea*. Springer.

Macit, F. (2014). *Caspian Energy Outlook*. Caspian Strategy Institute. https://www.academia.edu/12345287/Caspian_Energy_Outlook

Mamedov, R. (2001). International Legal Status of The Caspian Sea: Issues of Theory and Practice. *The Turkish Yearbook*, *32*, 217-259.

Mehdiyoun, K. (2000). Ownership of Oil and Gas Resources in the Caspian Sea. *American Journal of International Law*, *94*(1), 179-189.

Mehtiyev, E. (2015). The Caucasus: The Current Development and Expectations and Perspectives for the Next Decade. In A. Yalçınkaya & Ş. Yazğan (Eds.), *4. Blue Black Sea International Congress Proceedings* (pp. 27-45). Gündoğan Yayınları.

Michel, C. (2015, May 31). *Caspian Agreement: Rare Good News for Central Asia Relations*. The Diplomat.

http://thediplomat.com/2015/05/caspian-agreement-rare-good-news-for-central-asia-relations/
Oğan, S. (2001). Hazar'da Tehlikeli Oyunlar: Statü Sorunu, Paylaşılamayan Kaynaklar ve Silahlanma Yarışı. *Avrasya Dosyası*, *7*(2), 143-183.
Özbay, F. (2007). Realpolitik, Pragmatizm, Ulusal Çıkarlar ve Nükleer Program Ekseninde Dünden Bugüne Rusya-İran İlişkileri. In K. Dağcı & A. Sandıklı (Eds.), *Satranç Tahtasında İran: "Nükleer Program"* (pp. 151-218). TASAM.
Poyraz, Y. (2011). Hazar'ın Hukuki Rejimine İlişkin Sorunlar ve Kıyıdaş Devletlerin Çözüm Çabaları. *Uluslararası Hukuk ve Politika*, *7*(28), 27-55.
President of Russia (2018a, August 12). *Convention on the Legal Status of the Caspian Sea*. http://en.kremlin.ru/supplement/5328
President of Russia. (2018b, August 12). *Fifth Caspian Summit.* http://en.kremlin.ru/events/president/news/58296
TANAP. (n.d.-a). *Major Shareholder in the Project of the Century!* Retrieved August 17, 2019, from https://www.tanap.com/media/press-releases/major-shareholder-in-the-project-of-the-century/
TANAP. (n.d.-b). *Turkey: Historic TANAP gas pipeline project goes live.* Retrieved August 17, 2019, from https://www.tanap.com/media/news/turkey-historic-tanap-gas-pipeline-project-goes-live/
TANAP. (n.d.-c). *Why TANAP?* Retrieved August 17, 2019, from https://www.tanap.com/tanap-project/why-tanap/
Terzioğlu, S. S. (2008). Hazar'ın Statüsü Hakkında Kıyıdaş Devletlerin Hukuksal Görüşleri. *OAKA*, *3*(5), 26-47. https://docplayer.biz.tr/31308070-Hazar-in-statusu-hakkinda-kiyidas-devletlerin-hukuksal-gorusleri.html
TRACECA. (n.d.). *TRACECA – Restoration of the Historic Silk Road.* Retrieved July 15, 2019, from http://www.traceca-org.org/en/countries/azerbaijan/azerbaijan-in-traceca/
World Bank. (n.d.). *Trans-Anatolian Natural Gas Pipeline Project.* Retrieved August 17, 2019, from http://projects.worldbank.org/P157416/?lang=en&tab=overview
Yalçınkaya, A. (2019). *Özbekistan'ın Türk Cumhuriyetleriyle İşbirliği Stratejisi ve Hazar'ın Statüsü.* III. Uluslararası Hocalı Soykırımı ve Türk Dünyası Sempozyumu, Giresun Üniversitesi.

CHAPTER SIX

ENERGY POLICY OF THE BLACK SEA BASIN AND TAX PRIVILEGES PROVIDED FOR ENERGY INVESTMENTS

MELTEM IRTEŞ GÜLŞEN*

Introduction

As a result of mechanization with the industrial revolution and the need for the high amount of energy used in mechanization, it was necessary for states to determine new strategies both economically and politically, within and outside the country. The lower level of energy required for the most natural heating and nutritional needs of people and the higher level of energy requirements for machines have survived to the present day. Initially, quality coal reserves in the UK were opened up as the energy source needed by the industrial revolution. Later, other countries, with the effects of the industrial revolution outside the UK, also needed coal. Due to the inability to meet the demand for coal, the priority of coal was replaced by oil, an alternative source of energy, and oil was then replaced by the use of natural gas as a result of price increases created by the oil crises. Despite the fact that oil prices were kept under control in the 1980s, since natural gas production was not sufficient, the energy supply security problem gained importance again in the 2000s due to the increase in both oil and natural gas prices. Solving this problem is of great importance in terms of preventing many economic, social, and political problems (Ercümen, 2016; Bohi & Toman, 1996, p. 12).

One of the issues that today's states attach great importance to in their foreign policies is to ensure their production by protecting their energy resources and controlling the market. Energy has become a strategic tool. In

* Assoc. Prof. Meltem Irteş Gülşen, Open Education Faculty, Anadolu University. E-mail: mirtes@anadolu.edu.tr.

order to control the market, it is necessary to control the energy transmission routes. Controlling the energy market and the transit routes will be one of the main drivers of countries' future foreign and national policies. In the short term, the goal of energy policies is to ensure that energy resources reach the market in the shortest time and at the most affordable prices. In the long term, the subject of energy policies is development plans and policies. Although these plans are not a problem in terms of reserves, they will continue to be an important problem affecting relations between countries on a global basis, such as with regard to finding and producing alternative energy sources, as well as supplying them to the market (Ercümen, 2016).

The most important sources in the world's energy production are coal, oil, and natural gas, which are the consumable energy sources obtained from hydrocarbon sources, which constitute more than two-thirds of the energy resources consumed. Today, 90% of energy production is met by these sources, namely fossil fuels. The remaining 10% is provided by nuclear and renewable energy sources.

In recent years, the need for energy has increased with the increasing population and income increases as developing countries entered the rapid industrialization process. This situation increased the consumption demand for oil and natural gas, which are the primary sources of energy. Therefore, competition is more intense in regions where the energy demand is high. In other words, having an energy source and directing the energy trade is becoming more and more important. This has a significant impact on the energy policies of the countries that have these resources and those countries that want to have a say in the transfer of these resources to the countries in need.

Purpose and Method

In this study, the energy policies of the countries in the Black Sea Basin, which have an important role in transferring primary energy resources between the countries that have important reserves in Central Asia and the Middle East and the Western countries that need these energy resources, and the tax privileges granted to energy investments to support these policies will be examined. Firstly, the energy sources of the countries in the Black Sea Basin will be briefly analyzed. Then, the importance of the countries in the Black Sea Basin in terms of energy supply and the similarities and differences of the tax privileges provided in these countries will be investigated. Thus, by identifying the potential cooperation areas of the countries in the Black Sea Basin, the aim is to guide the common policies that can be developed on energy supply.

Energy Resources of Countries in the Black Sea Basin

All types of energy, which means power generated from various sources, constitute the energy supply. Oil, coal, and natural gas are ranked in the top three of the world's primary energy supply. The share of nuclear energy in the primary energy supply is quite low (EYODER, 2017). In terms of energy resources' consumption, the breakdown is 33% oil, 30% coal, 24% natural gas, 7% hydroelectricity, 4% nuclear energy, and 2% renewable energy (IEA, 2013). According to ExxonMobil's "2018 Outlook for Energy: A View to 2040" report, due to the effect of non-OECD countries, global energy demand is expected to increase by 25% by 2040. Global natural gas demand is estimated to increase by approximately 40% (ExxonMobil, 2018). As can be seen from these data, the level of fossil fuel production and consumption on a global scale, and thus dependence on electrical energy, is remarkable.

Today, due to the problems experienced in energy supply globally, providing supply diversity is an important part of energy policies. Therefore, investments are made in alternative energy sources. According to reports prepared by BP in 2016 on this subject, renewable energy used in electricity generation increased by 15.2% in 2015 compared to 2014. This constitutes 6.7% of global production. Its share in world energy consumption has reached 2.8%. In other words, in the last decade, global electricity generation has largely been met by renewable energy (BP, 2016). The data show that, among all regions and fuels, the choices made by governments in their energy policies will shape the energy system of the future (Birol, 2018). As a result, the energy resources of Bulgaria, Romania, Turkey, Georgia, Russia, and Ukraine in the Black Sea Basin will be discussed. In the following sections, the extent to which renewable energy resources in the energy systems of the future are supported by the state will be examined.

Bulgaria

Bulgaria generates 61% of its primary energy supply from coal and nuclear power generation. Thus, it can reduce its dependence on external energy. 32% of the energy supplies consists of oil and natural gas, most of which is met through imports. The aging of Bulgaria's energy infrastructure, the fact that 32% of its energy supply is dependent on external sources, and its low

GDP increase the importance of Bulgarian energy policies for the national economy.

Romania

Romania is a country with oil and gas reserves. However, despite the increase in domestic demand, there is a decrease in reserves, and therefore in oil and natural gas production. This increases energy imports. Three-quarters (79%) of Romania's energy supply consists of oil, natural gas, and coal. On the other hand, Romania also produces domestic shale gas.

Turkey

Turkey receives about 90% of its primary energy supply from natural gas, coal, and oil. Half of its coal and almost all of its oil and natural gas (91-97%) are imported. There is no supply of nuclear energy in Turkey. Therefore, Turkey's dependence on external energy is very high. Among the OECD countries, Turkey is ranked first in terms of energy demand growth. This increase is mainly caused by natural gas imports. This increases the importance of energy supply security in Turkey.

According to TÜİK data, "*In 2017, Turkey met 37% of its electricity needs from natural gas, 33% from coal, 20% from hydroelectricity, 6% from wind, 2% from geothermal energy, and 2% from other energy sources*" (Türkiye.gov, 2019).

Georgia

A large portion of Georgia's primary energy supply consists of oil and natural gas. However, Georgia's supply of most of its energy resources, namely 97% of its oil and almost all of its natural gas supply, comes through imports. This is an indication that Georgia's dependence on external sources in terms of energy is very high. Georgia also exports electricity to various countries. However, the electricity produced domestically is not sufficiently utilized in the country. Georgia uses only 10% of the generated hydroelectric energy. Therefore, it cannot meet its own needs. Russia supplies natural gas via Turkmenistan and Azerbaijan (Kaytez vd, 2018: 94).

The country's oil and gas reserves are quite limited. Magnesium and perlite mines are being mined. The richest manganese deposits in the world are in the Chiatura region of Georgia. Zinc, lead, and gold are being extracted from other mines. The total area of forests concentrated in the foothills of the Caucasus Mountains is around 3 million hectares, and timber has an important place in Georgia's export potential (Ege Bölgesi Sanayi Odası, 2018, pp. 1-19).

In Georgia, there are many problems facing the energy sector. In addition, while the need for energy has increased in Georgia in the last ten years, the existing hydropower plants (HPPs) have been rehabilitated and new HPPs have been installed. Georgia, which previously imported electricity, started to export electricity in recent years. The establishment of new power plants in Georgia is being encouraged (Dış Ekonomik İlişkiler Kurulu, 2018).

Russia

Russia is one of the countries with the world's richest oil reserves. It is also the world's second-largest supplier of natural gas and has rich coal reserves. However, its actual production is limited. 90% of the energy supply in the country is covered by primary energy sources. On the other hand, the country also produces nuclear energy.

Ukraine

Approximately 80% of the Ukrainian energy supply consists of primary energy sources. Due to a lack of sufficient reserves, it is dependent on imports of oil and natural gas. It is dependent on Russia, especially for its natural gas supply, and largely imports natural gas (Orta Karadeniz Kalkınma Ajansı, 2010., p. 7). As the existing energy infrastructure is old infrastructure from the Soviet Union period, energy efficiency is adversely affected. On the other hand, the energy transmission lines in the country consisting of gas and oil lines have given Ukraine a strategic position. Coal production ranks second in primary energy supply.

As Ukraine has energy-intensive sectors, energy consumption in the country is still quite high. The country's energy resources can only cover 20% of consumption. In this respect, Ukraine ranks third in the world after the USA and Russia in gas consumption and imports large amounts of natural gas (Orta Karadeniz Kalkınma Ajansı, 2010, p. 14).

Summary

As can be seen from the brief explanations above, the primary energy supply of the countries in the Black Sea Basin is predominantly fossil fuels. The countries in the region, other than Russia, are energy-dependent. Therefore, the countries in the Black Sea Basin are required to regulate their energy policies in order to ensure energy supply security. As the domestic resources of Turkey, Bulgaria, Georgia, Romania, and Ukraine are limited, it is necessary to increase diversity both among the energy sources consumed and among the countries where energy is imported in order to secure energy supply. As a result, these countries are turning to reserve research, alternative energy sources, and policies that increase energy efficiency and therefore save money. They are trying to ensure energy supply security by creating alternatives by increasing the energy transmission lines and the number of countries to which they supply energy.

The Importance of Black Sea Basin Energy Politics

Energy is one of the most important requirements for the sustainability of daily life as well as for the execution of economic policies. States wishing to have a say on world energy policies are striving to control their energy resources and transport routes. The Black Sea Basin is a region with rich natural resources in terms of energy and energy transmission lines (Tüysüz, 2014, pp. 81-82). It is located on the trade routes between Asia and Europe. Today, this situation causes conflicts. Socio-cultural differences between the countries around the Black Sea Basin are another cause of conflict. It increases competition in the international system with the contributions of globalization. However, for countries that do not have sufficient energy resources, it is very important to reach the energy resources under the most favorable conditions, that is, to ensure the security of energy supply. This, in other words, the desire to meet energy needs in a short time, cheaply, and in the most reliable ways, shapes the policies regarding the Black Sea Basin of both the energy-supplying countries and the importing countries (Pamir, 2003, p. 137).

Energy supply security is defined in the EU Commission as follows: "*To provide uninterrupted physical access to the energy products market at all prices for all consumers within the framework of the goal of sustainable development for the well-being of the whole society and a well-functioning economy*" (European Commission, 2010).

Although the strategic importance of the Black Sea Basin in the 20th century remains dormant, its geopolitical importance has not been forgotten (Blouet, 2005). Halford Mackinder states that "*the power that holds control of the natural resources will control an area within the Black Sea region, which is necessary to control the whole world*" (Mackinder, 1962, p. 150).

The United States has a policy of managing all energy resources for the world leadership. Therefore, the Black Sea Basin is one of the most important regions for the United States in terms of energy resources. The

United States wants to guide the world's energy policies through the Middle East, Caucasus, Caspian Basin, and the Black Sea Basin, which also have the world's richest natural resources and energy transportation lines, and to overcome its economic difficulties (İrge, 2017, pp. 14-15).

In the same way, the EU wants to be a neighbor to the Black Sea coast and realize cooperations with its countries to ensure the security of the energy supply of the Union and to have a say on the transition routes. At the same time, EU member countries, which have foreign-dependent energy policies, depend on Russia for their energy imports. More than half of their natural gas needs are met from Russia (U.S. Energy Information Administration, 2018). Russia, which has two-thirds of the world's oil reserves, wants to maintain its former Cold War-era regional power. Russia is not only a supplier country but also a transit country due to the pipelines that transport natural gas in the Caspian Basin to Europe. Russia's direct interventions in Georgia in 2008 and Ukraine in 2014 are results of its policy to have regional power and become the dominant power in the transfer of energy resources (Erbaş, 2012, p. 4). Therefore, the Black Sea Basin has become the center of the power struggles of global powers. For this reason, it is important to ensure the stability and security of the Black Sea Basin (Tüysüz, 2014, p. 81; Yorulmaz, 2019).

Russia, on the other hand, wants to use energy as a means of repression in its foreign policy in order to make good use of its legacy from the Soviets. It seeks to maintain its influence in the Caspian Basin and to have the authority to determine prices and control in the energy market.

Alexander Goncharenko stated the importance of the Black Sea Basin as follows: "*According to classical geopolitical theories, the Black Sea Basin is one of the most important cornerstones of order and security in Eurasia. This region is a very sensitive area with its natural resources, energy and transportation lines. Domination over the Black Sea Basin region will bring Eurasian sovereignty. Therefore, the Black Sea Basin is in the interest of all global actors in political, military, financial and other similar fields*" (Goncharenko, 2005, p. 23). This statement shows the geopolitical and geostrategic importance of the Black Sea Basin. The countries of the region are fortunate in terms of their geostrategic area. However, the lack of balance in the distribution of energy resources between countries can cause crises from time to time. This requires extensive cooperation.

While the Black Sea Basin is the subject of competition between global and regional powers on the one hand, the problems and instability arising from the ethnic conflicts and border problems between the countries of the Balkans and Caucasus region on the other hand directly affect the security of the region (Oğan, 2009, p. 12). The South Ossetian Crisis can be considered as an example. Therefore, since the instability and chaos that may occur in the Black Sea Basin will affect the coastal countries as well as the non-coastal countries, it is of great importance that the region is peaceful (Tüysüz, 2014, pp. 74-75)

In his study of Russia's regional energy policies, Kantörün (2010) stated, "It is quite difficult to deliver the natural gas extracted from these regions to European markets without pipelines passing through the territory controlled by the Russian state" (Kantörün, 2010, p. 2). Naturally, this makes it difficult for European countries to recover from their energy dependence on Russia. At the same time, other coastal countries in the Black Sea Basin, such as Turkey, Georgia, and Bulgaria, which also serve as bridges for the transfer of energy resources, are of indispensable importance. The security and stability of the regions that provide energy to the EU need to be ensured. Therefore, like many countries in the world, the EU member states, which do not want to experience problems in energy supply, are in search of alternative sources for energy.

Existing Energy Lines in the Black Sea Basin

The main priority of energy policies for all countries is to ensure the security and diversity of their energy supply. Therefore, besides the existing pipelines, new large- and medium-scale projects are also supported. The energy potential of the Black Sea region, which was not very noticeable during the Cold War period, has just begun to be discovered. This has caused the energy transmission lines and planned projects in the Black Sea Basin to gain importance every day in eliminating the energy deficits faced by countries and increasing the diversity of supply. While transit routes and markets of both oil and gas pipeline projects in the Black Sea Basin have been identified, countries attempt to exclude neighboring countries and other countries in the region. Some of the existing and planned pipelines in the Black Sea Basin are as follows:

- Trans-Caspian Pipeline
- Baku-Tbilisi-Ceyhan Pipeline
- South Caucasus Pipeline
- Trans-Siberian Pipeline
- Blue Stream Pipeline
- Blue Stream II Pipeline
- South Stream Pipeline
- TurkStream Pipeline

Blue Stream is the first pipeline in the world to be installed at a depth of 2,150 m (Gazprom, 2019). The line has a length of 1,213 km. The fact that the pipeline passes through the dense hydrogen sulfide-filled base of the Black Sea and will create a dependence on Russia for energy has caused controversy in the Turkish public opinion (Öztürk, 2017).

Blue Stream II is a project that aims to carry Russian natural gas through Turkey to Israel, Syria, Lebanon, as well as Cyprus by building a parallel line to the existing Blue Stream line (Uluatam, 2010, p. 63-64).

The South Stream gas project aimed to connect the Russian Federation to Bulgaria and Serbia through a 900 km pipeline, which would pass under the Black Sea. Compared to the Nabucco project developed by the EU for the security of natural gas supply, South Stream became an attractive project since it had no financing and supplier country problems (Tüysüz, 2014, p. 84). However, the project was canceled by Russia on the grounds that it was not practicable (Sabah Gazetesi, 2014).

Another project is the TurkStream pipeline involving Turkey and Russia. The agreement was signed in Istanbul on October 10, 2016 (Demirci, 2019). TurkStream is planned to be 2,100 km shorter than the proposed South Stream line (the South Stream pipeline would have been 2,386 km, 931 km of which would have been under the Black Sea and 1,455 km on European land).

When we consider Ukraine, it can be seen that 80% of the natural gas imported by the EU from Russia is supplied by seven pipelines passing through Ukraine. The pipelines pass through Soyuz, Brotherhood, and Northern Lights and connect to the Transgas pipeline in Slovakia. The gas is then distributed to many European countries. Ukraine has become Europe's natural gas distribution center with its pipelines. This advantage is sometimes used to resist Russian policies (Uluatam, 2010, p. 66). The White Stream project also aims to connect Georgia to Ukraine via a natural gas pipeline. The biggest problem with the project is the uncertainty of the countries that will be its financiers and suppliers, as with the Nabucco project (Uluatam, 2010, pp. 65-66).

Turkey, on the other hand, has an important role to play in the transfer of energy resources, even though it is not an energy supplier country. It is in a very important strategic position in this regard. Turkey is an important transit country for the transportation of oil and gas demand to the market through the Straits. A significant amount of oil in Russia and the Caspian region is transported to European countries through the Turkish Straits. International and regional policies play an important role in cross-border pipelines. In this context, both Russian-Ukrainian relations and Russian-

European relations are important for the TurkStream pipeline planned by Gazprom.

The Turkey-Greece-Italy pipeline is 290 km long. It is a natural gas pipeline agreement that supplies natural gas from the Caspian Sea and the Middle East to Europe. Turkey supplies natural gas from Azerbaijan, Russia, and Iran and delivers it to Greece through this pipeline.

The length of the Trans-Balkan natural gas pipeline is more than 965 km. This line supplies Russian gas to Southeast Europe and Turkey, meeting the energy need in these regions. Natural gas from here is also transmitted from Turkey to Ukraine, Moldova, Romania, and Bulgaria.

The 692-km-long East Caucasus pipeline transports natural gas from Azerbaijan to Georgia and Turkey. The East Caucasus pipeline was constructed using the Baku-Tbilisi-Ceyhan (BTC) corridor. The line was generally built to bring the gas produced at the Shah Deniz natural gas field to the Turkey-Georgia border.

The planned Arab gas pipeline, intended to transport Egyptian gas to Europe, is designed to include Lebanon, Jordan, Syria, and Turkey. With this pipeline, it is aimed to bring Egyptian natural gas to Turkey.

The Trans-Adriatic Pipeline (TAP) is a project to transport Azerbaijani gas through Turkey to Italy via Greece and Albania. The line is 870 km long. It is the continuation of the TANAP project. Its target market is Italy and Southern European countries.

The purpose of the Trans-Anatolia (TANAP) project is to transport the natural gas produced in Azerbaijan's Shah Deniz 2 gas field in the Caspian Sea and in other fields in the south of the Caspian Sea to Turkey and then to Europe. Upon completion, TANAP will join the South Caucasus pipeline and the TAP to form the Southern Gas Corridor. The supplier is Azerbaijan. The recipients are the countries of Southeast Europe (Erbaş, 2012, p. 10).

Tax Incentives Provided by Countries in the Black Sea Basin for Energy Investments

It is important that states have a diversity of resources and countries for energy supply security. Renewable energy resources have become one of the most important energy policy issues of countries in the last two decades. In order to increase renewable energy investments, more than 100 countries are applying tax incentive policies in order to encourage renewable energy investments. Some countries apply tax exemptions and exceptions, while others apply reductions in research and development expenditure. In a study conducted by Çelikkaya, it is stated that almost every country has provided various tax incentives in order to increase the share of renewable energy investments in the energy industry around the world and that Russia and Ukraine make little use of renewable energy (Çelikkaya, 2018, p. 373).

The tax privileges imposed by the countries in the Black Sea Basin for renewable energy investments are described in the following sections.

Bulgaria

The tax incentives for investments in Bulgaria in general are as follows:

- Partial granting of corporate income tax (CIT) due for the performance of agricultural activities;
- Additional tax deductions for the hiring of long-term unemployed, handicapped, or elderly persons;
- Granting back of up to 100% of the CIT due for investment in regions with high unemployment;
- Investments to improve energy efficiency consist of the production of equipment and devices that are part of the initial investment or purchase, and accelerated depreciation is applied as a tax incentive for machinery. The annual tax depreciation rate is up to 50% (PWC, 2019.-a).

Incentives within the scope of the Renewable and Alternative Energy Sources Act are as follows:

- Mandatory purchase at preferential prices of the electricity generated by renewable energy sources;
- Feed-in tariffs set by the State Energy and Water Regulatory Commission;
- Priority connection to the electricity grid;
- Certificates of origin (Invest Bulgaria, 2019).

Romania

Romania's energy strategy for the period 2007-2020 highlights its future energy strategy. It targets the need for energy for an adequate modern market economy both now and in the medium- and long-term at as low a price as possible. Strategies such as ensuring a high civilized living standard, security of supply, the development of competitive markets, and respect for sustainability principles are being developed (Chirila, 2013, p. 19).

The Green Certificate System, which is a part of the Renewable Energy Act, provides incentives for certain types of renewable energy. Green Certificates are processed in parallel with the energy produced. Although Green Certificates are intended to provide an additional revenue source for renewable energy producers, revisions to the support system have created instability in renewable investment environments. Energy-intensive industry consumers are exempt from obtaining a Green Certificate. In March 2017, the government revised its renewable energy support legislation (RCCG, 2017).

Incentives provided in the tax laws are as follows:

- 16% fixed tax
- Possibility of quick depreciation (50% depreciation for the first year)
- Possibility to account for losses for up to 5 years
- Land and construction tax exemption for up to 5 years
- Tax exemption in industrial parks
- Incentives for the recruitment of new graduates
- Financial support for investments exceeding €30 million

"*With the exception of penalties and protocol expenses as a general rule, raw materials, materials, machinery, equipment, work safety and accident protection costs, advertising, training, business travel, market research, communication infrastructure volumes and expenses arising from natural disasters*" can be reduced in terms of cost (RCCG, 2017).

Turkey

There are a number of tax incentives for energy investments in Turkey. According to the law, "*Investments for energy efficiency, which are designed to save energy by at least 20% according to the current situation and which will be provided with energy savings, with a maximum return period of 5 years, will benefit from the incentives provided for investments to be made in the fifth region regardless of the region in which the investment will be made. The incentives to be utilized are value added tax exemption, customs duty exemption, tax deduction, insurance premium employer share support, interest support and investment place allocation*" (ETKB, 2019).

The following are the investment issues of special importance that will be supported by the fifth region elements, regardless of the region in which they are located:

- Investments in electricity generation in which the mines in the 4-b group of Article 2 of Mining Law No. 3213 are used as input within the scope of a valid mining license and permission issued by the Ministry of Energy and Natural Resources;
- Investments for the energy efficiency project, which is designed to save at least 20% energy according to its current state and which has a return period of 5 years and less, will be realized in existing manufacturing industrial plants with an annual minimum consumption of 500 TOE (tonne(s) of oil equivalent);
- Investments in the manufacture of turbines and generators for the production of renewable energy and the manufacture of blades used in wind power generation;
- Integrated investments in the production of aluminum flat products by direct cooling slab casting and hot rolling method;
- Nuclear power plant investments (Invest In Turkey, 2019).

More detailed incentives are provided for renewable energy: "*In addition to general, regional, priority, and strategic investment incentives for investments in the energy sector, the government provides specific incentives for electricity generation investments based on renewable energy sources*." These are as follows:

- 100% exemption from customs duty and VAT
- 10-year tariff guarantee (FiT) application
- Network connection priorities
- Lower license fees
- Various practical facilities for project preparation and land acquisition (Invest In Turkey, 2019)

Georgia

Georgia is a very rich country in terms of water resources and is one of the largest hydropower exporters in the world. Georgia offers significant investment opportunities for HPPs. Investment Tax Credit (ITC) is applied in its solar energy system. This policy can reduce the cost of its solar energy system by 30% (Energysage, 2019).

The business environment in Georgia is investor-oriented. The Georgian investment climate has improved in recent years. Less tax is imposed and procedures for opening a business have been significantly simplified. Great steps have been taken to eliminate the bureaucracy that exists at every level of government in Georgia. The conditions of investment in the large HPPs are subject to the approval of the Government of Georgia, which offers a number of tax advantages:

- There is no payroll tax or social insurance tax;
- There is no capital gains tax;
- There is no wealth tax, inheritance tax, or stamp tax;
- Foreign income for individuals is completely tax-free (Georgia Energy Electricity Industry, 2012).

Russia

The tax privileges granted to investments in Russia are as follows:

- Regional incentives provided by regional or local authorities;
- Special tax regimes in special economic zones (SEZs);
- Regional investment projects and private investment contracts;
- Advanced development zones (ADZs);
- Free port of Vladivostok;
- Incentives related to specific activities;
- Incentives for special projects (e.g. the Skolkovo Innovation Center or 2018 FIFA World Cup) (PWC, 2019-b).

Many industrial regions of Russia offer numerous tax and non-tax incentives and benefits to investors. Regional incentives (primarily the CIT portion of the specified region, property tax, and transport tax) in the form of lowering tax rates are given to certain taxpayer classes, usually to large investors or organizations operating in certain sectors. The discounted regional rates will be applied until January 1, 2023. Local land tax incentives are also often available to regional investors. The size of the investment is between about 50 million RUB and 150 million RUB. For some regions, this amount is less, and in others, a certain amount is not specified but is subject to negotiation.

Credit reduction is granted for foreign taxes paid up to the amount of Russian tax debt to be paid in the same amount in accordance with Russian rules (PWC, 2019-c).

A property tax exemption is available for energy-efficient assets (including buildings) for three years, starting from the date of the asset's entry into operation, with no preapproval from the tax or any other authorities. In practice, the application of this incentive has thus far been very limited.

Renewable energy investments include a climate change tax, a property tax exemption for three years, and a double depreciation of standard practice (Deloitte, 2016).

Ukraine

In Ukraine, businesses are provided with incentives to attract investments to priority sectors of the economy (Deloitte, 2017, p. 4). According to the Tax Code of Ukraine, between 2017 and 2021, taxpayers with an annual income of less than 3 million UAH were allowed to apply for tax holidays. Tax holidays are implemented in line with restrictions on certain types of activities, provided they meet the requirements for the average number of employees and payroll amount (PWC, 2019-d).

In addition to the global trend, Ukraine attracts the attention of local and foreign investors as it provides special legal support for renewable energy projects within the framework of the Government of Ukraine's Energy Efficiency Program 2010-2015. In order to ensure the development of renewable energy facilities in Ukraine, the green tariff regime is implemented within the framework of the Electrical Power Industry Law. This tariff applies specifically to electricity generated from renewable energy sources, including solar and wind energy.

According to the said law, for renewable energy facilities which started to operate after 2019 and 2024, the green tariff indices applied will be reduced by 20% and 30%, respectively, and in general, the concept of green tariffs will continue until January 1, 2030.

The following exemptions apply in relation to operations with equipment working on renewable energy sources; materials and equipment used in renewable energy production or the production of alternative fuel types; energy-efficient materials and equipment; and measuring, controlling, and managing energy and fuel costs:

- A full exemption from CIT is envisaged for profits from the core activities of companies generating electricity solely from renewable energy sources until 2021. Also, a partial CIT exemption (applicable to 80% of the profits) applies to the profits of companies from the sale of certain self-produced goods.
- A temporary exemption from VAT and customs duties for specified transactions in imports (for use in their own production) until 2019.
- A 75% discount on land tax on the land used to install power plants that generate electricity from renewable energy sources (KPMG, 2015, pp. 9-80; Deloitte, 2017).

- A CIT exemption (and other similar incentives) for profits of companies from the sale of equipment powered by renewable energy sources; raw materials, equipment, and components used in renewable energy production; and energy-saving equipment and materials which enable the rational consumption of fuel resources (Boboshko, 2013; Kharenko, 2019).

Conclusion

Energy is one of the most strategic tools that can be used to achieve development and prosperity. Energy policies are a factor regulating the relations between the states that import and export energy. Therefore, it has an important place in the international system. The willingness of states to control their energy transmission routes is one of the obvious reasons for conflicts between countries. Furthermore, one of the main reasons for the rapid recovery from the aircraft crisis between Turkey and Russia in the recent past is the TurkStream and Akkuyu nuclear power plant projects.

The Black Sea Basin is an important bridge between east and west. It is of strategic importance between the producer countries, which have the majority of the world's primary energy resources, and the consumer countries. It is a route that carries energy products to developed and developing countries in need of energy and enables them to be delivered to global markets. With this role, it has increased the importance of Black Sea Basin countries in ensuring power balances internationally and in determining energy policies. It is especially the problems experienced in the transportation of energy resources in Central Asia and the Caspian Basin to Europe and the power conflicts between the USA and Russia that reveal the geopolitical importance of the Black Sea Basin.

Although the countries in the Black Sea Basin are on the transition line of energy resources, other than Russia, they are not producing countries. Their energy supply security also depends on external sources. Therefore, in the growth model based on energy production, targets such as reducing dependence on external energy, increasing resource diversity, and increasing the use of alternative energy sources are important for the importing countries in the Black Sea Basin.

When we look at the world energy view, it can be seen that fossil fuels have been replaced by renewable energy. According to World Economic Outlook data from 2015, it is estimated that renewable energy will be used as the primary source of electricity generation in the next decade. The fact that the supply of energy resources is met with externally dependent imported energy sources is not sustainable. Therefore, nowadays, renewable energy is an inevitable choice in terms of the economy and the environment. Therefore, reducing fossil fuel consumption, which is the dominant energy resource in the world, will result in a change of energy policies in the world. The expansion of renewable energy sources will reduce the current account deficit problem of external-dependent countries, as well as reduce the harmful effects of fossil fuels on the environment.

The fact that renewable energy sources have become one of the most important energy policy issues of the world's countries has led to the need to promote this issue. In order to increase the competitiveness of renewable energy, serious public support is needed in the initial phase. Today, many countries are implementing both non-tax incentives as well as various tax incentive policies specific to renewable energy investments for the promotion of renewable energy investments. Some countries apply tax exemptions and exceptions, while others apply cost reductions in research and development expenditure.

The Black Sea Basin countries, which are the subject of our review, have also taken necessary measures in this regard. As in the rest of the world, it has been observed that various tax incentives have been provided in order to increase the share of renewable energy in the energy mix of Black Sea Basin countries. These incentives are mainly exemptions from corporation tax, value-added tax, and real estate tax. Accelerated depreciation and the implementation of regional privileges are other notable incentives. In each of the countries in the Black Sea Basin, it is found that important tax regulations are included in energy policies for renewable energy investments. Maintaining this support in line with the countries' energy policies will enable the transfer of sustainable energy policies to future generations.

References

Birol, F. (2018). The Gold Standard of Energy Analysis. *World Energy Outlook 2018*. Retrieved June 25, 2019, from https://www.iea.org/weo2018/

Blouet, B. W. (2005). *Global Strategy: Mackinder and the Defence of the West*. Frank Cass.

Boboshko, A. (2013). *Legal and tax incentives for solar and wind projects in Ukraine*. Financier Worldwide. https://www.financierworldwide.com/legal-and-tax-incentives-for-solar-and-wind-projects-in-ukraine#.YKQzFKhKiUk

Bohi, D. R., & Toman, M. M. (1996). *The Economics Of Energy Security*. Kluwer Academic Publisher.

BP. (2016). *Statistical Review of World Energy 2016.*
Chirila, N. (2013). *Renewable Energy In Romania, January 2013.* https://www.flandersinvestmentandtrade.com/export/sites/trade/files/market_studies/249130212154437/249130212154437_1.pdf
Çelikkaya, A. (2018). Dünyada Yenilenebilir Enerji Yatırımlarına Sağlanan Vergi Teşviklerinin Değerlendirilmesi. *Afyon Kocatepe Üniversitesi Sosyal Bilimler Dergisi*, *20*(1), 357-384.
Deloitte. (2016). *Tax Incentives In Russia.* https://www2.deloitte.com/content/dam/Deloitte/ru/Documents/tax/tax-incentives-inrussia-2016-en.pdf
Deloitte. (2017). *Ukraine Taxation and Investment 2017.* https://www2.deloitte.com/content/dam/Deloitte/global/Documents/Tax/dttl-taxukraineguide-2017.pdf
Demirci, M. C. (2019, January 28). *Türk Akımı mı, Rus Akımı mı? Boru hattı en çok kime yarıyor?* Euronews. https://tr.euronews.com/2019/01/28/turk-akimi-mi-rus-akimi-mi-dogal-gazboru-hatti-en-cok-kime-yariyor
Dış Ekonomik İlişkiler Kurulu. (2018). *Gürcistan Bülteni 2018.* https://www.deik.org.tr/uploads/gurcistan_bulten_2018.pdf
Ege Bölgesi Sanayi Odası. (2018). *Uluslararası İlişkiler Şefliği, Gürcistan Ülke Raporu*. https://www.ebso.org.tr/ebsomedia/documents/gurcistan-ulke-raporu_27761727.doc
Energysage. (2019). *Go Solar With Georgia's Great Solar Rebates and Incentives*. Retrieved May 5, 2019, from, https://www.energysage.com/solar-panels/solar-rebates-incentives/ga/
Enerji Ve Tabii Kaynaklar Bakanlığı (ETKB) (2019). *Enerji Verimliliği Desteği.* Retrieved April 3, 2019, from https://www.enerji.gov.tr/trTR/Sayfalar/Enerji-Verimliligi-Destekleri
Erbaş, G. (2012). *Klasikten Eleştirel Jeopolitiğe Karadeniz Jeopoliğin Dönüşümü* [Unpublished doctoral dissertation]. Ankara Üniversitesi.
Ercümen, M. A. (2016, September 9). *Doğu Akdeniz Enerji Rekabeti*. İHH İnsani ve Sosyal Araştırma Merkezi. https://insamer.com/tr/dogu-akdeniz-enerji-rekabeti_366.html
European Commission. (2010). *Towards A European Strategy For Energy Supply Security 2010.* http://www.europarl.europa.eu/sides/getDoc.do?pubRef=-//EP//TEXT+TA+P7-TA2010-0441+0+DOC+XML+V0//EN
ExxonMobil. (2018). *2018 Outlook for Energy: A View to 2040*. Retrieved June 17, 2019, from https://corporate.exxonmobil.com/Energy-and-innovation/Outlook-for-Energy/Outlook-for-Energy-A-perspective-to-2040

EYODER. (2017). *Ulusal Enerji Verimliliği Eylem Planı 2017-2023.* http://www.eyoder.org.tr/UlusalEVEP.pdf

Gazprom. (2019). *The Blue Stream Natural Gas Pipeline.* Retrieved May 11, 2019, from http://www.gazprom.ru/eng/articles/article8895.shtml

Georgia Energy Electricity Industry. (2012). *Georgia Energy Electricity Industry Overview June 28, 2012.* http://www.energy.gov.ge/projects/pdf/pages/Elekroenergiis%20Sektoris%20Mimokhilva%20Da%20Eksportis%20Shesadzleblobebi%2014%20geo.pdf

Goncharenko, A. (2005). The wider Black Sea area: New geopolitical realities, regional security structures and democratic control: A Ukrainian view. *NATO Defense College Occasional Paper*, *11*(2), 23-32.

IEA. (2013). *World Energy Outlook 2013.* https://www.iea.org/publications/freepublications/publication/WEO2013.pdf

Invest Bulgaria. (2019). *Bulgarian Investment Incentives.* Retrieved May 5, 2019, from http://www.investbulgaria.com/BulgarianInvestmentIncentives.php

Invest In Turkey (2019). *Teşvikler*. Retrieved April 4, 2019, from http://www.invest.gov.tr/trTR/investmentguide/investorsguide/Pages/Incentives.aspx

IRENA (2019). *The International Renewable Energy Agency.* Retrieved July 12, 2019, from. http://resourceirena.irena.org/gateway/dashboard/?topic=4&subTopic=54

İrge, N. F. (2017). Karadeniz Havzası Jeopolitiğinde Güç Mücadelesinin Arka Planı ve Bölgesel Güvenliğin Uluslararası Önemi. *Marmara Üniversitesi Siyasal Bilimler Dergisi*, *5* (April, Special Issue).

Kantörün, U. (2010). *AB'nin Güvenlik Politikasında Türkiye'nin Yeri.* Bilge İnsanlar Stratejik Araştırmalar Merkezi. Retrieved June 2, 2019, from http://www.bilgesam.org/incele/787/-ab%E2%80%99ninguvenlik-politikasinda-turkiye%E2%80%99nin-yeri/#.XTmMOflzayo

Kaytez, F. M., Taplamacıoğlu, C., Gözde, H., & Küçük A. O. (2018). Yenilenebilir Enerjide Bölgesel Fırsatlar: Türkiye ve Gürcistan PotansiyDurum Değerlendirmeleri ve Öneriler. *Güç Sistemleri Konferansı, Ankara* (pp. 93-98).

Kharenko, S. (2019). *Foreign Investments – Tax Incentives.* https://www.sk.ua/sites/default/files/foreign_investments_230_230.pdf

KPMG. (2015, September 22). *Taxes And Incentives For Renewable Energy.* https://home.kpmg/in/en/home/insights/2015/09/taxes-and-incentives-for-renewable-energy-2015.html

Mackinder H. J. (1962). *Democratic Ideals and Reality: A Study in the Politics of Reconstruction.* Norton and Company.
Oğan, S. (2009). *Rusya-Ukrayna Doğalgaz Krizi ve Çıkarılacak Dersler.* Türkiye Uluslararası İlişkiler ve Stratejik Analizler Merkezi. Retrieved April 2, 2019, from http://turksam.org/rusya-ukrayna-dogalgazkrizi-ve-cikarilacak-dersler
Orta Karadeniz Kalkınma Ajansı (2010). *Ukrayna Ülke Raporu.* https://www.oka.org.tr/Documents/Ukrayna_Ulke_Raporu.pdf
Öztürk, Ö. (2017, December 21). *Karadeniz'de Petrol, doğalgaz ve Stratejik Boru Hatları.* http://ozhanozurk.com/2017/12/21/karadeniz-petrol-doğalgaz-boru-hatti/
Pamir, A. N. (2003). *Dünya'da ve Türkiye'de Enerji, Türkiye'nin Enerji Kaynakları ve Enerji Politikaları, Mayıs.*
PWC (2019.-a). *Worldwide Tax Summaries, Bulgaria.* Retrieved May 5, 2019, from http://taxsummaries.pwc.com/ID/BulgariaCorporate-Tax-credits-and-incentives
PWC (2019.-b). *Worldwide Tax Summaries, Georgia.* Retrieved May 5, 2019, from http://taxsummaries.pwc.com/ID/GeorgiaCorporate-Tax-credits-and-incentives
PWC (2019.-c). *Worldwide Tax Summaries, Russian Federation.* Retrieved May 5, 2019, from http://taxsummaries.pwc.com/ID/RussianFederation-Corporate-Tax-credits-and-incentives
PWC (2019.-d). *Worldwide Tax Summaries, Ukraine.* Retrieved May 5, 2019, from http://taxsummaries.pwc.com/ID/UkraineCorporate-Tax-credits-and-incentives
Romania Country Commercial Guide (RCCG) (2017). *Romania Industrial Policies.* https://www.export.gov/article?id=Romania-Industrial-Policies
Sabah Gazetesi. (2014, December 12). *'Güney Akım' resmen kapatıldı!* Sabah Gazetesi. 12.12.2014, http://www.sabah.com.tr/ekonomi/2014/12/12/guney-akim-resmen-kapandi
Türkiye.gov. (2019). *Türkiye İstatistik Kurumu Başkanlığı (TÜİK).* Retrieved July 12, 2019, from https://www.turkiye.gov.tr/turkiye-istatistik-kurumu-baskanligi-tuik
Tüysüz, E. (2014). Karadeniz Güvenliği ve Bunun AB Güvenliğine Etkileri – Security Of The Black Sea And Its Effects Of The EU Security. *Dicle Üniversitesi İktisadi ve İdari Bilimler Fakültesi Dergisi, 2*(6), 73-91.
U.S. Energy Information Administration (2018). *International.* http://www.eia.gov/countries/cab.cfm?fips=RS

Uluatam, E. (2010). Yenilenebilir Enerji Teşvikleri. *Ekonomik Forum, 10,* 34-41.

Yorulmaz, R. (2019). *Doğu Akdeniz'de Yeni Enerji Kaynaklarının Ekonomi Politiği*. Ortadoğu Araştırmaları Merkezi. Retrieved May 22, 2019, from https://orsam.org.tr/tr/dogu-akdenizde-yeni-enerjikaynaklarinin-ekonomi-politigi/

PART III:

THE EFFECT OF GLOBAL ENERGY POLICIES ON DEVELOPING COUNTRIES

CHAPTER ONE

THE EFFECTS OF CHANGES IN OIL PRICES ON DEVELOPING COUNTRIES' ECONOMIES

GÜLDEN ÜLGEN,* İPEK M. YURTTAGÜLER** & SİNEM KUTLU HORVATH***

Introduction

The concept of energy has different definitions and types, but in general it means the capacity to do business. Therefore, it is widely used in physics and engineering sciences. In the economic sense, the concept of energy differs. While other sciences are concerned with the quantity and quality of energy that emerges, economists are concerned with the way energy is used in production processes.

Although energy is the most important input for social and economic development worldwide, it also has a major impact on macroeconomic indicators. In today's world, where population and technology increases are intense, the importance of energy is increasing day by day. The use of energy factor and energy is also important for countries to put their macroeconomic indicators on solid ground and thus protect them from economic crises that may be experienced.

Due to the different geographical structures of countries and the different energy sources they have, energy dependencies are changing. While in some countries there may be a dependency on imported energy, in others, the problem of the inefficient use of the resources they have may

---

* Prof. Dr. Gülden Ülgen, Department of Economics, Faculty of Economics, Istanbul University. E-mail: gulgen@istanbul.edu.tr.
** Asst. Prof. İpek M. Yurttagüler, Department of Economics, Faculty of Economics, Istanbul University. E-mail: ipeksa@istanbul.edu.tr.
*** Asst. Prof. Sinem Kutlu Horvath, Department of Economics, Faculty of Economics, Istanbul University. E-mail: sinemkut@istanbul.edu.tr.

come up. For all these reasons, the concept of energy is a very important one that directly affects the economies of countries.

It is known that, with the realization of industrialization, petroleum became the main input in the production process and the most important energy factor required for economic growth. Therefore, the importance of changes in oil prices is emphasized in the literature. The aim of our study is to reveal to what extent changes in oil prices affect the macroeconomic indicators of developing countries.

The Concept of Energy

The concept of energy is divided into two: non-renewable and renewable. According to their transformability characteristics, primary and secondary energy sources are classified into two groups. The primary energy source can be used directly as it exists in nature without any conversion. Sources such as oil, natural gas, coal and wood are such energy sources. Secondary energy sources are those that can be converted from primary sources to more useful forms. For example, electric energy obtained from coal and wind from primary energy sources are secondary energy sources.

When the process regarding the primary energy consumption of the world between 1965-2018 is examined, the consumption of primary energy sources has increased continuously over the years. Especially when the data related to recent years are analyzed, it can be seen that primary energy consumption increased by 1.2% in 2016 and 2.2% in 2017. In recent years, the countries with the highest demand for these resources are China and India, which are not OECD members. The economic growth experienced by these countries as a result of the acceleration in their industrialization processes also increased their primary energy demand.

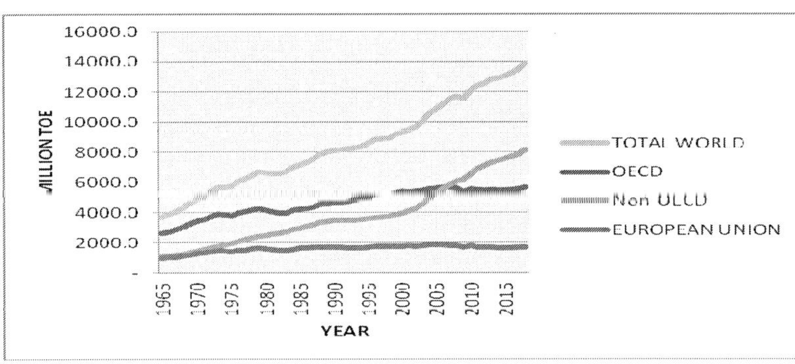

Figure 1: Global Primary Energy Consumption (1965-2018). Source: BP, 2018.

While the primary energy consumption of the world is continuously increasing, which of these resources are used extensively is also important. At this point, primary energy sources, especially petroleum, are important for the sustainability of production for countries in the process of industrialization. As can be seen in Figure 2, the share of petroleum in primary energy resource consumption was 34.19% in 2017, compared to 33.62% in 2018. In this view, oil is the most consumed resource among the primary energy sources. Oil is followed by coal with a rate of 27.20% and natural gas with a rate of 23.86%, respectively. Hydroelectric and nuclear energy are observed as the next highest.

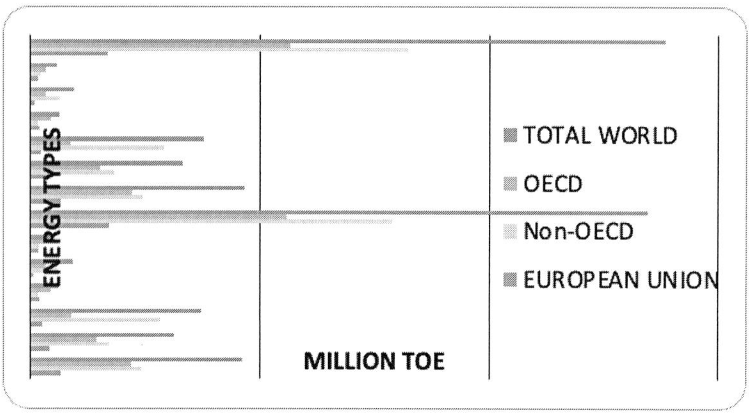

Figure 2: Distribution of Primary Energy Types. Source: BP, 2018.

Crude oil is used as raw material or intermediate material in different sectors, especially in industry and transportation, after various refining processes. It is also known that crude oil is an input to meet heating needs after the distillation process. The largest oil refining capacity in the world belongs to the USA. China, on the other hand, ranks second in the world's largest refined capacity list after the US.

When all these reasons are evaluated in the historical process and the developments of recent years are observed, it is noteworthy that the use of oil has gained importance, especially for the realization of production in the industrial sector. For this reason, the formation, change and economic effects of oil prices are very important. In this study, how the price is formed in the oil market and what results it creates on different variables of the economy are discussed.

The Importance of Oil and the Historical Process

With the beginning of the industrialization process, petroleum, which then started to settle on the world agenda, has been the subject of research in different disciplines such as international politics, political history and economics. Oil, which plays an active role in the industrialization of countries due to its raw material input and energy source characteristics, has directly or indirectly been the focus of power wars between countries throughout history for these reasons. It is known that wars, embargoes, political agreements and disagreements have been experienced throughout history in order for a country to have this important energy source.

The Industrial Revolution, which began in the United Kingdom in the 18th century and then spread throughout Europe first and then to the entire world, was manifested by the mechanization of looms, particularly in England. The introduction of steam-powered and coal-powered machines increased mobility and helped to transform production into a large-scale process. In this period, which was defined as the first Industrial Revolution, steam, coal and iron, used as energy sources, also played an active role as raw materials in the construction of railways. In this way, the first steps were taken to make the world a more integrated structure, and capital accumulation increased. The process that was experienced from the second half of the 19th century was defined as the second Industrial Revolution, and the energy sources used in this period also changed their shape. Steam, coal and iron resources, which were actively used in the beginning, were replaced by steel, oil and electricity. Especially with the introduction of oil in the production process, industry became more developed, and the competition for industrialization among countries was marked. In today's world (especially after World War II), the rapid advances in information and communication technologies, defined as the third Industrial Revolution, and the tendency toward renewable energies are noteworthy.

Despite all these new developments, it can be observed that oil is still widely used, especially in production processes, and, therefore, it is accepted that changes in oil prices will affect national economies. Looking at the developments in world trade, although the share of oil in total global energy consumption has decreased slightly in recent years, it is still the most widely used type of energy in the world. For this reason, it is clear that any crisis or imbalance in the oil market will be reflected on the entire energy market and thus on national economies.

When changes in oil prices are taken into consideration in the historical process, it can be seen that there have been huge fluctuations. In certain periods, shocks were experienced that had both global and sectoral effects. Among these shocks, which have affected most of today's economies, is the oil crisis of 1973-1974. During this period, after Egypt and Syria attacked Israel on October 6, 1973, on October 17, Arab members of the Organization of Petroleum Exporting Countries (OPEC) imposed an embargo on oil exports on the countries on the Israeli side. OPEC then significantly reduced its total oil production, leading to a significant increase in oil prices.

In 1980, the total decrease in oil production after the Iran-Iraq War was around 6% of the world's production at that time. During the OPEC embargo, the Iranian Revolution and the Iran-Iraq War, oil production decreased considerably and, consequently, oil prices increased. In response to price increases since the 1970s, world oil demand has declined considerably. This led to a downward trend in oil prices over time, while Saudi Arabia, which aimed to increase its market share in the global oil market in the mid-1980s, increased its production. Therefore, the downward trend in oil prices in the mentioned period is remarkable.

By the late 1990s the East Asian financial crisis was noticeable. This financial crisis, which started in Thailand in 1997 and then spread to other East Asian countries such as South Korea and Indonesia, brought economic and financial pressures. Subsequently, oil prices fell by a significant margin. After the crisis had lasted for about two years, as the growth figures accelerated again as of the beginning of the 2000s, oil prices returned to an upward trend.

Oil prices, which showed a slow increase in the 2000s, decreased by 78.1% in the July-December period during the 2008 global financial crisis. The Middle East was also affected by the so-called Arab Spring in 2011, and oil prices entered another upward trend. However, although oil production is expected to decline due to the conflicts in Iraq and Libya, the increasing trend in production and OPEC's decision not to reduce its production quota are considered to be the most important reasons for the price decreases observed in the following years (Eraydın, 2015, p. 1). On the other hand, the slowdown in global growth trends, the inability of OPEC countries to make concurrent decisions, and the increase in oil production in recent years can also explain the decreases in oil prices.

Price Formation in the Oil Market

The formation of oil prices varies in the short, medium and long terms. In the short term, the interaction of supply and demand determines the severity and frequency of fluctuations of the prices set for crude oil. In other words, prices are determined by fluctuations between supply and demand. In the medium term, the structure of the oil market may allow a dominant group of actors to implement a strategy that leads to an increase in oil prices, aiming to isolate the market from competitive forces. The structure of the sector also determines how compatible prices are with competitive prices. Finally, in the long run, the price of oil reflects the actual cost of producing enough oil to meet demand. In other words, the marginal cost of production in line with world oil demand plays an important role (Angelier, 1991, pp. 217-218).

The short term can be defined as a short enough time to prevent significant changes in supply or demand capacities. Oil demand is considered to be inelastic in this period. In other words, the amount requested will vary less than a change in price. The inelasticity of demand is explained by the fact that non-durable final consumption constitutes a large part of oil demand. The reason for this is related to the fact that consumers do not pay much attention to the prices of non-durable consumer goods. On the other hand, demand is influenced by factors other than the price, such as the climate and the current level of economic activities. Another important variable that mediates the relationship between price and demand is the size of stocks. Large stocks increase the demand for oil more sharply, whereas low stocks reduce this demand. Oil supply is also inelastic in terms of prices. One of the main reasons for this is the structure of producer prices. On the other hand, the available production volume depends to a large extent on the decisions of oil-producing countries. Countries manage their resources differently from firms that consider how they can affect the return on a capital investment. In the short term, supply and demand are inelastic with respect to prices, which makes it an ineffective market adjustment tool. In other words, in order to make any changes in supply and demand, it is necessary to create large changes at a price level (Angelier, 1991, pp. 217-219).

The medium term is a period in which significant adjustments can be made in production and consumption capacity. The structure of the oil industry is more stable in the medium term. Companies determine their strategies according to the structure of the sector, and the performance of the sector, price level and the quantity of product are affected by these strategies. The fact that the oil industry has a small number of firms or a small number of producing countries brings about an oligopolistic structure in the sector. In oligopoly markets, firms must consider how other competitors will react when determining price or production output levels. For this reason, in the oligopoly market, firms have a mutually interdependent relationship and there is a necessity to act strategically. In consequence, OPEC was established on September 14, 1960 as a result of the motivation to act strategically in line with the oligopolistic structure of the sector.

OPEC was first established by Venezuela, Iran, Iraq, Saudi Arabia and Kuwait, which came together to stop the decline in crude oil prices, and these countries were later joined by Qatar (1961), Libya (1962), Indonesia (1962), the United Arab Emirates (1967), Algeria (1969), Nigeria (1971), Ecuador (1973), Gabon (1975) and Angola (2007). OPEC countries, which control the world's oil production and provide about half of the world's total oil, have two-thirds of the crude oil reserves and one-third of the natural gas reserves. OPEC has been characterized as a cartel because it is a corporation where oil-exporting countries come together and act as monopolies. Although originally OPEC was founded as a cartel, later it lost some of its features as some of the countries gained the right to set independently their own prices and quantities supplied. For this reason, it is observed that member countries often do not comply with the decisions taken and are not considered as cartels. It is known that the period when OPEC showed a cartel character was the period of the oil crises.

In the long term, changes may occur in production technologies, oil consumption and production regions. In the long run, the cost of production is a critical variable because the market price may not deviate much from this value. When the market price falls below the cost of production, profitability ceases and producers with the highest costs will reduce their supplies and put upward pressure on prices. On the other hand, when the market price is higher than the cost of production for a considerable period, new capital will flow into the industry, increase supply and exert downward pressure on prices. Therefore, in the long run, the market price is around the cost of production. On the other hand, in addition to geological, economic and strategic factors, another aspect that affects long-term oil production costs is the technology level. Most of the price increases which were needed to ensure the profitability of new fields used to meet the increased global demand for oil have been used as a source tofinance the development of new technologiesin oil industry.

Reasons for and Economic Impacts of Oil Shock

Changes in oil prices can be attributed to different reasons. In particular, among the causes of the shocks in 1970 and beyond, external political events in the Middle East, wars in this region, the formation and policies of cartels such as OPEC, global macroeconomic conditions, and changes in the expectations about the oil market can be cited. Generally speaking, it is accepted that the unpredictable exogenous political shocks in the Middle East have caused sudden and major oil price changes. However, this approach can be refuted if recent history is examined due to the fact that oil price increases are also observed in periods when Middle East problems did not exist. This is why oil prices change in the absence of political shocks (Barsky & Killian, 2004, p. 125).

It is accepted that wars in the Middle East mainly affect the amount of oil supplied. The discontinuation of crude oil production due to wars affects oil prices and thus the amount of demand. At this point, it is estimated that oil supply elasticity is an important indicator. If the supply of oil is not flexible, increases in oil demand will lead to high increases in prices. According to Barsky and Killian (2004), the main reason for this change in demand is that consumers, who realize that the supply of oil will be limited, tend to start oil stocking. In other words, the uncertainty of the environment increases the demand, and thus oil prices rise.

Apart from the uncertainty created by the war environment, political instabilities are also very important in the formation of oil shocks. Both the lack of consensus on the compliance of oil-producing countries with the decisions they have taken and the insecure and uncertain environment created by the presence of such practices as embargos pave the way for fluctuations in oil prices. It should not be forgotten that all these developments are not independent of global macroeconomic conditions.

It is undisputed that oil shocks have effects on the global economy. At this point, it is also accepted that there is an inverse relationship between oil prices and economic activities, and this relationship is gathered under three different channels. The first of these is called the real balance channel, in which an increase in oil prices will create inflation and, as a result, the purchasing power of individuals will decrease and the real balance level will decrease. Decreasing real balances, on the other hand, can lead to a stagnant economy through the monetary transmission mechanism. The second channel is the cost channel, also known as the supply channel. In this channel, production costs increase due to the oil shocks, and therefore the real production and real income levels decrease. The third channel is the demand-side channel. This channel analyzes the effects of the differences in oil prices on consumption and investment areas. As a result of the inflationary effect of the rise in oil prices, purchasing power decreases and thus disposable income decreases. As a result, a contraction in consumption is inevitable. The global impact of the oil shocks varies depending on the nature and magnitude of the change in oil price and the extent to which it is reflected on oil users. This demand-side channel has shown that the damage caused by the oil shocks will increase as the duration increases. On the other hand, in addition to the negative economic effects that oil shocks can create, such as cost increases, contraction in investment and consumption levels, it is inevitable that the welfare level will be disrupted against one side by disrupting the foreign trade balance (Akıncı et al., 2012, pp. 2-3; Yalçin Erik & Koşaroğlu, 2016, p. 130; Husain et al., 2015, p. 8).

Apart from these channels, which express the relationship between oil prices and economic activities, it is possible to explain the possible stagnation caused by oil shocks by two different mechanisms. The first of these mechanisms was developed by Hamilton (1988) and analyzes sectoral effects. Accordingly, price shocks adversely affect the labor market and increase the level of unemployment. Under these conditions, unemployed people will transfer to sectors that are positively affected by the oil shock rather than waiting for the conditions of their sector to improve. Thus, the recovery process of the sector, which is adversely affected by the oil shock, will be extended. The second mechanism was proposed by Bernanke (1983), and it was developed from the idea that uncertainty in oil prices is an important factor affecting economic life. Accordingly, failure to predict the future level of oil prices forces firms to postpone their investment decisions. The increase in uncertainty over oil prices will lead to a decrease in investments, and this will bring stagnation in the economy (Akıncı et al., 2012, p. 3).

In addition to the direct impact of oil shocks on the general level of prices, there are secondary effects such as strict nominal wages and price and wage indexing on the labor market. Higher wage pressure and weaker demand create a reduction in employment. Moreover, the deterioration in stock market reactions may increase the effects of shocks. On the other hand, economies are affected by changes in the international environment created by shocks in oil prices. Rising import prices cause deterioration in trade conditions and accelerate welfare losses. At this point, it should also be said that all these findings are valid for oil-importing countries (Schneider, 2004, p. 27).

Effects of Changes in Oil Prices on Developing Countries' Economies

The formation of oil prices and the effects of oil shocks are gaining importance, especially in developing countries. The level of countries' development varies depending on the resources held, the nature of their industrial structures, and their degree of dependence on external economic forces. The economic growth potential of a country is greatly influenced by the wealth of physical and human resources. Developing countries are characterized by relatively low levels of labor productivity due to low levels of physical and human capital. Agriculture plays a fundamental role in economic activity, particularly for the professional distribution of the labor force, but its contribution to the gross national product varies between countries. However, the industrial structures of these countries are compared depending on the relative importance of agriculture, manufacturing and services. With regard to resource endowment and industrial structure, the degree of external dependence of a country on foreign economic powers is also relevant. Most developing countries are highly dependent on foreign trade with developed countries. At this point, it can be observed that they are especially dependent on the importation of foreign production technologies (West & Desai, 2002, p. 52).

Since raw or partially processed goods are often the most important exports of developing countries, income from these has a significant impact on their economies. Export pricing decisions for developing countries are often subject to market conditions. They have relatively low production and technology opportunities, resulting in higher production costs. Generally, they may have to sell their products below the cost of production because of their weak bargaining power. On the other hand, it is known that their products have less added value compared to developed countries. In this context, exporters in developing countries are generally price buyers rather than price determinants. On the export side, they generally follow a market-based pricing strategy.

It is known that especially developing countries need oil as the main input of production as a result of the existing resource problems. Therefore, a change in oil prices will have a direct impact on the economic structures of developing countries. In this respect, the effects of oil prices, especially on growth, balance of payments, stock market and inflation rate, will be analyzed with regard to developing countries.

The Effect of Changes in Oil Prices on Growth

Traditional trade theories are based on the argument that the production of goods or services, subject to international trade, is mainly dependent on the intensive production factors that countries have. For this reason, the geographical imbalances of natural resources disappear with the realization of the international division of labor and specialization. It is accepted that natural rcsourccs play an active role in the first stage of industrialization and growth and that rich countries started the race for growth. However, unlike this generalization, observations and statistical studies, especially from the last forty years, show that natural resources do not provide the expected economic benefits. On the contrary, it has been shown that many countries with rich natural resources are adversely affected in terms of trade, economic growth and prosperity levels. On the other hand, developing countries, which export natural resources and depend on the income obtained from this field, have been found to be at a disadvantage compared to their commercial partners (Sarr et al., 2011, pp. 51-52; Demiral et al., 2016, p. 86).

In the literature, despite the abundance of natural resources, the fact that economic growth is not at similar levels is defined as the resource curse. This concept was first used by Richard Auty in 1993 and was labeled in the literature as the paradox of abundance. This paradox relates to how countries rich in natural resources cannot use their existing wealth to develop their economies, achieve economic growth and increase their welfare levels and therefore show lower development performance than countries with fewer resources (Auty, 1993; Stiglitz, 2004; Frankel, 2010, pp. 3-4).

In the resource curse paradox, there is an inverse relationship between natural resource wealth and economic growth. At this point, it can be observed that growth performances are far behind when looking at the countries that are natural resource exporters and depend on the income to be earned from this trade relationship. Unlike economies that depend on production, these countries obtain only natural resource exports. In such an economic understanding, the links that make up the tax-based state-society relationship are broken and a different order is formed in which the state earns its income independently from the public. In such a system, the state does not earn its income from the domestic economy and therefore departs from the economic and social policies followed by production-based states (Karl, 2005, pp. 25-26).

Another reason why countries that are rich in natural resources do not perform as highly as expected is the theory that has been named in the literature as the Dutch syndrome or Dutch disease. This approach, which was developed based on the Dutch case, was introduced with the discovery of gas and oil in the North Sea of the Netherlands. The discovery of natural gas resources led to an increase in the value of the guilder, the Dutch currency, and exports decreased. Therefore, the existence of natural resources, which can be considered as a positive development in terms of economics, deteriorated the foreign trade balance of the Netherlands and brought about economic contraction.

The concept of the Dutch syndrome, which was developed specifically for the Netherlands and explains the effects of fluctuations in the price of natural gas, has been developed and generalized over time. Accordingly, although oil and other natural resources appear as sources of wealth, they cannot create jobs on their own and generally exclude other economic sectors. Following the discovery of natural resources, foreign currency inflow into the country increases with the export of these resources and the domestic currency appreciates. As a result, the goods produced in the country become expensive and the real exchange rate increases. As the foreign competitiveness of the country weakens, it becomes disadvantageous for foreign trade, especially in sectors with foreign dependence, such as the real sector or manufacturing. In such an environment, the rise of unemployment is inevitable. Due to the increased exchange rate as a result of the increase in natural resources, countries cannot export manufactured or agricultural products, while domestic producers cannot compete with an import attack. So, to prevent this situation, policymakers adopt strong protective policies in order to maintain non-competitive economic activities and to place the fund load in the oil sector, and this situation makes other sectors within the country more dependent on oil exports. Therefore, according to Stiglitz, the richness of natural resources generally creates rich countries with poor people (Stiglitz, 2004; Karl, 2005, pp. 23-24). To summarize, the existence of sources such as oil or natural gas and the exportation of these resources cause the manufacturing industry to shrink. When natural resources are discovered, the country is enriched, but problems such as unemployment and unfairness of income distribution arise.

Looking at current studies, it can be seen that there is no clear consensus on whether natural resources bring economic growth. According to one approach, which sees natural resources as an advantage over other countries, the existence of these resources will trigger growth by increasing both real production and investment capital due to the easy and cheap access to raw materials. According to another approach, which considers the existence of rich natural resources as a misfortune, excess resources destroy the export structure of the country and limit its economic and political institutions. In this respect, there is an inverse relationship between richness in natural resources and economic growth.

Today, especially in developing countries, it can be observed that the economic growth of oil-rich countries is not at the expected level. The dominance of a state order is evident, in which a significant portion of their growth is based on oil exports, and therefore the real sector remains limited, technological developments cannot be kept up, distribution of income is unfair, and economic and political institutions do not develop.

Changes in oil prices are also important for oil-importing countries. As it is a cost item for oil-importing countries, a change in price directly affects the real sector. A decrease in oil prices leads to higher cash for the investor over cost and for the consumer over household income, which leads to an increase in demand and triggers growth due to the multiplier effect.

According to the IMF's World Economic Report, the growth rate of developed countries was estimated to be 2.1% in 2019, while it was 2.4% in 2018. In developing countries, it is foreseen to remain stable at 4.7% in the period of 2018-2019 and to achieve similar growth in the medium term. One of the most important reasons for the fact that 2018 ended with a positive growth rate in the world arises from the fact that oil prices have been at their lowest level in recent years. Oil prices started to decline, especially in 2017, and they followed a similar trend in 2018 as well. On the other hand, the increase in demand for renewable energy types in the world also brought about a decline in oil prices, and thus the increase in growth rates was inevitable. To summarize, in the case of oil-exporting countries where the real sector is not supported, it can be observed that a low level of growth based on oil income is realized. On the other hand, it can also be concluded that the decrease in oil prices positively affects the growth rates of the oil-importing developing countries.

The Effect of Changes in Oil Prices on Current Accounts

The current account is the most important item on the balance of payments. The balance of payments is an indicator of macroeconomic life. The analytical representation of all economic activities between the inhabitants of one country and the inhabitants of another country in a given account is carried out on the balance of payments. In this way, all foreign payment instruments entering the country and all domestic payment instruments exiting the country are recorded. This balance sheet, which is generally prepared on an annual basis, also shows the foreign exchange supply and demand values of the countries. The balance of payments generally consists of the current account, capital account and financial account. Of these, the current account is the most important one and the most followed item.

The current account is one of the most important main accounts of the balance of payments, and it is composed of foreign trade (export-import balance), services (service purchases-service sales), investment (net factor), revenues (foreign investment income-foreign investment expenses) and current transfers (unrequited transfer of external income and external expenses). As can be seen, the current account balance in general terms includes trade in goods, trade in services and unrequited transfers. Therefore, fluctuations in oil prices affect the foreign trade balance and thus the current account.

It is known that an increase in oil prices will create a current account surplus in oil-exporting countries and a current account deficit in oil-importing countries. The effect of the increase in oil prices on the current account balance depends on whether this increase is expected or unexpected or whether the oil shock is permanent or not. While temporary shocks in oil prices worsen the current account balance, the impact of permanent shocks on the current account balance is uncertain. In other words, permanent oil shocks may cause the current account balance to deteriorate or improve, while temporary shocks have an impact on disrupting this balance (Marion, 1981, pp. 1-2). On the other hand, as the financial development of a country increases, the effects of oil price shocks on the current account balance decrease. In addition, rising oil prices are not the main driving force of the current account surplus of more financially developed oil-exporting countries; they only play an important role in the economies of less developed countries (Allegret et al., 2014, p. 198). On the other hand, demand- and supply-side shocks have a negative impact on the current account balance of oil-importing countries. It has been determined that shocks to oil supplies have a relatively small and short-term effect on the oil trade balance and shocks to oil demand cause large and permanent oil trade deficits in oil-importing countries. It is accepted that supply shocks in the oil market have a short-term effect on crude oil prices and therefore have a limited impact on macroeconomic variables (Kilian et al., 2009, pp. 190-193; Allegret et al., 2015, pp. 232-233). To sum up, if shocks to oil prices increase real oil prices, it is expected that oil-exporting countries will have a current account surplus and that oil-importing countries will have a current account deficit.

The first effect of an increase in oil prices is the inequality of income resulting from the flow of money from the importing country to the exporting country. Developing countries are especially affected by these fluctuations because of their import dependency. As a result, the value of imports rises and the value of exports falls, and thus the balance of payments deteriorates with such effects. Developing countries, which mostly finance their budget deficits by debt, are more affected by this situation. On thc othcr hand, the fact that developing countries have mostly energy-intensive sectors and are highly dependent on oil causes their economies to be affected more negatively than others. The main reason for this is explained by the fact that as the price of oil increases, firms purchase less energy and therefore reduce national income by decreasing production, capital and labor productivity. On the other hand, a decline in oil prices causes imported goods to become cheaper and increases the value of exported goods, while it positively affects the balance of payments of oil-importing countries and causes an increase in the national income (Güngör et al., 2016, p. 31).

The Effect of Changes in Oil Prices on the Stock Market

Oil is one of the most important commodities in foreign trade due to the fact that it is the main input of production. Therefore, oil directly affects the balance of payments of importing and exporting countries and directs the capital flow between countries. In other words, it is observed that it affects not only real sectors but also capital markets. There is a capital transfer from oil-importing countries to oil-exporting countries, and this transfer affects all sectors of the economy as well as the stock markets. On the other hand, the fact that oil is being used as an investment instrument also triggers the interest of investors. Oil attracts investors' interest since it is fed by speculative movements, its price can be determined by different political developments, and it is affected by issues such as war, disaster and geopolitical risks.

Although volatility in oil prices has a direct or indirect impact on many macroeconomic variables, the underlying effect of these impacts is uncertainty created by price changes. Changes in oil prices bring about risk and uncertainty in the economy, and stock markets are particularly affected by this environment of uncertainty. There are several reasons for this environmental uncertainty. The first is that OPEC does not act on a common and systematic consensus, especially in recent years. There is uncertainty for oil-importing countries where the member countries can implement their own policies, there is no control at this point, and the countries' different amounts of oil production mean that they do not follow common decisions. Secondly, the differences between the internal dynamics of the importing countries differentiate the effects of the volatility in oil prices. The uncertainty of these fluctuations will be higher in economies with a highly fragile structure. On the other hand, the expectations of economic decision-makers in an environment of uncertainty are negatively affected. This situation is also reflected in the investment decisions and thus the behaviors in the stock market.

Changes in oil prices and stock prices are explained by the asset pricing model. The Intertemporal Capital Asset Pricing Model, which was first developed by Merton in 1973, evolved into a multi-factor asset pricing model over time, and it suggests that macroeconomic variables may be important determinants of asset return. Although changes in oil prices do not seem statistically significant in a multi-factor asset pricing model, Hamilton (1983) evaluated the direct link between changes in oil prices and real production. Afterward, the relationship between oil prices and stock prices was developed by applying the asset pricing model (Pollet, 2005, pp. 2-3).

The effect of oil prices on the stock market was first analyzed in the literature by Jones and Kaul (1996) and Huang et al. (1996). Huang et al. suggested that if futures and stock markets are efficient, oil prices and stock prices are simultaneously correlated, as other markets react quickly to information shocks and investor expectations can be capitalized. If the markets are efficient, each market will react quickly to information shocks in other markets, and oil prices and stock prices will behave simultaneously (Huang et al., 1996, p. 2).

With the asset pricing model, the aim is to evaluate the cash flow risk, to calculate the cost of capital and to estimate the expected rate of return before the investment decision is made and determine whether the investment decision should be taken. At this point, it is noteworthy that fluctuations in oil prices can be associated with stock investments.

Increasing costs with a rise in oil prices will be reflected in the general level of prices, and cost-push inflation will occur. An inflationary environment decreases the purchasing power of households and thus reduces total demand and investment. Central banks intervene in the economy within the scope of the strategy to fight inflation, and there are different methods of intervention for the monetary authority. In this respect, it can be observed that higher interest rates are frequently applied. Along with the interest rate rise, investors seek investment instruments (treasury bills, government bonds, etc.) where they can earn interest income, and therefore the demand for stocks decreases. As a result of this decrease in demand, it is observed that stock prices move downward (Abdioğlu & Değirmenci, 2014, p. 3). At this point, the total impact created in the stock market differs depending on whether the country is an oil importer or exporter. This adverse relationship is expected to be realized in oil-importing countries.

The simultaneous effect of changes in oil prices on stock prices can be more clearly observed in developed countries with deeper capital markets. For the developing countries, there is no consensus in the literature. In some empirical studies, it has been found that the simultaneous effect between stock prices and oil prices is more limited than in developed countries, and sometimes there is no relationship. This limited relationship is mainly attributed to the relatively shallow capital markets in these countries. On the other hand, there are also studies that argue that changes in oil prices have a significant impact on stock prices in developing countries. According to these studies, developing countries do not have the capacity to rapidly turn to alternative energy sources despite the changes in oil prices. Therefore, it is accepted that changes in oil prices affect stock prices.

The Effect of Changes in Oil Prices on Inflation

Inflation is an important part of macroeconomic stability, and it is also an important variable that is taken into consideration when making investment decisions. In particular, due to the duty of monetary authorities to maintain price stability, which is currently their main objective, it is necessary to monitor inflation rates. A change in oil prices directly affects inflation rates due to both the increase in costs and the increase in final goods' prices. Therefore, knowing the inflationary effects of shocks will help policymakers to analyze the results. Therefore, it is necessary to pay attention to price stability in order to attract investments in the country, and thus, the interaction between oil prices and inflation gains importance.

Sharp and permanent increases in oil prices have led policymakers and macroeconomists to draw attention to this area. It is also known that the volatility in oil prices has a direct impact on many macro variables of the economy. The most significant of these effects are expected to have an influence on inflation. Since almost all sectors of the economy are dependent on oil input, it is a cost item for all producers. That is why the creation of an environment of inflation will subsequently be expected. Although there is no clear consensus as to whether oil shocks cause an economic recession, oil price shocks are considered to be partly justified by inflation.

When we look at the world economy in general terms, we can see some eras when changes in oil prices have directly affected inflation. It has been pointed out that before the 1973 oil crisis, inflation rates were informative about the development of future oil prices. However, there is no clear evidence that oil prices directly affected macroeconomic variables in the period following the 1973 OPEC embargo (Gisser & Goodwin, 1986, p. 102). On the other hand, volatility in oil prices has increased more particularly since the 2000s, and both direct and indirect effects on inflation have been observed. Understanding the empirical link between oil prices and inflation rates is important because most monetary authorities try to keep inflation under control. Information about the inflationary effects of the rise in oil prices will help monetary authorities to adopt appropriate policies to address these shocks.

The effect of a change in oil prices on inflation was defined by Fernald and Trehan (2005) as inflation tax on domestic users, and it varies according to the country's dependence on oil. While the main determinants of inflation in countries with high oil dependence are the real exchange rate and production costs, they are the domestic output level and production costs in countries with low oil dependency. For this reason, a change in oil prices affects the inflation rate, but the extent of this effect varies. At this point, while the countries with low oil dependence are directly affected by changes in oil prices, an indirect effect is mentioned for countries with high dependence. A rise in oil prices increases the production cost of producers, which is reflected in the price levels and thus creates an environment of inflation (Sek et al., 2015, p. 635).

When the studies are examined in general terms, the fact is that there is a link between oil prices and inflation, and this differs according to the development levels of the countries. Recent studies have shown a decline in the inflationary effects of oil price increases. In other words, it was concluded that changes in oil prices had a lower impact on inflation in the 2000s than in the 1970s. According to Chen (2009), the reason for the decreasing effect of oil prices on inflation is the appreciation of the domestic currency. According to Bernanke, Gertler and Watson (1997), it is the implementation of a more active monetary policy in response to inflation. According to Pain et al. (2006), it is associated with the degree of freedom in trade (Chen, 2009, pp. 132-133). On the other hand, Blanchard and Gali (2007) show that reliable monetary policy and higher wage flexibility are the reasons for the decrease in transitivity. An alternative to these reasons, according to De Gregorio et al. (2007), is that the differentiation of energy intensity and the introduction of different and renewable energy sources weakened the relationship between oil prices and inflation, especially in terms of the developed countries.

On the developing countries' side, their high oil dependence and their fragile economic structure affect the relationship between oil prices and inflation rates. It is possible to say that as the trade liberalization levels of developing countries that meet their oil needs through imports fall, they will be more affected by fluctuations in oil prices. On the other hand, the reliability of monetary authorities in developing countries and the independence of central banks are important criteria. The lack of an independent central bank and the failure to implement a reliable monetary policy will both increase the effect of oil price changes and create an environment of inflation. Moreover, the effectiveness of monetary policies to be implemented in such an economy will be weak. For this reason, the existence of a reliable monetary authority is the main determinant of the degree to which oil shocks affect inflation.

As a result of these studies, it can be observed that developing countries that have a foreign trade surplus are rarely or never affected by oil shocks. In other words, the negative effects of oil shocks are solved by acquiring a foreign trade surplus. That is why the inflationary impact of oil shocks is felt more intensively in countries with a trade deficit. Another feature that needs to be emphasized is the existence of a tendency toward the privatization of companies in the energy sector in developing countries. Following privatization in this sector, it has been pointed out that the establishment of enterprises that seek profit makes these effects of inflation more apparent.

Conclusion

Although the concept of energy is a widespread research subject in sciences such as physics and engineering, it is also a very important concept that determines economic life. Economists concentrate on the impact of energy on the production process and thus investigate how macroeconomic indicators are shaped. With the increase in population and in the use of technology, the use of energy has increased. Oil has a different place in the existing energy types. The main reason for this difference is the increase in the amount of production with industrialization, and the main energy type required to achieve this increase is oil. This is why a change in oil prices directly or indirectly affects macroeconomic indicators. This effect is different in developed and developing countries. In our study, the effects of changes in oil prices in developing countries have been emphasized.

The general characteristics of developing countries are relatively low labor productivity, external dependency on raw materials and intermediate production and external dependency on imports of production technologies. For this reason, a change in oil prices will have an especially great impact on the economies of developing countries. It has been determined that a decrease in oil prices positively affects growth in oil-importing developing countries. The first effect of an increase in oil prices is the income injustice resulting from the flow of money from the importing country to the exporting country. In particular, developing countries face the effect of disrupting the balance of payments as a result of this flow. Developing countries do not have the capacity to rapidly turn to alternative energy sources following changes in oil prices. Therefore, it is accepted that changes in oil prices affect stock prices. The extent of this impact varies depending on how deep the capital markets are. It is possible to say this as the trade liberalization levels of developing countries that meet their oil needs through imports will be more affected by fluctuations in oil prices. On the other hand, both the lack of an independent central bank and the failure to implement a reliable monetary policy will increase the effect of oil price changes and create an inflationary environment.

References

Abdioğlu, Z., & Değirmenci, N. (2014). Petrol Fiyatları-Hisse Senedi Fiyatları İlişkisi: Bist Sektörel Analiz. *Kafkas Üniversitesi İktisadi ve İdari Bilimler Fakültesi Dergisi*, *5*(8), 1-24.

Akıncı, M., Aktürk, E., & Yılmaz, Ö. (2012). Petrol Fiyatları ile Ekonomik Büyüme Arasındaki İlişki: OPEC ve Petrol İthalatçısı Ülkeleri İçin Panel Veri Analizi. *Uludağ Üniversitesi İİBF Dergisi*, *XXXI*(2), 1-17.

Allegret, J. P., Couharde, C., Coulibaly, D., & Mignon, V. (2014). Current accounts and oil price fluctuations in oil-exporting countries: The role of financial development. *Journal of International Money and Finance*, *47*, 185-201.

Allegret, J. P., Mignon, V., & Sallenave, A. (2015). Oil price shocks and global imbalances: Lessons from a model with trade and financial interdependencies. *Economic Modelling*, *49*, 232-247.

Angelier, J. P. (1991). The Determinants of Oil Prices. *Energy Studies Review*, *3*(3), 217-226.

Auty, R. (1993). *Sustaining Development in Mineral Economies: The Resource Curse Thesis.* Oxford University Press.

Barsky, R. B., & Killian, L. (2004). Oil and the Macroeconomy Since the 1970s. *Journal of Economic Perspectives*, *18*(4), 115-134.

Bernanke, B. (1983). Irreversibility, Uncertainty and Cyclical Investment. *The Quarterly Journal of Economics*, *98*(1), 85-106.

Bernanke, B., Gertler, M., & Watson, M. (1997).Systematic Monetary Policy and the Effects of Oil Price Shocks. *Brookings Papers on Economic Activity*, *28*(1), 91-157.

Blanchard, O. J., & Galí, J. (2007). The Macroeconomic Effects of Oil Price Shocks: Why are the 2000s so different from the 1970s? *NBER Chapters, içinde: International Dimensions of Monetary Policy*, 373-421.

BP. (2018). *BP Statistical Review of World Energy*. https://www.bp.com/content/dam/bp/business-sites/en/global/corporate/pdfs/energy-economics/statistical-review/bp-stats-review-2018-full-report.pdf

Chen, S. S. (2009). Oil Price Pass-through Into Inflation. *Energy Economics*, *31*(1), 126-133.

Demiral, M., Bal, H., & Akça, E. (2016). Petrol Gelirleri ve Ekonomik Büyüme: Seçilmiş Petrol Zengini Gelişmekte Olan Ülkeler Üzerine Bir Panel Veri Analizi. *Sosyoekonomi*, *24*(27), 85-102.

De Gregorio, J., Landerretche, O., Neilson, C., Broda, C., & Rigobon, R. (2007). Another Pass-Through Bites the Dust? Oil Prices and Inflation, *Economía*, *7*(2), 155-208.

Eraydın, K. (2015). Petrol Fiyatlarındaki Düşüşün Nedenleri ve Etkileri. *Türkiye İş Bankası İktisadi Araştırmalar Bölümü*, 1-22.

Fernald, J., & Trehan, B. (2005). Why Hasn't the Jump in Oil Prices Led to a Recession? *FRBSF Economic Letter*, *2005-31*, 1-3.

Frankel, J. A. (2010). *The Natural Resource Curse: A Survey*. NBER Working Paper No. 15836.

Gisser, M., & Goodwin, T. H. (1986). Crude Oil and the Macroeconomy: Tests of Some Popular Notions: Note. *Journal of Money, Credit and Banking*, *18*(1), 95-103.

Güngör, S., et al. (2016). Petrol Fiyatlarındaki Değişimlerin Türkiye'nin Cari İşlemler Açığına Etkileri. *Maliye Finans Yazıları*, *106*, 29-48.

Hamilton, J. D. (1983). Oil and the macroeconomy since World War II. *Journal of Political Economy*, *91*(2), 228-248.

Hamilton, J. D. (1988). A Neoclassical Model of Unemployment and the Business Cycle. *Journal of Political Economy*, *96*(3), 593-617.

Huang, R. D., Masulıs, R. W., & Stoll, H. R. (1996). Energy Shocks And Financial Markets. *The Journal of Futures Markets*, *16*(1), 1-27.

Husain, A., et al. (2015). *Global Implications of Lower Oil Prices*. IMF Staff Discussion Note.

Jones, C. M., & Kaul, G. (1996). Oil and the Stock Markets. *The Journal of Finance*, *51*(2), 463-491.

Karl, T. L. (2005). Understanding the Resource Curse. In S. Tsalik & A. Schiffrin (Eds.), *Covering Oil A Reporter's Guide to Energy and Development* (pp. 21-26). Open Society Institute.

Kilian, L., Rebucci, A., & Spatafora, N. (2009). Oil shocks and external balances. *Journal of International Economics*, *77*, 181-194.

Marion, N. P. (1981). *Anticipated and Unanticipated Oil Price Increases and the Current Account*. NBER Working Paper No. 759.

Pain, N., Koske, I., & Sollie, M. (2006). *Globalisation and Inflation in the OECD Economies*. OECD Economics Department Working Papers No. 524. OECD Publishing.

Pollet, J. M. (2005). Predicting Asset Returns With Expected Oil Price Changes. *SSRN*. https://ssrn.com/abstract=722201

Sarr, M., Bulte, E., Meissner, C., & Swanson, T. (2011). Sovereign Debt and the Resource Curse. In R. W. Kolb (Ed.), *Sovereign Debt: From Safety to Default (Kolb Series in Finance)* (pp. 51-61). Wiley.

Schneider, M. (2004). The Impact of Oil Price Changes on Growth and Inflation. *Monetary Policy & The Economy*, *2*, 27-36.

Sek, S. K., Teo, X. Q., & Wong, Y. N. (2015). A Comparative Study on the Effects of Oil Price Changes on Inflation. *Procedia Economics and Finance*, *26*, 630-636.

Stiglitz, J. (2004, August 18). *We can now cure Dutch disease*. The Guardian. https://www.theguardian.com/business/2004/aug/18/comment.oilandpetrol

West, J., & Desai, P. (2002). *Diverse Structures and Common Characteristics of Developing Nations*. Oxford University.

Yalçın Erik, N., & Koşaroğlu, Ş. M. (2016). Tarihsel Süreç Boyunca Değişen Petrol Fiyatları; Şeyl Gazı Etkisi Ve Bazı Öngörüler. *C.Ü. İktisadi ve İdari Bilimler Dergisi*, *17*(2), 119-143.

CHAPTER TWO

THE EFFECTS OF CASPIAN ENERGY RESOURCES ON KAZAKHSTAN'S FOREIGN POLICY

GİRAY SAYNUR DERMAN*

Introduction

The Caspian Basin emerged as a new problem area when the Soviet Union collapsed in 1991. The basin has given rise to numerous conflicts, especially over the sharing of the Caspian Sea's energy resources and exporting them to world markets. One of the main causes of the conflict is the potential route for the transmission of oil and natural gas. Transporting the region's energy resources to world markets is a critical question due to economic and commercial reasons as well as political concerns. In addition to the regional countries, other powers also have geopolitical and economic concerns and interests in the Caspian Sea.

> Indeed, oil's economic importance also gives it a tremendous strategic importance for the countries in the Caspian Basin. Therefore, regional countries have focused on improving their relations with Western partners by means of their energy resources, besides decreasing their dependence on Russia and moderating Moscow's influence. (Sultanov, 2013, p. 64)

In discussions initiated about the energy potential of the region after the dissolution of the Soviet Union, it was claimed that Azerbaijan is the "Kuwait of the Caucasus" while Kazakhstan is the "Second Saudi Arabia". The Caspian Basin contains vast oil and natural gas reserves, raising the

---

* Prof. Dr. Giray Saynur Derman, Department of Public Relations and Publicity, Faculty of Communication, Marmara University. E-mail: saynurderman@gmail.com.

region's strategic profile. Both Azerbaijan and Kazakhstan have discovered significant offshore energy reserves there. In this context, some authors have called the competition among governments and companies "the Second Great Game" or "the Greater Middle East Project". Oil and natural gas contracts, pipelines, energy routes, and energy consortiums are regarded as the rewards of the "New Great Game" or the project. With its potential energy resources, Kazakhstan captured the interest of American oil companies immediately after gaining independence. Today, large oil companies are making major investments in Kazakhstan's oil fields, developing operational fields, and realizing various projects to transport Kazakh oil to world markets. In addition, Kazakhstan has both territorial and onshore-offshore oil reserves (Tokayev, 2001, p. 360).

In this paper, Kazakhstan's role in the world by means of its oil and natural gas, with a special emphasis on the Caspian Basin, is evaluated first.

The second part of the article examines the energy policy of Kazakhstan after it declared independence. The role and influence of global and regional powers are also included in the analysis of Kazakhstan's energy policy. President Nursultan Nazarbayev's successful energy strategies in maintaining a balance gave the opportunity to China, Russia, and the US to make investments in Kazakhstan. Multinational oil companies have invested heavily in Kazakhstan with the goal of meeting market demand by exploring and developing oil reserves (Friedland et al., 1975, p. 437) and controlling the market and the potential supply to prevent excessive competition over pricing (Emeklier, 2010, p. 61). States regard multinational companies as threats to their sovereignty because of the intensity of their in-country operations and presence. As noted above, Nazarbayev pursued a balanced foreign policy to protect his country against such threats.

The third part deals with relations between Kazakhstan and Russia, as well as Russia's primary role in Kazakhstan's foreign policy, with a focus on energy (Derman, 2013, p. 243). Among the former Soviet Republics, Kazakhstan ranks second in terms of oil production after Russia, which illustrates the critical importance of energy for the country.

The fourth part emphasizes the importance of energy in Kazakhstan-US relations with a focus on US companies' operations and investments in the country. It should be noted that Kazakhstan is a key regional partner for the US in terms of energy reserves.

Kazakhstan and its Energy Role in the World

Kazakhstan is located in the heart of Eurasia. According to the Statistical Agency of Kazakhstan, the population is 19,189,022 million, which saw a 1.5 percent increase in 2020. This natural increase is to be expected, as the number of births exceeded the number of deaths by 257,179. The proportion of ethnic Kazakhs in the population was around 45 percent during the final years of the Soviet Union; this has now increased to 67 percent (Countrymeters, n.d.). Russians make up 22 percent of the population, a figure that has decreased year-on-year since independence (Purtaş, 2006, p. 2). Kazakhstan is one of the wealthiest countries among the Central Asian republics, which is mostly due to its rich energy resources, with a per capita income of $13,610 in 2020.

The energy sector constitutes at least two-thirds of Kazakhstan's export revenue, and it was the most important source of foreign currency in the country's transition to the free market. Today, the Kazakh economy is dependent on oil, natural gas, and mining (Öz & Gülten, n.d.). Approximately two-thirds of the state budget came from energy exports in 2013-2014. It is estimated that Kazakhstan has 30 billion barrels of oil and 2.4 trillion cubic meters of natural gas reserves (İsmayilov & Budak, 2015, p. 1). Kazakhstan ranks 12th in the world in terms of oil reserves and 20th for natural gas reserves. There are around 172 oil and 42 natural gas fields in Kazakhstan (Ismayilov & Budak, 2015, p. 2).

Following Kazakhstan's declaration of independence, Kazakh Tengizchevroil LLP (TCO) signed an agreement with Chevron in April 1993 (Nikolayev, 2011). The current partners are Chevron (50 percent), KazMunaiGas (20 percent) (Karabalin, 2014, p. 29), ExxonMobil Kazakhstan Ventures Inc. (25 percent), and LukArco (5 percent) (Fluor, n.d.). In 2013, Tengizchevroil produced 27.1 million tons of oil in the Tengiz field (Sumarokov, 2010, p. 58), which dropped to 26.7 million tons in 2014. The company sold 1.3 million tons of liquefied gas and 7 billion cubic meters of gas in 2014. Oil produced from the Tengiz field is exported to Novorossiysk via the CPC pipeline, to Odessa and Taman by railway, and then onward to the ports of Aktau, Batum, and Kulevi (İsmayilov & Budak, 2015, p. 4).

The Kashagan field, located in the southeast part of the Caspian, is the largest offshore oil field in the country and is estimated to hold 16 billion barrels of oil (Balgınbayev, 1996, p. 36). A consortium consisting of ENI (Italy), BP (UK), ExxonMobil (USA), RoyalDutch Shell (UK/Netherlands), Total (France), PhillipsPetroleum (USA), Statoil (Norway), and Inpex (Japan) hastened exploration in 1998. Production started in September

2013 but then stopped one month later due to a malfunction in the pipeline, and the recommissioning date was postponed until the second half of 2016 (İsmayilov & Budak, 2015, p. 3).

The Tengiz and Karachaganak projects account for half of the country's oil production with their daily production capacity of 1.70 million barrels of liquid petroleum (Evnina, 2014, p. 12). As an oil producer, Kazakhstan's economic development is dependent upon three major projects: Karachaganak, Kashagan, and Tengiz. According to data published by the Energy Information Agency, Kashagan – the country's third-largest project, holding between 7 and 13 million barrels of oil – was expected to start operations in 2016 or 2017 (EIA, n.d.). Kazakhstan, having produced 83.4 million tons of oil in 2013, was projected to produce 110 million tons of oil in 2018 (İsmayilov & Budak, 2015, pp. 2-3).

More than three-quarters of Kazakhstan's crude oil exports go to European markets via the Caspian Sea, and only 16 percent of its oil is transported to China via pipelines. Kazakh crude oil flows from Atasu through the Alataw Pass into Xinjiang in Western China via a 1000-kilometer-long pipeline. Moreover, it is estimated that Chinese companies directly participated in the 40 percent of oil production in Kazakhstan's oil fields in 2014 (EIA, n.d.).

Kazakhstan's state-owned gas and oil company KazMunaiGas (KMG) was established in 2002. It has shares in Karachaganak (10 percent), Kashagan (16.8 percent), and Tengiz (20 percent). In the last decade, with Kaztransoil, KMG has been one of the leading national oil-producing companies in Kazakhstan. In 2008, KMG took another step toward developing the transportation system of the Trans-Caspian project by signing a significant agreement with the State Oil Company of the Azerbaijan Republic (SOCAR) on connecting the pipeline to Georgian ports and the BTC. The parties to the agreement emphasized the importance of export routes backed by the West, but ultimately the Kazakh president refused to sign the final declaration (Guliyev & Akhrarkhodjaeva, 2008, p. 3)

It is estimated that 20 million tons of Kazakh oil will be transported via the BTC in 2018-2020. At present, a small amount of Kazakh oil is transmitted to Russia and China by railway. In total, more than 1.5 billion tons of oil and 741 billion cubic meters of natural gas were produced in Kazakhstan during the the years of independence (since 1991). Total oil revenue in Kazakhstan in 2019 worth 31.6 trillion tenge (approximately 81.6 billion dollars). With each new project, the oil industry increased its production, turnover and potential during the years of independence. Since then, Kazakhstan became among the leading oil exporting countries.

According to Kanat Bozumbayev, current Minister of Energy of the Republic of Kazakhstan, the annual oil production, which was 25 million tons in 1991, increased 3.5 times to 90 million tons. He said "*The oil and natural gas transportation system was created. The Caspian oil pipeline is the shortest route for oil export from Tengiz, Karaçaganak and Kashagan oil fields and it provides economic and suitable conditions. Oil exports to 36 countries increased by 5 times and reached 66 million tons.*"

Saying that the annual oil production volume is expected to increase to 105 million tons in 2025, Bozumbayev added that investment projects worth 75 billion dollars will be implemented in the oil and natural gas sector in the medium term (Raimbekova, 2019).

Three major Kazakh refineries have an annual oil production capacity of 18 million tons. These are:

- JSC "Atyrau Refinery" (ANPZ)
- JSC "Pavlodar Petrochemical Facility" (PPCP)
- "Shymkentnefteorgsintez" (SHNOS) Refineries

These refineries are located in the south, west, and north of the country, respectively. The total processing capacity of these national refineries is approximately 18 million tons annually. Annual output of a minimum of 9.5 million tons of oil would be sufficient to meet domestic demand. The Atyrau refinery in the west of the country processes the crude oil that is delivered from Kazakhstan's northwest reserves, while the Shimkent refinery in the south mainly processes the oil coming from the Kumkol area. The Pavlodar refinery in the north is connected to the pipeline coming from Western Siberia (Evnina, 2014, p. 17).

In Kazakhstan, foreign investors constitute around 71 percent of oil production. These are mostly Russian, American, European, and Chinese multinational companies, including ExxonMobil, Chevron, Agip, BG, BP/Statoil, Shell, Total, INPEKS, Philips, Lukoil, Eni, etc. Kazakhstan's oil and gas sector has long attracted both national and foreign investors. The country is a safe bet for investors thanks to its rich Kashagan, Tengiz, and Karachaganak resources in the Caspian Basin (Derman & Ongarova, 2014, pp. 82-83).

Kazakhstan's Energy Policy in the Post-Independence Period

When analyzing the role of Caspian energy resources in Kazakhstan's foreign policy, it is helpful to first recognize that energy is a focal issue for other regional and non-regional actors, and in this regard it shapes the Kazakh foreign policy together with its increasing geopolitical significance. With regard to the Caspian's energy resources, Kazakhstan pursues a foreign policy based on multilateral and pragmatic cooperation. Due to its multilateral policy, Kazakhstan has good relations with each of the world's great powers. The country is not isolated and is open to interaction both in the East-West and South-North directions. Nursultan Nazarbayev has previously said, *"How much we control and eliminate our problems does not matter; the only way to economic development is integration."* Nazarbayev took significant steps to ensure integration and to strengthen the economic basis he created. Similarly, he was dedicated to creating an integration-based common market by developing market economy conditions (Nogayeva, 2011, p. 77).

According to Nazarbayev, "*In the 21st century, Kazakhstan, Russia, Central Asian countries and the Caucasus made a great effort to transform Eurasia into a common market in order to create the infrastructure for a modern market and ensure strategic communication among transport routes.*" In this context, former states of the USSR expressed their interest in communicating between the East and West. Their efforts in the field of energy are particularly diversified in Eurasia (Dugin, 2005, p. 117).

Nazarbayev sought to project a pragmatic and open-to-cooperation image, taking into consideration the country's financial capability and limitations. When examining the country's energy policy, the 2014-2020 Foreign Policy Concept Paper, which sets forth the country's main foreign policy goals, must also be scrutinized. Strategic priorities, the economy, and the "humanitarian aspect" of international relations are all analyzed within the concept. Moreover, the importance of energy security is emphasized in terms of Kazakhstan's energy strategy, given that the country is not only an energy producer but is also located along the transit route (Kavas, 2014).

Nazarbayev was re-elected for his fifth consecutive term in the Presidential elections held on April 26, 2015 (BBC, 2015). In this new term, he faced important economic challenges. Aware of this, during the run-up to the elections, he published a new program stipulating various reforms for transforming the economic structure. After the elections, the first item on the agenda was the "*restructuring of a raw material-based economy by focusing on high technology and value added production*". Crude oil exports constitute 69 percent of total exports in Kazakhstan, and so the Kazakh economy is directly affected by developments in the international oil market. In his new term, President Nazarbayev's primary aim was to create a robust economic model that is resilient to fluctuations in oil markets; he planned to achieve this by diversifying the sources of income (Mutlu, 2015). But this new term clearly holds some challenges and problems. For instance, the sustainability of the Eurasian Union project posed a great challenge for Nazarbayev as one of the architects of this project (Nazarbayev, 2007, p. 116). Russian President Vladimir Putin regards the Eurasian Union as not only an economic union but also a corporate infrastructure that will contribute to political unity in the future. Although Nazarbayev's participation in the union is interpreted as a political maneuver, it is still unclear to what extent Astana will follow its balancing policy between Russia and the West in the post-Ukraine crisis era (Mutlu, 2015). When presenting Kazakhstan's 2014-2020 foreign policy, Nazarbayev clearly indicated that the Eurasian Union is "an organization based on the principle of economic cooperation, not a political organization" (Weitz, 2014).

The main objective of the Kazakh government's economic policies is to minimize the impact of changes and fluctuations in oil prices by developing the non-energy sector.

Thus, the country is aiming to keep the annual GDP growth rate at over 8 percent and is focusing on ensuring economic diversification within the framework of the 2003-2015 Innovative Industrial Development Strategy (Er, 2013). Kazakhstan has the aim of becoming a key energy actor in the region and is striving to derive maximum political and economic profit from the various international strategies toward Central Asian energy resources, including those of Russia, the US, the EU, and China. It is therefore open to the different projects proposed by these various countries (Has, 2013, p. 2).

The National Programme for Accelerated Industrial and Innovation Development of the Republic of Kazakhstan was applied for the period from 2010 to 2014. One of the main targets of this program was to reduce energy intensity of industry in order to achieve competitiveness of Kazakhstan's economy. In determining the strategic priorities of Kazakhstan's oil and gas industry, this program has been taken into consideration. The national oil and gas development program, which was approved by the President as part of Kazakhstan's Strategic Development Plan (which runs until 2020), is also taken into account. Kazakhstan's Ministry of Oil and Gas has developed intersectoral industry plans through 2020 with the participation of KazMunaiGas. These are:

- Creating a logistics corridor for oil and gas exports in new transportation

- Completion of Kazakhstan's oil and gas multi-vector system
- Developing the tanker fleet on the Caspian Sea and open seas (Black Sea, Mediterranean, etc.)
- Effective use of energy-efficient technologies
- Developing a regulatory framework for oil and gas complexes
- Implementation of European fuel standards (KazMunaiGas, n.d.)

The Role of Energy in Kazakh-Russian Relations

Russia's interest in the Caspian Sea has political, economic, and security dimensions. The region was completely under its sway during the Soviet era, and Moscow is keen to maintain its political influence on the newly independent republics as part of the "near abroad" doctrine it has pursued throughout the post-USSR period. Trying to expand its grip and counter the West's influence in the region, Russia's aim is to achieve full authority over the energy resources of the Caspian region and to ensure the security of its southern part.

Putin's integration-centered policies as well as the pragmatic strategic partnership between Moscow and Astana have a major impact on Kazakhstan's political and economic sustainability (Dukenbayev, 1996, p. 37). Of all the Central Asian countries, Kazakhstan has the closest relations with Russia in every sector. Accordingly, Kazakhstan pursues a balancing policy between global powers while at the same time following Russia's lead. "Moscow-Astana relations also form the basis for regional cooperation and organizations established in Eurasia under the leadership of Russia" (Has, 2013, p. 13). In Kazakhstan, Russia has four military shooting ranges in addition to the Baikonur cosmodrome, the operating time of which has been extended until 2050 (Has, 2013, pp. 4-5). Russia and Kazakhstan also signed various agreements for the establishment of joint military-industrial enterprises between 2013 and 2015.

"Coal mined in Kazakhstan's Ekibastuz town is transferred to power plants in Russia's Ural and Siberia regions. Kazakhstan receives back the electricity generated in these plants, and in this way it meets some of its energy needs. Similarly, Kazakhstan sends some of its raw materials such as oil and natural gas for processing in the industrial zones of South Ural, Samara, Orenburg and Bashkortostan, and in return it buys processed products from Russia" (Has, 2013, pp. 7-8). The Russian-Kazakh border is Kazakhstan's longest border, and as two energy-rich countries, they share significant economic interests.

In 2002, Lukoil and KazMunaiGaz established a joint company named KazRosGaz. The company transmits Kazakh natural gas to third countries through Russia (Zakon.kz, 2014). Gazprom also delivers Kazakh natural gas to Orenburg (Polovinkin, 2004, p. 44). Russia's most important achievement after the dissolution of the Soviet Union is the Caspian pipeline, which transports Kazakh oil to Novorossiysk Port. The Russian oil company Lukoil operates the Karachaganak field in Kazakhstan and also takes an active role in other projects such as in Aksay, Kumkolya, and North Buzachi (İsmayilov & Budak, 2015, p. 4).

"The infrastructure established during the Soviet period is highly important for the transportation of Kazakh oil and natural gas to international markets, therefore Russia has a significant transit role for Kazakhstan. For instance, almost all of the natural gas that Kazakhstan sold in 2012 (11 billion cubic meters) was transported to Russia via pipelines or to other markets through Russia." Russia is also pursuing new opportunities with Gazprom and Rosneft in terms of oil and natural gas supplies to Kazakhstan. The parties have made significant progress toward their shared goal of increasing the volume of Kazakh and Russian oil transported by the Caspian Pipeline Consortium to 67 million tons by 2016 (Has, 2013, pp. 12-13).

Russia's policies for maintaining its political presence in the region are damaging to Kazakhstan's influence in the energy sector. Therefore, investments by Russian companies in the Kazakh oil and natural gas sector remain much lower than those of their Western and Chinese counterparts (Cohen, 2005, p. 21). Although it does not seem like there is major competition between the West and Russia over Kazakhstan's hydrocarbon resources, the Astana government has been trying to develop cooperation with the West and China in order to balance Russian influence in its national energy sector (İsmayilov & Budak, 2015, p. 8).

The biggest problem for Russia is the potential development of Kazakhstan's independent relations with the West. Kazakhstan's dependence on Russia for military-technical support has come to an end now that Astana is actively developing its ties both with NATO and bilaterally. This has been a cause for concern in both Moscow and Beijing, Kazakhstan's partners in the Shanghai Cooperation Organization. These concerns also stem from the fact that the US, the UK, and Germany have all been involved in the modernization of Kazakhstan's air defense system. Initially, Russia was indifferent to Kazakhstan's statement regarding its participation in the Baku-Tbilisi-Ceyhan oil pipeline. But when these abstract plans became a reality, Russia started to feel uncomfortable. However, Kazakhstan has fully supported Russia's integration efforts, remaining loyal to Russian politics within the SCO, CIS, CSTO, EurAsEC, and SES. In addition to their economic and humanitarian cooperation, Kazakhstan and Russia share common interests on national security:

- Kazakhstan hosting part of Russia's strategic infrastructure;
- Various agreements regarding security within the framework of CSTO;
- Unilateral and bilateral military-industrial relations;
- Russia's geopolitical interests in the Caspian Sea;
- Russia's primary nuclear and strategic potential being located close to the Kazakh-Russian border.

Russian leaders Boris Yeltsin, Vladimir Putin, and Dimitri Medvedev all visited Kazakhstan officially several times. The Russian leadership clearly appreciates Nazarbayev's contribution to the development of Kazakh-Russian relations (Laumulin, 2009, p. 44).

Presence and Investments of US Companies in Kazakhstan

The US regards the Caspian region as a door to Central Asia, where it is trying to increase its influence. For this reason, Washington maintains relations with the Central Asian and Caucasus states in every field. It is asserted that the US will support the rapid and uninterrupted flow of oil from the region, closely monitor and control Iran's policies toward the region, ensure the security of energy resources in the Caspian Basin, improve democracy in regional countries, maintain peace among the regional countries, create free-market economies, and better integrate those countries with the international community. The US wants to be more active and influential in the region as a counterpoint to Russia. The most recent operations of the US administration, aimed at strengthening its economic and military hegemony, disturbed the fragile balance in Eurasia and had terrible impacts on regional and global stability with the potential to stir up new dangerous and destructive conflicts in the region. At the same time, a new era has started that would change the political frame of the region. In comparison to the other regional countries, Kazakhstan has the most important and largest reserves for US companies. Investments in Kazakhstan's huge oil and gas in Tengiz have already been pioneered by US companies (Zhaissenbayev, 2004, p. 100).

After the Central Asian states were incorporated into NATO's Partnership for Peace (PfP) program, American companies such as Chevron, Amaco, ExxonMobil, and Arco came to the region to bring the region's hydrocarbon reserves to world markets. (Menon, 1998, p. 44). According to the US Department of Energy, Kazakhstan has the largest proven oil reserves in the Caspian region, holding 9 to 29 billion barrels. The Tengiz oil field, which holds more than half of Kazakh reserves, has been operated by a consortium including ExxonMobil and under the leadership of Chevron-Texaco since 1993. Chevron-Texaco is also a part of the consortium that operates the Karachaganak field, which holds an estimated reserve of 2.4 billion barrels of oil (Hersh, 2005). Moreover, oil and natural gas operations on Kazakhstan's Caspian shores are managed by a consortium that includes ExxonMobil (Nichol, 2005).

The US supported alternative pipelines aimed at ending or preventing Russian influence over Kazakh energy resources, while Kazakhstan pursued a balancing policy between the two major powers. The US played an influential economic role, whereas Russia exerted its influence on political and strategic aspects. The entrance of Chevron-Texaco, the former workplace of former US Secretary of State Condoleezza Rice, into Kazakhstan (Engdahl, 2007, p. 64) was interpreted as a new sign of America's engagement in the region.

Richard Morningstar, who has served in different positions in the region and worked as a special consultant for implementing President Bill Clinton's Caspian Basin Energy Diplomacy in 1998,[1] listed four strategic objectives for the energy resources in the Caspian region at a 1999 Senate Subcommittee meeting on international economic policies:

1. Contributing to strengthening the independence, sovereignty, and level of wealth of new states and encouraging them to make political and economic reforms;
2. Assisting in solving regional conflicts by establishing economic ties among newly independent states;
3. Ensuring the flow of energy resources from the Caspian region to the world market without any dependence or restraint, and in this way contributing to increasing the energy security of America and its allies; and
4. Raising commercial opportunities for American companies (Özkan, 2005, p. 147).

A report prepared by the US National Energy Policy Development Group during the George W. Bush era stated that the American

---

[1] Richard Morningstar served as US Ambassador to Azerbaijan from 2012 to February 2015.

administration should support the BTC pipeline project and the transmission of Kazakh oil through this line for the purpose of creating alternative routes for energy transport (National Energy Policy Development Group, 2001, pp. 8-12). The report emphasized that America's energy security must be given priority in foreign policy, energy dependence on a single region should be eliminated, and the US government should give aid and assistance for the construction of pipelines, including preparing and protecting the infrastructure necessary for transporting Caspian energy resources to the West (Özkan, 2005, p. 149).

As another step in this strategy, the US wants to extend the Southern Corridor pipeline to Europe through Turkey in order to bring Iraq and Turkmen gas online (U.S. Senate, 2012, p. 2).

Kazakhstan's 2014-2020 Foreign Policy Concept underscored the importance of further developing relations with the US (President of the Republic of Kazakhstan, 2020; Ministry of Foreign Affairs of Kazakhstan, n.d.). Washington wants to ensure the control and security of its oil, prevent nationalization that would harm the interests of American companies, and limit the influence of an unfriendly regional power (Iran) or a non-regional hegemon (Russia and China).

Along with the US, the EU is also encouraging Kazakhstan and Turkmenistan to build pipelines that will bypass Russia, such as Trans-Caspian. Although Caspian energy resources are very important for European energy security, the EU's influence on Caspian and Central Asian energy resources will be limited – at least in the medium term – due to member states' failure to create a common foreign and security policy and a common energy policy (Derman, 2014, pp. 3-19).

Conclusion

The Caspian Sea is historically, geopolitically, and commercially important for the small number of regional countries that surround it. However, in recent decades, its geopolitical significance has increased. A large number of regional as well as external actors exert influence in the Caspian Basin and have interests there, leading to different balances of power. This is largely due to the vast oil and natural gas resources in the Caspian Basin. Although there are various projects being developed by a range of multinational and national companies, Russia remains the dominant player when it comes to the region's energy reserves.

The EU and Turkey, dependent on Russia for energy, are trying to find export routes from the Caspian that do not go through Russia. Thus, they are focusing on different projects to transport Caspian resources to the

West, such as the Baku-Tbilisi-Ceyhan oil pipeline and the Trans-Anatolian natural gas pipeline. In addition, there are also efforts to create an alternative route to the giant Chinese market through Kazakhstan. Russia and Iran are blocking all these efforts, aiming instead to reach a settlement that will enable them to share the Caspian for their own interests (O'Lear, 2004, p. 175). The littoral states have started to produce oil and natural gas in the areas close to their coasts, ignoring any negative reactions from their neighbors. Today, there is a North-South conflict; Russia, Azerbaijan, and Kazakhstan in the north, and Iran and Turkmenistan in the south (Neftegaz, 2013). It is also known that the issue of the legal status of the Caspian has not been resolved for good. There are ongoing negotiations regarding the resolution of different problems in the Caspian. In the absence of a common solution, states sometimes reach bilateral agreements on certain issues. In addition, there are also certain projects that are quite difficult to realize (Lee, 2005, p. 44), for instance, opening a canal to connect the Caspian to the Black Sea and thus creating a link to international waters. The most fair and reasonable solution seems to be to accept the Caspian as a sea, divide it among the five coastal countries and create five national sectors on the basis of the principle of equal distance from the shore, and share the seabed on that basis (Joyner & Walters, 2006, pp. 190-191). The implementation of various pipeline projects could end Russia's regional monopoly and create an alternative for the world market, especially for Turkey and the US. Caspian energy can be used more efficiently by looking after the interests of all coastal states rather than a couple of national hegemons.

In conclusion, Kazakh energy resources, which are mostly located in the Caspian Basin, attract large oil companies and continue to be an important focal point for Western and Eastern states. With its ever-developing energy transport network and increasing foreign investments, Kazakhstan supports major projects for developing and producing its energy resources. Due to its strategic location at the crossroads between the East and West, Kazakhstan pursues a multidimensional foreign policy. It has adopted a "win-win" strategy in its energy initiatives, based on cooperation and mutual interest.

References

Balginbayev, N. (1996). *Nefti Gaz Kazakhstana (Нефтьи Газ Казахстана).* Kazakhstan i Vsemirnoye Soobshestvo.

BBC. (2015, April 26). "Presidential Election in Kazakstan / *Kazakistan'da Cumhurbaşkanlığı seçimi.* https://www.bbc.com/turkce/haberler/2015/04/150426_kazak_secim

Cohen, A. (2005). *Kazakhstan: Energy Cooperation with Russia – Oil, Gas and Beyond.* Kogan Page Business Book.

Countrymeters. (n.d.). *Population of Kazakhstan 2020.* Retrieved April 13, 2020, from http://countrymeters.info/en/Kazakhstan

Derman, G. S. (2013). "Black Sea Regional Policies of Russia and the United States after September 11." In G. S. Derman (Ed.), *Blue Black Sea: New Dimensions of History, Security, Strategy, Energy and Economy* (pp. 241-265). Cambridge Scholars Publishing.

Derman, G. S. (2014). Avrupa Birliği ve Orta Asya Ülkeleri ile İlişkiler ve Avrupa Birliği'nin Bölgeye Yönelik Stratejisi. *TURAN-SAM, 6*(22), 3-19.

Derman, G. S., & Ongarova, Y. (2014). Kazakistan'ın Enerji Politikası. *TURAN-SAM, 6*(22), 81-91.

Dugin, A. (2005). *Evraziskaya Missia Nazarbayev (Евразийская Миссия Назарбаева, ENU Издательство ENU İzdatelstva).* Astana.

Dukenbayev, K. (1996). *Energetika Kazahstane i Puti Ee İntegracii v Mirovuyu Ekonomiku.* İzdatelstvo Gylym.

EIA. (n.d.). *Kazakhstan.* Retrieved April 10, 2020, from http://www.eia.gov/countries/analysisbriefs/Kazakhstan/kazakhstan.pdf

Emeklier, B. N. E. (2010). Petrolün Uluslararası İlişkilerindeki Yeri: Jeopolitik Teoriler ve Petropolitik. *Bilgi Strateji, 2*(3), 59-85.

Engdahl, F. W. (2007). ABD Avrasya Enerji Politikalarında Kuşatılmakta mı? *Sürdürülebilir Kalkınma ve Bağımsızlık İçin Stratejik Bir Unsur ENERJİ, 71*, 64-67.

Er, Ö. (2013). *Değişim Sürecinde Kazakistan Ekonomisinin Yeni Parametreleri ve Türkiye ile Ticari-Ekonomik İlişkileri.* İzmir Chamber of Commerce. http://www.izto.org.tr/portals/0/pusuladergisi/2013/degisimsurecinde.pdf

Evnina, Y. (2014). *Analiz Neftedobivayuşey Otrasli, RK (Анализ Нефтедобывающей Отрасли РК).* RFSA.

Fluor. (n.d.). *Tengizchevroil Future Growth Project - Wellhead Pressure Management Project.* https://www.fluor.com/projects/tengizchevroil-future-growth-project

Friedland, E., Seabury, P., & Wildavsky, A. (1975). Oil and the Decline of Western Power. *Political Science Quarterly*, *90*(3), 411-437.

Guliyev, F., & Akhrarkhodjaeva, N. (2008). *Transportation of Kazakhstani Oil Via Caspian Sea (TKOC) Arrangements, Actors and Interests.* RussGasp Working Paper.

Has, K. (2013). *Orta Asya'nın Bölgesel Dinamikleri Çerçevesinde Rusya-Kazakistan İlişkileri (USAK Analiz 23)*. USAK.

Hersh, S. M. (2001, July 9). *The Price of Oil.* The New Yorker. https://www.newyorker.com/magazine/2001/07/09/the-price-of-oil

İsmayilov, E., & Budak, T. (2015). Bağımsızlık Sonrası Kazakistan'ın Enerji Politikası. *Bilgesam Analiz*, *1189*, 1-2.

Joyner, C., & Walters, K. Z. (2006). The Caspian Conundrum: Reflections on the Interplay Between Law, the Environment and Geopolitics. *The International Journal of Marine and Coastal Law, 21*(2), 173-216.

Karabalin, U. (2014). *Osnovnıye Mestorojdenya Nefti v Kazakhstane (Основные Месторождения Нефти в Казахстане).* FNB Samruk-Kazna.

Kavas, A. Y. (2014, September 3). "*Kazakistan'da Rusya-Çin Rekabeti"/ Russia -China Rivalry in Kazakstan*. Bilgesam. http://www.bilgesam.org/incele/1758/-kazakistan'da-rusya-cin-rekabeti/#.VU4WQI7tmko

KazMunaiGas. (n.d.). *KazMunaiGas*. Retrieved April 12, 2014, from https://kmg.kz/

Laumulin, M. (2009). *Tsentralnaya Aziya V Zarubejnom Politologii i Mirovoy Geopolitike, Tsentralnaya Aziya V XXI Stoletii (Центральная Азия в Зарубежной Политологии и Мировой Геополитике, Центральная Азия В XXI Столетии)*. KİSİ.

Lee, Y. (2005). Toward a New International Regime for the Caspian Sea. *Problems of Post-Communism*, *52*(3), 37-48.

Menon, R. (1998). Treacherous Terrain: The Political and Security Dimensions of Energy Development in the Caspian Sea Zone. *The National Bureau of Asian Research Analysis*, *9*(1), 1-44.

Ministry of Foreign Affairs of Kazakhstan. (n.d.). *Foreign Policy Concept for 2014-2020 Republic of Kazakhstan*. http://mfa.gov.kz/index.php/en/foreign-policy/foreign-policy-concept-for-2014-2020-republic-of-kazakhstan

Mutlu, G. (n.d.). *Kazakistan Seçimleri ve Kapıdaki Ekonomik Durgunluk.* USAK.

National Energy Policy Development Group. (2001). *National Energy Policy.* http://www.wtrg.com/EnergyReport/National-Energy-Policy.pdf

Nazarbayev, N. (2007). *Tarih Tolkınında (Тарих Толкынында).* ENU.

Neftegaz. (2013, August 5). *3-я нитка Трансазиатского МГП Туркменистан - Китай может быть проложена по территории Киргизии.* http://neftegaz.ru/news/view/112066/

Nichol, J. (2005). *Central Asia: Regional Developments and Implications for U.S. Interests.* Congressional Research Service.

Nikolayev, S. (2011). Central Asia in Geopolitics: The American Vector (1991-2008). *International Affairs, A Russian Journal of World Politics, Diplomacy and International Relations*, *57*(2), 47-63.

Nogayeva, A. (2011). *Orta Asya'da ABD, Rusya ve Çin: Stratejik Denge Arayışları.* USAK.

O'Lear, S. (2004). Resources and Conflict in the Caspian Sea. *Geopolitics*, *9*(1), 161-186.

Öz, E., & Gülten, S. (n.d.). *Enerji Politikaları Bağlamında Türkiye ve Kazakistan Ekonomik İlişkileri.* http://www.ersanoz.com/sunumlar/enerji-politikasi-kazakistan.pdf

Özkan, G. (2005). "Türk-Amerikan İlişkilerinde Kafkasya Faktörü"/ The Caucasus Factor in Turkish American Relations . "*Türkiye-ABD İlişkileri"/ Turkey- USA Relations, Eurasia Strategic Research Center (ASAM)*, *11*(2), 145-149.

Polovinkin, M. (2004). *Evraziskaya Ruskaya v İstorya-Kultura-Pismo (Евразийская Руская в История-Культура-Письм).* Obyom.

President of the Republic of Kazakhstan. (2020, March 9). On the Concept of the Foreign Policy of the Republic of Kazakhstan for 2020-2030. https://www.akorda.kz/en/legal_acts/decrees/on-the-concept-of-the-foreign-policy-of-the-republic-of-kazakhstan-for-2020-2030

Purtaş, F. (2006). *Kazakistan'da Sivil Toplum Kuruluşları, İç ve Dış Politika Etkileri.* USAK. http://www.usak.org.tr/dosyalar/dergi/72mzaGl872S0isSiOZsp1L6Ng8URNE.pdf

Raimbekova, A. (2019). *Kazakistan'da 28 yılda 1,5 milyar ton petrol üretildi.* aa.com.tr. https://www.aa.com.tr/tr/dunya/kazakistanda-28-yilda-1-5-milyar-ton-petrol-uretildi-/1573664.

Sultanov, B. K. (2013). *Kaspiski Regyon: Aktualnoye Problemi Razvitiya (Каспийский Регион: Актуальные Проблемы Развития).* KİSİ.

Sumarokov, L. (2010). *Evrazya Kenistigindegi Kazakhstan (Еуразия Кенистигиндеги Казахстан).* Egemen Kazakistan.

Tokayev, K. (2001). *Kazakistan Cumhuriyeti'nin Dış Politikası.* Kazakhstan Al-Farabi National University Publications.

U.S. Senate. (2012). *Energy and Security from the Caspian to Europe: A Minority Staff Report prepared for the use of the Committee on*

Foreign Relations, United States Senate, 112th Congress, second session, 12 December 2012. U.S. Government Printing Office.

Weitz, R. (2014). President Nazarbayev Discusses Kazakhstan's Foreign Policy Priorities. *Eurasia Daily Monitor, 11*(30). http://www.refworld.org/docid/5301c7e04.html

Zakon.kz. (2014, April 8). *Доклад Министра нефти и газа на правительственном часе в Мажилисе (г.Астана, 7 апреля 2014 года)*. http://www.zakon.kz/4615031-doklad-ministra-nefti-i-gaza-na.html

Zhaissenbayev, K. (2004). *Hazar Havzası Enerji Kaynakları ve Bölgesel Politikalar 1991–2004* [Unpublished Master's thesis]. Ankara University Institute of Social Sciences.

CHAPTER THREE

EVALUATION OF THE TURKSTREAM PIPELINE IN TERMS OF THE ENERGY POLICIES OF TURKEY AND RUSSIA

MERAL BALCI[*] AND SERKAN YAVUZ[**]

Introduction

Since the Industrial Revolution, energy has become one of the most important requirements in the world. However, energy sources are not distributed in equal amounts among every region of the world. As a result, countries with energy sources generate revenue by exporting those resources to other countries.

While Russia is a country rich in energy resources, especially natural gas, Turkey is a very poor country in this respect. Russia derives much of its GDP from energy exports. Turkey, on the other hand, is a country that depends heavily on energy.

Russia is constantly developing its strategy in the region to ensure energy demand security. Turkey and EU countries make up most of Russia's total natural gas demand, and Russia has been using this situation as a political strategy. As a result of Russia's annexation of Crimea, the straining of relations between the western states and Russia brought about the TurkStream project, which gave Turkey an opportunity to increase its energy supply security. Moreover, thanks to this project, Turkey has had the chance to increase its mission to be a central country in energy by using its geopolitical position. Russia, on the other hand, has provided energy demand security with the project and eliminated transit countries, especially

[*]Assoc. Prof. Dr. Meral Balcı, Faculty of Political Sciences, Marmara University. E-mail: mbalci@marmara.edu.tr.
[**]Res. Assist. Serkan Yavuz, Sakarya University. E-mail: serkanyavuz@sakarya.edu.tr

Ukraine, for the transportation of energy to Europe.

After the collapse of the Union of Soviet Socialist Republics (USSR), Russia emerged in the world order as the successor of the USSR. In Russia, the transition from a socialist economic order to a capitalist economic order started through privatization. However, during this privatization, state control was maintained in many sectors, particularly in the energy sector. While the state became the capital shareholder of the established energy companies, the state's representatives became the managers, and thus control over the energy companies was achieved. The most important reason for the government to maintain control in the energy sector is the size of the sector. The political and economic problems that may arise from the seizure of energy resources by other states caused the government to implement more conservative policies in terms of energy (Baysoy, 2009, pp. 56-64). It is seen as a necessity for Russia to retain energy control when considering the strategies based on the relationship with and the interests of the United States and the EU in the region.

At Russian National Security Council meeting in 2005, Russia set out its goal of becoming an "energy superpower" and made this goal clear to the world. Especially after Vladimir Putin came to power, Russia has established its foreign policy on energy resources and taken important steps in this regard (Durmuşoğlu, 2016, p. 294).

Russia's main objective on the energy issue is to use the energy factor to become the most important actor in the political and economic field in the world. As a matter of fact, Russia can reach the desired target if it uses these resources correctly. Despite the United States and the EU, Russia engages in statist policies to achieve these goals (Al & Gül, 2018, p. 65).

The increase in production potential due to technological developments in the world gives the energy-owning countries an economic advantage. In this respect, Russia is a lucky country in terms of energy resources. Russia had 14.5 billion tons of proven oil reserves as of 2017. This figure amounts to 6.3% of the world's oil reserves. Russia extracted 554.4 million tons of oil from these reserves in 2017, producing 12.6% of the world's total oil. Based on this production, Russia is one of the most important oil exporter countries. In 2017, of the 277 million tons of crude oil Russia exported, 170 million were sent to Europe, 60 million were sent to China, and 9 million were sent to Japan. Of the 145 billion tons of total processed oil exports, 84 million were sent to Europe, 16 million were sent to the US, and 13 million were sent to Singapore (BP, 2018, pp. 12-24).

Russia is one of the most important natural gas suppliers in the world. As of 2017, Russia owns 18.1% of the world's total natural gas reserves with its 35 trillion cubic meters of natural gas reserves. Of these reserves, with its annual production of 636 billion cubic meters of natural gas, Russia contributes 17.3% of the world's natural gas production. Moreover, Russia ranks first in the world's natural gas exports with its exports of 215 billion cubic meters per year (BP, 2018, pp. 26-44). Most of Russia's natural gas production is carried out by Gazprom: 72% of Russian natural gas and 17% of the world's total natural gas are produced by this company (World Energy Council, n.d.). A 38.37% share of Gazprom, Russia's largest joint-stock company, is owned by the Russian state (Gazprom, n.d.).

The increase in energy demand and the lack of self-sufficiency due to the production capacities of European countries provide advantages to Russia. Due to this situation, European countries are severely affected by possible disruptions to Russia's gas supply. Indeed, European countries are aiming to reduce their reliance on undependable transit countries and Russia and want to increase their energy supply diversity (Kim & Blank, 2015, p. 2).

Maintaining supremacy in the gas production and distribution sector through pipelines is Russia's main energy policy. In this sense, the implementation of statist policies is also seen as an important requirement for Russia. However, Russia both uses its own natural resource reserves and makes bilateral agreements with countries such as Turkmenistan, Kazakhstan, and Uzbekistan that may emerge as competitors (Bayraç, 2009, p. 127).

Turkey's Energy Policies and Profile

Turkey has an ever-increasing need for energy due to its economic growth. However, it is not a self-sufficient country in terms of energy resources. Nevertheless, it seeks to address the need for energy by using its geopolitical position and renewable energy sources (Durmuşoğlu, 2016, p. 297). Turkey acts as a bridge between the countries that supply energy and the countries that demand energy. Thanks to this geopolitical advantage, energy supply security is provided by diversifying resources (İlter & Kınık, 2017, p. 187).

The energy policies implemented by Turkey tend to be influenced by the overall structure of the world energy sector. Although there are all kinds of energy sources in Turkey, its reserves of fossil fuels other than lignite are small, and consequently its production is very low (Bayraç, 2009, p. 134). Turkey ranks second in the world in energy demand growth after China. With regard to this demand, Turkey obtains 98% of the natural gas, 92% of the oil, and 50% of the coal it consumes from outside its borders (Ulusoy, 2018). Due to this situation, Turkey has to meet approximately 70% of its energy demand with imports (Ulutaş, n.d.). Also, since 2002, Turkey's electricity demand has been the highest among OECD countries (Republic of Turkey Ministry of Foreign Affairs, n.d.).

The continuous increase of Turkey's energy demand and its dependence on external sources are the most important characteristics of its energy markets. Therefore, it aims to reduce this dependency in line with domestic and national strategies. Turkey's energy policy objectives can be grouped into four main categories (Republic of Turkey Ministry of Foreign Affairs, n.d.):

- Ensuring the diversity of the countries it imports energy from and the security of supply routes
- Increasing the share of renewable energy
- Increasing energy efficiency
- Developing nuclear energy activities

One of the first issues that comes to mind as a result of the evaluation of Ibn Khaldun's "geography is destiny" axiom regarding Turkey is its geopolitical position in terms of energy. Turkey's fate is closely related to its proximity to regions where oil and natural gas resources are abundant.

Turkey aims to become an energy corridor and energy center country by ensuring energy supply security and using its geopolitical position. Although Turkey has a large dependence on energy imports, its current geopolitical position provides a number of advantages. The most important advantage is that it is close to Central Asia and the Middle East, which are the most important regions of the world in terms of energy resources, and to Europe, where the energy demand is high. This proximity is important for achieving its goal of being an energy corridor between these regions (Durmuşoğlu, 2016, p. 299).

Turkey also aims to improve its relations with Central Asian countries in order to ensure energy supply security. In relation to this situation, the support of the United States and the EU on this issue helps Turkey to develop its energy supply policy. In particular, energy transport projects developed with Azerbaijan make Turkey an energy corridor for the delivery of energy resources in the region to the world (Durmuşoğlu, 2016, p. 294).

Furthermore, Turkey is aiming to strengthen its position in both the east-west and north-south energy corridors. The pipelines envisioning the transport of Caspian Basin and Middle Eastern natural gas resources to Europe are considered as the Southern Gas Corridor. The South Caucasus pipeline, the Baku-Tbilisi-Erzurum gas pipeline, and the Turkey and Greece Interconnector are operating in this context. The Trans-Anatolian natural gas pipeline (TANAP), the most important project of the Southern Gas

Corridor, opened on June 12, 2018. With the completion of the Trans-Adriatic Pipeline (TAP) in 2019, the transport of Azerbaijani gas to Europe began (Republic of Turkey Ministry of Foreign Affairs, n.d.). The addition of the TurkStream project, which foresees the transportation of Russian gas from the Black Sea to Turkey and from Turkey to Europe, serves Turkey's mission to become an energy corridor.

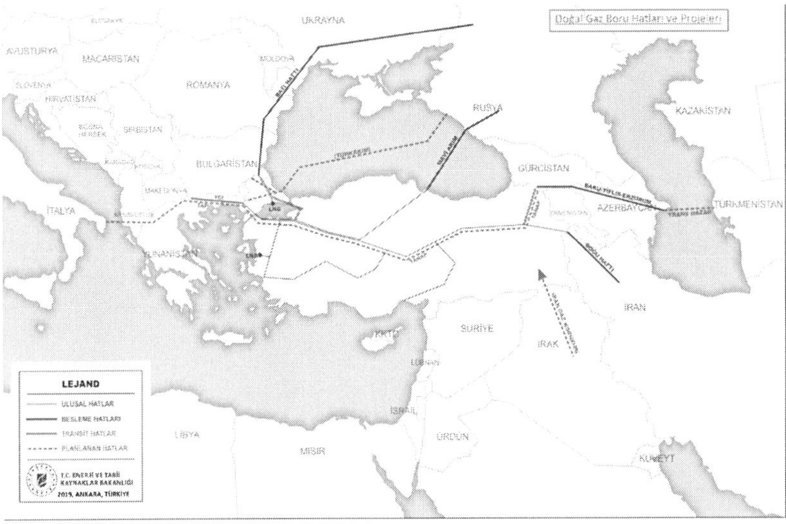

Figure 1: Natural Gas Pipelines and Projects Passing Through Turkey. Source: Republic of Turkey Ministry of Energy and Natural Resources, n.d.

Besides natural gas pipelines, Turkey has a strategic position regarding oil pipelines. The importance of oil pipelines is also seen when it is considered that approximately 3% of the world's total oil consumption passes through the Straits (Republic of Turkey Ministry of Foreign Affairs, n.d.).

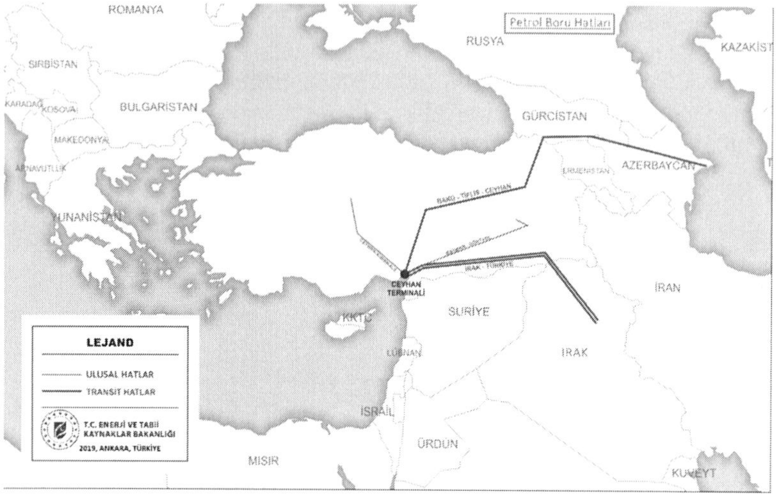

Figure 2: Oil Pipelines Passing Through Turkey. Source: Source: Republic of Turkey Ministry of Energy and Natural Resources, n.d.

From South Stream to TurkStream

The South Stream project, which was launched in 2007 and planned to be operational in 2015, was a project that would transport Russian gas to Europe under the Black Sea. With this project, a very serious energy transport agreement was formed between the EU and Russia. The South Stream project was supported by the EU because Russian gas would be directly connected to the EU without a shortage of funding and supplier countries (Tüysüz, 2014, p. 82). In other words, the fact that Russian gas is being transmitted to the EU via Ukraine and the search for alternative routes made the South Stream project important. Although the EU did not increase its diversity of resources with this project, it aimed to increase the diversity of supply routes. As a matter of fact, considering that the EU imports half of the gas it demands, it is very important for the EU to increase its diversity of routes in terms of its energy supply security (Yorkan, 2019).

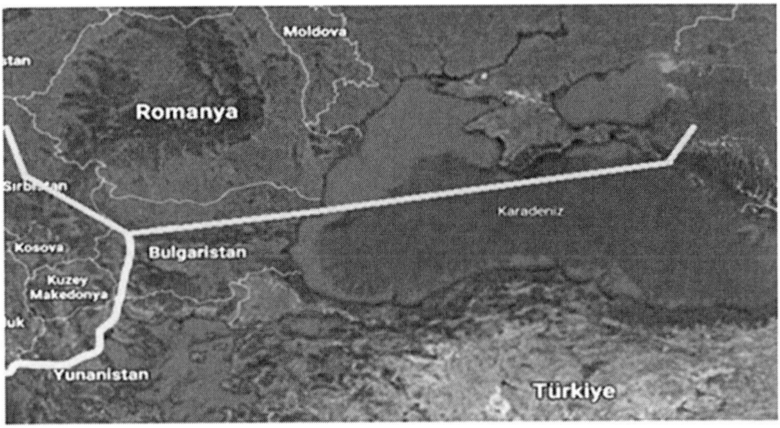

Figure 3: Route of the Cancelled South Stream Project, Source: This figure was drawn by Serkan Yavuz.

However, Russia's annexation of Crimea and the outbreak of civil war in Ukraine in 2013 caused Russia's relations with the western world, particularly with the United States and the EU, to be strained. After the collapse of the Soviet Union in 1991, cold war-like blocs re-emerged when Russia annexed Crimea (İlter & Kınık, 2017, p. 194). Because Ukraine is quite important to Russian geopolitics, the idea that Ukraine should be kept under Russia's control is consequently common among Russians. In other words, it can be said that Ukraine is a country that threatens the geopolitical security of Russia (Dugin, 2018, pp. 176-206). As a matter of fact, in response to Russia's annexation of Crimea, the USA and the EU decided to impose trade embargoes against Russia. Indeed, Russia also gave up on the South Stream natural gas pipeline that would have passed through the Black Sea to Europe (İlter & Kınık, 2017, p. 194).

The embargoes significantly affected the Russian economy. The Russian ruble depreciated by about 50% against the US dollar. As a matter of fact, the Central Bank of Russia raised interest rates from 10.5% to 17% in order to prevent the further depreciation of the ruble (BBC News, 2014). In addition to the falling oil prices, the Russian company Gazprom was seriously affected by the embargoes imposed by the US and the EU. The company, which made a profit of $21 billion in 2013, had a profit of just $3 billion in 2014 (AA, 2015).

In the face of the trade embargoes imposed by western states against Russia, President Putin announced the cancellation of the South Stream project to the world during his visit to Turkey on December 1, 2014.

However, he used his energy trump card by saying that the TurkStream project, which had a wide impact in the European press, would be implemented instead. The South Stream project had envisioned the transport of Russian gas to Europe via Bulgaria. However, the fact that Bulgaria was on the same side as the EU when sanctions were made against Russia was one of the most important reasons for the cancellation of the project. Furthermore, the fact that the cost of TurkStream is lower than that for South Stream was also one of the reasons for the cancellation of the South Stream project. In other words, the shortening of the pipeline with the TurkStream project can be considered as an opportunity for Russia, which has been subjected to various economic embargoes (Karagöl & Kızılkaya, 2015, p. 2).

Although the TurkStream project was suspended as a result of the crisis following the downing of a Russian aircraft in Turkey in 2015, this subject came to the fore again with the improvement of relations between the two countries in the following period. Indeed, following the approval of the project on December 2, 2016 in the Turkish Grand National Assembly (TGNA) and on January 20, 2017 in the Russian State Duma, the project was implemented (Al & Gül, 2018, p. 77).

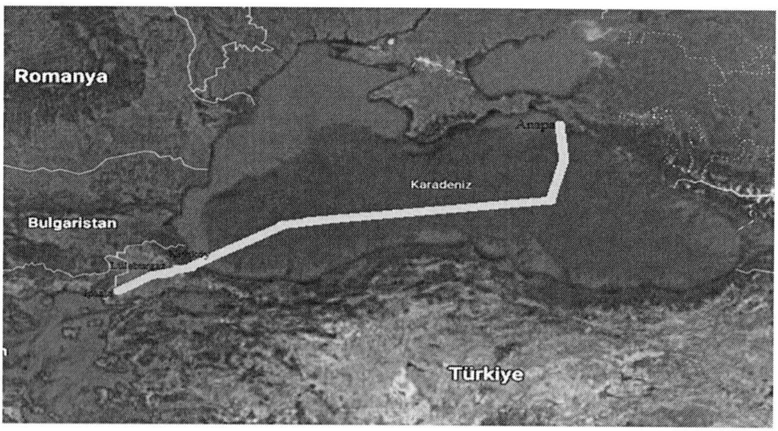

Figure 4: Route of the TurkStream Project. Source: This figure was drawn by Serkan Yavuz.

Evaluation of TurkStream from the Perspectives of Turkey and Russia

With the implementation of the TurkStream project, bilateral and political relations between Turkey and Russia are expected to develop. Although the TurkStream project is preferred for political reasons, it also costs less than the South Stream project. Therefore, this situation is seen as an important advantage for Russia, which is experiencing economic difficulties. In addition, with this project, Russia can maintain its position in the European natural gas market in the medium and long term. Russia transports about 40% of the gas exported to Europe via Ukraine. With the implementation of the TurkSteam project, Russia has found a new, alternative route. With this project, Russia has direct access to the European market, bypassing transit countries (Budak, 2017, p. 6).

Turkey, which has had occasional problems with Russia on issues such as Syria and Cyprus, is looking for ways to become an energy hub and increase its geo-economic influence (Kim & Blank, 2015, p. 4). Turkey has taken an important step toward becoming an energy center with the TANAP line, which enables Azerbaijani gas to reach Europe. This project is very important in the energy supply security of both Turkey and the EU. After the TANAP project, the TurkStream project, which foresees the transfer of Russian gas to European countries via Turkey and the Balkans, is seen as the project that will further enhance Turkey's status as an energy hub (Karagöl, 2015).

In addition to having a strategic political value, TurkStream is an important project because it is a project that can meet Turkey's growing energy demand. Ensuring a safe energy supply is seen as another issue that can serve Turkey's purpose (Karagöl & Kızılkaya, 2015, p. 3).

Turkey is aiming to reduce the percentage of natural gas in its total energy use. However, demand for natural gas is expected to increase due to increased energy consumption even if this goal is realized (Franza, 2015, p. 45). TurkStream is one of the most important projects that will contribute to meeting this demand.

Turkey, which imports more than half of the gas it buys from Russia, expects a drop in natural gas import prices with this project. Furthermore, the change of the route of a portion of the gas taken from Russia stands out as an element that will increase energy supply security. However, with this project, Turkey has the opportunity to import the gas it receives from Russia without any transit countries. This means that Turkey's energy supply security will not be adversely affected if Russia experiences political crises with other transit countries, especially Ukraine, and the absence of transit countries will reduce the cost of exports (Budak, 2017, p. 6).

The TurkStream project provides a number of advantages to Turkey thanks to the change of route. Turkey's dependence on Russia for natural gas does not increase with this project. Also, given that Ukraine received a $2.7 toll per 100 km from Russia for every 1,000 cubic meters of natural gas in 2015, Turkey will generate that revenue in the absence of this country (Times of Crimea, 2016). In other words, Turkey, which has diversified its energy supply routes, has the opportunity to gain some advantages from natural gas prices with this project (Karagöl, 2015). Indeed, Turkey is expected to import gas from Russia at about a 6% cheaper cost with this project (Kim & Blank, 2014, p. 11).

Turkey's steps toward becoming a central country in energy are leading the country from being a regional power to being a global actor. Although it is not known how long the tension between the west and Russia will last, it can be seen that Turkey will profit from this project (Karagöl & Kızılkaya, 2015, p. 4).

There are many alternative routes that allow the transport of Russian gas to Europe. Most of these routes pass through Ukraine. Due to this reason, crises with Ukraine cause many problems (Hafnar et al., 2015, pp. 2-4).

As a result of the political crises with Ukraine, Russia wants to remove Ukraine from the natural gas consortium involving Russia, Ukraine, and Europe. Although this situation is unacceptable for Ukraine, Russia is trying to diversify the routes by which natural gas is transmitted to Europe (Hafnar et al., 2015, p. 7). The TurkStream project serves this purpose for Russia.

As Figure 5 shows, Ukraine is critical in the transportation of Russian natural gas to Europe. As a matter of fact, the importance of Ukraine is diminished with the TurkStream project, and Russia thus obtains both economic and political gain.

Russia will also maintain its tendency to control the Central Asian countries and prevent gas from being exported from these countries to Europe (Kim & Blank, 2015, p. 10). As a matter of fact, this project serves this purpose significantly by providing the transport of Russian gas to Europe.

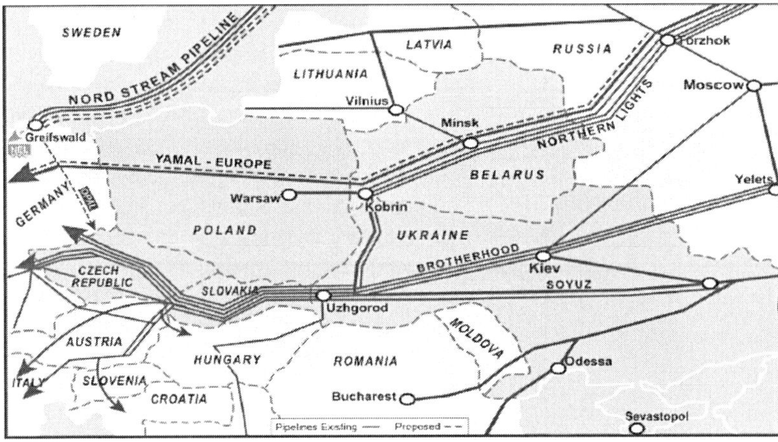

Figure 5: Routes of Russia's Gas Exports. Source: Hafner & Tagliapietra, 2015, p. 2.

Conclusion

The continuous increase of the population of the world, the development of industrialization, and technological developments increase the need for energy every day. While the purpose of countries with energy sources is to ensure energy demand security, the aim of countries with scarce facilities in terms of energy resources is to ensure energy supply security. This raises transit countries between countries with energy sources and countries without energy sources to an important position. Turkey has a very strategic position in its location. However, it has to import a large part of the energy it consumes. Due to this situation, Turkey aims to ensure energy supply security by diversifying the countries and routes it imports energy from. It also aims to have the right to have a say in the field of energy by using its location geostrategically.

The transit countries between Turkey and Russia were eliminated by the implementation of the TurkStream project. Thus, Turkey has prevented Russia from being affected by political crises with these countries. In addition, this project strengthens Turkey's role of being an energy center. In other words, thanks to this project, Turkey is becoming an indispensable country for the EU and Russia in terms of providing energy. The implementation of this project after TANAP strengthens Turkey's hand in the field of energy. However, despite all these gains, it is not possible to say that Turkey's high dependency on foreign energy sources has disappeared.

Through this project, Russia has developed an alternative route to moving its natural gas to Europe via Ukraine, where it is experiencing political problems. Russia responded to the economic embargoes imposed by the USA and the EU with the TurkStream project. It is clear that Russia views Turkey as a reliable partner despite its historic rivalry with Turkey. In addition, a cost advantage was achieved by canceling the South Stream project and implementing TurkStream. Russia aims to ensure energy demand security through the TurkStream project. In other words, maintaining the EU's energy dependence on Russia is seen as one of Russia's most important goals.

References

Al, A., & Gül, U. (2018). Küresel Enerji Denkleminde Türkiye'nin Rolü: Türk Akımı ve Tanap Analizi. In A. Al & M. Balcı (Eds.), *Uluslararası İlişkilerde Güncel Çalışmalar 2.* Savaş Yayınevi.

Bayraç, H. N. (2009). Küresel Enerji Politikaları ve Türkiye: Petrol ve Doğalgaz Kaynakları Açısından Bir Değerlendirme. *Eskişehir Osmangazi Üniversitesi Sosyal Bilimler Dergisi*, *10*(1), 115-142.

Baysoy, E. (2009). Rusya, AB, ABD İlişkileri Bağlamında Enerjinin Ekonomi Politiği ve Küreselleşmenin Jeopolitiği. *Güvenlik Stratejileri Dergisi*, *10*, 59-81.

Budak, T. (2017). Türkiye'nin Enerji Politikasında Tanap ve Türk Akımı. *Bilgesam Analiz*, *1364*.

Dugin, A. (2018). *Rus Jeopolitiği Avrasyacı Yaklaşım.* Küre Yayınları.

Durmuşoğlu, S. (2016). 21. Yüzyılın Enerji Denklemi ve Türkiye. *İstanbul Ticaret Üniversitesi Sosyal Bilimler Dergisi*, *29*, 283-303.

Franza, L. (2015). *From South Stream to Turk Stream Prospects for Rerouting Options and Flows of Russian Gas to Parts of Europe and Turkey*. Clingendael International Energy Programme (CIEP).

Hafner, M., & Tagliapietra, S. (2015). *Turkish Stream: What Strategy for Europe?* Fondazione Eni Enrico Mattei.

İlter, E., & Kınık, H. (2017). Türkiye'nin Enerji Denklemi: Trans Anadolu Doğalgaz Boru Hattı ve Türk Akımı. *Uluslararası İktisadi ve İdari İncelemeler Dergisi*, *18*, 185-200.

Karagöl, E. T. (2015, August 3). *Türkiye'nin Yeni Enerji Perspektifi ve Türk Akımı*. SETA. http://www.setav.org/turkiyenin-yeni-enerji-perspektifi-ve-turk-akimi/

Karagöl, E. T., & Kızılkaya, M. (2015). *Rusya-AB-Türkiye Üçgeninde Türk Akımı.* SETA Perspektif, 105.

Kim, Y., & Blank S. (2015). The New Great Game of Caspian Energy in

2013-2014: 'Turk Stream', Russia and Turkey. *Journal Of Balkan and Near Eastern Studies*, *18*(1), 37-55.
Tüysüz, E. (2018). Karadeniz Güvenliği ve Bunun AB Güvenliğine Etkileri. *Dicle Üniversitesi İktisadi ve İdari Bilimler Fakültesi Dergisi, 2*(6), 73-91.
Ulutaş, M. (n.d.). *Küresel enerji savaşları ve Türkiye'nin konumu.* Retrieved May 24, 2019, from http://www.emo.org.tr/ekler/830f71ff178b369_ek.pdf?dergi=500
Ulusoy, M. K. (2018, September 17). *Rakamlarla Türkiye'nin Enerji Görünümü.* Stratejik Düşünce Enstitüsü. https://www.sde.org.tr/merve-karacaerulusoy/genel/rakamlarla-turkiyenin-enerji-gorunumu-kose-yazisi-7155
Yorkan, A. (2019). *Güney Akım'da Son Gelişmeler- Nabucco Nasıl Etkilenecek?* Bilgesam. Retrieved May 1, 2019, from http://www.bilgesam.org/incele/801/-guney-akim%E2%80%99da-son-gelismeler-%E2%80%93-nabucco-nasil-etkilenecek-/#.XPjMZxYzbIU

Internet Sites

AA. (2015, April 29). *Gazprom'u Ruble Vurdu.* https://www.aa.com.tr/tr/ekonomi/gazpromu-ruble-vurdu/52547
BBC News. (2014, December 16). *Russia makes drastic rate rise to 17% to stem rouble decline.* https://www.bbc.com/news/business-30490082
BP. (2018). *BP Statistical Review of World Energy.* https://www.bp.com/content/dam/bp/business-sites/en/global/corporate/pdfs/energy-economics/statistical-review/bp-stats-review-2018-full-report.pdf
Gazprom. (n.d.). *Stock.* Retrieved May 21, 2019, from http://www.gazprom.com/investors/stock/
Republic of Turkey Ministry of Energy and Natural Resources (n.d.). *Natural Gas Pipelines and Projects.* Retrieved May 17, 2019, from https://www.enerji.gov.tr/tr-TR/Sayfalar/Dogal-Gaz-Boru-Hatlari-ve-Projeleri
Republic of Turkey Ministry of Foreign Affairs. (n.d.). *Turkey's Energy Profile and Strategy*. Retrieved May 21, 2019, from http://www.mfa.gov.tr/turkiye_nin-enerjistratejisi.tr.mfa
Times of Crimea. (2016, October 10). *Türk Akım, Türkiye'ye Milyarlar Kazandıracak.* http://www.timesofcrimea.com/turk-akim-turkiyeye-milyarlar-kazandiracak.html
World Energy Council. (n.d.). *Russia*. Retrieved May 20, 2019, from https://www.worldenergy.org/data/resources/country/russia/gas

CHAPTER FOUR

THE IMPORTANCE OF CYPRUS IN THE CONTEXT OF EASTERN MEDITERRANEAN ENERGY SECURITY

FURKAN KAYA*

Introduction

The Eastern Mediterranean geography has placed it in a significant geopolitical and geostrategic position for a new world order and energy security. The political and international structures of Mediterranean energy have a great impact on regional actors, the US and the Russian Federation. Accordingly, the East Mediterranean continues to direct its countries' national interests, and this has led to the struggle for dominance in the Cyprus issue. The increasing political tension during the Arab Spring period, the ongoing civil war in Syria, and the growing power of Turkey's intervention capability over the region have paved the way for the attention of powerful states' to be drawn to the local geography. The geopolitics of energy for a region is determined by its geographical position and role in the supply, transit or demand for energy resources. The gas reserves found in the Aphrodite gas field off Cyprus and the Tamar and Leviathan areas off Israel have had an important role for other states since 2009. Since the total of 140 bcm of gas found on the island of Cyprus is not considered as commercially viable for export to European markets, the total of 900 bcm of Israeli reserves is viewed as commercially suitable for exportation to Europe. Therefore, many alternatives to improve energy policies have been seen, including the EastMed Pipeline, liquefied natural gas facilities, and a prospective Israeli-Turkish pipeline. The first options are considered as commercially unprofitable due to high

* Assist. Prof. Dr. Furkan Kaya, Department of History, Faculty of Arts and Sciences, Yeditepe University. E-mail: kayafurkan@gmail.com.

costs and security concerns. In that sense, the Turkish-Israeli pipeline project is mostly preferred. Therefore, energy resources may cause effective collaborations or conflicts among regional actors. For better or worse, regional states ought to search for interim and permanent agreements for initiating regional cooperation in the Eastern Mediterranean. Mutual dependence in the context of energy cooperation may pave the way for finding permanent solutions to chronic problems. More importantly, there cannot be a permanent solution unless international agreements that have been made are operatively accepted by other states.

The Significance of the Eastern Mediterranean and Cyprus in Eurasian Geopolitics

The Mediterranean is located in the middle of Afro-Eurasia, which is accepted as the mainland of the world, and is considered to be the world's largest inland sea, located in the wide territory from the Strait of Gibraltar in the west to Turkey, Syria, Lebanon, Israel and Egypt in the east (Turhan, 2016, pp. 20-21). The Eastern Mediterranean is regarded as being in a particular location within this geography. It would not be wrong to state that this is the section of the Mediterranean region that connects its three continents. Therefore, the Eastern Mediterranean is an important transit route for world maritime trade due to it being an intersection. In addition, it has an important place in opening energy to the world since it hosts energy basins. The Eastern Mediterranean, which has been the scene of important geopolitical power wars throughout history, has important historical, economic and natural resource characteristics.

In particular, hydrocarbon explorations around the island of Cyprus during the 2000s have had a significant impact in determining the economic and other benefit areas of the countries of the region. It has been observed that Turkey, Israel, Greece, Egypt, Lebanon, the Greek Cypriot Administration (GCA) and Syria, which have coasts on the Eastern Mediterranean, play a strategic, tactical and operational role dictated by energy geopolitics. One of the most important developments that shaped the geostrategic importance of the Eastern Mediterranean was the opening of the Suez Canal in 1869. In the early 2000s, the hydrocarbon discoveries made in the region added another dimension to the regional power and sovereignty of the Eastern Mediterranean nations. In recent years, the states are particularly active regarding the exclusive economic zone (EEZ) within the frame of the sharing of energy and maritime areas in the Eastern Mediterranean (Yaycı, 2012, pp. 13-30). New natural gas reserves discovered off Cyprus and Israel in the Eastern Mediterranean should play a positive role in resolving the Cyprus issue fairly and peacefully. For instance, it will make a positive contribution to the solution of the Cyprus problem through energy dynamics as the European Union (EU) often brings its dependence on Russia regarding energy onto the agenda due to the Ukrainian crisis. Turkey, which has an important position in the Eastern Mediterranean's geopolitics with its responsibility of being the "energy terminal", one of the most important foreign policy parameters in recent years, can strengthen its geostrategic position in the eyes of the Western world by undertaking the transfer of energy resources from Asia through the Eastern Mediterranean to Europe (Örmeci, 2014, p. 381). The US, on the other hand, can increase its influence on the local geography because American companies are strong in the region.

The major reasons why the Eastern Mediterranean has been designated as a center of gravity by the great powers are the existence of Tamar, discovered in 2009 in offshore Israel, Leviathan, discovered in 2010, and the natural gas discovered by the GCA in 2012 in the Aphrodite gas field in the so-called EEZ. It has become an important center of attention where a power struggle between regional states, international energy companies and global powers has begun (Danış, 2017). There is no doubt that it would not be wrong to evaluate the geopolitical importance of the Eastern Mediterranean and the island of Cyprus with economic and political parameters. The region has not attained stability for many years, and the territory – the site of issues such as the Arab Spring, the Arab-Israeli conflict, migrant issues and terrorist activities – is geography that countries such as the USA, Russia and China want to control due to its geopolitical position.

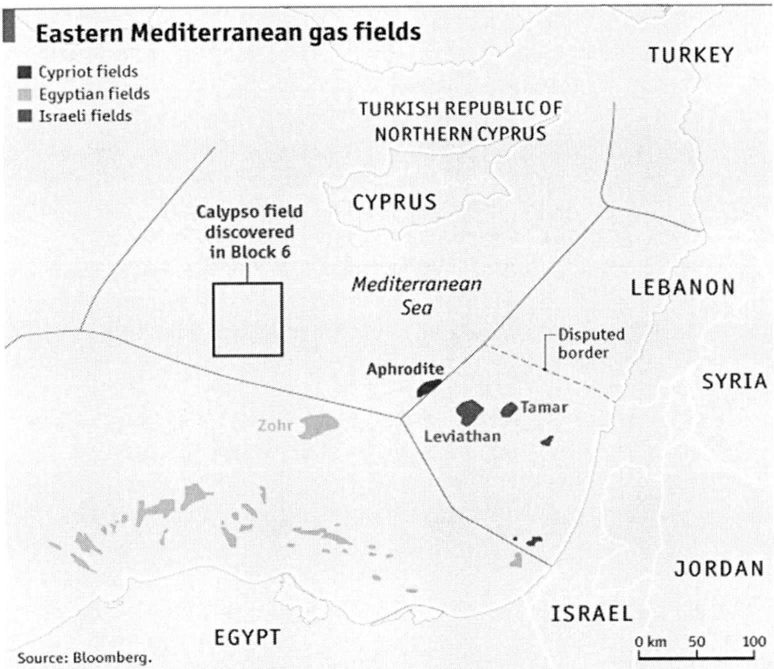

Figure 1: Eastern Mediterranean Gas Fields. Source: The Economist Intelligence Unit, 2018.

Cyprus, which is strategically the most important point of the Eastern Mediterranean, is an important area for the UK due to its proximity to the coasts of Anatolia and Syria and its proximity to Egypt and the Suez Canal. Therefore, Cyprus is significant for the continuaition of the Middle East and North Africa strategies located on the imperial route of the UK.

The emergence of natural gas deposits in the Eastern Mediterranean since the 2000s has led to changes in the policies of countries that have coasts in the region. It is stated that there are hydrocarbon reserves equivalent to 60 billion barrels of oil with a total value of $3 trillion in the Mediterranean. These are numbers that will meet the natural gas demands of Turkey for 572 years and of Europe for 30 years. Another important feature that increases the strategic importance of the region is its indispensable role in transit energy transport. Recently, about 5 billion barrels of crude oil have been transported to Western markets by means of the Suez Canal through the Eastern Mediterranean geography (Kedikli & Deniz, 2015). In this context, in addition to the rich energy reserves it has, the Eastern

Mediterranean is also an important junction point as a transfer and transit route for energy exports from the Middle East and Caspian regions to the West (Aksoy, 2016, pp. 1-3).

The natural gas reserves that have been discovered in the Mediterranean Sea around Egypt, Israel and Greece redesigned Europe's energy policy. The energy discoveries in the Eastern Mediterranean have influenced Russia's position as the main gas supplier. Therefore, this situation has caused the emergence of other energy actors, namely Turkey, Egypt, the island of Cyprus and Israel, over the region. Egypt has also been one of the most significant gas suppliers and importers of natural gas since 2016. However, the discovery of gas in 2015 has the capacity to give Egypt the area's most important gas hub in the Zohr field, which is the Mediterranean's largest gas field.

Another important energy actor in the region is Cyprus, which is suitable for energy exploration, and huge gas discoveries were made in the recent period. For instance, the Aphrodite gas field was discovered in 2011 and is estimated to provide revenue of $9.5 billion over 18 years from the sale of energy through Egypt's Idku terminal.

Energy Diplomacy Between Turkey and the Russian Federation

Turkey is one of the critical and important energy actors in the Eastern Mediterranean region. Ankara has been trying to make big gas discoveries in the Eastern Mediterranean and has sent ships into the coastal waters of the island of Cyprus to drill for gas. Turkey points out that the energy reserves that are placed around Cyprus should be used by all Cypriot people. In response, the EU indicates that Turkish drillships are violating international law and that it is going to expose Turkey to economic and political sanctions. Turkey has a legal right to conduct gas exploration according to the 1959 Zurich and London agreements. Thus, Turkey has been protecting its geographical rights within the scope of international agreements. The Fatih, Yavuz and Baraoros Hayrettin Paşa drillships and the Oruç Reis seismic research ship have all been sent to the Eastern Mediterranean to conduct seismic research for gas around Cyprus.

Although Turkey is a poor country in terms of energy reserves, it has a unique position between energy producers and consumers. Turkey is a bridge country that provides cheap and secure energy transportation. However, Turkey's strategic position brings some risks because of the political instabilities in the region, terrorism and global threats. In this sense, Turkey considers the Eastern Mediterranean as strategic geography and important for its national security due to the Cyprus question. However, Greece and Southern Cyprus have pursued some policies that have been violating international law and acted unilaterally. Moreover, they have tried to legitimize the process by involving the EU.

Turkey's Foreign Minister, Mevlüt Çavuşoğlu, has pointed out that Turkey intends to increase its activities in the region and continue to send other oil drillships to the region (Middle East Monitor, 2019). Southern Cyprus and the EU consider these Turkish actions provocative and illegal, but Turkey's response is obvious. All these actions are legitimate as the licenses for the Turkish Petroleum Corporation's (TPAO) exploration were granted by the Turkish Republic of Northern Cyprus. Turkey defends its right within the framework of international law in the region. However, the great powers, the US and Russia, do not consider anything other than their national interests in the region in spite of all the calls from Turkey for international collaboration to protect itself and the Turkish Republic of Northern Cyprus.

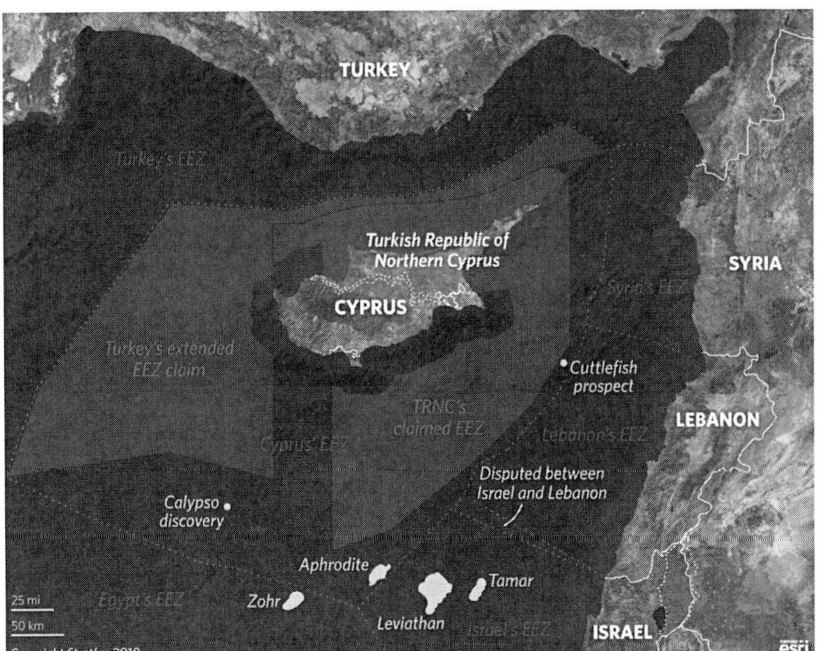

Figure 2: Maritime Disputes in the Eastern Mediterranean. Source: Stratfor, 2018.

The problem of the energy security of Eastern Mediterranean states is a very sophisticated and omnidirectional one. The understanding of the balance of power is adopted by regional states that have national interests in that region due to its fragile political system. The Russian Federation and the US have a great interest in the new energy discoveries in the Eastern Mediterranean. These two great powers have an aim to provide energy diversification in order not to lose their dominant position in energy markets. Naturally, the augmentation of supply resources reduces the effect of deterioration in supply from one source by getting alternatives serving the interests of both energy producers and consumers (Yergin, 2006, pp. 69-82). The gas fields around the Eastern Mediterranean have caught the attention of Russia, which is one of the global leaders in gas production and the gas trade. There is also the struggle between Turkey and the Turkish Republic of Northern Cyprus and, on the other side, Southern Cyprus, Greece, Israel and Egypt, which have been supported by the US, the EU and global corporations. However, Moscow has not revealed its national strategies in this regard yet.

Russia has two possible options for Eastern Mediterranean diplomacy. Firstly, Moscow may follow a policy of non-intervention since its significant strategic interest in energy has been directed toward the Arctic Basin. Therefore, Russia's adoption of an active policy in the Eastern Mediterranean could lead to tension between Turkey and Russia in affairs involving regional and Western states, namely the UK and France. The UK is trying to expand its air force on the island, and France has signed an agreement with Southern Cyprus on the construction of a naval base in the area of the village of Marie (Starodubstev, 2019). The national corporate interests of Turkey and Russia will lead them to be wary of any undesirable steps. Russia has not opted to support Southern Cyprus, nor does it want to have any cooperation either. However, Moscow could support Turkey and the Turkish Republic of Northern Cyprus in the Eastern Mediterranean energy dispute. It ought to be pointed out that Turkey and Russia have been in serious cooperation in the Astana process for peace in Syria – this is a success story of these two partners. Consequently, Moscow is aiming to establish long-term institutions in military-political cooperation with Ankara. Turkey and Russia have important strategic projects that intensify bilateral affairs in the economic and political spheres as well. Moscow has been conscious of the fact that the Astana process and the S-400 deal pave the way to an opportunity for Russia to improve its affairs.

As is well-known, the significance of the Middle East's energy resources is placed in a position of priority for US foreign policy. However,

Washington has begun to pay attention to the Eastern Mediterranean geography because of the new discoveries of natural gas there. As the US has a great potential to be the strongest gas producer in the world, it is trying to hinder Russian hegemony over the region's energy resources that will be vital for EU countries to end their energy dependence on Russia. Eastern Mediterranean energy reserves are alternative resources to the Russian monopoly (Demir & Tekir, 2017, p. 667). Noble Energy, which is a private American company, has an important role in the discovery of energy, and it has shareholdings of 40% in the Leviathan region, 36% in the Tamar region, and 7% in the Aphrodite region (Karagiannis, 2016, pp. 1-11).

Conclusion

The sharing of the energy resources of the Eastern Mediterranean has been the most important energy politics issue for international relations in recent years. The geopolitical position of Turkey requires it to pay more attention to the region and to defend its regional and international rights in the context of international law. As is well-known, the sea border disputes between the Turkish Republic of Northern Cyprus and Southern Cyprus have not been solved yet. Therefore, the improvement of energy security and the stability of the region cannot be ensured, and this will influence regional energy production and consumption that threaten the activity of the commercial and energy infrastructure.

Significant issues are experienced in the Eastern Mediterranean region to the extent that they may not be encountered in any other part of the world and in such a way that is relevant to other parts of the world. These events tend to develop rapidly and reach dimensions that affect security.

References

Aksoy, M. (2016). *Doğu Akdeniz Enerji Rekabeti.* İNSAMER. http://insamer.com/rsm/files/Dogu-Akdeniz-Enerji-Rekabeti.pdf

Danış, E. E. (2017, May 8). *Türkiye'den D. Akdeniz'de oyun değiştirici iki hamle.* PetroTurk. http://petroturk.com/makale/dogu-akdeniz-gazi

Demir, N., & Tekir, O. (2017). Sharing Energy Resources of Eastern Mediterranean: Regional and Global Dynamics. *Economic and Environmental Studies*, *17*(4), 651-674.

Karagiannis, E. (2016). Shifting Eastern Mediterranean Alliances, The *Middle East Quarterly*, Spring, 1-11. https://www.meforum.org/meq/pdfs/5877.pdf

Kedikli, U., & Deniz, T. (2015). Enerji Kaynakları Mücadelesinde Doğu Akdeniz Havzası ve Deniz Yetki Alanları Uyuşmazlığı / Maritime Jurisdiction Dispute Within The Scope of East Mediterranean Energy Sources. *Alternatif Politika*, *7*(3). http://alternatifpolitika.com/makale/enerji-kaynaklari-mucadelesinde-dogu-akdeniz-havzasi-ve-deniz-yetki-alanlari-uyusmazligi

Kokkinidis, T. (2019, July 18). Turkey Sends Third Drillship Off Cyprus. *Greek Reporter.* https://greece.greekreporter.com/2019/07/18/turkey-sends-third-drillship-off-cyprus-video/

Middle East Monitor. (2019, July 17). *FM says Turkey to send 4th drillship to eastern Mediterranean.* https://www.middleeastmonitor.com/20190717-fm-says-turkey-to-send-4th-drillship-to-eastern-mediterranean/

Örmeci, O. (2014). Kıbrıs Müzakerelerinde Yeni Dönem: Enerji Jeopolitiği ve Akdeniz Birliği Olgusu / New Period in Cyprus Talks: Energy Geopolitics and The Mediterranean Union. *Uluslararası Sosyal Araştırmalar Dergisi (The Journal of International Social Research)*, *7*(31), 376-385. http://www.sosyalarastirmalar.com/cilt7/sayi31_pdf/2tarih_uluslararasi iliskiler_siyaset_sanattari hi_arkeoloji/ormeci_ozan.pdf

Starodubtsev, I. (2019, May 26). *Will Russia Back Turkey in the Eastern Mediterranean?* The New Turkey. https://thenewturkey.org/will-russia-back-turkey-in-the-eastern-mediterranean

Stratfor. (2018, February 22). *The Eastern Mediterranean's New Great Game Over Natural Gas.* https://worldview.stratfor.com/article/eastern-mediterraneans-new-great-game-over-natural-gas

The Economist Intelligence Unit. (2018, February 23). *Egypt holds keys to East Mediterranean gas.* http://www.eiu.com/industry/article/1466463730/egypt-holds-keys-to-east-mediterranean-gas/2018-02-23

Turhan, A. (2016). Doğu Akdeniz ve Karadeniz'de Meydana Gelen Jeopolitik Kırılmalar ve Türkiye Jeopolitiği. *Uluslararası Afro-Avrasya Araştırmaları Dergisi*, *2*, 19-25. http://dergipark.gov.tr/download/article-file/342887

Yaycı, C. (2012). Doğu Akdeniz'de Deniz Yetki Alanlarının Paylaşılması Sorunu ve Türkiye / The Problem of Delimitation of Maritime Areas in Eastern Mediterranean and Turkey. *Bilge Strateji*, *4*(6), 1-70. http://www.bilgesam.org/Images/Dokumanlar/0-159-2014040713bs-2012-1-1-70.pdf

Yergin, D. (2006). Ensuring energy security. *Foreign Affairs*, *85*, 69-82.

CHAPTER FIVE

RENEWABLE ENERGY IN DEVELOPING COUNTRIES

BILGIN BIRLIKSEVEN*

Introduction

According to the classification of the United Nations, there are a total of 107 developing countries in 11 regions (UN, 2014). However, among the developing countries, the BRICS countries, which consist of Brazil, Russia, India, China and South Africa, stand out in terms of both development and renewable energy, especially China. The Western world, on the other hand, has been industrialized through the great advantage of fossil fuels over approximately the last two centuries. The Malthusian Theory (Ashraf & Galor, 2008, pp. 4-5) also lost its validity with the transition to a carbon-based economy. As a relatively small and advantaged population in terms of population on a global scale, the fossil fuels that the West benefits from appear to be the most important source of momentum in the welfare and development of these countries. Developing countries also want to benefit from fossil fuel opportunities, but they are faced with obstacles. At this point, it is especially the renewable energy moves of China and India that attract attention. Other developing countries can also monitor these two countries and increase their level of development (OECD, 2016).

Green energy has an important place not only in the agenda of developing countries but also in the future plans of developed countries. According to a report published in 2019, the portion of electricity used in the USA, for the first time in its history, that derived from renewable

* Bilgin Birlikseven, Ph.D. Candidate (International Political Economy), Institute of Social Sciences, Marmara University. E-mail: bilgin.birlikseven@hotmail.com.

energy was greater than coal's share. In the report, made in line with the monthly data, it is maintained that 20% of the electricity used in the USA is obtained from coal, while 23% of it is supplied from renewable energy (Cassella, 2019). Green energy has become a rising phenomenon all over the world, primarily due to climate change and air pollution, and also because it has the potential to serve as an answer to the boom in energy demand in the world. Developing countries stand out as the countries that most benefit from these developments concerning green energy.

The topic of this article concerns the impacts of renewable energy policies on developing countries. While developing countries will be discussed in general, the main focus regarding green energy will be on China and other BRICS countries. The article will focus on renewable energy, climate change, developing countries and China. The most recent reports, analyses and news published on the subject were utilized in the preparation of the article. The article is designed as follows: In the first section, the question "why renewable energy?" is asked, and the motives of the green energy revolution are mentioned; in the second section, developments and breakthroughs in the developing countries regarding renewable energy are touched upon, and it also tries to reveal the renewable energy investments made and the developing countries 'global position in this regard; in the third section, the future of green energy is evaluated in terms of the developing countries; and in the fourth section, the impact of renewable energy policies on both the developing countries and China, more precisely their interaction processes, are mentioned, and China's hegemonic state in green energy is expressed.

Why Renewable Energy?

Climate Change

While there are many reasons that have triggered the move toward renewable energy, climate change can be mentioned as the most important among them. While the world is warming day by day and population growth continues, the air, which is the source of life, is also dangerously polluted. Nine out of 10 people breathe polluted air, and around 7 million people die every year from air pollution (WHO, 2019). According to another study (HEI, 2018), it is maintained that more than 95% of the world's population lives in unhealthy weather conditions, and nearly 6.1 million people lost their lives in 2016 due to this pollution. Today, air pollution stands out as the fourth-highest cause of death in the world (McCarthy, 2018). Climate change and the associated negative conditions have reached levels that cannot be ignored anymore, and this issue has started to be voiced in all media as a matter that the whole world needs to pay attention to. China and India take the lead among the countries that cause most climate change, but also, in this sense, take significant precautions and make big investments. The intense use of fossil fuels and the serious health problems of their people require these two countries to address the climate change issue in more depth.

Developing countries make cost-effective emission reductions by taking steps in the context of green energy and energy efficiency (UN Environment, 2017, p. vii). It is a fact that despite the successful steps taken by these countries in the field of renewable energy, they are far from reaching their targets that aim at completely carbon-free energy (BloombergNEF, 2018, p. 4). According to the 2016 data, 1.61 million people in India and 1.58 million people in China lost their lives due to reasons related to air pollution. With these figures, India and China stand out as the top two countries in the world in terms of deaths caused by air pollution (McCarthy, 2018). Therefore, it seems unlikely that there will be promising developments in the near future regarding the threat of climate change in the world. More effort and more international cooperation are needed to make the world a more livable place. At this point, climate change has been stimulating the developing countries as a very important impulse regarding renewable energy.

China stands out from all developing countries and occupies a special position within the context of renewable energy. China's energy policy preferences are of great global importance. Yet, China is the world's largest energy consumer and alone accounts for one-fifth of all global energy consumption. By 2030, China's energy consumption is projected to have increased by 60%. Therefore, China's steps toward renewable energy will play a decisive role in global climate change (IRENA, 2014, p. 1). Even though China has taken major steps in the field of renewable energy and is a pioneer in this field, in recent years, an increase in its coal and oil use has been observed. Therefore, the air quality is low in most of the big cities and public health conditions in this sense have deteriorated. There is no path on the horizon by which China can get immediate results in the near or medium term for cleaner air. Nevertheless, the efforts based on the motto "make the skies blue again" have now reached an inevitable and central position for the Chinese administration (IEA, 2017). Although China has been making progress in solar, wind and hydroelectric energy, it has to develop strong policies to address high CO_2 emissions (Pathak & Shah, 2019, p. 1). According to one study, China is confronted with 1.6 million early deaths per year due to air pollution (Stanway, 2018).

According to another study, air pollution causes about 1 million people to die annually in China, and 20 million tons of rice, wheat, corn and soy are rendered inconsumable annually due to air pollution. The annual cost of financial losses caused by air pollution to the Chinese economy is 38 billion dollars (Kao, 2018). Within the context of the amount of energy that China produces, consumes and needs, its current situation forces it to become a locomotive country at an international level in the struggle against climate change. Otherwise, it is inevitable that steps to be taken at the international level that are not taken by China and then by India will be ineffective in the fight against air pollution.

In recent years, Beijing has fallen outside the list of the 100 most polluted cities in Asia, and overall the pollution level of China's cities is 10% lower in 2018 than in 2017. (Griffiths, 2019). The deteriorating air quality and other environmental threats, especially in China's industry-intensive regions, have rendered the goal of China's development model to strengthen the framework of environmental management and form an energy policy more significant (Gippner & Torney, 2017, p. 650). While governments, project implementers and organizations supporting these projects can achieve sustainable development goals, they also need to identify policies and programs that can truly meet the climate change objectives determined in the Paris Agreement (UN Environment, The 1 Gigaton Coalition, 2017, p. 76). Achieving the Paris Convention's climate change goals can save the lives of about 1 million people a year by 2050 with only a reduction in air pollution. The economic dimension of the fight against air pollution is also noteworthy. It is estimated that the health expenses of the 15 countries that emit the most greenhouse gases in the world cost more than 4% of the total GDP of these countries (WHO, 2019). All these data and information reveal why the struggle with climate change is crucial. Success in the struggle with climate change will provide normal climatic conditions, ensure that any kind of agricultural activity is performed efficiently and with the lowest loss, decrease the deaths that occur due to air pollution by fixing the deteriorated health conditions, and free both states and individuals from people's growing, huge health expenses.

Decrease in Renewable Energy Costs

Green energy has become a strategic choice at an international level to solve the problem of environmental pollution and the energy crisis and to ensure sustainable development (He et al., 2016, p. 695). Green energy, which is the fastest-growing energy source and contributes to half of the increasing global energy supply, is expected to be the largest energy source by 2040 (BP, 2019, p. 7). The ratio of electricity generated from renewable energy sources such as wind, solar, biomass, waste, geothermal and hydroelectric power to the electricity produced in the world increased from 11% in 2016 to 12.1% in 2017. Thus, it was also possible to avoid the emission of about 1.8 gigatonnes of carbon dioxide (UN Environment, 2018, p. 11). Developments show that the future of the world will inevitably surrender to renewable energy. One of the most important reasons behind this is the sharp decreases in renewable energy costs.

What made the renewable energy revolution possible was neither the taxes on carbon emissions nor the subventions provided for green energy; the actual reason for the renewable energy revolution was the decrease in the costs of the production of energy obtained from solar, water and wind, as mentioned above, and it is becoming more cost-effective than coal (OECD, 2016). Therefore, the decrease in renewable energy costs year by year appears as one of the most important reasons for this sector's growth, and it is gaining momentum. In 2017, this situation continued, and in this sense, renewable energy and especially solar energy came to the fore. The cost of electricity generation from solar energy decreased by 15% in 2017 when compared to the previous year and by 72% in total from 2009 to 2017. This decrease stems from both the decrease in the costs stemming from production and the developments regarding energy efficiency (UN Environment, 2018, p. 11). Wind energy costs fell by 60% between 2009 and 2014 (Lazard, 2014). While the costs of mining, drilling or extraction operations are relatively low in the process of obtaining fossil fuels, investments in green energy decrease the costs of renewable energy production rapidly, ensure the adoption of this technology, expand the market and render the subsequent investments more attractive (OECD, 2016). The decrease in the installed coal capacity also had a significant effect on the increase of renewable energy capacity. Together with the significant progress made by developing countries in renewable energy, the US, Australia and Europe are now pioneers in renewable energy technologies (Enel Green Power, 2019). Although there are still some problems that have not been solved in and of themselves, as can be seen from the data above, the production costs of renewable energy, the foremost sources being solar and wind energy, show great decreases together with technological advances. This, in turn, leaves no choice other than green energy for developing economies like China and India, which already have a huge deficit in their energy supply.

Economic Advantages

While the steps taken in the name of renewable energy and energy efficiency contribute to the reduction of carbon emissions of developing countries, they also lend a great impetus to their sustainable economic growth (UN Environment, 2019, p. 47). Renewable energy attracts attention as a major industrial sector in its own right. At this point, it can be stated that China and India have a great weight in the sector. It can be argued that the approaches of these two countries to renewable energy are mostly in the context of industrialization. Interest in renewable energy eases the balance of payments of leading countries in this sector, reduces unemployment and, most importantly, increases energy security. Thus, renewable energy contributes to emerging giants such as China and India and other developing countries as a response to their economic obligations. As China and India move their economic weight to more green energy, these two countries trigger a global chain reaction that will gain them favor and may allow them to serve as role models for many other developing countries (OECD, 2016). Especially in the case of China, which has become the world's production base, renewable energy has grown as a very important and very large sector due to its low labor and other costs, and it has become one of the most important markets in the world.

Renewable energy offers great opportunities for industrial development. Countries with abundant green energy resources can use this sector and its technologies to accelerate their industrial development. Among the developing countries, those who are coming up from behind in green energy can follow examples such as China and India, which are relatively advanced in this technology, and apply their technologies. While renewable energy systems such as wind turbines and solar panels can be built in order to have clean energy and a clean sky and energy security can be strengthened, the problem of the balance of payments can also be solved (OECD, 2016). It has been observed that, within the body of BRICS, there is a strong will aimed at ensuring that renewable energy contributes initially to the economies of BRICS countries and then to those of developing countries. In today's world, where the contributions of green energy to the development of countries 'industries and hence their economies are recognized throughout the whole world, the demand for green energy has also been gaining momentum, and this economic advantage appears to be an important triggering factor for clean energy.

Energy Security

Another important dimension related to renewable energy is energy security. Undoubtedly, the dependence of countries on energy regarding both their daily lives and within the context of the improvement of their industry and thus their economy is a matter of survival. Energy security appears to be a necessity for the social and economic growth of all countries globally. At this point, green energy is a prominent and effective topic that comes to the fore within the scope of energy crises (Pathak & Shah, 2019, p. 1). With regard to the energy deficit, it can be observed that China and India are in very sensitive situations, and therefore it is mostly these countries that make energy moves in order to establish energy security.

In general, developing countries will develop their own energy security solutions by investing in this field to reach the capacities they need to produce wind turbines, solar panels and other renewable energy sources (OECD, 2016). In today's world, where fossil fuels are limited and difficult to supply and where developing economies that make great moves in green energy production become prominent, the energy security phenomenon has become even more important and has had a significant impact on the formation of energy policies.

Developing Countries

General Evaluation

Even though it is not easy to measure, in the reports published, the developing countries appear as leaders in renewable energy transformation (BloombergNEF, 2018, p. 1). The main reason for this remarkable change regarding developing countries is seen in the increase and size of new transmission line projects constructed (Enel Green Power, 2019). According to the reports published, the reason why renewable energy is catching up with fossil fuels in developing countries is not only the abundant resources but also because the economic competition capacity of wind and solar energy no longer has to rely on subventions (Enel Green Power, 2019). It is not surprising that developing countries are ahead in renewable energy. Both the fact that there are huge differences between energy production and consumption values and the concentration of air pollution in these countries naturally lead to this result.

The majority of global renewable energy capacity added in 2017 was built in developing countries. It can be seen that these countries added 186

GW to their systems and that nearly more than half of this capacity is formed by wind and solar energy. The green energy network has been growing the fastest in developing countries. While the rate of increase in annual renewable energy construction is 20.4% in developing countries, it can be observed that this rate decreases by 0.4% when compared to the previous year in the more developed countries, instead of increasing (BloombergNEF, 2018, p. 1).

Although China has a general superiority in the field of renewable energy, according to a piece of research in which various criteria were considered for 2017, it can be seen that Chile, which is among the developing countries, comes to the fore due to factors such as its solid energy policies, its experience in managing clean energy investments and the permanent commitment it sets forth despite its energy grid limitations (BloombergNEF, 2018, p. 23). China, on the other hand, fell to seventh place in this report due to reasons such as the discontinuation of solar subventions (BloombergNEF, 2018, p. 4). Chile is followed by India, Jordan, Brazil, Rwanda and the Philippines (BloombergNEF, 2018, p. 23). However, the BRICS countries, which come to the fore in the data and rankings regarding developing countries, are very important. Among these countries, China and India take the lead.

BRICS Countries

BRICS countries, which make up about 40% of the world's population, are among the top ten global energy consumers. As the leading developing countries, BRICS is at the center of a major transformation, and their economies have been growing gradually. It can be stated that BRICS countries have the power to reshape the international system in general because of factors such as mineral resources, low-cost labor, and the technological innovations that they have (Pathak & Shah, 2019, p. 1). According to 2015 data, BRICS countries rank first in total renewable energy capacity. The capacity concerned is almost twice that of the EU and about four times that of the US (Pathak & Shah, 2019, p. 14). Regarding the reason for this, it can be argued that the West's ability to access fossil fuels and control the market has an effect.

As another country that attracts attention in the field of renewable energy and has steady energy policies, Brazil was a leading country in hydroelectric power and bio-fuel production until 2014. In addition, solar and wind power generation was supported by applying special taxes. In the context of renewable energy, it can be argued that among the BRICS countries, South Africa and Russia have relatively more steps to take than

China, India and Brazil. South Africa needs to determine the steps it must follow in order to increase its renewable energy and reduce coal mining according to the countries that have advanced in the field of renewable energy and to infer the lessons it needs to learn accordingly. Russia should offer more incentives for renewable energy policies and develop its legal and regulatory framework (Pathak & Shah, 2019, p. 1). Consequently, whereas the BRICS countries have a very important place among developing countries and even in the world within the context of renewable energy, China has a more developed image than all the developing countries in this sense.

When the total amount of energy produced and needed between 2010 and 2016 in BRICS countries is analyzed, it can be seen that the countries are at different levels. Hence, it can be observed that there is a great difference between the total energy produced and needed in China and India, that there is a relative balance between Brazil and South Africa's production and consumption per capita, and that Russia produces more than it needs. The reasons underlying these differences can be expressed as technological progress, population size, geographical location and other factors (Pathak & Shah, 2019, p. 1). This result also demonstrates why China and India, which have major energy deficits, are leaders by necessity in the field of renewable energy.

Together with the differences within the scope of renewable energy among BRICS countries, joint steps are being taken to increase the levels of development in this field and other issues. The New Development Bank, which was established by BRICS countries in 2014 to mobilize resources for infrastructure and sustainable development projects, including renewable energy in BRICS and other developing countries, represents one of the most important examples of this. In the period of 2016-2017, the New Development Bank provided over 3.4 billion dollars in financial aid loans for a range of projects, including renewable energy (New Development Bank, 2019). In 2019, another 300 million dollars of credit increase was provided for renewable energy in South Africa, to which the contribution of the New Development Bank was considerable (Phakathi, 2019). Kundapur Vaman Kamath, president of the New Development Bank, announced in a statement that the bank would double its loan amount of 8 billion dollars during 2019. According to the president, 80% of these loans are used in environmental protection and urban development sectors such as renewable energy and transportation (Xinhua, 2019). In addition to all this, BRICS countries need to redefine their energy policies, considering the existing geographic, economic, social and environmental conditions that will help regulate global energy policies and greater financial stability (Pathak & Shah, 2019, p. 1). Renewable energy for BRICS countries, as rising powers, is both cause and effect. In these countries, which have made progress in their production and development levels, increases in energy demand have gained momentum, and therefore the demand for renewable energy increased greatly. However, green energy has become a mandatory choice for countries where air pollution is intense due to fossil fuel use, particularly in China and India.

China

Since the beginning of the 21st century, China has achieved more growth than the sum of all OECD countries in line with its goal of becoming a superpower in green energy, together with its approach to renewable energy that emphasizes both industrialization and energy security. China has outperformed all developing countries in the field of renewable energy. By utilizing water, wind and sun, it established a renewable energy capacity of 378 GW as of 2014. It also aims to have a renewable energy capacity of at least 750 GW within the framework of the Five-Year Plan (OECD, 2016). According to data from 2014, 22.16% of China's total energy production consists of renewable energy sources (He et al., 2016, p. 696). China's efforts toward clean energy continue to gain momentum. However, despite all this, these breakthroughs are not enough. In China, both the continuation of its energy deficit and the intense health problems due to air pollution are concerning.

According to the China National Renewable Energy Center, with an improved economic outlook, the expansion of China's solar and wind energy sectors is expected to increase significantly by 2030, and renewable energy is expected to form the basis of China's energy system by 2050 (CNREC, 2018, p. 1). The steps China will take on renewable energy will have a major impact on achieving shared global goals such as global markets, trade and investment flows, technology costs and climate change. China is responsible for a significant portion of global investment in many green energy technologies such as electric vehicles and batteries (IEA, 2017). Besides, within the context of the global integration and harmonization of renewable energy initiatives, the approaches of China and the EU have become more harmonious in recent years, and there has been an increasing trend toward renewable energy in China's energy investments in the EU (Gippner & Torney, 2017, p.649). China appears to have a decisive and dominant role regarding climate change and renewable energy. China is one of the most important actors of the sector in renewable energy, the foremost sources being solar and wind.

India

In India, which is trying to expand its access to energy by adopting a lower carbon route, the annual capacity increase of new coal in 2012-2016 was 17 GW, while this figure decreased to 4 GW in 2017 (BloombergNEF, 2018, p. 1). However, it is a fact that this step is not sufficient because India still supplies about 75% of its electricity from coal. Given the significant share of coal in contributing to air pollution in India, the government's position in energy policies is still very important. In India, around 1.2 million people died in 2017 due to air pollution (Lewis & Defterios, 2019). In India, dependence on coal is greater than in China. India is also ahead in deaths due to air pollution.

For the desired level in the field of renewable energy to be achieved, India needs to update its energy policies and provide additional incentives for research, development and energy generation technologies (Pathak & Shah, 2019, p. 1). Nevertheless, it can be stated that the administration in India is showing sensitivity to this issue, at least in terms of intent and discourse. At the G20 summit held in Osaka in 2019, Indian Prime Minister Narendra Modi called for more investment in renewable energy resources and infrastructure projects in developing countries (Sputnik, 2019). Modi also stated that the New Development Bank should give priority to renewable energy programs and the physical and social infrastructure of member countries for sustainable and inclusive development (India Today, 2019). As can be seen, both in developing countries in general and in China and India in particular, it is a fact that a great effort toward renewable energy is being made in discourse and practice, but much more needs to be done for them to reach a promising level regarding the future.

Renewable Energy Investments

Renewable energy investments have been spreading to more countries in the world than before. At this point, there is a remarkable increase in the investments being made by developing countries in renewable energy. For example, as of the end of the year 2017, at least one wind plant investment was made on the network scale by 54 countries, and financial support was provided for solar energy projects in 76 countries. It can be said that renewable energy investments were 20 times higher for wind plants and three timcs higher for solar energy in 2017 than about ten years previously (BloombergNEF, 2018, p. 1). While renewable energy investments by developing countries accounted for 54% of global investment in 2016, this amount increased to 63% in 2017 (UN Environment, 2018, p. 20).

Although there has been a decline in investments in recent years due to the impact of the decline in renewable technology costs, the figures relating to renewable energy investments in developing countries have been remarkable. Even though the amount of investment in 2017, which was 143 billion dollars, was approximately the same in 2016, the much higher investment amount of 178 billion dollars in 2015 is noteworthy. It can be said that local development banks in China and Brazil have a significant impact on renewable energy investments in developing countries (BloombergNEF, 2018, p. 2). It is foreseen that global investment in renewable energy and the technology related to this sector will gain further momentum in the future (He et al., 2016, p. 697).

It can be stated that China, India and Brazil have a major share of the investments made in renewable energy. The total renewable energy investments of these three leading developing countries in 2017 account for more than half of global investments, excluding hydro energy. In 2016, China alone represented 35% of global investments, while in 2017 this share increased to 45% (UN Environment, 2018, p. 20). In 2017, China played a leading role in the sector with 126.6 billion dollars of renewable energy investment. Solar (86.5 billion dollars) and wind (36.1 billion dollars) energy investments constitute significant portions of this amount (UN Environment, 2018, p. 27). Within the scope of renewable energy, solar energy investments in particular can be observed to have experienced a big boom in 2017 in China. Solar panels with a capacity of 53 GW were installed, and solar investments increased by 58% (UN Environment, 2018, p. 11).

The amount of foreign direct investment supporting green energy has also reached the highest levels of all time. The amount of foreign direct investment increased from 13.9 billion dollars in 2016 to 21.4 billion dollars in 2017. Regionally, EU-centered investments account for the largest share with 9.6 billion dollars, followed by the United States with 5.1 billion dollars and Asia with 4.8 billion dollars. Private foreign capital also has an increasing role in foreign direct investment in renewable energy. Whereas investments from development banks were similar in 2016 and 2017, funds provided by international institutions, project developers and commercial banks increased to 9.8 billion dollars in 2017 (BloombergNEF, 2018, p. 2).

International support for investments in renewable energy and energy efficiency is vital for carbon reduction. Thanks to this support, crucial resources can then be provided for green energy, and appropriate conditions may be formed for the future of the global climate. In a report published by the UN in 2017, it is stated that international support constitutes 10% of all global renewable energy and energy efficiency activities and expenditures. Undoubtedly, this support has a significant effect in reducing the future impacts of climate change. Internationally supported renewable energy and energy efficiency projects implemented in developing countries between 2005 and 2016 are aimed at reducing CO_2 by 0.6 gigatons annually by 2020 (UN Environment, The 1 Gigaton Coalition, 2017, p. 7). Furthermore, due to the profit margin provided by renewable energy, new projects are financed with great appetite by European public institutions, especially in the Latin American market (Enel Green Power, 2019). Even though renewable energy and energy efficiency projects and policies in this direction are gaining momentum in developing countries, problems continue in terms of insufficient data flow and information sharing that prevent countries and international organizations supporting renewable energy from systematically evaluating the effects of their work (UN Environment, The 1 Gigaton Coalition, 2017, p. 7).

Global Position in Renewable Energy

The increase in demand for electricity and the decline in renewable energy technology costs enable developing countries to lead the transition to a global clean energy. This shows that many of the leading investments and moves of the developed countries in the field of renewable energy in the early 21st century are being reversed. Wind, solar, geothermal and other types of green energy were considered to be very expensive technologies for collecting and spreading energy for developing countries in the era concerned (BloombergNEF, 2018, p. 1).

The reasons for developing countries to get ahead of developed countries in renewable energy capacity may be categorized as the steady increase in electricity demand, the implementation of innovative energy policies, the presence of many investments in this area, and low technology costs. As a whole, such factors actualized this result, which was thought to be science fiction a few years ago and, for the first time, made it possible for developing countries to get ahead of developed countries (Enel Green Power, 2019).

Looking at the 2017 data, it can be seen that most of the zero-carbon green energy capacity has been established in developing countries. In contrast to the installed capacity of 114 GW in developing countries, a total capacity of 63 GW has been formed in developed countries, resulting in the capacity difference of the former being almost double that of the latter (BloombergNEF, 2018, p. 1). Within this 114 GW value, wind and solar energy serve as the locomotives of renewable energy because 94 GW of 114 GW is supplied by these two energy sources. These data stand out as the all-time records. In addition, this situation is not only good news for the global climate; it also serves as great support for the balance of payments generated by the energy bills of each country (Enel Green Power, 2019). This difference between developed and developing countries is largely based on the difference between energy demands, the proportions of energy needs being met by fossil fuels, and the health-threatening aspect of air pollution.

The Future of Renewable Energy

Problems Encountered in the Transition to Clean Energy

The increase in coal capacity in developing countries is tending to decline. After the new capacity increase reached a peak of 97 GW in 2015, this figure decreased to 48 GW in 2017 (BloombergNEF, 2018, p. 1). Although the coal-fired energy capacity increases were at the lowest level in the last decade in 2017, coal production is observed to have increased by almost 4% in 2017 compared to the previous year. Likewise, there was a 3% increase in natural gas production. According to the 2017 data, an increase of 193 GW coal capacity is continuing in developing countries. 86% of this capacity is expected to be constructed in developing countries such as China, India, Indonesia and South Africa (BloombergNEF, 2018, p. 4). Therefore, despite their remarkable renewable energy moves, it can be stated that especially China and India still have a serious dependence on coal and lignite (Enel Green Power, 2019). Given the high amounts of coal reserves of China and India, the reason for this can be understood (EIA, n.d.).

Global energy demand reached its peak in the last decade in 2018, increasing by 2.3%, and 30% of this demand was met by renewable energy, while the remaining 70% was met by fossil fuels. Despite the significant developments in renewable energy, economic growth in developing countries still encourages the intensive use of fossil fuels. While attempts are trying to be made to replace coal's use with natural gas in developed countries, in developing countries, coal is seen as a force multiplier for their growing economies. Factors such as coal being cheaper and that it is easy to install coal plants and transfer coal come to the fore when choosing coal (Conca, 2019).

There are long-term problems that cannot be solved easily in order for green energy to replace existing coal-fired power plants. Within the context of these problems, China and India are especially prominent because China supplies two-thirds of the energy it needs from coal and India supplies three-quarters of it from coal. Between 2010 and 2017, the total coal capacity added by these two countries reached 432 GW. Considering the fact that the total available coal capacity of the USA is 260 GW, it can be seen that the above figure is very big (BloombergNEF, 2018, p. 4). Regarding other fossil fuels such as oil and natural gas, there is also a similar situation for China. By 2040, about 30% of the oil that is subject to international trade and about a quarter of the gas that is treated over long distances are expected to flow into China (IEA, n.d).

In addition, at least 81% of the total coal power capacity in developing countries is concentrated in China (68%) and India (13%). Since India contributes to access to energy, China helps to access energy at affordable prices, and they are subject to pressure in relation to these factors, it can be considered that it is not possible for the executives of these two countries to shut down coal power plants in the foreseeable future. Another important problem with renewable energy is how to integrate large volumes of energy into existing energy markets. This is because green energy, which is included in liberal energy markets, will lower the prices of all types of energy. In the short term, renewable energy can both keep carbon emissions under control and accelerate the disappearance of fossil fuels that yield less efficiency. However, the failure to manage this process properly and the penetration of renewable energy into energy markets in this way can lead to imbalance. In particular, the lack of a balanced overlap of green energy with the energy demand may increase this imbalance (BloombergNEF, 2018, p. 5).

Today, it does not seem possible to remove the financial burden of a rapid transition from fossil fuels to renewable energy in the world (Smith, 2019). In the context of renewable energy, the compliance framework is of great importance. Compliance framework analysis refers to policies that link renewable energy production and transmission with end-user management. There is a need for integrated system-oriented policies aimed at decarbonization in all sectors (UN Environment, The 1 Gigaton Coalition, 2017, p. 76). The inadequate integration of China's renewable energy capacity in use into the Chinese energy system in general may be presented as a good example of this. Due to this structural problem, China cannot use about 15% of its solar and wind energy (IEA, 2017). If there is excess capacity in some parts of China, wind and solar power plants are interrupted and replaced by coal power plants (BloombergNEF, 2018, p.

5). Another problem area related to renewable energy has a legal origin, as in China and Russia. In the related literature, it is stated that the laws and supporting measures of the energy market are flawed and therefore these mechanisms and policies remain insufficient to support the development of renewable energy (He et al., 2016, p. 695).

What Can Be Done?

The problems with renewable energy do not only apply to developing countries. Similar problems exist in developed countries. There are some proposed solutions to the kinds of problems listed above. For example, the implementation of total energy market reforms to regulate subventions for renewable energy producers, the establishment of extended demand programs to encourage the reduction of electricity consumption in significant time periods, the expansion and development of energy storage technologies such as batteries, and the development of transmission lines in order to transfer more energy from various remote regions where efficient wind and solar energy production is provided stand out as measures to be implemented for these problems. These solutions are being carefully implemented by some developing countries. Brazil plans to put in tenders for the transfer of energy from its regions with significant renewable energy sources. The World Bank also provides support at this point. The Scaling Solar program in Madagascar can be given as an exemplar in this respect. Again, it should be noted in this regard that a public institution of South Africa has a storage target of 800 MWh by 2019 (BloombergNEF, 2018, p. 5).

There is no doubt that further studies are underway to address the current problems of renewable energy. Green energy costs continue to decline and the spread of green energy has been expanding. The renewable energy systems of developing countries should not only provide comprehensive availability to developed countries 'energy networks but should even reach a position in which they surpass this because they need more energy and pollute the air more. It is imperative that developing countries make joint efforts, including advanced policy development, investment and the implementation of new technologies, to reach this position. At this point, it is also a fact that there will be important market opportunities for companies in the sector and financial institutions (BloombergNEF, 2018, p. 5).

It is predicted that, throughout the 21st century, developing countries will represent almost all the energy demand growth in the world. These countries need to align their development goals with global climate targets.

At this point, international support stands out as a necessity for the success of developing countries (UN Environment, The 1 Gigaton Coalition, 2017, p. 76). In order for developing countries to strengthen their efforts on renewable energy and energy efficiency and to accelerate the process, issues such as sharing experiences, providing expert support in a political and technical context, ensuring the transfer of advanced technologies to developing countries and providing financial support are of great importance (UN Environment, The 1 Gigaton Coalition, 2017, p. 76).

There are some steps these countries can take within the context of air pollution, which is one of the most important reasons why renewable energy has emerged as a growing sector, especially in countries such as China and India. In 2016, CO_2 emissions from fossil fuels and other industrial sources reached 34 billion metric tons. It is estimated that these gases, which hold heat and cause global climate change, remain in the atmosphere for almost a hundred years and accumulate there. From this point forth, economic efficiency, that is, the proper taxation of individual fuel uses according to the CO_2 emission factor within the context of the emergent costs, comes to the fore as a generally accepted implementation. There are several approaches to the economic assessment of CO_2 emissions. In one of these approaches, the aim is to determine the social cost of carbon, which is the value of the global damage that will be caused by climate change in the future in relation to the additional ton of carbon emissions.[1] According to this approach, a social cost of approximately 35 dollars per ton is proposed for 2015 emissions. Another approach is to estimate global emission prices in a way that meets the temperature compensation targets at a low cost. According to a recent study conducted on this topic, a global CO_2 emission pricing rate of 40 to 80 dollars per ton is foreseen by 2020. The third approach is to make carbon pricing consistent with countries 'carbon reduction commitments (Coady et al., 2019, pp. 8-9).

[1] For detailed information on the social cost of carbon and the calculation of the social cost of carbon, see United States Environmental Protection Agency 2014, 2016.

Renewable Energy and Developing Countries

The Impact of Renewable Energy Policies on Developing Countries

In the process of the world evolving to use green energy, many parameters have to adapt to this change. While the efforts of a transition to green energy in developing countries continue with great momentum, different factors can slow down or prevent this transition. The primary problem for these countries is the existence of an energy source that complies with their growing economy. Therefore, there is still a great dependency on fossil fuels. As such, the existence of some deficiencies of green energy resources, which are both structural, legal and regulatory, prevents the use of these energy types from being raised to the desired level in accordance with the developing economies 'growth rates. It also seems important to maintain the balances in the world energy market. The maintaining of these balances will be closely monitored by countries with large amounts of fossil fuel resources, developed countries that control the fossil fuel market, and large international companies. Otherwise, green energy rapidly coming to dominate the energy market may cause other problems in the financial context.

Renewable energy policies are developed meticulously in developing countries, especially under the leadership of BRICS. When BRICS countries 'share in global energy demand is taken into consideration, it is easy to understand why they lead the way in renewable energy policies. The renewable energy sector stands out as an area of necessity and a cause of economic growth for developing countries and especially for BRICS countries. So here, both a necessity and a great motivation are at stake. Green energy policies stimulate and improve the industry, production and therefore the economy of developing countries. While the green energy sector is a fast-growing industrial sector in the world, BRICS countries in particular are pioneers in this sector with cheap labor and technological developments. Renewable energy appears as a necessity, both in the sense that it has the potential to be an answer to the huge energy deficits of BRICS countries and because air pollution resulting from fossil fuels causes very serious health problems in the societies of these countries.

The China Factor in the Renewable Energy Context

China's primary role in renewable energy is also easily understood when the data put forth on the serious health problems and mortality rates experienced due to energy demand, energy generation, energy deficit and intensive fossil fuel use are studied. Since China has a very important place in the sector, when we talk about international renewable energy policies, it is often necessary to refer to China's policies. For example, China is by far the leader in the production of solar panels in the global market. Likewise, when we look at the data listed above regarding the green energy breakthroughs of developing countries, it can be seen that the contributions made by China alone represent a large part of the total. Therefore, it can be said that international renewable energy policies are directing and being directed by China. At this point, the fact that China is under the pressure of the international community regarding global warming also directs China's renewable energy policies.

The development of renewable energy policies is still not at a sufficient level for China. There are many steps remaining to be taken. Of course, it will not be enough for China to act alone, and international cooperation and joint policies will pave the way for renewable energy. In the context of China, especially green energy transmission and infrastructure deficiencies can be mentioned as two of the biggest problem areas. These problems cause China to continue to use fossil fuels, the foremost being coal, at significant rates. The dilemma of necessity and motivation mentioned above in relation to renewable energy is much more valid for China. For all these reasons, China, which is compelled to use green energy, is a country that shapes renewable energy policies both among developing countries and internationally. Due to air pollution, both health-related costs and those arising from the damage to agricultural products put a heavy burden on the Chinese economy and motivate China in terms of renewable energy.

Conclusion

Negative, economically based claims aimed at renewable energy sources such as their being expensive, interrupted from time to time, or their insufficient concentration can easily be rebutted. Although the adversaries of renewable energy are a large mass, it can be argued that their main motivation is to maintain the status quo formed by fossil fuels and nuclear energy rather than about the pollution of the Earth with wind turbines or solar farms. It seems unlikely that the simple economic argument formed against renewable energy will constitute an impediment for this technology and the sector (OECD, 2016).

The current frightening picture that emerges regarding air pollution and climate change has mobilized the entire international community and developing countries such as China, which seem to be the most responsible for this issue. China's pioneering role in renewable energy also sets an example for other developing countries, and efforts are underway to take joint steps in renewable energy policies under BRICS and through institutions such as the New Development Bank. Thus, emerging and developing renewable energy policies and the sector are shaped by developing countries, led by China, but these policies also affect their future plans. So there is a mutual interaction. In this process, the main determinants for developing countries can be listed as climate change, energy deficits where fossil fuels are insufficient, energy security, and the extraordinary contribution of the renewable energy sector to the economic growth of developing countries. Consequently, renewable energy contributes greatly to the progress of developing countries in terms of climate change and air pollution, particularly in the case of China, and to the development and growth of their industrial sectors and economies within the context of reducing energy imports and increasing renewable energy production. Another important point related to renewable energy is the increase in the competitiveness of developing countries with developed countries, and even the former getting ahead of the latter in some areas.

References

Ashraf, Q., & Galor, O. (2008). *Malthusian Population Dynamics: Theory and Evidence.* https://www.econstor.eu/obitstream/10419/62638/1/571838952.pdf

BloombergNEF (2018). *Emerging Markets Outlook 2018.* http://global-climatescope.org/assets/data/reports/climatescope-2018-report-en.pdf

BP. (2019). *BP Energy Outlook 2019 Edition.* https://www.bp.com/content/dam/bp/business-sites/en/global/corporate/pdfs/energy-economics/energy-outlook/bp-energy-outlook-2019.pdf

Cassella, C. (2019, June 28). *Renewable Power Exceeded Coal For The First Time in US History And None of Us Noticed.* Science Alert. https://www.sciencealert.com/renewables-exceeded-coal-for-first-time-in-us-history-with-no-noticeable-difference

CNREC. (2018). *China Renewable Energy Outlook 2018,*

http://boostre.cnrec.org.cn/wp-content/uploads/2018/11/China-Renewable-Energy-Outlook-2018-Folder_ENG.pdf

Coady, D., Parry, I., Le, N.-P., & Shang, B. (2019, May 2). *Global Fossil Fuel Subsidies Remain Large: An Update Based on Country-Level Estimates*. IMF. https://www.imf.org/en/Publications/WP/Issues/2019/05/02/Global-Fossil-Fuel-Subsidies-Remain-Large-An-Update-Based-on-Country-Level-Estimates-46509

Conca, J. (2019, July 20). *So You Think We're Reducing Fossil Fuel? Think Again*. Forbes. https://www.forbes.com/sites/jamesconca/2019/07/20/so-you-think-were-reducing-fossil-fuel-think-again/

EIA. (n.d.). *How much coal is left*. Retrieved June 17, 2019, from https://www.eia.gov/energyexplained/index.php?page=coal_reserves

Enel Green Power. (2019). *Developing countries are the new leaders in renewables*. Retrieved June 11, 2019, from https://www.enelgreenpower.com/stories/a/2019/01/developing-countries-and-renewable-energy-for-a-sustainable-future

Gippner, O., & Torney, D. (2017). Shifting policy priorities in EU-China energy relations: Implications for Chinese energy investments in Europe. *Energy Policy*, *101*, 649-658.

Griffiths, J. (2019, July 10). *China has made major progress on air pollution. Wuhan protests show there's still a long way to go.* CNN. https://edition.cnn.com/2019/07/10/asia/china-wuhan-pollution-problems-intl-hnk/index.html

He, Y., Xu, Y., Pang, Y., Tian, H., & Wu, R. (2016). A regulatory policy to promote renewable energy consumption in China: Review and future evolutionary path. *Renewable Energy*, *89*, 695-705.

HEI (Health Effects Institute). (2018). *State of Global Air 2018. Special Report*. Boston, MA: Health Effects Institute. https://www.stateofglobalair.org/sites/default/files/soga-2018-report.pdf

IEA. (2017). *World Energy Outlook 2017: China*. Retrieved June 26, 2019, from https://www.iea.org/weo/china/

India Today. (2019, June 28). *G20 Summit: PM Modi give 5 suggestions to tackle challenges like unilateralism, protectionism*. https://www.indiatoday.in/india/story/pm-modi-5-suggestions-tackle-unilateralism-protectionism-1557745-2019-06-28

IRENA. (2014). *Renewable Energy Prospects: China*. https://www.irena.org/-/media/Files/IRENA/Agency/Publication/2014/Nov/IRENA_REmap_China_report_2014.pdf.

Kao, E. (2018, October 2). *Air pollution is killing 1 million people and costing Chinese economy 267 billion yuan a year, research from CUHK shows*. South China Morning Post. https://www.scmp.com/news/china/science/article/2166542/air-pollution-killing-1-million-people-and-costing-chinese

Lazard. (2014, September 18). *Levelized Cost of Energy v8 Abstract*. https://www.lazard.com/perspective/levelized-cost-of-energy-v8-abstract/

Lewis, N., & Defterios, J. (2019, July 11). *Can India kick its coal addiction?* CNN. https://edition.cnn.com/2019/07/11/business/india-energy-coal/index.html

McCarthy, N. (2018, April 18). *Air Pollution Contributed To More Than 6 Million Deaths In 2016 [Infographic]*. Forbes. https://www.forbes.com/sites/niallmccarthy/2018/04/18/air-pollution-contributed-to-more-than-6-million-deaths-in-2016-infographic/

New Development Bank. (2019). *About Us*. Retrieved July 19, 2019, from https://www.ndb.int/about-us/essence/history/

OECD. (2016). *Developing countries and the renewable energy revolution*. Retrieved May 18, 2019, from https://www.oecd.org/dev/developing-countries-and-the-renewable-energy-revolution.htm

Pathak, L., & Shah, K. (2019). Renewable energy resources, policies and gaps in BRICS countries and the global impact. *Frontiers in Energy*, *13*, 1-16. https://doi.org/10.1007/s11708-018-0601-z

Phakathi, B. (2019). *Renewable energy sector receives $300m loan boost.* Business Day. https://www.businesslive.co.za/bd/national/2019-04-01-renewable-energy-sector-receives-300m-loan-boost/

Smith, G. (2019, May 14). *The U.S. Spends More To Subsidize Dirty Fuels Than on Defense.* EWG. https://www.ewg.org/energy/22648/us-spends-more-subsidize-dirty-fuels-defense

Sputnik. (2019, June 28). *India's Modi Calls for Boosting Investment in Infrastructure Projects*. https://sputniknews.com/world/201906281076076932-chinas-xi-says-developed-countries-protectionism-poses-biggest-risk-intl-community/

Stanway, D. (2018, April 17). *China cuts smog but health damage already done: study.* Reuters. https://www.reuters.com/article/us-china-pollution-health/china-cuts-smog-but-health-damage-already-done-study-idUSKBN1HO0C4

UN Environment. (2017). *The Emissions Gap Report 2017, A UN Environment Synthesis Report.* https://wedocs.unep.org/bitstream/handle/20.500.11822/22070/EGR_2017.pdf?sequence=1&isAllowed=y
UN Environment, The 1 Gigaton Coalition. (2017). *Renewable Energy and Energy Efficiency in Developing Countries: Contributions to Reducing Global Emissions.* https://wedocs.unep.org/bitstream/handle/20.500.11822/22149/1_Gigaton_Third%20Report_EN.pdf?sequence=1&isAllowed=y
UN Environment. (2018). *Global Trends in Renewable Energy Investment 2018.* https://europa.eu/capacity4dev/file/71900/download?token=57xpTJ4W
UN Environment. (2019). *Renewable Energy and Energy Efficiency in Developing Countries: Contributions to Reducing Global Emissions.* https://wedocs.unep.org/bitstream/handle/20.500.11822/22149/1_Gigaton_Third%20Report_EN.pdf
UN. (2014). *Country classification.* https://www.un.org/en/development/desa/policy/wesp/wesp_current/2014wesp_country_classification.pdf
United States Environmental Protection Agency. (2014). *The Social Cost of Carbon Made Simple.* https://www.epa.gov/sites/production/files/2014-12/documents/the_social_cost_of_carbon_made_simple.pdf
United States Environmental Protection Agency. (2016). *Social Cost of Carbon.* https://www.epa.gov/sites/production/files/2016-12/documents/social_cost_of_carbon_fact_sheet.pdf
WHO. (2019). *How air pollution is destroying our health.* Retrieved June 18, 2019, from https://www.who.int/air-pollution/news-and-events/how-air-pollution-is-destroying-our-health
Xinhua. (2019, April 2). *BRICS New Development Bank to double loan approval book in 2019.* http://www.xinhuanet.com/english/2019-04/02/c_137942743.htm